Fourth Edition

Philosophical Documents in Education

Fourth Edition

Philosophical Documents in Education

Tony W. Johnson

The Citadel: The Military College of South Carolina

Ronald F. Reed

Late of Texas Wesleyan University

Boston   Columbus   Indianapolis   New York   San Francisco   Upper Saddle River
Amsterdam   Cape Town   Dubai   London   Madrid   Milan   Munich   Paris   Montréal   Toronto
Delhi   Mexico City   São Paulo   Sydney   Hong Kong   Seoul   Singapore   Taipei   Tokyo

Vice President and Editor in Chief: Jeffery W.
  Johnston
Senior Acquisitions Editor: Ann Castel Davis
Editorial Assistant: Penny Burleson
Vice President, Director of Marketing: Margaret
  Waples
Senior Marketing Manager: Christopher Barry
Senior Managing Editor: Pamela D. Bennett
Senior Production Editor: Mary M. Irvin
Project Manager: Susan Hannahs

Senior Art Director: Jayne Conte
Cover Designer: Suzanne Duda
Cover Art: Fotosearch
Full-Service Management: Jerusha Govindakrishnan/
  PreMediaGlobal
Composition: PreMediaGlobal
Text and Cover Printer/Bindery:
  R. R. Donnelley/Harrisonburg
Text Font: Garamond 10/12 pts

Credits and acknowledgments borrowed from other sources and reproduced, with permission, in this textbook appear on the appropriate page within the text.

Every effort has been made to provide accurate and current Internet information in this book. However, the Internet and information posted on it are constantly changing, so it is inevitable that some of the Internet addresses listed in this textbook will change.

Library of Congress Cataloging-in-Publication Data

Philosophical documents in education / [edited by] Tony W. Johnson, Ronald F. Reed.—4th ed.
    p. cm.
  Includes bibliographical references and index.
  ISBN-13: 978-0-13-708038-0
  ISBN-10: 0-13-708038-7
  1. Education—Philosophy.   I. Johnson, Tony W.   II. Reed, Ronald F.
  LB7.P5432 2012
  370.1—dc22   2010053140

10 9 8 7 6 5 4 3 2 1

www.pearsonhighered.com

ISBN 10: 0-13-708038-7
ISBN 13: 978-0-13-708038-0

In Memoriam

Ronald F. Reed died suddenly and unexpectedly of a heart attack on August 23, 1998. Ron Reed was many things—a devoted husband and father, a down-to-earth friend and colleague, and an outstanding scholar and thinker, but, most of all, he was a teacher. He combined a "natural" ability to work with people of all ages and backgrounds with a willingness to reexamine his own teaching in a never-ending quest for better, more effective ways of helping others to think and learn. Philosophical Documents in Education, *by inviting and enabling potential and practicing teachers to participate in the conversation concerning the nature and purpose of education, contributes to and continues Ron's educational legacy.*

Much like the great minds included in this volume, Ron truly impacted the lives of all who knew him. We miss him, but, through such works as Philosophical Documents in Education, *his teaching voice continues to be heard.*

TONY W. JOHNSON

for Fran Johnson and Ann Reed

BRIEF CONTENTS

CONTENTS

PREFACE

The largely positive responses to the first three editions of *Philosophical Documents in Education* are gratifying. To build on the success of the earlier editions, included in the fourth edition are historical documents chronicling conflicting educational visions and their continuing legacy. A subtle but significant change of focus from the ideally educated individual to the question of what it means to be educated characterizes this fourth edition. We believe that as classroom teachers and other educational professionals grapple with the different responses to this essential question, their own vision of what it means to be educated will begin to crystallize and, in turn, will increasingly influence their professional activity in the classroom and beyond.

We continue to think that education students and professional educators are capable of dealing directly with great philosophical literature in and about education. We understand that such literature is not easy and that it is hard work to create an environment in which topics such as Plato's "Allegory of the Cave" are meaningful for contemporary students and applicable to current educational problems. When such an environment is created, the payoff is substantial. Imagine being able to ask Aristotle, Rousseau, Maxine Greene, or Martin Luther King for advice about classroom practice. The selections included in *Philosophical Documents in Education* enable prospective and practicing educators to engage these great minds in meaningful conversations about education and its importance.

Finally, as we suggest in the Introduction, we think of *Documents* as an invitation for prospective and practicing educators to interact with these great minds and to engage them in a serious conversation about what it means to be educated. The great minds included in the fourth edition continue to reflect our perspectives, but by inviting the reader to go beyond the information given, the largely Western, pragmatic, and somewhat contemporary worldviews of these great minds are expanded and become—as we suggest in the Introduction—"interestingly complex."

NEW TO THIS EDITION

Changes to this fourth edition are substantive and also mundane. Timelines have been updated to reflect accomplishments since the publication of the previous edition in 2008. Questions at the end of several chapters have been reviewed and modified as needed. Introductory essays for specific chapters have been revised to provide relevant new material and to remove unnecessary or redundant material. More substantive changes have also been made:

- Chapters on Augustine, Erasmus, Hannah Arendt, and Cornel West have been eliminated since—as the reviewers indicated—these chapters do not appear to be relevant for many students.
- New chapters—*Conflicting Educational Visions: The Puritans and Thomas Jefferson; Local versus Centralized Control of Schooling; Traditional versus Progressive Education: The Great Debate;* and *Education: The Panacea for African Americans*—have been added to offer readers a better understanding of the historical antecedents of contemporary education.

- An essentially new chapter has been added on Philosophy for Children that replaces the Matthews and Egan chapters and integrates their contributions to Lipman's response to what it means to be educated.
- The introductory chapter has been revised substantially and the selections in the John Dewey and Jane Roland Martin chapters have been reduced to reflect the subtle shift in focus of the text and to achieve greater balance in the length of each chapter.
- A topical table of concepts is offered to assist the reader in aligning the contributions found in the documents with more contemporary educational issues.

Our goal for this edition, as it was for previous editions of *Philosophical Documents in Education,* is to foster an appreciation of philosophy among prospective and practicing educational professionals. We believe that philosophy is very important in the education of those who are to be educators; but we also believe that philosophy—the sense of wondering, of seeking explanations, of trying to figure things out, of determining what is worthy of belief and action—is a birthright of all students, young as well as old. Our hope is that *Philosophical Documents in Education* will be used to help achieve that birthright.

ACKNOWLEDGMENTS

Anthologies are the most collaborative of efforts. Although it is relatively easy to describe this work—an anthology of primary sources that can be read with profit by prospective and practicing educators—turning this description into the fourth edition of *Philosophical Documents in Education* has been achieved only through the efforts of many people.

We acknowledge and deeply appreciate the permission of philosophers and publishers to reprint their work. Specific acknowledgments are presented at the beginning of each excerpt or section.

A very special thank you is due the staff of The Citadel's School of Education for their assistance in the many tasks associated with compiling this work. Special recognition is due Judy Hagen and Kathy Triggs for their overall support of this effort, and to Meredith Petty, Heather Burke and Shannon Crow, graduate assistants in the School of Education, for their work in securing permissions and in proofreading the manuscript.

We are also grateful to the following individuals for their recommendations for this fourth edition: Patricia Walsh Coates, Kutztown University; Joyce E. Miller, Texas A&M University-Commerce; and Andrew Milson, University of North Texas.

TABLE OF CONCEPTS

Concept	Where It Is Addressed
1. What It Means to Be Educated	
• The Critic or Gadfly	Introduction and Chapter 1
• The Guardian	Introduction and Chapter 1
• The Rational Animal	Introduction and Chapter 2
• The Humanist	Introduction and Chapter 9
• Locke's Gentleman	Introduction and Chapter 3
• The Biblical Commonwealth	Introduction and Chapter 6
• The Natural Aristocracy	Introduction and Chapter 6
• The Natural Man	Introduction and Chapter 4
• The Benevolent Being	Introduction and Chapter 5
• Education for the "child races"	Introduction and Chapter 10
• Education for the Elite	Introduction and Chapters 1 and 10
• The Scientists	Introduction and Chapters 2 and 8
• The Autonomous Human Being	Introduction and Chapters 11 through 14
• Reproductive Education	Chapters 12 and 14
• The Critical Thinker	Introduction and Chapters 1, 15, and 16
2. Relationship of Education to Society	Introduction and Chapters 1, 4, 6, 7, and 8
3. Relationship of Democracy and Education	Introduction and Chapters 6, 8, and 11
4. Gender and Race Issues in Education	Introduction and Chapters 5, 10, 12, and 14
5. Importance of Dialogue in Education	Introduction and Chapters 1, 8, 15, and 16

Introduction

Philosophical Documents in Education rests on a very basic assumption that students of education, and potential and practicing educational professionals, can learn something of significance in terms of both theory and practice from reading, thinking about, and discussing the great historical and philosophic tradition in education. This book attempts to bring that tradition to you in such a way that you may understand it and use it to formulate your own vision of the ideally educated person and how to foster it.

We recognize that philosophical writing is not the easiest thing to read and understand. Frequently, it is rife with technical language, refers back to unfamiliar books and articles, and has a density and rigor of presentation and argumentation that is not typical of much of the other writing to which students of education are exposed. In selecting the works to be included here, efforts have been made to keep the technical language to a minimum. You will not need an extensive philosophical vocabulary to read and understand these selections.

Still, students need to be aware that a powerful philosophical argument or position cannot be captured in a succinct sentence or paragraph without loss of force, evocativeness, and beauty. As students of the history and philosophy of education, we tend to distrust brief summaries, and as editors, we have avoided them. Recognizing that students have a limited amount of time and energy, our goal is to offer a deliberately lean text of a limited number of selections that invite the reader to more serious study. The level of difficulty of certain selections may challenge some readers, and we suggest that you treat these selections much as you would poetry: Read them slowly, carefully, and frequently.

The text comprises sixteen chapters and includes selections ranging from such classical thinkers as Plato, Aristotle, Rousseau, and Dewey; more contemporary theorists such as Martin Luther King, Maxine Greene, Nel Noddings, and Parker Palmer; and related historical material. One benefit of the obvious contemporary slant to the selections is that it exposes readers to the views of women and minorities, views that have been largely ignored in previous anthologies.

Accompanying each selection is a brief, informal essay on the thinker or theme designed as a kind of an advanced organizer to assist the reader in placing the selection in its historical and social context. The theme that ties the introductory essays and the historical and philosophical selections together is that each selection responds in a unique way to the question of what does it mean to be educated. A time line highlighting the events, lives, and accomplishments introduces each chapter, and each chapter concludes with a series of questions designed to aid the students in grasping the significance of these great minds and/or historical movements.

Anthologies, of necessity, are selective and reflect the interests, values, perspectives, and biases of the compilers. They are always open to legitimate criticism: Why this philosopher and not that? Why this excerpt instead of another? Why—in this anthology, the *Apology* but no reference to the *Meno?* Though efforts have been made in this edition to provide a more balanced selection of classic and contemporary thinkers, it is not and cannot be a comprehensive treatment of the area of study or even of the central question of what it means to be educated. It is meant to serve as an *invitation* to a tradition of scholarship focused on this question. If the reader accepts the invitation to go beyond the information provided, to use the selections as stepping stones for further reading, our purpose will be achieved.

We ask that readers view this anthology as an invitation to enter a room in which an extended conversation is taking place. The conversation revolves around differing views on what it means to be educated and involves great minds of both the past and the present. The room has specific historical, philosophical, and geographic characteristics—it is Western, pragmatic, progressive, and so on—but once you have entered it, things become interestingly complex. Read any of the selections included here, take them seriously, go beyond these brief excerpts, study the contexts that produced these works, and almost inevitably, you will embark upon a journey that more than compensates for the limitations inherent in this or any other anthology. Reading Dewey will lead the inquiring mind to Whitehead or James and perhaps on to Richard Rorty. Engaging Plato's *Apology* will whet the appetite for the *Meno* and other Platonic dialogues. Becoming familiar with largely Western conceptualizations of what it means to be educated leads to questions of how these are similar to and different from the views of other parts of the world. This anthology invites and enables you to enter a room that is almost without limits—a room in which a dynamic conversion about the nature and purpose of education is taking place.

To accompany and support you as you enter this room, we offer the following brief historical and social commentary placing the thinkers and themes included here in context. We suggest that you begin by reading the following overview in its entirety before tackling the chapters that follow. We also encourage you to move back and forth, rereading the appropriate sections of the overview as you grapple with the educational ideas presented in the selections of specific classical and contemporary thinkers.

DIFFERING PERSPECTIVES ON WHAT IT MEANS TO BE EDUCATED

The Fallible Human Being

Some have characterized the competing visions of the ideally educated human being as a "battle for the mind," and that battle has a long history. It originated at least 2,400 years ago when the Athenians killed Socrates for corrupting the youth by his teaching. In his own defense, Socrates tried to explain to the Athenians that "he was a teacher unlike any they had ever known."[1] Many Athenians recognized Socrates as a wise man, though he denied it, professing to possess "no wisdom, small or great." After years of questioning politicians, poets, artisans, and others claiming to be wise and discovering that they were not, Socrates recanted. Perhaps he was wiser than others, he reasoned, since at least he knew that he knew nothing. Socrates' awareness of his own ignorance made him wiser than other fallible human beings who claimed to be wise. He dedicated his life to questioning these individuals and revealing their ignorance to them.

Although his method was less than diplomatic, Socrates believed that it contributed to the improvement of their souls. By helping others to see their own mistakes, Socrates provided these fallible human beings the necessary first step toward improving themselves. Socrates refused to tell his students what to think. Instead, he helped them improve their thinking by identifying problems and/or weaknesses in their reasoning.

Socrates was right. The Athenians had never known a teacher like him and did not always understand or appreciate his tendency to challenge established truths. They did not understand or did not agree that such a negative approach is the only way for fallible

---

[1]Henry J. Perkinson, *Since Socrates: Studies in the History of Western Educational Thought* (New York: Longman, 1980), p. 2.

human beings to improve their souls. From this perspective, fallible human beings can never know what is absolutely right, good, or true. Progress is possible only by humans discovering the errors and foibles in our established norms and truths, and using such discoveries to improve themselves and the world they inhabit. According to Socrates, it is only through recognizing and learning from our mistakes that we can improve our souls.

The Critic or Gadfly

The Athenians turned a deaf ear to Socrates' apology, perhaps because of the catastrophes they had experienced during his lifetime. The Spartans had defeated the Athenians in the Peloponnesian War, breaching the walls of the city and establishing a puppet government there in 401 BC. When democracy was restored three years later, many Athenians longed for a return to normalcy and abandoned the critical inquiry of Socrates. Accusing him of—among other things—leading the youth of Athens astray, he was tried, convicted, and sentenced to drink the hemlock for his transgression. Refusing to flee the city, Socrates dies as he lived—as a critic helping his fellow Athenians improve themselves and their society by making them aware of their mistakes. In becoming a martyr, Socrates demonstrates for his and future societies the injustices involved in silencing critics.

The Guardian

Witnessing the death of his beloved teacher at the hands of a democratic government, Plato recognized how vulnerable intellectuals were in Athens. Plato's solution was to replace the Socratic critic with the benevolent and omniscient authority or expert as the ideally educated individual. Instead of the intellectual as a critic, Plato advocated for the intellectual as a wise, all-knowing philosopher king. Concerned about the Athenian's suspicions of him because of his affiliation with Socrates, Plato replaced the idea of the intellectual as critic or gadfly with the guardian whose absolute mastery of truth and goodness merits political power and allegiance. In replacing the critic with the authority or expert as the ideal for the educated individual, Plato argues that there is a universal reality and that it is possible for certain gifted individuals to achieve certain knowledge of that reality through multiple years of guided, rigorous study.

According to Plato, there is a world of ideas that transcends the material or physical world. Unlike the material world that is accessible to us through our senses, the "real" world or world of ideas is accessible to us only through the intellect. That which is known by the intellect is universal, absolute, and perfect, while that which is known through the senses is temporal, relative, and flawed. Most of us are destined to deal with imperfect copies or images of reality rather than the pure abstractions or conceptualizations that are—according to Plato—the ultimate reality.

Since only the gifted few can be guided to see with the mind's eye the ultimate reality, Plato suggested that these few special individuals merited a special place in the social order as the guardians, overseeing and directing the masses to live in accordance with these ultimate truths. In Plato's ideal state or society, those who genuinely know the truth are the guardians or philosopher kings. These mighty intellects are little concerned with earthly pleasures but have committed themselves and their lives to their pursuit of true, absolute knowledge. Plato argues that all people benefit when the truly wise is in charge. His ideal society is one governed by an omniscient and all-powerful philosopher king.

From Plato's perspective, the intellectual or philosopher merits the position of authority for he or she alone knows what is good and true. Motivated, at least in part, by what happened to Socrates, Plato abandoned the critic as a practical model of the ideally educated individual. Plato joins Socrates in thinking of intellectuals as teachers, but for Plato teaching took on a much more conservative function. For Plato, the goal of education is to identify and guide a gifted few to the truth and to sort and socialize those less intellectually gifted into lesser roles in life.

In Socrates and in his most famous pupil, we encounter opposing visions of what it means to be educated. While the Socratic ideal of the fallible intellectual as critic continues to inspire, its success is overshadowed by the educational and political authoritarianism that began with Plato's philosopher king.

The Rational Animal

The final member of the Greek triumvirate of philosophers still influencing our vision of the ideally educated individual is Aristotle. Recognized in his day and ours as Plato's most famous student, Aristotle joined with his mentor in providing the intellectual foundations for a rather conservative worldview that continues to dominate much of the world. Aristotle joined Plato in believing in an absolute reality and in an ultimate force that transcends the world that humans inhabit, but Aristotle's process for reaching these ultimate generalizations differed dramatically from that of Plato. Characterized by some as the philosophical grandson of Socrates, Aristotle exhibited little of Socrates' humility, having never uttered the phrase "I don't know." Believing that the world could be understood at its most fundamental level through the careful and detailed observation and cataloging of phenomenon, Aristotle employed this approach in developing major treatises on virtually all fields of knowledge. The treatises produced are the results of careful study including an examination of what had been previously written or said on a topic, an analysis of the extant opinions on the subject, and a systematic investigation of all related subjects and material. Refusing to think of the world in abstract terms the way Plato did, Aristotle reasoned inductively, observing as many examples as possible before reaching and embracing an overarching general principle or generalization. This fundamental empirical process employed by Aristotle has become the foundation for our modern scientific method.

Employing this empirical method, Aristotle eventually concluded that human beings are—by nature—rational animals. On the basis of his observations of and reflections on the world around him, he concluded that the characteristic that distinguishes humans from all other things—both animate and inanimate—is the ability to contemplate the universe and wonder about the meaning of the world. Although the potential for reason is inherent in every human being, it is actualized in varying degrees in each individual. For Aristotle, education's role is to create an environment that nurtures the individual's rational potential and actualizes it to the highest degree possible. Using data derived from careful observations of the surrounding universe, Aristotle suggests that human beings—by reflecting upon these data and relating it to or connecting it with other previously acquired data—develop increasing complex and abstract conceptualizations that are consistent with and explain our empirical observations.

Though Aristotle arrived at this point through an entirely different path than did Plato, both embraced the life of the mind as the human being's ultimate quest. Plato is often associated with the origins of idealism and Aristotle with the origins of realism, but collectively they established the liberally educated, rational human being as the exemplar of what it means to be educated.

Idealists versus Realists

While both Plato and Aristotle believed in a universal reality that transcended the temporal and finite world that humans inhabit, their perceptions of the essence of this transcendent reality differed dramatically. Plato believed in the existence of a cosmic soul or absolute mind comprised of all eternal ideas and that human beings possessed a microscopic version of this absolute mind or soul within their being. This belief resulted in Plato and his followers looking inward for the truth and seeking to unfold from within the innate knowledge that resides within each individual. As a result of this belief, Platonists or idealists thought of education as a birthing process, a movement from the inside out. As a result of this inward focus, idealists tend to focus on the affective, the spiritual, the artistic, and the intuitive, even the mystical in the pursuit of the ultimate, more abstract realities.

In contrast, Aristotelians or realists look outside the individual in their pursuit of truth and knowledge. Realists focus on informing the mind using data derived from the world around them. In short, realists focus on the external, the cognitive, the behavioral, and the scientific. While the realists emphasize the study of things through the fields of science and mathematics, the idealists emphasize the study of ideas through literature, history, philosophy, and religion.

Happiness: The Life of the Mind

It should be noted at this point that the Greeks and especially the Romans were largely concerned with the education of leaders or rulers and secondarily with the education of citizens. Whether Platonists, Aristotelians, or advocates of the more pragmatic schools of oratory associated with Isocrates and Quintillian, Graeco-Roman education emphasized the life of the mind through the study of the liberal arts and the humanities. For the Greeks and to a lesser extent for the Romans, happiness in this world was the quintessential goal, and happiness was equated with the life of the mind. Whether it meant exercising the intellect, gaining understanding or true knowledge of the universe, or using knowledge to solve real problems and/or to guide one's life, happiness—since the time of Socrates—became the ultimate educational goal of the Graeco-Roman world.

When the Romans supplanted the Greeks as the dominant political force of the period and region, happiness through education took on added significance. As the Roman Empire expanded and incorporated many diverse populations into its boundaries, culture increasingly became the defining characteristic of what it meant to be a Roman. Being a Roman meant acquiring the Graeco-Roman culture through the study of the literary arts and philosophy. Through such studies, one became civilized, that is, human and free. By studying and embracing this Graeco-Roman culture, one became a Roman and—by embracing the life of the mind—Romans experienced, in varying degrees, happiness in this world.

Happiness as Otherworldly Salvation

As Christianity evolved and emerged into a powerful force throughout the empire, the question of whether one could or should be both a Christian and a Roman began to take on added significance. The conflict between the Christian and the Graeco-Roman or pagan cultures was real and seemingly beyond reconciliation. While the Graeco-Romans sought happiness in this world, the Christians sought salvation in the next. Most Christians eschewed membership in the intellectual culture of the Romans for a kind of mystical universal brotherhood that one achieves not through education but as a result of God's grace.

In short, while the Romans sought happiness through wisdom, honor, and/or glory in this world, the Christians sought happiness through salvation in the next world.

Paradoxically, many Christians wanted to be Romans too, in spite of their abhorrence of Roman culture and education. In reality, their only real choice was either to be a civilized Roman or an ignorant barbarian. At this point, the question became: Can there be a synthesis of Christian and classical cultures? Is it possible to be both a Christian and a Roman? It is at this point that Augustine enters the picture.

Romans and/or Christians

Like many of his contemporaries, Augustine converted to Christianity as an adult (in his thirties). Prior to this conversion, he experienced the worldly materialism associated with well-educated, affluent Romans of the day. He studied rhetoric (literary studies) in Carthage and later became a municipal professor of rhetoric in Milan. Like many of his contemporaries, he cherished the Greek and Latin classics for their literary merits, and he reluctantly and only partially abandoned them once he became a Christian. Realizing that these Greek and Roman classics often glorified gods doing ungodly things (adultery, rape, murder, etc.), Augustine championed a pragmatic compromise, rejecting the questionable morality that filled the pages of classical literature while embracing their literary skills as a tool for preaching the gospel.

Becoming the Bishop of Hippo in AD 395, Augustine contributed to a growing body of Christian literature focused on church doctrine and on describing the saintly exploits of religious leaders worthy of emulation. Following Augustine's pragmatic compromise, Christians embraced the eloquence of the classical scholars as a tool for spreading the gospel of Jesus Christ.

As Christianity grew in popularity, many people questioned the relevancy of inquiry, assuming that Jesus Christ was the answer to all philosophical questions. Since faith in Christianity resulted in possession of the ultimate and divine truth, speculative philosophy seemed irrelevant. Unwilling to abandon his first love completely, Augustine took the lead in developing what is best described as a uniquely Christian philosophy.

Following the lead of the Greek philosophers in their attempt to explain the nature and origins of the universe and the role of humans in this universe, Augustine explained how the answer to each of the basic philosophical questions is god. Augustine agrees with the Greek and the Romans that happiness is the quintessential goal of humankind, but he parts company with them in suggesting that happiness is related more to the will—to what he calls love—than to the life of the mind.

Primarily as a result of the fall of Adam (original sin), humans do not know who or what to love. Given a multitude of options and without god's grace, the human being flounders, pursuing one meaningless desire after another. Through god's grace in the form of Jesus Christ, humans can achieve genuine happiness by choosing a loving union with god.

Though his reasoning may appear circular to our modern sensibilities, Augustine succeeded—by cherry-picking from the Greek and Roman literary tradition—in establishing a plausible intellectual framework in support of Christianity. Reminiscent of Plato, Augustine suggests that there are two kinds of human communities. One (the city of man) is the secular world consisting of those pursuing the pleasure of the flesh. The other comprises those pursuing a spiritual life (the city of god).

Obviously, the goal for Augustine is for humans to choose the city of god over the city of man. For this to happen, the individual must experience directly this ultimate or spiritual reality. No one can teach or transmit knowledge of such a reality, but humans—through divine illumination—are capable of experiencing the abstract and spiritual absolutes that transcend the temporal and finite world.

By participating in the development of a uniquely Christian literature and philosophy, Augustine contributed to Christianity's becoming the dominant social, political, and religious force in the West in the centuries following the fall of Rome. During the period—sometimes referred to as the Dark Ages—much of the Greek and Roman learning was lost to the Western world and replaced with a belief in faith and revelation. In the twelfth and thirteenth centuries—thanks in part to the expansion of the Moslems into Spain and other parts of Europe—Aristotelian and Neoplatonic ideas were revived and with them the tension between Hellenic and Christian thinking.

Aquinas, Aristotle, and the Renaissance

With the re-emergence of Greek and Roman thought and with the founding of universities to prepare religious leaders, scientists, and other professionals, questions regarding the compatibility of the newer, more scientific way of thinking and the settled theological beliefs began to emerge. In response to such challenges to established Christian doctrine, church leaders—most notably Thomas Aquinas—embraced Aristotelian thought and used it to buttress faith in Christianity. Much like Augustine's efforts centuries earlier, Aquinas sought to reconcile Christian doctrine with Greek thought. In doing so, Aquinas and the scholastic method he embraced considered Aristotelian thought to be more compatible with Christian doctrine than were the ideas of Plato.

Whether Aquinas succeeded in reconciling faith and reason remains an open question, but this monumental effort has contributed significantly to the civilization of the Western world. In addition, through the efforts of Aquinas and other scholastics, the legacy of Hellenic thought—most especially Aristotelian—was rekindled to burn brightly, once again, during the time of Erasmus and other Renaissance thinkers.

In part as a result of their intellectual power and skill, St. Thomas Aquinas and other scholastics established the Catholic or universal Church as the dominant institution in the Western world. But the success of the Church led to abuses and corruptions that, along with the collapse of medieval feudalism, created conditions conducive to the changes that began to appear in Europe during the latter part of the fifteenth century. Often referred to as the Renaissance, intellectual commotion characterized this period of Western civilization. A time of religious turmoil that culminates in the polarizing protest of Martin Luther, the Renaissance also suggests a rebirth or a reawakening of the classical Greek learning. Medieval ways of thinking were being challenged, and, reminiscent of classical Greece, education became a major focus. In emulation of Greeks of the fourth and fifth centuries, the leaders of the Renaissance offered relief from the suffocating ascetics of medieval Scholasticism and from a mindless acceptance of Church doctrine. Much like the earlier Greeks, the ideally educated person of the Renaissance was a free thinker, an inquirer, a lover of classical literature and philosophy, a gentler, kinder version of the Socratic gadfly.

The Renaissance Humanist

There is no better exemplar of the renaissance humanist than Desiderius Erasmus. Aware that his beloved European community of scholars was in danger of being overrun by the nationalistic and religious passions of the time, Erasmus remained steadfast in his belief that the elusive middle ground could be found or created. Erasmus believed that faith and reason could be reconciled through Christian piety and classical scholarship. Though no less caustic than Martin Luther in his condemnation of the abuses of the Catholic Church, Erasmus believed that the Church could be salvaged—even strengthened—by grounding Christianity in the truths found in its classical sources. Tragically, history has shown that such a naive faith in reason is no match for the fanaticism of emotions.

Still, Erasmus has much to teach us. He was the true citizen of the world, bounded by neither borders nor geography and blessed with an insatiable curiosity. One of the foremost learned thinkers of his time, Erasmus showed little interest in ritual, formality, or pomp. His description of his friend Thomas More could easily serve as a self-portrait. Like More, Erasmus did not slavishly follow convention but employed good common sense in virtually all situations. Erasmus and the Renaissance humanists shared the ancients' belief in the natural goodness of human beings. This natural human goodness—when educated properly—results in humans doing the right thing. While history has not always supported this optimistic view of human nature, it remains—if not a basic human characteristic—at least a goal worthy of emulation.

The humanist or Renaissance interest in a revival of the classics and in challenging the religious authority of the scholastics received reinforcement in the form of an inductive, investigative mode of thinking often referred to as "scientific inquiry." Relying more and more on natural rather than supernatural explanations of observable events, this growing confidence in the scientific way of thinking enveloped all aspects of life.

Locke's Gentleman

John Locke is representative of this new, more scientific approach, applying this new way of thinking to both politics and education. Often thought of as an enlightenment thinker, Locke looked to his traditional, aristocratic roots in tapping the landed gentry as his ideally educated individual. Largely accepting the established class structure of his day, Locke's social vision of a society governed by a landed gentleman continues the humanist or Renaissance legacy of a hierarchical social order dominated by the educated elite.

Still, Locke's educated gentleman is no Platonic philosopher king. Rather than an omniscient and omnipotent ruler, Locke envisioned rule by a contractual arrangement between the governors and the governed. Grounded in the natural law, this contract guaranteed the governed certain natural rights (life, liberty, property, etc.), and the governors usurped these natural rights at their own peril. Locke's ideal government resembled a political think tank committed to discovering the laws of human nature and to ruling in accordance with them. Absent such a utopia, the next best thing—according to Locke— is rule by an educated landed class. For as Locke asserts in the preface to his *Some Thoughts Concerning Education,* once gentlemen were "by their Education once set right, they will quickly bring all the rest into Order."

Basing his vision on what it means to be educated on the characteristics required of the successful landed gentry in eighteenth-century England, Locke's gentleman ruler was religious, affable, and prudent in both his personal and public affairs. Almost the antithesis of Plato's philosopher king, Locke's gentleman places virtue, wisdom, and breeding above knowledge and learning. For Locke, wisdom was a virtue acquired through commonsense experience. This view of wisdom as an active virtue, naturally acquired, has it is roots in both the Renaissance thought and in the emerging new empiricism. The wisdom necessary for effective leadership was—suggests Locke—as much the product of "good natural temper" and experience as it was the result of the "application of the mind."

Still, the properly educated gentleman—the one whose mind had been set right— was free of intolerance, prejudice, and passion. Of more importance, the leader with the mind set right could both make wise decisions and lead others to decide wisely. In extolling the virtues of the human mind set right by education, Locke—in spite of his class and gender prejudices—deserves Bertrand Russell's characterization of him as the most influential if not the most profound of modern philosophers.

Education and Society: Conflicting Visions

As long as education remained a parental or familial responsibility, parents and guardians of means could determine the nature of education available to their children and youth. Once education became a societal affair, conflicts between personal and societal visions of what it means to be educated began to emerge.

For the Puritans—the intellectual heirs of both the Renaissance and the Reformation—education was so crucial to their vision of a biblical commonwealth that it had to be more than a familial responsibility. For their vision of a theocracy (rule by religious men) to become a reality, everyone must be able to read, understand, and follow societal laws derived from the word of god.

Such a theocracy was an anathema to Jefferson, but education—the ability to read and appreciate the lessons of history—was equally important for his vision of the ideal society as a secular, democratic republic. While their visions of the ideal society are antithetical to one another, the Puritans and Jefferson are alike in that education was so crucial for their respective societal visions that it had to be more than just a parental or family responsibility. Herein lies the roots of the idea that education is a societal or state responsibility, and—due to the nature of their conflicting visions—to the origins of the continuing conflict between religion and education in contemporary education.

Rousseau's Émile and Sophie

With a literary flair reminiscent of Erasmus' in *The Praise of Folly,* Jean Jacques Rousseau lambasted virtually all civil institutions of his time for denying and destroying humankind's natural freedom and goodness. Like the ancients but in obvious conflict with Christian beliefs, Rousseau considered humans to be naturally good. The debasement of this natural goodness—so evident in the Europe of the eighteenth century—is, Rousseau suggests, the product of so-called advances in the arts and sciences.

To correct this decline in the moral fiber of humankind and to regain the personal freedom and goodness that characterizes humankind's natural state, Rousseau called for creating an education environment that allows—indeed requires—that humans develop in accordance with their nature. In such an environment, the child experiences directly the limitations of nature and readily accepts them. By exposing the child to a carefully constructed "natural" environment, Rousseau believed that the natural capacity for freedom could be preserved, allowing each human's natural goodness to develop and to eventually blossom into both a good human being and a good citizen.

Suggesting that contemporary human beings had been corrupted by modern civilization, Rousseau sought to create a new, more natural human being who was both a good person and a good citizen. These new humans, Émile and Sophie, were to be isolated from the corrupting institutions of modern civilization and free from the artificial conventions of society. By creating such an ideal, natural environment, Émile and Sophie, learned that with freedoms came responsibilities, for actions freely chosen had consequences.

At times, it appears as if Rousseau champions the individual when conflicts with society arise, while on other occasions, he seems to embrace a totalitarian collective that severely limits human freedom. In reality, what Rousseau does is to confront the individual/collectivity problem directly. In short, Rousseau believed that—by properly educating future generations—it was possible to create a society where individual desires and societal demands were joined.

By creating a society of his ideally educated human beings—a society comprising Émiles and Sophies—Rousseau believed that it was possible to develop boys and girls into both good men and good women and good citizens. In the selection from *Émile* included here, Rousseau's advocacy of different kinds of education for boys and girls clearly offends our more contemporary sensibilities. And as indicated in the selection included from Rousseau's contemporary—Catharine Macaulay—a more gender-equal vision of the ideally educated individual appeared in 1790.

Macaulay's Benevolent Being

In *Letters on Education with Observations on Religious and Metaphysical Subjects,* Catharine Macaulay offered a counterpoint to Rousseau's commonly accepted view that there are essential differences between men and women and that these differences are complementary. Though well-known and respected for her history of the English civil war of the seventeenth century, Macaulay's educational ideas were largely ignored in her own time, and her quarrel with the educational ideas of Rousseau, Locke, and Plato have not been included in the study of educational thought through the ages. Jane Roland Martin—a present-day philosopher of education—argues that women's responses to such questions as what constitutes an educated individual have been excluded from the philosophical canon and their contributions to the field marginalized. According to Martin, "the disciplines (including educational philosophy) exclude women from their subject matter; they distort the female according to the male image of her; and they deny the feminine by forcing women into a masculine mold."[2] The failure to entertain Macaulay's contribution as a worthy counterpoint in the debate regarding the ideally educated human being adds credence to Martin's argument that women's ideas have been ignored to the detriment of all human beings.

Macaulay's *Letters on Education* published in 1790 effectively refutes the more conventional views on gender and education represented in Rousseau's work. Arguing that there is a single human essence composed of what has been labeled as feminine and masculine attributes, Macaulay suggests that both boys and girls need to be reeducated to overcome the false gender images fostered by society. Rather than just emphasizing a new and an improved education for women, Macaulay proposes that the education of both men and women be refashioned into an integrated whole that fosters a genderless human nature in emulation of a more divine nature. Macaulay has great faith that the right kind of education will produce human beings committed to the virtues of reason and benevolence.

Macaulay's ideas on what it means to be educated merit serious consideration. To the extent that she effectively counters Rousseau's advocacy of different and supposedly complementary education programs for boys and girls, her ideas offer a new perspective through which to consider the thought of those significantly influenced by Rousseau: Pestallozzi, Froebel, Montessori, Dewey, and others. Macaulay was—in many ways—ahead of her time as similar ideas appear in more contemporary forms in the works of Paulo Freire, Jane Roland Martin, and Nel Noddings.

[2]Jane Roland Martin, "Excluding Women from the Educational Realm," *Harvard Educational Review* 52 (1982): 35.

Local versus Centralized Control of Education

As suggested above, education took on added significance during the Age of Enlightenment, but who or what is responsible for it. Is education a private or public responsibility? Is education the primary responsibility of the local community or should the larger society assume responsibility for educating the children and youth? What is or should be the relationship between education and the state? Should education promote nationalism? If so, how is this to be done? The role of education in defining what it means to be an American became an especially poignant question during the first half of the nineteenth century. During this period the "pure little democracies"—or district or public schools—emerged as the dominant educational institution in the United States. Beginning in the 1830s, Horace Mann successfully challenged the idea of local control of schooling, effectively succeeding where Jefferson failed in establishing a statewide system of the education.

Though the United States does not have a national or federal system of education, Horace Mann and other nineteenth century school reformers achieved a remarkable consensus on what it means to be educated from Massachusetts to California. Following Massachusetts's lead, almost every state had a Mann-like figure championing the virtues of the common school. By 1848, twenty-four of the thirty states in the union had named a chief state school officer and were in the process of establishing what came to be known as the "one best system" of education. Simply put, these school reformers fashioned a new U.S. institution. Known as the common or public school, it was to be free (supported by tax dollars) and open and attractive to (almost) all people. The curriculum emphasized basic skills (the three R's) and purportedly the values common to all Americans.

Education: The Panacea for African Americans?

The common school originated in New England, spread rapidly throughout the Mid-Atlantic and Midwestern states, and established a foothold on the West Coast prior to the Civil War. As the war came to end, the next generation of common school crusaders hoped that a truly integrated common school system could help reunite the wayward South and reduce, if not eliminate, the racial divisions largely responsible for this conflict. With the inevitable failure of this effort to transform the South into clones of the North and West, reformers lost faith in the efficacy of the common school for all children. Based on their experiences in the post-Civil War South , school reformers concluded that Negroes or African Americans were inferior and embraced industrial education as the most appropriate training for the so-called "child races."

Schooling—whether the accomodationist industrial training advocated by Booker T. Washington or the more elitist "talented tenth" approach championed by William E. B. Du Bois—remained the solution for the nation's "Negro" problem well into the twentieth century. It was not until the non-violent protests of the 1950s and 60s that the focus shifted from appropriately educating the "child races" to educating the white population to the horrors of racism in America. This shift, led by the Reverend Martin Luther King, Jr., provided momentum for a civil rights movement admonishing the nation to live up to its creed.

Darwin, Huxley, and Dewey: The Challenge of Modern Science

Paralleling the social and political conflicts described above, a new mode of scientific inquiry emerged to challenge traditional ways of thinking and the worldviews upon which they were based. Stressing inductive, experimental methods of investigation, these new scientists increasingly sought natural rather than supernatural explanations for the mysteries of life. While this new scientific way of thinking—focusing on natural causes of observable phenomena—certainly influenced the thought of Locke, Rousseau, and even Macaulay, the real challenge to the religious and/or absolutist worldview exploded on the world stage with the publication of Charles Darwin's *Origins of Species* in 1859.

Though the culture of science has its roots in the Renaissance and enlightenment eras, the nineteenth century—with its emphasis on technology and industrialization—ushered in what came to be known as the scientific age. By championing Darwin's theory of evolution and the scientific thinking that produced it, Thomas Henry Huxley assumed the mantra of "Darwin's bulldog" and became the first spokesperson for this scientific age.

In Huxley we encounter a vision of the ideally educated individual as a scientific humanist, that is, one who is fascinated by the natural order of things and committed to discovering and understanding the natural laws that govern such phenomena. As a proponent of this new scientific way of thinking, Huxley considered science as a liberator, freeing humankind from an unnatural dependence on false or unsubstantiated beliefs. While Huxley and Herbert Spencer championed this new scientific approach in Great Britain and Europe, John Dewey would soon emerge—first in the United States and eventually worldwide—as the most significant advocate of a reflective scientist as the ideally educated human being.

From Absolutism to Experimentalism

Born in the year that Darwin published his theory of evolution, John Dewey lived through the transformation of the United States from a largely agrarian, divided republic into the major military and industrial power in the world. Growing up in a puritan New England dominated by a religious culture, Dewey gradually abandoned his religious foundations, and—as he explains in "From Absolutism to Experimentalism"—transformed his metaphysical idealism into pragmatic naturalism. Earning his doctorate in philosophy from Johns Hopkins University, Dewey reconciled his religious upbringing with his intellectual journey by embracing the absolutist metaphysics of Hegelian idealism.

By the early 1890s, Dewey distanced himself from the metaphysical absolutists. Keenly aware of the intellectual ferment created by Darwin's challenge to an absolutist worldview, Dewey gradually developed a philosophy of experience that utilized the new scientific way of thinking in support of his commitment to social justice and democracy. Dewey's embrace of experimentalism was not done cavalierly, but, by the time he became the chair of the Department of Philosophy, Psychology, and Pedagogy at the University of Chicago (1894), he concluded that a commitment to democratic principles could be sustained by grounding them in experience. Having achieved a degree of comfort with this reconciliation, Dewey spent the remainder of his life working out the implications of this philosophical shift for his social, political, and educational ideas.

Dewey appreciated the quality of Plato's thought, but he rejected the either/or (Aristotelian or Platonic) worldview that dominated the Western world for centuries. From this rather traditional perspective, knowledge is innate, that either is, inside the individual at birth awaiting the right mnemonic device to bring it to consciousness or is external to human beings awaiting our discovery. In either case, an absolute is implied, resulting in the imposition of knowledge and values upon each generation. Dewey suggests that such a worldview may be appropriate for a monarchy or some other form of autocracy, but it is antithetical to education in a democracy.

Dewey proposed a "new education" grounded in experience. In distinguishing good or educative experiences from bad or miseducative experiences, Dewey suggests that an educative experience is characterized by both interaction and continuity. To Dewey, reality was neither innate nor outside the human being, but is a human construct produced by human beings as they interacted with an ever-changing world, a universe of endless possibilities. Much like Socrates, Dewey suggests that for humans to grow or improve, they must encounter problematic situations.

As the human mind interacts with a universe with the lid off, a problem is identified, possible hypotheses or plans for action are developed, potential consequences are considered, and action is taken based on the most desirable choice. Keeping in mind that the most desirable plan of action is the one that fosters long-term growth, the ideally educated human chooses and acts upon a course of action and then evaluates the actual consequences produced by the action. For Dewey the ideally educated person is one who does more than just react to external stimuli. Such an individual thinks and reflects before acting, responds intelligently to a problematic situation, and finally assesses the consequences of a chosen plan of action to determine its efficacy in addressing the problem.

With the possible exception of the influence of Plato and Aristotle, Dewey's influence on the educational thought of the modern world is unprecedented. Falsely and sometimes foolishly criticized for the foibles of progressive education, Dewey's legacy remains strong as both contemporary critics and followers cite his work either as a foil to illuminate their differing views or to suggest that their ideas stand on the shoulders of this philosophical giant.

Traditional versus Progressive Education: The Continuing Debate

To better understand the various and sometime competing views of the differing conceptions of what it means to be educated in the twentieth century, the intellectual debates between followers of Dewey and their more conservative challengers merit attention. Sometimes referred to as the "classicists versus the experimentalists," these intellectual sparring matches dominated the educational journals of the 1930s and 1940s. The chief protagonists—John Dewey and Robert M. Hutchins—agreed that children need to read, to understand the past, and to experience literature, but they disagreed over the appropriate means to achieve these ends.

Hutchins favored a great books curriculum with students' reading and engaging the great minds of the Western world as they struggled with the perennial philosophical questions of humankind. Dewey countered that the "attempt to re-establish linguistic skills and materials as the center of education and to do so in the guise of 'education for freedom' is directly opposed to all that democratic countries cherish as freedom." He saw the major fallacy of classicism as its supposition "that the subject matter of liberal education is fixed in itself."[3]

This debate between what is sometimes referred to as the traditionalist or conservatives versus progressive educators has continued through the generations manifesting itself in slightly different forms. In the 1950s, for example, academics like Arthur Bestor, a history professor from the University of Illinois, gained notoriety by denouncing public education in America. Bestor, in his critique titled *Educational Wastelands,* attacks progressive education in general and "life adjustment" curricula in particular. Reminiscent of positions articulated by Hutchins, Bestor and others called for a return to a classical curriculum that fostered intellectual discipline in the individual and that sought to transmit the essential—if not eternal—truths and values to each new generation of students. Such

[3]John Dewey, "Challenge to Liberal Thought," *Fortune,* 30:2 (August 1944): 156.

conservative thought dominated America education for most of the twentieth century and remains influential today.

Whether the critic is Robert M. Hutchins, Mortimer Adler, Arthur Bestor, or—more recently—Allan Bloom or E. D. Hirsch, the culprit is often John Dewey and a version of progressive education that only sometimes is derived from Dewey's thought. Most of these conservative critics espouse a vision of what it means to be educated derived more from the thought of Plato and Aristotle than from that of John Dewey and his followers.

Existentialism in Ascendancy

Existentialism is not a philosophy in the way that idealism, realism, or even pragmatism is said to be. It is not systematic and does not aspire to be. At best, it is an approach to philosophy that is fixated on what it means to be human in a world without certainty. Gaining popularity in the aftermath of World War II, existentialists are perhaps best associated with the phrase, *existence precedes essence*. At its core, the phrase suggests that there is no common or universal characteristic that prescribes and describes human nature. From the existentialist point of view, each individual human being is alone in a world without meaning and defines oneself through the choices that the individual freely makes. Humans are often in a state of despair and experience significant anguish since there is no one or no thing to guide or direct them. They are here, alone, and—as Sartre says—"condemned to be free."

As to be expected, themes of anguish, despair, and alienation dominate the thought of many of these thinkers, but some existentialists choose a more hopeful or optimistic perspective. As Maxine Greene suggests, there is something liberating about awakening to the realization that you are an autonomous creature responsible for creating your own unique essence through the choices you freely make. To the extent that existentialists concern themselves with education, they tend to embrace humanistic studies, because it is in the various art forms that human existence is portrayed in all its splendid poignancy.

Maxine Greene is one of the preeminent American educational philosophers of the twentieth and twenty-first centuries. For almost half a century, Greene has invited students and colleagues to "do philosophy in their own voices, to become more aware of their situations, to resist what they find unacceptable." Now in her nineties, Maxine Greene has never stopped teaching, purposely shocking her students and colleagues into an awareness of the taken for granted in hopes of enabling them to become more critical and humane beings in an uncertain world. Greene continues—as she explains—"asking, imagining, writing, teaching, I try with my companions, with my students, with live and wide-awake people . . . (in my own fashion) to awaken." Very much aware that others may wonder why she bothers, Greene answers that " . . . I have to resist meaningless along with objectness and cruelty and injustice. Otherwise, why live?"[4]

Pragmatism and/or Existentialism

Richard Rorty has suggested that there are few, if any, significant differences between the thought of pragmatists and of existentialists. There are those prepared to take issue with this assertion, but for our purposes it is reasonable to suggest that several of the remaining thinkers included in this volume have—in developing their visions of what it means to be educated— been significantly influenced by the thought of both pragmatists and existentialists. Among these thinkers are Jane Roland Martin, Paulo Freire, and Nel Noddings.

[4]William Ayers and Janet L. Miller, eds., *A Light in Dark Times: Maxine Greene and the Unfinished Conversation* (New York: Teachers College Press, 1998), p. x.

In countering the male chauvinism that has dominated the field of educational philosophy for much of its history, Jane Roland Martin calls for a gender-sensitive approach to developing the ideally educated person. In her view, to be educated is to engage in a conversation that stretches back in time, that enables today's students of both sexes to converse with scholars—men and women—of the past. From Martin's point of view, education is the development of intellectual and moral habits through the give-and-take of the conversation, the place where one comes to know what it means to be a person.

As one of the most influential thinkers of the late twentieth and early twenty-first centuries, Paulo Freire—the Brazilian philosopher and educator—is known for his advocacy of dialogue as a key component of the pedagogy of the oppressed. In contrast to the "banking" method of education in which those privileged to know the truth deposit it in the appropriate amount and form into the empty and limited minds of the unwashed, Freire—much like Dewey—favors a problem-posing approach to education. Known for his work in helping Brazilian illiterates to read, Freire helped peasants to understand that they too were creators of culture and that they could contribute to the transformation of their own reality.

Nel Noddings—a prominent contemporary educational theorist—asserts that had the disciplines been developed by women rather than men, the fields of study would have been organized around the stages of life. For example, philosophy—a male-dominated field—focuses on questions of death and an afterlife. In the tradition of Catharine Macaulay and in tune with the thought of Jane Roland Martin, Professor Noddings suggests that questions of birth would be more prominent in a feminist-oriented philosophy of education. In language similar to that of Martin, Noddings reminds us that a rigorous and academically challenging curriculum could be developed around the question: What does it mean to make a home? By focusing on caring as an educational goal, Noddings shines a spotlight on the ethical and moral foundations of education.

The Critical Thinker: The Fallible Human Being Revisited

As we conclude this essay, it is altogether fitting that we revisit the notion that there is a "battle for the mind" between competing visions of the ideally educated human being. Tim LaHaye, a leading contemporary proponent of the Religious Right, suggests that there is a conflict between those who wish to indoctrinate humankind to do the right thing and those seeking to educate human beings to think for themselves. In this battle, the Religious Right and advocates of critical thinking as the educational ideal are natural enemies.

By its very nature, critical thinking requires questioning of conventional attitudes and keeping an open mind. But it is this championing of a healthy skepticism, of open-mindedness, that makes this movement the natural enemy of the Religious Right. To the Religious Right, "open mindedness is not some inviolate concept that every educator has the duty or even the right to encourage." Many Christian fundamentalists believe that anything that encourages questioning of traditional values has no place in education. Articulating a point of view that is still representative of the Religious Right, Alice Moore of the Kanawa County (West Virginia) textbook controversy, proclaims her belief "in indoctrinating my children." Beginning with the assumption that god exists; she explains that "concerning my children's rearing, I am doctrinally dogmatic and dictatorial."[5]

Consider a different approach. Even when we believe that traditional values are the best, it is important that we allow them to be accepted or rejected by each new generation.

[5]Joe Kincheloe, *Understanding the New Right and Its Impact on Education* (Bloomington, Indiana: Phi Delta Educational foundation, 1983), p. 17.

Modern-day proponents of critical thinking as an educational ideal—Lipman, Matthews, Noddings, Egan, and others—embrace the Socratic notion that the arguments favoring traditional values should be given the fullest expression by one capable of presenting the best possible case for them. Such thinkers favor providing all points of view a fair and equitable hearing. Those championing the critical thinker as the ideally educated individual have faith in both human nature and the power of education to assist each individual in identifying the strongest argument and in making the right choices.

The notion of the critical thinker as the ideally educated person is rooted in humility, in the recognition that while progress toward knowing the truth is possible, absolute certainty is not. Those adhering to this point of view are open to opinions different from their own. By considering other points of view, they may encounter additional evidence that refutes all or part of their original stance. After carefully examining the additional evidence, they may find it incorrect or irrelevant, thus enhancing their original position. Or they may, as Parker Palmer suggests, become paradoxical thinkers adept at celebrating contradictions.

Matthew Lipman, Gareth Matthews, and Kieran Egan embrace—in slightly different ways—the critical thinker as the ideally educated individual. Parker J. Palmer adds a spiritual dimension to their versions of the critical thinker. Lipman—by developing a philosophically sophisticated curriculum—has successfully dramatized philosophy, making it accessible to children and youth. Matthews—by personally engaging children and youth in philosophically rich conversations and capturing them in print—illustrates how a child's natural inquisitiveness can be employed in developing a thoughtful and critical thinker. Egan, in championing the role that imagination plays in the educational process, demonstrates how imagination supports the cognitive development of children and youth. While the Philosophy for Children approach employs a more formalized strategy, Matthews and Egan join Lipman in supporting a Socratic community of inquiry as the primary vehicle for developing children and youth into critical thinkers. Palmer employs similar language in proposing a community of truth as the best means for developing individuals into thoughtful, critical thinkers who are willing to struggle with life's most profound paradoxes and contradictions.

As suggested in this brief historical overview, humankind continues to struggle to improve ourselves and our worlds through education. These struggles are often influenced by differing and—at times—competing responses to the question of what does it mean to be educated. While the definitive answer to that question is not forthcoming, the quest is and should be never-ending. Perhaps it is this quest—this journey to Ithaca and not the arrival—that is the essence of education. It is our hope that this brief cultural discussion of the thinkers and themes included in this volume will entice you—as prospective and practicing educators—to join in this never-ending quest for what it means to be educated and how to foster it.

1
Socrates and Plato

Time Line for Socrates

470 BC	Is born in Athens, Greece, the son of Sophroniscus, a stonemason, and Phaenarete, a midwife.
470–400	Grows up during the "golden age" of Greece—his father, an intimate friend of the son of Aristides the Just, provides Socrates an acquaintanceship with the members of the Pericles circle.
	Serves with valor in the Peloponnesian War.
	Marries Xanthippe. They have seven or eight children.
	Is declared the wisest man by the Oracle at Delphi.
	Is put on trial for corrupting the minds of the youth of Athens.
399	Is found guilty and forced to drink hemlock.

Socrates wrote nothing. All that we know of him is from the writings of Aristophenes (The Clouds), *Plato, and Xenophon.*

Time Line for Plato

427 BC	Is born in Athens, Greece, to a prominent family. Following his father's death, his mother marries Pyrilampes, a close friend of Pericles.
405–400	Studies with Socrates.
399	Attends the trial and execution of Socrates.
387	Establishes the Academy. Later, Eudoxius, respected mathematician, unites his school, located at Cyzicus, with the Academy.
367	Accepts Aristotle into the Academy.
347	Dies in Athens.

Although scholars continue to debate the time frame of Plato's writings, the following are generally attributed to each period:

Early Period	Works, usually referred to as Socratic dialogues, focus on ethics. Included in this period are *Apology, Crito, Charmides, Laches, Euthyphro, Euthydemus, Cratylus, Protagoras,* and *Gorgias.*

Middle Period	Works focus on theory of ideas and metaphysical doctrines. Included in this period are *Meno, Symposium, Phaedo, The Republic,* and *Phaedrus.*
Late Period	Works focus on a reconsideration of the middle period, most notably the theory of ideas. Included in this period are *Theaetetus, Parmenides, Sophist, Statesman, Philebus, Timaeus,* and *The Laws.*

INTRODUCTION

Philosophy begins in the West with a group of philosophers variously known as the natural philosophers or the pre-Socratics. Men—and the history of Western philosophy has been dominated by males—such as Thales, Anaximander, Anaximenes, Parmenides, Empedocles, and Heraclitus were all engaged in an attempt to discover the secrets of the natural world, to reduce the mass of phenomena to a few manageable principles, and to understand their natural environments. What held them together was a belief that one could reason one's way to the truth, that by looking at natural effects one could deduce their causes. What distinguished one from the other was that they each reasoned their way to different causes. For some, the natural world was reducible to one immovable substance. For others, there were four basic elements (earth, air, fire, and water). Others saw five or six or even more basic causes.

This led a group of philosophers, the Sophists, to react against the program of the natural philosophers. Whereas the natural philosophers assumed that an educated person, a wise person, was one who knew the *truth* about things *natural,* the Sophists claimed that since "reason" generated so many different conclusions, there was something unreliable about reason itself. If, the Sophists suggested, reason were a reliable tool, it should always yield the same results. It did not; hence, the Sophists shifted inquiry away from an attempt to discover the truth about the natural world to an attempt to teach a useful skill.

The Sophists were the first professional teachers. They went around to the families of young boys—again, notice this orientation toward males—and offered to teach those boys how to argue persuasively. The Sophists said, in effect: We don't care what your position is. We don't care whether you are telling the truth or not. We will teach you how to make your case and how to win arguments. This was an especially valuable skill because eventually those boys would, as heads of households, have to speak in the public forums that constituted Greek democracy. If they could not speak well, their family's fortune would suffer.

Into this mix—a mix that included a switch from the educated person as she or he who knew the truth about the natural world to the educated person as she or he who could argue persuasively regardless of the truth or falsity of the position—came the character Socrates.

If one reads the dialogue *Apology* carefully, one will see that two of the accusations against Socrates suggest that Socrates was both a natural philosopher and a Sophist at the same time. Certainly, since one was a reaction against the other, Socrates cannot be both. But what was Socrates? What was his doctrine? Why was he so important? We will try to answer those questions in the second part of this introduction.

Most of what we know about Socrates comes from three sources. Socrates did not write; indeed, he distrusted the written word, and so we must rely on the plays of Aristophenes and the dialogues of Xenophon and Plato.[1] For our purposes, we will concentrate on those writings that are clearly the most important, both philosophically and historically, that is, the writing of Socrates' student, Plato.

Most commentators divide Plato's writing into three major periods. In the early dialogues, *Apology, Charmides,* and *Phaedo,* for example, Plato gives a fairly accurate portrayal of Socrates. Plato was almost like a "fly on the wall" or a tape recorder, and one "hears" dialogues that may actually have taken place. This is the place to go to find out what Socrates was about and what he was teaching. In the middle period, *The Republic* is a good example of Plato's using Socrates to espouse his (Plato's) own doctrine. That doctrine is called the Theory of the Forms, and the middle period is the place to go if one wants to see what the mature Plato thought. Toward the end of his career, Plato had some doubts about his theory; in later dialogues like *Parmenides, Theaetetus,* and *Sophist,* one sees Plato rethinking and, perhaps, rejecting the theory. At the same time, because Socrates was Plato's mouthpiece in the middle period, the character of Socrates now becomes a minor figure, becomes a figure of ridicule and scorn, or drops out altogether. The later dialogues are not the place to go to get an accurate picture of Socrates.

So who was Socrates, and what did he espouse? The dialogue *Apology* is probably the best place to start. As mentioned previously, Socrates was on trial for his life. After rejecting a number of the more far-fetched accusations (accusations that suggested he was a natural philosopher and a Sophist), Socrates wonders what the real charge against him is. He settles on the charge that he is guilty of corrupting the morals of the youth of Athens.

As one will see, "Socratic irony" is an apt description. Socrates, in the company of his students, engaged those with a reputation for wisdom in a dialogue. Over the course of those dialogues, Socrates discovered, and so did his students and the people who were questioned, that those with a reputation for wisdom did not always deserve it. Socrates was wiser than the "wisest" people because he knew his own limits: he knew that he did not know, while they mistakenly thought they did. For Socrates, the educated person is precisely the person who knows her or his limitations, who knows that she or he does not know.

There are two points that are worthy of consideration. The first is that this person, whom many consider to be one of the two great teachers in the Western tradition (Jesus is the other), professed to have virtually no doctrine and said that what he knew was unimportant. Over and over again, in the *Apology,* the *Phaedrus,* and the *Charmides,* Socrates suggests that true wisdom is the property of the gods, and that what he has—this human wisdom, this knowledge of his own limitations—is worth hardly anything at all.

The second point is that Socrates puts an enormous amount of weight, some might call it faith, on the power of the dialogue, that back-and-forth linguistic motion between speakers, to uncover the truth. When Socrates discusses ideas with those with a reputation for wisdom, a truth always emerges from the dialogue. The dialogue allows the truth to emerge—in the excerpt from *The Republic,* the truth is about some mistaken

---

[1]A dialogue is perhaps best understood as a focused attempt by a group of speakers to solve a limited number of problems or to answer a few questions.

claims to knowledge. Socrates is different from the Sophists because he thinks there is a "truth" to be discovered. He is different from the natural philosophers because the method that he uses—discourse, dialogue, conversation—is public and communal; it is open to scrutiny in a way that reasoning, as a purely mental activity, is not.

Plato, as one would expect from a student, took much from his teacher Socrates. For Plato, education is a matter of leading a person from mere belief to true knowledge. In his classic "Allegory of the Cave," Plato suggests that we, as uneducated persons, are chained in a cave, seeing shadows on the wall and mistakenly believing that the shadows (and the cave itself) are the real things. Education involves breaking those chains and leading a person from the cave into the bright sunshine. The good teacher does this through the dialectical process, leading the student as far as she or he is capable. The best students—those most philosophical, those best educated—will use the dialectical process to discover true beauty, goodness, and justice. Plato is different from his teacher, Socrates, precisely because the wisdom that Plato's students would discover is worth a good deal; that is, it involves knowledge of objective standards (the Forms) that will enable people to lead good, productive lives.

The following selections include one from the *Apology* and two from *The Republic*. The first section from *The Republic* presents an introduction to the Theory of the Forms. In the second, Plato presents a story, "The Allegory of the Cave," which is meant to shed light on the theory.

FROM PLATO'S *APOLOGY* (CA. 399 BC)

I dare say that someone will ask the question, "Why is this, Socrates, and what is the origin of these accusations of you: for there must have been something strange which you have been doing? All this great fame and talk about you would never have arisen if you had been like other men: tell us, then, why this is, as we should be sorry to judge hastily of you." Now I regard this as a fair challenge, and I will endeavor to explain to you the origin of this name of "wise," and of this evil fame. Please to attend then. And, although some of you may think that I am joking, I declare that I will tell you the entire truth. Men of Athens, this reputation of mine has come of a certain sort of wisdom which I possess. If you ask me what kind of wisdom, I reply, such wisdom as is attainable by man, for to that extent I am inclined to believe that I am wise; whereas the persons of whom I was speaking have a superhuman wisdom, which I may fail to describe, because I have it not myself; and he who says that I have, speaks falsely, and is taking away my character. And here, O men of Athens, I must beg you not to interrupt me, even if I seem to say something extravagant. For the word which I will speak is not mine. I will refer you to a witness who is worthy of credit, and will tell you about my wisdom—whether I have any, and of what sort—and that witness shall be the God of Delphi. You must have known Chaerephon; he was early a friend of mine, and also a friend of yours, for he shared in the exile of the people, and returned with you. Well, Chaerephon, as you know, was very impetuous in all his doings, and he went to Delphi and boldly asked the oracle to tell him whether—as I was saying, I must beg you not to interrupt—he asked the oracle to tell him whether there was any one wiser than I was, and the Pythian prophetess answered, that there was no man wiser. Chaerephon is dead himself; but his brother, who is in court, will confirm the truth of this story.

Why do I mention this? Because I am going to explain to you why I have such an evil name. When I heard the answer, I said to myself, What can the god mean? and what is the interpretation of this riddle? for I know that I have no wisdom, small or great. What then can he mean when he says that I am the wisest of men? And yet he is a god, and cannot lie; that would be against his nature. After long consideration, I at last thought of a method of trying the question. I reflected that if I could only find a man wiser than myself, then I might go to the god with a refutation in my hand. I should say to him, "Here is a man who is wiser than I am; but you said that I was the wisest." Accordingly, I went to one who had the reputation of wisdom, and observed him—his name I need not mention; he was a politician whom I selected for examination—and the result was as follows: When I began to talk with him, I could not help thinking that he was not really wise, although he was thought wise by many, and wiser still by himself; and I went and tried to explain to him that he thought himself wise, but was not really wise, and the consequence was that he hated me, and his enmity was shared by several who were present and heard me. So I left him, saying to myself, as I went away: Well, although I do not suppose that either of us knows anything really beautiful and good, I am better off than he is,—for he knows nothing, and thinks that he knows. I neither know nor think that I know. In this latter particular, then, I seem to have slightly the advantage of him. Then I went to another who had still higher philosophical pretensions, and my conclusion was exactly the same. I made another enemy of him, and of many others besides him.

After this I went to one man after another, being not unconscious of the enmity which I provoked, and I lamented and feared this: but necessity was laid upon me—the word of God, I thought, ought to be considered first. And I said to myself, Go I must to all who appear to know, and find out the meaning of the oracle. And I swear to you, Athenians, by the dog I swear!—for I must tell you the truth—the result of my mission was just this: I found that the men most in repute were all but the most foolish; and that some inferior men were really wiser and better. I will tell you the tale of my wanderings and of the "Herculean" labors, as I may call them, which I endured only to find at last the oracle irrefutable. When I left the politicians, I went to the poets; tragic, dithyrambic, and all sorts. And there, I said to myself, you will be detected; now you will find out that you are more ignorant than they are. Accordingly, I took them some of the most elaborate passages in their own writings, and asked what was the meaning of them—thinking that they would teach me something. Will you believe me? I am almost ashamed to speak of this, but still I must say that there is hardly a person present who would not have talked better about their poetry than they did themselves. That showed me in an instant that not by wisdom do poets write poetry, but by a sort of genius and inspiration; they are like diviners or soothsayers who also say many fine things, but do not understand the meaning of them. And the poets appeared to me to be much in the same case; and I further observed that upon the strength of their poetry they believed themselves to be the wisest of men in other things in which they were not wise. So I departed, conceiving myself to be superior to them for the same reason that I was superior to the politicians.

At last I went to the artisans, for I was conscious that I knew nothing at all, as I may say, and I was sure that they knew many fine things; and in this I was not mistaken, for they did know many things of which I was ignorant, and in this they certainly were wiser than I was. But I observed that even the good artisans fell into the same error as the poets;—because they were good workmen they thought that they also knew all sorts of high matters, and this defect in them overshadowed their wisdom—therefore I asked myself on behalf of the oracle, whether I would like to be as I was, neither having their knowledge nor their ignorance, or like them in both; and I made answer to myself and the oracle that I was better off as I was.

This investigation has led to my having many enemies of the worst and most dangerous kind, and has given occasion also to many calumnies. And I am called wise, for my hearers always imagine that I myself possess the wisdom which I find wanting in others: but the truth is, O men of Athens, that God only is wise; and in this oracle he means to say that the wisdom of men is little or nothing; he is not speaking of Socrates, he is only using my name as an illustration, as if he said, He, O men, is the wisest who, like Socrates, knows that his wisdom is in truth worth nothing. And so I go my way, obedient to the god, and make inquisition into the wisdom of any one, whether citizen or stranger, who appears to be wise; and if he is not wise, then in vindication of the oracle I show him that he is not wise; and this occupation quite absorbs me, and I have no time to give either to any public matter of interest or to any concern of my own, but I am in utter poverty by reason of my devotion to the god. . . .

From Hamilton, Edith. *Plato.* © 1961 by Princeton University Press, renewed 1989. Reprinted by permission of Princeton University Press.

From Plato's *The Republic* (ca. 366 bc)

Book VI

Conceive then, said I, as we were saying, that there are these two entities, and that one of them is sovereign over the intelligible order and region and the other over the world of the eyeball, not to say the sky-ball, but let that pass. You surely apprehend the two types, the visible and the intelligible.

I do.

Represent them then, as it were, by a line divided into two unequal sections and cut each section again in the same ratio—the section, that is, of the visible and that of the intelligible order—and then as an expression of the ratio of their comparative clearness and obscurity you will have, as one of the sections of the visible world, images. By images I mean, first, shadows, and then reflections in water and on surfaces of dense, smooth, and bright texture, and everything of that kind, if you apprehend.

I do.

As the second section assume that of which this is a likeness or an image, that is, the animals about us and all plants and the whole class of objects made by man.

I so assume it, he said.

Would you be willing to say, said I, that the division in respect of reality and truth or the opposite is expressed by the proportion—as is the opinable to the knowable so is the likeness to that of which it is a likeness?

I certainly would.

Consider then again the way in which we are to make the division of the intelligible section.

In what way?

By the distinction that there is one section of it which the soul is compelled to investigate by treating as images the things imitated in the former division, and by means of assumptions from which it proceeds not up to a first principle but down to a conclusion, while there is another section in which it advances from its assumption to a beginning or principle that transcends assumption, and in which it makes no use of the images employed by the other section, relying on ideas only and progressing systematically through ideas.

I don't fully understand what you mean by this, he said.

Well, I will try again, said I, for you will better understand after this preamble. For I think you are aware that students of geometry and reckoning and such subjects first postulate the odd and the even and the various figures and three kinds of angles and other things akin to these in each branch of science, regard them as known, and, treating them as absolute assumptions, do not deign to render any further account of them to themselves or others, taking it for granted that they are obvious to everybody. They take their start from these, and pursuing the inquiry from this point on consistently, conclude with that for the investigation of which they set out.

Certainly, he said, I know that.

And do you not also know that they further make use of the visible forms and talk about them, though they are not thinking of them but of those things of which they are a likeness, pursuing their inquiry for the sake of the square as such and the diagonal as such, and not for the sake of the image of it which they draw? And so in all cases. The very things which they mold and draw, which have shadows and images of themselves in water, these things they treat in their turn as only images, but what they really seek is to get sight of those realities which can be seen only by the mind.

True, he said.

This then is the class that I described as intelligible, it is true, but with the reservation first that the soul is compelled to employ assumptions in the investigation of it, not proceeding to a first principle because of its inability to extricate itself from the rise above its assumptions, and second, that it uses as images or likenesses the very objects that are themselves copied and adumbrated by the class below them, and that in comparison with these latter are esteemed as clear and held in honor.

I understand, said he, that you are speaking of what falls under geometry and the kindred arts.

Understand then, said I, that by the other section of the intelligible I mean that which the reason itself lays hold of by the power of dialectic, treating its assumptions not as absolute beginnings but literally as hypotheses, underpinnings, footings, and springboards so to speak, to enable it to rise to that which requires no assumption and is the starting point of all, and after attaining to that again taking hold of the first dependencies from it, so to proceed downward to the conclusion, making no use whatever of any object of sense but only of pure ideas moving on through ideas to ideas and ending with ideas.

I understand, he said, not fully, for it is no slight task that you appear to have in mind, but I do understand that you mean to distinguish the aspect of reality and the intelligible, which is contemplated by the power of dialectic, as something truer and more exact than the object of the so-called arts and that those who contemplate them are compelled to use their understanding and not their senses, yet because they do not go back to the beginning in the study of them but start from assumptions you do not think they possess true intelligence about them although the things themselves are intelligibles when apprehended in conjunction with a first principle. And I think you call the mental habit of geometers and their like mind or understanding and not reason because you regard understanding as something intermediate between opinion and reason.

Your interpretation is quite sufficient, I said. And now, answering to these four sections, assume these four affections occurring in the soul—intellection or reason for the highest, understanding for the second, belief for the third, and for the last, picture thinking or conjecture—and arrange them in a proportion, as their objects partake of truth and reality.

I understand, he said. I concur and arrange them as you bid.

Book VII

Next, said I, compare our nature in respect of education and its lack to such an experience as this. Picture men dwelling in a sort of subterranean cavern with a long entrance open to the light on its entire width. Conceive them as having their legs and necks fettered from childhood, so that they remain in the same spot, able to look forward only, and prevented by the fetters from turning their heads. Picture further the light from a fire burning higher up and at a distance behind them, and between the fire and the prisoners and above them a road along which a low wall has been built, as the exhibitors of puppet shows have partitions before the men themselves, above which they show the puppets.

All that I see, he said.

See also, then, men carrying past the wall implements of all kinds that rise above the wall, and human images and shapes of animals as well, wrought in stone and wood and every material, some of these bearers presumably speaking and others silent.

A strange image you speak of, he said, and strange prisoners.

Like to us, I said. For, to begin with, tell me do you think that these men would have seen anything of themselves or of one another except the shadows cast from the fire on the wall of the cave that fronted them?

How could they, he said, if they were compelled to hold their heads unmoved through life?

And again, would not the same be true of the objects carried past them?

Surely.

If then they were able to talk to one another, do you not think that they would suppose that in naming the things that they saw they were naming the passing objects?

Necessarily.

And if their prison had an echo from the wall opposite them, when one of the passers-by uttered a sound, do you think that they would suppose anything else than the passing shadow to be the speaker?

By Zeus, I do not, said he.

Then in every way such prisoners would deem reality to be nothing else than the shadows of the artificial objects.

Quite inevitably, he said.

Consider, then, what would be the manner of the release and healing from these bonds and this folly if in the course of nature something of this sort should happen to them. When one was freed from his fetters and compelled to stand up suddenly and turn his head around and walk and to lift up his eyes to the light, and in doing all this felt pain and, because of the dazzle and glitter of the light, was unable to discern the objects whose shadows he formerly saw, what do you suppose would be his answer if someone told him that what he had seen before was all a cheat and an illusion, but that now, being nearer to reality and turned toward more real things, he saw more truly? And if also one should point out to him each of the passing objects and constrain him by questions to say what it is, do you not think that he would be at a loss and that he would regard what he formerly saw as more real than the things now pointed out to him?

Far more real, he said.

And if he were compelled to look at the light itself, would not that pain his eyes, and would he not turn away and flee to those things which he is able to discern and regard them as in very deed more clear and exact than the objects pointed out?

It is so, he said.

And if, said I, someone should drag him thence by force up the ascent which is rough and steep, and not let him go before he had drawn him out into the light of the sun, do you not think that he would find it painful to be so haled along, and would chafe at it, and when he came out into the light, that his eyes would be filled with its beams so that he would not be able to see even one of the things that we call real?

Why, no, not immediately, he said.

Then there would be need of habituation, I take it, to enable him to see the things higher up. And at first he would most easily discern the shadows and, after that, the likenesses or reflections in water of men and other things, and later, the things themselves, and from these he would go on to contemplate the appearances in the heavens and heaven itself, more easily by night, looking at the light of the stars and the moon, than by day the sun and the sun's light.

Of course.

And so, finally, I suppose, he would be able to look upon the sun itself and see its true nature, not by reflections in water or phantasms of it in an alien setting, but in and by itself in its own place.

Necessarily, he said.

And at this point he would infer and conclude that this it is that provides the seasons and the courses of the year and presides over all things in the visible region, and is in some sort the cause of all these things that they had seen.

Obviously, he said, that would be the next step.

Well then, if he recalled to mind his first habitation and what passed for wisdom there, and his fellow bondsmen, do you not think that he would count himself happy in the change and pity them?

He would indeed.

And if there had been honors and commendations among them which they bestowed on one another and prizes for the man who is quickest to make out the shadows as they pass and best able to remember their customary precedences, sequences, and coexistences, and so most successful in guessing at what was to come, do you think he would be very keen about such rewards, and that he would envy and emulate those who were honored by these prisoners and lorded it among them, or that he would feel with Homer and greatly prefer while living on earth to be serf of another, a landless man, and endure anything rather than opine with them and live that life?

Yes, he said, I think that he would choose to endure anything rather than such a life.

And consider this also, said I. If such a one should go down again and take his old place would he not get his eyes full of darkness, thus suddenly coming out of the sunlight?

He would indeed.

Now if he should be required to contend with these perpetual prisoners in 'evaluating' these shadows while his vision was still dim and before his eyes were accustomed to the dark—and this time required for habituation would not be very short—would he not provoke laughter, and would it not be said of him that he had returned from his journey aloft with his eyes ruined and that it was not worth while even to attempt the ascent? And if it were possible to lay hands on and to kill the man who tried to release them and lead them up, would they not kill him?

They certainly would, he said. . . .

Questions

1. What is Socrates' definition of wisdom in the *Apology?*
2. Do you think Socrates was treated fairly? Explain.
3. Was Socrates really surprised by the charges brought against him? Explain.
4. Should he have been surprised? Explain.
5. What do you think of Socrates' teaching style?
6. Have you had teachers like Socrates?
7. If so, did you learn much from them? Explain.
8. Draw a picture representing the story of the cave, and then explain the picture to your neighbor.
9. Would those persons chained in the cave have reason to believe the person who returned to the cave? Explain.
10. Assume you were the person who had escaped. How would you explain the world outside the cave to the prisoners?
11. Restate the Theory of the Forms in your own words.
12. How is the definition of wisdom offered in *The Republic* different from that offered in the *Apology?*
13. In what ways is the educational system implicit in *The Republic* similar to (or different from) the American system?
14. In what ways is it better (or worse)?
15. Formulate your own definition of an educated person.

2

Aristotle

Time Line for Aristotle

384 BC   Is born in Stagira, Chalcidice, to Nicomachus, the court physician to Amyntas II, king of Macedonia. Is brought up by Proxenus, a guardian, following the death of his father.

367   Enters Plato's Academy.

347   Leaves Academy following Plato's death. Accepts invitation of Hermeias, ruler of Assos (which is near Troy), to join his court.

Studies, writes, and teaches during the time at court.

Marries Hermeias' niece and adopted daughter, Pythias. Fathers a daughter.

345   Moves to Mytilene on the island of Lesbos. During this time, he conducts zoological research.

342–339   Serves as tutor for son of Philip II of Macedon—Alexander the Great—at Pella.

335   Returns to Athens and opens the Lyceum. Shortly after arriving in Athens, his wife dies and he takes a mistress, Herpyllis. The union produces one son, Nicomachus.

323   Is charged with impiety (the death of Alexander the Great gave rise to anti-Macedonian sentiment).

Flees Athens to Chalcis.

322   Dies in Chalcis, Euboea.

Time Line of His Writings

367–347   Reflect empathetic and enthusiastic support of Platonism. Included in this period are *Eudemus* and *On the Good.*

347–335   Are critical of Platonic thought, in particular, the Theory of the Forms. Included in this period is *On Philosophy.*

335–322   Reject essential features of Platonic thought. His thinking becomes based on empirical science; included in this period are *Metaphysics, Politics,* and *Nicomachean Ethics.*

INTRODUCTION

Characterized by Dante as "the master of those who know," for centuries, Aristotle was called "The Philosopher." He is generally recognized as the best-educated individual of his or any time, and his mastery of all the world's knowledge places him on "the shortest of lists of the giants of Western thought." As Renford Bambrough explains:

> All studies in formal logic until very recent times were footnotes to his work. In the study of ethics, politics, and literary criticism he set standards of sanity, urbanity, and penetration by which his successors two thousand years later may still be severely judged. . . . There is no problem in any of the branches of what is still called philosophy—ontology, epistemology, metaphysics, ethics— on which his remarks do not continue to deserve the most careful attention from the modern inquirer.[1]

Born in the Macedonian town of Stagira in 384 BC, Aristotle acquired his taste for biology and the other sciences from his father, the physician to the court of the Macedonian king. Known today as the philosophical grandson of Socrates, Aristotle never gained full acceptance as a true Greek. Though honored and revered by subsequent generations, his contemporaries often referred to him, somewhat pejoratively, as "the son of the physician from Stagira" or as the "Stagirite philosopher."

Despite losing both parents at an early age, Aristotle received an outstanding education. At age 18, his guardian, Proxenus, sent him to Athens to study at Plato's Academy. For 20 years he studied with Plato, who described him as "the mind of the Academy." Upon Plato's death in 347 BC, Aristotle left Athens and spent the next few years traveling in the Aegean Islands. A crucial turning point occurred in 343 BC with his appointment as tutor to Prince Alexander, the heir to the Macedonian throne. Although the relationship between Aristotle and his soon-to-be-famous student was often strained, their association proved mutually beneficial. Alexander, the eventual conqueror of the Hellenic world, shipped back to his former teacher an enormous amount of information from those parts of the world about which the Greeks knew little or nothing. Included in this bounty were constitutions and descriptions of the culture and customs of the people encountered during these exploits. Biological and botanical specimens were also sent back, affording Aristotle and his students the opportunity to systematize and categorize the whole spectrum of human knowledge.

By this time, Aristotle had established in Athens the Lyceum, a school located near a favorite meeting place of Socrates. Here, for more than a decade, Aristotle lectured to students on philosophic and scientific topics in the morning and on more general topics to a more popular audience in the afternoon. A creature of habit, Aristotle often walked while he talked, with his students following close behind. Here, too, Aristotle composed his most significant works, summing up in an encyclopedic fashion the results of a life of all-embracing study and thought.

These very productive years ended all too soon as word reached Athens of Alexander's death. Longing for their cherished freedom, Athenians moved quickly to cast off the yoke of the hated Macedonians. Partly because of his association with the Macedonians, the Athenians charged Aristotle with crimes similar to those brought against Socrates several generations earlier. Refusing, as he put it, to allow the

---

[1]Renford Bambrough, *The Philosophy of Aristotle* (New York: New American Library, 1963), p. 11.

Athenians to sin a second time against philosophy, Aristotle withdrew to the Macedonian community of Chalcis, dying there of natural causes in 322 BC.

The body of data available to him enabled Aristotle to develop a "number of amazingly wide-ranging and precisely argued treatises, which have had an enormous influence upon the Western world."[2] In his early works, Aristotle mimicked the style of his mentor, Plato, but in these later, more mature works, Aristotle refuses to allow the human mind to impose its intuitive patterns on the natural world. For Aristotle, as for Plato, there are absolutes or universals, but the method Aristotle employed to attain those absolutes differs significantly from Plato's. Believing that as much data as possible should be collected and analyzed before drawing a conclusion, Aristotle placed his trust in the careful observation and analysis of nature as our best hope of arriving at the truth.

Spending his mature years observing and analyzing a body of knowledge "never before available to one man,"[3] Aristotle concluded that all things possess an essence or nature. Inherent in this essence or nature is the potential to be actualized in accordance with that nature. For example, every acorn has the potential to be actualized as a giant oak tree. Whether and to what extent the potential is actualized depend upon the conditions enhancing or impeding the acorn's natural inclination to become an oak tree.

After a lifetime of study, Aristotle concluded that every substance, whether found in the natural world or created by human agency, is unique in that each is striving toward an *end* consistent with its nature or essence. To understand any substance, one must understand the end that particular substance seeks. Each substance has certain characteristics or performs certain functions that no other substance has or can perform. For example, just as animals are a special kind of organism because they perform certain functions that plants do not, human beings are unique animals in that they perform certain functions no other animal is capable of. The defining characteristic of human beings is their ability to ask general questions and to seek answers to them through observation and analysis. In short, human beings are rational animals, that is, questioning and thinking animals, capable of philosophical thought.

For a variety of reasons, not all acorns fulfill their potential of becoming oak trees, and, obviously, too few humans attain the ideal of becoming rational, contemplative beings. Just as a forester or a farmer, by nurturing the acorn at the right time in the right way, can enhance the acorn's chances of fulfilling its inherent potential, an educator—by appropriately exposing human beings to the great minds struggling with the perennial problems of humankind—can enhance the human being's natural desire to know.

A human being who, through education, has cultivated this natural desire to know comes as close as it is possible in this world to actualizing the human potential. When engaged in contemplation—not as a means to some other end but as an end in itself—humans become godlike, no longer moving from potentiality toward actuality. While the union of potentiality and actuality is not possible in this world, it remains the ideal or aspiration of humankind to "soar after the wings of God, [our] maker, the cause of all things."[4]

---

[2]Paul Nash, *Models of Man: Explorations in the Western Educational Traditions* (New York: John Wiley & Sons, Inc., 1968), p. 33.

[3]Ibid.

[4]Robert Ulich, ed., *Three Thousand Years of Educational Wisdom: Selections from Great Documents* (Cambridge, MA: Harvard University Press, 1979), p. 88.

Aristotle implies that human beings, at their most sublime, are the most complex substances known in this world. Given this exalted status, it is appropriate for human beings to seek the highest good. As discussed in the selection from the *Nicomachean Ethics,* Aristotle suggests that the highest good "is to be found in human happiness." Since human beings are essentially rational creatures, Aristotle argues that they attain true happiness to the extent that they act in accordance with reason. In continuing the largely Greek idea that to know the good is to do the good, Aristotle suggests that, ideally, an educated person unites morality and reason in virtuous action. Although the potential for such virtuous being is present at birth, that potential must be nurtured if it is to be actualized. For human beings to develop as they should demands that they be properly educated. Since, according to Aristotle, human beings achieve moral excellence by performing good acts, the development of good habits is a crucial part of their education. The ultimate goal of education is to assist human beings in developing their unique capacity to contemplate the world and their role in it. In addition to achieving human happiness, such individuals become ideal citizens ready and able to perform their duties as rational members of a community.

FROM *NICOMACHEAN ETHICS* (CA. 330 BC)

Book I

Our discussion will be adequate if it has as much clearness as the subject-matter admits of, for precision is not to be sought for alike in all discussions, any more than in all the products of the crafts. Now fine and just actions, which political science investigates, admit of much variety and fluctuation of opinion, so that they may be thought to exist only by convention, and not by nature. And goods also give rise to a similar fluctuation because they bring harm to many people; for before now men have been undone by reason of their wealth, and others by reason of their courage. We must be content, then, in speaking of such subjects and with such premises to indicate the truth roughly and in outline, and in speaking about things which are only for the most part true and with premises of the same kind to reach conclusions that are no better. In the same spirit, therefore, should each type of statement be *received;* for it is the mark of an educated man to look for precision in each class of things just so far as the nature of the subject admits; it is evidently equally foolish to accept probable reasoning from a mathematician and to demand from a rhetorician scientific proofs.

Now each man judges well the things he knows, and of these, he is a good judge. And so the man who has been educated in a subject is a good judge of that subject, and the man who has received an all-round education is a good judge in general. Hence a young man is not a proper hearer of lectures on political science; for he is inexperienced in the actions that occur in life, but its discussions start from these and are about these; and, further, since he tends to follow his passions, his study will be vain and unprofitable, because the end aimed at is not knowledge but action. And it makes no difference whether he is young in years or youthful in character; the defect does not depend on time, but on his living, and pursuing each successive object, as passion directs. For to such persons, as to the incontinent, knowledge brings no profit; but to those who desire and act in accordance with a rational principle knowledge about such matters will be of great benefit. . . .

Let us again return to the good we are seeking, and ask what it can be. It seems different in different actions and arts; it is different in medicine, in strategy, and in the other arts likewise. What then is the good of each? Surely that for whose sake everything else is done. In medicine this is health, in strategy victory, in architecture a house, in any other sphere something else, and in every action and pursuit the end; for it is for the sake of this that all men do whatever else they do. Therefore, if there is an end for all that we do, this will be the good achievable by action, and if there is more than one, these will be the goods achievable by action.

So the argument has by a different course reached the same point; but we must try to state this even more clearly. Since there are evidently more than one end, and we choose some of these (e.g. wealth, flutes, and in general instruments) for the sake of something else, clearly not all ends are final ends; but the chief good is evidently something final. Therefore, if there is only one final end, this will be what we are seeking, and if there is more than one, the most final of these will be what we are seeking. Now we call that which is in itself worthy of pursuit more final than that which is worthy of pursuit for the sake of something else, and that which is never desirable for the sake of something else more final than the things that are desirable both in themselves and for the sake of that other thing, and therefore we call final without qualification that which is always desirable in itself and never for the sake of something else.

Now such a thing happiness, above all else, is held to be; for this we choose always for itself and never for the sake of something else, but honour, pleasure, reason, and every virtue we choose indeed for themselves (for if nothing resulted from them we should still choose each of them), but we choose them also for the sake of happiness, judging that by means of them we shall be happy. Happiness, on the other hand, no one chooses for the sake of these, nor, in general, for anything other than itself.

From the point of view of self-sufficiency the same result seems to follow; for the final good is thought to be self-sufficient. Now by self-sufficient we do not mean that which is sufficient for a man by himself, for one who lives a solitary life, but also for parents, children, wife, and in general for his friends and fellow citizens, since man is born for citizenship. But some limit must be set to this; for if we extend our requirement to ancestors and descendants and friends' friends, we are in for an infinite series. Let us examine this question, however, on another occasion; the self-sufficient we now define as that which when isolated makes life desirable and lacking in nothing; and such we think happiness to be; and further we think it most desirable of all things, without being counted as one good thing among others—if it were so counted it would clearly be made more desirable by the addition of even the least of goods; for that which is added becomes an excess of goods, and of goods the greater is always more desirable. Happiness, then, is something final and self-sufficient, and is the end of action.

Presumably, however, to say that happiness is the chief good seems a platitude, and a clearer account of what it is still desired. This might perhaps be given, if we could first ascertain the function of man. For just as for a flute-player, a sculptor, or any artist, and, in general, for all things that have a function or activity, the good and the "well" is thought to reside in the function, so would it seem to be for man, if he has a function. Have the carpenter, then, and the tanner certain functions or activities, and has man none? Is he born without a function? Or as eye, hand, foot, and in general each of the parts evidently has a function, may one lay it down that man similarly has a function apart from all these? What then can this be? Life seems to be common even to plants, but we are seeking what is peculiar to man. Let us exclude, therefore, the life of nutrition and growth. Next there would be a life of perception, but *it* also seems to be common even to the horse, the ox, and every animal. There remains, then, an active life of the element that has a rational principle; of this, one part has such a principle in the sense of being obedient to one, the other in the sense of possessing one and exercising thought. And, as "life of the rational element" also has two meanings, we must state that life in the sense of activity is what we mean; for this seems to be the more proper sense of the term. Now if the function of man is an activity of soul which follows or implies a rational principle, and if we say "a so-and-so" and "a good so-and-so" have a function which is the same kind, e. g. a lyre-player and a good lyre-player, and so without qualification in all cases, eminence in respect of goodness being added to the name of the function (for the function of a lyre-player is to play the lyre, and that of a good lyre-player is to do so well): if this is the case, [and we state the function of man to be a certain kind of life, and this to be an activity or actions of the soul implying a rational principle, and the function of a good man to be the good and noble performance of these, and if any action is well performed when it is performed in accordance with the appropriate excellence: if this is the case,] human good turns out to be activity of soul in accordance with virtue, and if there are more than one virtue, in accordance with the best and most complete. . . .

With those who identify happiness with virtue or some one virtue our account is harmony; for to virtue belongs virtuous activity. But it makes, perhaps, no small difference whether we place the chief good in possession or in use, in state of mind or inactivity. For the state of mind may exist without producing any good result, as in a man who is asleep or in some other way quite inactive, but activity cannot; for one who has the activity will of necessity be acting, and acting well. And as in the Olympic Games it is not the most beautiful and the strongest that are crowned but those who compete (for it is some of these that are victorious), so those who act win, and rightly win, the noble and good things in life. . . .

Book II

Virtue, then being of two kinds, intellectual and moral, intellectual virtue in the main owes both its birth and its growth to teaching (for which reason it requires experience and time), while moral virtue comes about as a result of habit, whence also its name (ηθικη) is one that is formed by a slight variation from the word $\varepsilon\theta o\zeta$ (habit). From this it is also plain that none of the moral virtues arises in us by nature; for nothing that exists by nature can form a habit contrary to its nature. For instance the stone which by nature moves downwards cannot be habituated to move upwards, not even if one tries to train it by throwing it up ten thousand times; nor can fire be habituated to move downward, nor can anything else that by nature behaves in one way be trained to behave in another. Neither by nature, then, nor contrary to nature do the virtues arise in us; rather we are adapted by nature to receive them, and are made perfect by habit.

Again, of all the things that come to us by nature we first acquire the potentiality and later exhibit the activity (this is plain in the case of the senses; for it was not by often seeing or often hearing that we got these senses, but on the contrary we had them before we used them, and did not come to have them by using them); but the virtues we get by first exercising them, as also happens in the case of the arts as well. For the things we have to learn before we can do them, we learn by doing them, e.g. men become builders by building and lyre-players by playing the lyre; so too we become just by doing just acts, temperate by doing temperate acts, brave by doing brave acts.

This is confirmed by what happens in states: for legislators make the citizens good by forming habits in them, and this is the wish of every legislator, and those who do not effect it miss their mark, and it is in this that a good constitution differs from a bad one.

Again, it is from the same causes and by the same means that every virtue is both produced and destroyed, and similarly every art; for it is from playing the lyre that both good and bad lyre-players are produced. And the corresponding statement is true of builders and of all the rest; men will be good or bad builders as a result of building well or badly. For if this were not so, there would have been no need of a teacher, but all men would have been born good or bad at their craft. This, then, is the case with the virtues also; by doing the acts that we do in our transactions with other men we become just or unjust, and by doing the acts that we do in the presence of danger, and being habituated to feel fear or confidence, we become brave or cowardly. The same is true of appetites and feelings of anger; some men become temperate and good-tempered, others self-indulgent and irascible, by behaving in one way or the other in the appropriate circumstances. Thus, in one word, states of character arise out of like activities. This is why the activities we exhibit must be of a certain kind; it is because the states of character correspond to the differences between these. It makes no small difference, then, whether we form habits of one kind or of another from our very youth; it makes a very great difference, or rather *all* the difference. . . .

It is the nature of such things to be destroyed by defect and excess, as we see in the case of strength and of health (for to gain light on things imperceptible we must use the evidence of sensible things); both excessive and defective exercise destroys the strength, and similarly drink or food which is above or below a certain amount destroys the health, while that which is proportionate both produces and increases and preserves it. So too is it, then, in the case of temperance and courage and the other virtues. For the man who flies from and fears everything and does not stand his ground against anything becomes a coward, and the man who fears nothing at all but goes to meet every danger becomes rash; and similarly the man who indulges in every pleasure and abstains from none becomes self-indulgent, while the man who shuns every pleasure, as boors do, becomes in a way insensible; temperance and courage, then, are destroyed by excess and defect, and preserved by the mean.

But not only are the sources and causes of their origination and growth the same as those of their destruction, but also the sphere of their actualization will be the same; for this is also true of the things which are more evident to sense, e.g., of strength; it is produced by taking much food and undergoing much exertion, and it is the strong man that will be most able to do these things. So too is it with the virtues; by abstaining from pleasures we become temperate, and it is when we have become so that we are most able to abstain from them; and similarly too in the case of courage; for by being habituated to despise things that are terrible and to stand our ground against them we become brave, and it is when we have become so that we shall be most able to stand our ground against them. . . .

Virtue, then, is a state of character concerned with choice, lying in a mean, i.e. the mean relative to us, this being determined by a rational principle, and by that principle by which the man of practical wisdom would determine it. Now it is a mean between two vices, that which depends on excess and that which depends on defect; and again it is a mean because the vices respectively fall short of or exceed what is right in both passions and actions, while virtue both finds and chooses that which is intermediate. Hence in respect of its substance and the definition which states its essence virtue is a mean, with regard to what is best and right an extreme.

But not every action nor every passion admits of a mean; for some have names that already imply badness, e.g. spite, shamelessness, envy, and in the case of actions adultery, theft, murder; for all of these and suchlike things imply by their names that they are themselves bad, and not the excesses or deficiencies of them. It is not possible, then, ever to be right with regard to them; one must always be wrong. Nor does goodness or badness with regard to such things depend on committing adultery with the right woman, at the right time, and in the right way, but simply to do any of them is to go wrong. It would be equally absurd, then, to expect that in unjust, cowardly, and voluptuous action there should be a mean, an excess, and a deficiency; for at that rate there would be a mean of excess and of deficiency, an excess of excess, and a deficiency of deficiency. But as there is no excess and deficiency of temperance and courage because what is intermediate is in a sense an extreme, so too of the actions we have mentioned there is no mean nor any excess and deficiency, but however they are done they are wrong; for in general there is neither a mean of excess and deficiency, nor excess and deficiency of a mean. . . .

Book X

If happiness is activity in accordance with virtue, it is reasonable that it should be in accordance with the highest virtue; and this will be that of the best thing in us. Whether it be reason or something else that is this element which is thought to be our natural ruler and guide and to take thought of things noble and divine, whether it be itself also divine or only the most divine element in us, the activity of this in accordance with its proper virtue will be perfect happiness. That this activity is contemplative we have already said.

Now this would seem to be in agreement both with what we said before and with the truth. For, firstly, this activity is the best (since not only is reason the best thing in us, but the objects of reason are the best of knowable objects); and, secondly, it is the most continuous, since we can contemplate truth more continuously than we can *do* anything. And we think happiness has pleasure mingled with it, but the activity of philosophic wisdom is admittedly the pleasantest of virtuous activities; at all events the pursuit of it is thought to offer pleasures marvellous for their purity and their enduringness, and it is to be expected that those who know will pass their time more pleasantly than those who inquire. And the self-sufficiency that is spoken of must belong to the contemplative activity. For while a philosopher, as well as a just man or one possessing any other virtue, needs the necessaries of life, when they are sufficiently equipped with things of that sort the just man needs people towards whom and with whom he shall act justly, and the temperate man, the brave man, and each of the others is in the same case, but the philosopher, even when by himself, can contemplate truth, and the better the wiser he is; he can perhaps do so better if he has fellow-workers, but still he is the most self-sufficient. And this activity alone would seem to be loved for its own sake; for nothing arises from it apart from the contemplating, while from practical activities we gain more or less apart from the action. And happiness is thought to depend on leisure; for we are busy that we may have leisure, and make war that we may live in peace. Now the activity of the practical virtues is exhibited in political or military affairs, but the actions concerned with these seem to be unleisurely. Warlike actions are completely so (for no one chooses to be at war, or provokes war, for the sake of being at war; any one would seem absolutely murderous if he were to make enemies of his friends in order to bring about battle and slaughter); but the action of the statesman is also unleisurely, and—apart from the political action itself—aims at despotic power and honours, or at all events happiness, for him and his fellow citizens—a happiness different from political action, and evidently sought as being different. So if among virtuous actions political and military actions are distinguished by nobility and greatness, and these are unleisurely and aim at an end and are not desirable for their own sake, but the activity of reason, which is contemplative, seems both to be superior in serious worth and to aim at no end beyond itself, and to have its pleasure proper to itself (and this augments the activity), and the self-sufficiency, leisureliness, unweariedness (so far as this is possible for man), and all the other attributes ascribed to the supremely happy man are evidently those connected with this activity, it follows that this will be the complete happiness of man, if it be allowed a complete term of life (for none of the attributes of happiness is *in*complete).

But such a life would be too high for man; for it is not in so far as he is man that he will live so, but in so far as something divine is present in him; and by so much as this is superior to our composite nature is its activity superior to that which is the exercise of the other kind of virtue. If reason is divine, then, in comparison with man, the life according to it is divine in comparison with human life. But we must not follow those who advise us, being men, to think of human things, and, being mortal, of mortal things, but must, so far as we can, make ourselves immortal, and strain every nerve to live in accordance with the best thing in us; for even if it be small in bulk, much more does it in power and worth surpass everything. This would seem, too, to be each man himself, since it is the authoritative and better part of him. It would be strange, then, if he were to choose not the life of his self but that of something else. And what we said before will apply now; that which is proper to each thing is by nature best and most pleasant for each thing; for man, therefore, the life according to reason is best and pleasantest, since reason more than anything else *is* man. This life therefore is also the happiest. . . .

But that perfect happiness is a contemplative activity will appear from the following consideration as well. We assume the gods to be above all other beings blessed and happy; but what sort of actions must we assign to them? Acts of justice? Will not the gods seem absurd if they make contracts and return deposits, and so on? Acts of brave man, then, confronting dangers and running risks because it is noble to do so? Or liberal acts? To whom will they give? It will be strange if they are really to have money or anything of the kind. And what would their temperate acts be? Is not such praise tasteless, since they have no bad appetites? If we were to run through them all, the circumstances of action would be found trivial and unworthy of gods. Still, every one supposes that they *live* and therefore that they are active; we cannot suppose them to sleep like Endymion. Now if you take away from a living being action, and still more production, what is left but contemplation? Therefore the activity of God, which surpasses all others in blessedness, must be contemplative; and of human activities, therefore, that which is most akin to this must be most of the nature of happiness.

This is indicated, too, by the fact that the other animals have no share in happiness, being completely deprived of such activity. For while the whole life of gods is blessed, and that of men too in so far as some likeness of such activity belongs to them, none of the other animals is happy, since they in no way share in contemplation. Happiness extends, then, just so far as contemplation does, and those to whom contemplation more fully belongs are more truly happy, not as a mere concomitant but in virtue of the contemplation; for this is in itself precious. Happiness, therefore, must be some form of contemplation. . . .

Now he who exercises his reason and cultivates it seems to be both in the best state of mind and most dear to the gods. For if the gods have any care for human affairs, as they are thought to have, it would be reasonable both that they should delight in that which was best and most akin to them (i.e. reason) and that they should reward those who love and honour this most, as caring for the things that are dear to them and acting both rightly and nobly. And that all these attributes belong most of all to the philosopher is manifest. He, therefore, is the dearest to the gods. And he who is that will presumably be also the happiest; so that in this way too the philosopher will more than any other be happy. . . .

Now some think that we are made good by nature, others by habituation, others by teaching Nature's part evidently does not depend on us, but as a result of some divine causes is present in those who are truly fortunate; while argument and teaching, we may suspect, are not powerful with all men, but the soul of the student must first have been cultivated by means of habits for noble joy and noble hatred, like earth which is to nourish the seed. For he who lives as passion directs will not hear argument that dissuades him, nor understand it if he does; and how can we persuade one in such a state to change his ways. And in general passion seems to yield not to argument but to force. The character, then, must somehow be there already with a kinship to virtue, loving what is noble and hating what is base.

But it is difficult to get from youth up a right training for virtue if one has not been brought up under right laws; for to live temperately and hardily is not pleasant to most people, especially when they are young. For this reason their nurture and occupations should be fixed by law; for they will not be painful when they have become customary. But it is surely not enough that when they are young they should get the right nurture and attention; since they must, even when they are grown up, practise and be habituated to them, we shall need laws for this as well, and generally speaking to cover the whole life; for most people obey necessity rather than argument, and punishments rather than the sense of what is noble.

This is why some think that legislators ought to stimulate men to virtue and urge them forward by the motive of the noble, on the assumption that those who have been well advanced by the formation of habits will attend to such influences; and that punishments and penalties should be imposed on those who disobey and are of inferior nature, while the incurably bad should be completely banished. . . .

Now it is best that there should be a public and proper care for such matters; but if they are neglected by the community it would seem right for each man to help his children and friends towards virtue, and that they should have the power, or at least the will, to do this.

It would seem from what has been said that he can do this better if he makes himself capable of legislating. For public control is plainly effected by laws, and good control by good laws; whether written or unwritten would seem to make no difference, nor whether they are providing for the education of individuals or of groups—any more than it does in the case of music or gymnastics and other such pursuits. For as in cities laws and prevailing types of character have force, so in households do the injunctions and the habits of the father, and these have even more because of the tie of blood and the benefits he confers; for the children start with a natural affection and disposition to obey. Further, private education has an advantage over public, as private medical treatment has; for while in general rest and abstinence from food are good for a man in a fever, for a particular man they may not be; and a boxer presumably does not prescribe the same style of fighting to all his pupils. It would seem, then, that the detail is worked out with more precision if the control is private; for each person is more likely to get what suits his case.

But the details can be best looked after, one by one, by a doctor or gymnastic instructor or any one else who has the general knowledge of what is good for every one or for people of a certain kind (for the sciences both are said to be, and are, concerned with what is universal); not but what some particular detail may perhaps be well looked after by an unscientific person, if he has studied accurately in the light of experience what happens in each case, just as some people seem to be their own best doctors, though they could give no help to any one else. None the less, it will perhaps be agreed that if a man does wish to become master of an art or science he must go to the universal, and come to know it as well as possible; for, as we have said, it is with this that the sciences are concerned.

And surely he who wants to make men, whether many or few, better by his care must try to become capable of legislating, if it is through laws that we can become good. For to get any one whatever—any one who is put before us—into the right condition is not for the first chance comer; if any one can do it, it is the man who knows, just as in medicine and all other matters which give scope for care and prudence.

Reprinted from Aristotle's *Nicomachean Ethics* translated by W. D. Ross (1925) by permission of Oxford University Press.

Questions

1. What does Aristotle mean by happiness?
2. Is happiness intrinsically or instrumentally valuable? Explain.
3. What is the difference between intellectual and moral virtue?
4. What role, if any, does habit play in developing virtue?
5. What role, if any, does nature play in humankind's development of virtue?
6. Explain why habit plays such a significant role in Aristotle's educational scheme.
7. Why did Aristotle refuse to allow the Athenians to sin a second time against philosophy?
8. What is the relationship between virtue, happiness, and leisure?
9. In what ways is the philosopher like the just human being, the temperate human being, and the brave human being?
10. How does the philosopher differ from those human beings?
11. Do you think Aristotle would be pleased with the way contemporary human beings use their leisure time? Explain.
12. What argument does Aristotle offer in support of the statement that the most blessed and happy activity of the gods is contemplation?
13. According to Aristotle, what is it about human beings that make them unique?
14. How did Aristotle arrive at his beliefs about human nature or essence?
15. In what ways is Aristotle like his mentor, Plato, and in what ways does he differ from Plato?
16. In your own words, describe Aristotle's vision of the ideally educated human being.

3

John Locke

Time Line for Locke

1632	Is born in Wrington, Somerset, England, into a Puritan home.
1646	Enters the Westminister School, where he studies the classics.
1652	Is elected to a studentship at Christ's Church, Oxford.
1656	Receives his bachelor's degree and continues in residence for the master's degree.
1661	Receives small inheritance from father's estate and decides to study medicine.
1664	Is appointed censor of moral philosophy.
1667	Is appointed personal physician to Lord Ashley, Earl of Shaftesbury, who is the leader of the parliamentary opposition to the Stuarts.
1674	Is awarded medical degree and is licensed to practice medicine.
1675	Travels to France.
1679	Returns to England.
1683	Is denounced as a traitor and flees England for Holland.
1683–1688	Is involved in activities to place William of Orange on the throne of England.
1689	Publishes *First Letter Concerning Toleration* and *Essay Concerning Human Understanding*.
1689	Returns to England escorting the princess of Orange, who later becomes Queen Mary.
1690	Publishes *Two Treatises of Government*.
1691	Accepts position as commissioner on the Board of Trade and Plantations.
1693	Publishes *Some Thoughts Concerning Education*.
1695	Publishes *Reasonableness of Christianity,* followed by a response to its critics, *Vindiction of Reasonableness of Christianity*.
1697	Publishes second *Vindiction of Reasonableness of Christianity*.
1704	Dies at the home of Sir Francis and Lady Masham (October 28).

INTRODUCTION

John Locke (1632–1704) is one of the most influential philosophers of the modern era. His empiricism, which included an attack on innate ideas—ideas, say, of truth, beauty, and goodness—which were thought of as part of one's birthright as a human being, and his subsequent claim that all knowledge comes through the senses, set the stage not only for Anglo-American philosophy for the next two or three hundred years, but also for the flowering of the scientific method throughout the world.

His political writing, as presented in *Two Treatises of Government,* reads in many ways as a precursor of the revolutionary events in America during the eighteenth century. Locke was concerned with uncovering the sources and limits of political rights and responsibilities. To do this, he assumed a fictional place called a "state of nature," a place where the philosopher could imagine people in their natural condition and from that generate a theory of political rights and responsibilities.

In that "state," natural laws governed people's behavior and reasonable people would follow those laws. Unfortunately, not all people were reasonable. And, in this fictional state, there was no power of enforcement. To deal with these problems, people banded together and created civil society. They *contracted,* each with everyone, to create a sovereign power who would be in charge of protecting their rights (rights which were given by the natural law).

> Locke explicitly recognized, as the events during his lifetime had shown, that men may become tyrants to those whom they were bound to serve. It may be a king, an assembly, or a usurper that claims absolute power. In such cases the people have a right to rebellion if no other redress is possible. Locke was not unmindful of the fact that the executive needs latitude and prerogatives so that he may govern, and that the legislative body must be in the public good. The right to rebellion is warranted only in the most extreme conditions, where all other means fail. Locke did not believe that men would lightly avail themselves of this power, for men will suffer and endure much before they resort to rebellion.[1]

It is not hard to see why Locke would be so influential, why he would strike such a chord with colonists such as Thomas Jefferson and Alexander Hamilton. Locke was not a wide-eyed radical advocating revolution. There is something very bourgeois, very middle class, at the core of his thought. His argument goes something like this: We have created a sovereign to protect our rights. That sovereign must have the latitude to do what she or he thinks best. It is unreasonable to expect the sovereign to report to citizens in all matters. Still if, over an extended period of time, the sovereign does not live up to the demands of the contract, if, over an extended period of time, the sovereign does not protect our rights, then we, the citizens, have the right to rebel. We have the right to dump the tea in Boston Harbor.

Given the fact that Locke does strike such a resonant chord in the American political psyche, and given the fact that many of Locke's educational claims and arguments, as found in *Some Thoughts Concerning Education,* are now accepted as near commonplaces of contemporary educative thought, it is at least curious that Locke's understanding of the educated person should receive such little attention.

---

[1] James Gordon Clapp, John Locke in *Encyclopedia of Philosophy*, vol. 4, ed. Paul Edwards (New York: Macmillan Publishing, 1967), p. 500.

Consider, first, some of the "commonplaces":

1. Education is something that adults do to children. As such, the educative process is, at heart, hierarchical, with authority residing in the hands of the adult.
2. Education is dependent on the securing of right habits of thought and action. Children, especially young children, have not developed enough, intellectually and morally, to understand why they must perform certain activities. Indeed, the habitual performing of those is a necessary condition for children's, one day, understanding.
3. Children learn more by example than by mere telling. Thus, it is crucial to create an environment in which children can learn from the example of their elders. In effect, the teacher models correct behavior for her or his students.
4. Cognitive development in children tends to proceed from part to whole and from the concrete to the abstract. The curriculum, in turn, should mirror this developmental sequence, moving from part to whole, from the concrete to the abstract.

These commonplaces, of course, come under occasional review by critics, who have pointed out, for example, that children's most efficient learning seems to occur in the earliest years of their lives, and it is not at all clear that learning always proceeds from the concrete to the abstract. For example, children typically master a highly complex concept like "Mommy" or "Daddy" well before, say, they memorize the alphabet. Still, the commonplaces have a staying power, which makes all the more curious the fact that Locke's understanding of the educated person is largely ignored when it comes to the contemporary debate regarding education in the United States.

Locke was quite explicit regarding the nature of education. The first part of education Locke called "virtue." It was concerned, for the most part, with a twofold relationship, namely, a relationship with God and a relationship with other people. A virtuous person was one who believed in and worshiped God and who treated other people with respect, dignity, care, and so on. For Locke, this was the most important part of education.

The second most important part of education Locke called "wisdom." Here, it is helpful to recall Locke's affinity with the middle class. A wise person was one who could manage her or his affairs, primarily business affairs, in a fair and prudent manner. The wise person is that individual who can manage affairs in such a way that both family and community will prosper.

The third part of education Locke claimed for breeding, the ability to handle oneself in social situations. The well-bred person is the person who behaves fairly and without condescension to "inferiors" and honestly and without obsequiousness toward "superiors."

Finally—and Locke is explicit about this—is what is called "learning":

You will wonder, perhaps, that I put learning last, especially if I tell you I think it the least part. This may seem strange in the mouth of a bookish man, and this making usually the chief, if not only, bustle and stir about children, this being almost that alone which is thought on when people talk of education, makes it the greater paradox. When I consider what ado is made about a little Latin and Greek, how many years are spent on it and what a noise and business it makes to no purpose, I can hardly forbear thinking that the parents of children still live in fear of the schoolmaster's rod, which they look on as the only instrument of education, as a language or two to be its whole business. How else is it possible that a child should be chained to the oar seven, eight or ten of the best years of his life to get a language or two which, I think, might be had at a great deal cheaper rate of pains and time, and be learned almost in playing.[2]

Again, it is very curious that the philosopher who, in many ways, sets the contemporary educational agenda is ignored at precisely the moment he speaks about the characteristics of the educated person. Focus on the ethical and aesthetic qualities, try to create a person of decency, resourcefulness, and style, and the cognitive qualities can be developed "almost in playing." In an era dominated by the contemporary equivalent of the schoolmaster's rod—standardized tests—it may be the appropriate time to return to John Locke.

FROM *SOME THOUGHTS CONCERNING EDUCATION* (1693)

The well educating of their children is so much the duty and concern of parents, and the welfare and prosperity of the nation so much depends on it, that I would have everyone lay it seriously to heart; and after having well examined and distinguished what fancy, custom or reason advises in the case, set his helping hand to promote everywhere that way of training up youth, with regard to their several conditions, which is the easiest, shortest and likeliest to produce virtuous, useful and able men in their distinct callings; though that most to be taken care of is the gentleman's calling. For if those of that rank are by their education once set right, they will quickly bring all the rest into order.

A sound mind in a sound body is a short but full description of a happy state in this world. He that has these two has little more to wish for; and he that wants either of them will be but little the better for anything else. Men's happiness or misery is most part of their own making. He whose mind directs not wisely will never take the right way; and he whose body is crazy and feeble will never be able to advance in it. I confess there are some men's constitutions of body and mind so vigorous and well framed by nature that they need not much assistance from others; but by the strength of their natural genius they are from their cradles carried towards what is excellent, and by the privilege of their happy constitutions are able to do wonders. But examples of this kind are but few; and I think I may say that of all the men we meet with nine part of ten are what they are, good or evil, useful or not, by their education. 'Tis that which makes the great difference in mankind. The little or almost insensible impressions on our tender infancies have very important and lasting consequences; and there 'tis, as in the fountains of some rivers, where a gentle application of the hand turns the flexible waters in channels that make them

[2]John Locke, *Some Thoughts Concerning Education*, ed. F. W. Garforth (London: Heinemann, 1925), pp. 129–130.

take quite contrary courses; and by this direction given them at first in the source they receive different tendencies and arrive at last at very remote and distant places. . . .

That which every gentleman (that takes any care of his education) desires for his son, besides the estate he leaves him, is contained, I suppose, in these four things, virtue, wisdom, breeding and learning. I will not trouble myself whether these names do not some of them sometimes stand for the same thing, or really include one another. It serves my turn here to follow the popular use of these words, which, I presume, is clear enough to make me be understood, and I hope there will be no difficulty to comprehend my meaning.

I place virtue as the first and most necessary of those endowments that belong to a man or a gentleman, as absolutely requisite to make him valued and beloved by others, acceptable or tolerable to himself. Without that, I think, he will be happy neither in this nor the other world.

As the foundation of this there ought very early to be imprinted on his mind a true notion of God, as of the independent Supreme Being, Author and Maker of all things, from whom we receive all our good, who loves us and gives us all things. And consequent to this, instil into him a love and reverence of this Supreme Being. This is enough to begin with, without going to explain this matter any farther, for fear lest, by talking too early to him of spirits and being unseasonably forward to make him understand the incomprehensible nature of that Infinite Being, his head be either filled with false or perplexed with unintelligible notions of him. Let him only be told upon occasion that God made and governs all things, hears and sees everything, and does all manner of good to those that love and obey him; you will find that, being told of such a God, other thoughts will be apt to rise up fast enough in his mind about him, which, as you observe them to have any mistakes, you must set right. And I think it would be better if men generally rested in such an idea of God, without being too curious in their notions about a Being which all must acknowledge incomprehensible; whereby many, who have not strength and clearness of thought to distinguish between what they can and what they cannot know, run themselves in superstition or atheism, making God like themselves or, because they cannot comprehend anything else, none at all. And I am apt to think the keeping children constantly morning and evening to acts of devotion to God, as to their Maker, Preserver and Benefactor, in some plain and short form of prayer suitable to their age and capacity will be of much more use to them in religion, knowledge and virtue than to distract their thoughts with curious enquiries into his inscrutable essence and being.

Having laid the foundations of virtue in a true notion of God, such as the creed wisely teaches, as far as his age is capable, and by accustoming him to pray to him, the next thing to be taken care of is to keep him exactly to speaking of truth and by all the ways imaginable inclining him to be good-natured. Let him know that twenty faults are sooner to be forgiven than the straining of truth to cover anyone by an excuse. And to teach him betimes to love and be good-natured to others is to lay early the true foundation of an honest man; all injustice generally springing from too great love of ourselves and too little of others.

Wisdom I take in the popular acceptation for a man's managing his business ably and with foresight in this world. This is the product of a good natural temper, application of mind and experience together, and so above the reach of children. The greatest thing that in them can be done towards it is to hinder them as much as may be from cunning, which, being the ape of wisdom, is the most distant from it that can be. . . . Cunning is only the want of understanding, which, because it cannot compass its ends by direct ways, would do it by a trick and circumvention; and the mischief of it is, a cunning trick helps but once, but hinders ever after. No cover was ever made so big or so fine as to hide itself; nobody was ever so cunning as to conceal their being so; and when they are once discovered, everybody is shy, everybody distrustful of crafty men; and all the world forwardly join to oppose and defeat them, whilst the open, fair, wise man has everybody to make way for him and goes directly to his business. To accustom a child to have true notions of things and not to be satisfied till he has them, to raise his mind to great and worthy thoughts and to keep him at a distance from falsehood and cunning, which has always a broad mixture of falsehood in it, is the fittest preparation of a child for wisdom. The rest, which is to be learned from time, experience and observation and an acquaintance with men, their tempers and designs, is not to be expected in the ignorance and inadvertency of childhood or the inconsiderate heat and unwariness of youth. All that can be done towards it during this unripe age is, as I have said, to accustom them to truth and sincerity, to a submission to reason and, as much as may be, to reflection on their own actions.

The next good quality belonging to a gentleman is good breeding. There are two sorts of ill breeding, the one a sheepish bashfulness, and the other a misbecoming negligence and disrespect in our carriage; both which are avoided by duly observing this one rule, not to think meanly of ourselves and not to think meanly of others.

The first part of this rule must not be understood in opposition to humility but to assurance. We ought not to think so well of ourselves as to stand upon our own value and assume to ourselves a preference before others because of any advantage we may imagine we have over them, but modestly to take what is offered when it is our due. But yet we ought to think so well of ourselves as to perform those actions which are incumbent on and expected of us without discomposure or disorder in whose presence soever we are, keeping that respect and distance which is due to everyone's rank and quality. There is often in people, especially children, a clownish shamefacedness before strangers or those above them; they are confounded in their thoughts, words and looks, and so lose themselves in that confusion as not to be able to do anything, or at least not to do it with that freedom and gracefulness which pleases and makes them acceptable. The only cure for this, as for any other miscarriage, is by use to introduce the contrary habit. But since we cannot accustom ourselves to converse with strangers and persons of quality without being in their company, nothing can cure this part of ill breeding but change and variety of company and that of persons above us.

As the before-mentioned consists in too great a concern how to behave ourselves towards others, so the other part of ill breeding lies in the appearance of too little care of pleasing or showing respect to those we have to do with. To avoid this, these two things are requisite: first, a disposition of the mind not to offend others; and secondly, the most acceptable and agreeable way of expressing that disposition. From the one men are called civil; from the other well-fashioned. The latter of these is that decency and gracefulness of looks, voice, words, motions, gestures and of all the whole outward demeanor, which takes in company and makes those with whom we may converse easy and well pleased. This is, as it were, the language whereby that internal civility of the mind is expressed; which, as other languages are, being very much governed by the fashion and custom of every country, must, in the rules and practice of it, be learned chiefly from observation and the carriage of those who are allowed to be exactly well-bred. The other part, which lies deeper than the outside, is that general good will and regard for all people, which makes anyone have a care not to show in his carriage any contempt, disrespect or neglect of them, but to express, according to the fashion and way of that country, a respect and value for them according to their rank and condition. It is a disposition of mind that shows itself in the carriage, whereby a man avoids making anyone uneasy in conversation. . . .

You will wonder, perhaps, that I put learning last, especially if I tell you I think it the least part. This may seem strange in the mouth of a bookish man; and this making usually the chief, if not only, bustle and stir about children, this being almost that alone which is thought on when people talk of education, makes it the greater paradox. When I consider what ado is made about a little Latin and Greek, how many years are spent in it and what a noise and business it makes to no purpose, I can hardly forbear thinking that the parents of children still live in fear of the schoolmaster's rod, which they look on as the only instrument of education, as a language or two to be its whole business. How else is it possible that a child should be chained to the oar seven, eight or ten of the best years of his life to get a language or two which, I think, might be had at a great deal cheaper rate of pains and time, and be learned almost in playing?

Forgive me, therefore, if I say I cannot with patience think that a young gentleman should be put into the herd and be driven with a whip and scourge, as if he were to run the gauntlet through the several classes *ad capiendum ingenti cultum.* What then, say you, would you not have him write and read? . . . Not so, not so fast, I beseech you. Reading and writing and learning I allow to be necessary, but yet not the chief business. I imagine you would think him a very foolish fellow that shall not value a virtuous or a wise man infinitely before a great scholar. Not but that I think learning a great help to both in well-disposed minds; but yet it must be confessed also that in others not so disposed it helps them only to be the more foolish or worse men. I say this that when you consider the breeding of your son and are looking out for a schoolmaster or a tutor, you would not have (as is usual) Latin and logic only in your thoughts. Learning must be had, but in the second place, as subservient only to greater qualities. Seek out somebody that may know how discreetly to frame his manners; place him in hands where you may, as much as possible, secure his innocence, cherish and nurse up the good, and gently correct and weed out any bad inclinations and settle in him good habits. This is the main point, and this being provided for, learning may be had into the bargain, and that, as I think, at a very easy rate by methods that may be thought on.

From *Some Thoughts Concerning Education,* John Locke, edited by F. W. Garforth © 1925 by Heinemann Educational Books Ltd., Oxford, England, pp. 25–26, 122–127, 129–130.

Questions

1. Why, for Locke, should "errors in education be less indulged in than any"?
2. For Locke, how important is education?
3. Locke is concerned with the education of gentlemen. Do you think that what he says is applicable to the education of gentlewomen?
4. Why do you think Locke focuses on the education of one part of the population?
5. What are the four parts of education?
6. Why is learning the least important part of education for Locke?
7. Do you think Locke's criticisms are applicable to contemporary American educational practices?
8. Describe a Lockean classroom.
9. Respond to the teacher who says she or he has neither the time nor the right to do all of the things Locke recommends.
10. Locke uses the metaphor of the child being "chained to the oar." Do you think that is an appropriate metaphor for describing schooling? Can you think of others?
11. Do you think that a person can be learned but not educated? Do you think that a person can be educated but not learned?

Jean-Jacques Rousseau

Time Line for Rousseau

1712	Is born in Geneva. His mother dies following his birth, and he is brought up by his father and an aunt.
1712–1728	Receives little formal education.
	Lives two years with a country minister at Bossey.
	Returns to Geneva and lives with an uncle.
	Is apprenticed to a notary and then to an engraver who treats him badly.
1728	Leaves Geneva.
	Is befriended by Mme. de Warens.
	Serves as a lackey.
	Converts to Catholicism.
1729	Returns to Mme. de Warens.
1730–1742	Travels widely.
1742	Arrives in Paris to introduce a new system of musical notation.
1743	Is appointed secretary to French ambassador at Venice.
1750	Publishes *Discours sur les sciences et les arts* (*Discourse on the Sciences and the Arts*).
1754	Travels to Geneva and is reconciled with the republic and returns to Protestantism.
1755	Publishes *Discours sur l'origine de l'inégalité* (*Discourse on the Origin of Inequality*).
1762	Publishes *Émile* and *Contrat social* (*The Social Contract*).
1766	Arrives in England at the invitation of the philosopher David Hume.
1767	Leaves England following an argument with Hume.
1767–1770	Travels widely, spurred by the assumption that he is universally persecuted.
1770	Settles in Paris.
1770–1778	Writes a series of personal works: *Confessions, Rousseau juge de Jean-Jacques* (*Confessions: Rousseau Judges Himself*) and *Reveries do promeneur solitaire* (unfinished) (*Reveries of a Solitary Walker*).
1778	Dies suddenly on July 2 at the estate of the marquis de Girardin at Ermenonville.

INTRODUCTION

Jean-Jacques Rousseau remains, on the surface at least, an enigmatic figure in the history of modern thought. In spite of or perhaps because of his enigmatic nature, Rousseau's ideas are as relevant today as they ever were. In challenging the *philosophes* and other Enlightenment thinkers' faith in progress through reason, Rousseau, at times, presents himself as the unabashed champion of the individual in the inevitable clash with more powerful societal forces. At other times, he seems to favor a dominating if not totalitarian societal structure that all but eclipses individual freedom. In reality, what Rousseau has done is to attack the individual-collectivity problem head on. With such statements as "Man is born free; and everywhere he is in chains" and "Everything is good as it comes from the hands of the Maker of the World but degenerates once it gets into the hands of man," he seems to be calling for a return to a primitive life. A more careful reading suggests Rousseau believed that, by properly educating future generations, a society could be created that resolved the conflict between individual needs and societal demands. Recognizing that in the corrupt society of his time it was impossible to transform the boy into both a man and a citizen, Rousseau, when faced with the opportunity of reforming a society, did not hesitate in proposing an educational system aimed at making a good citizen.

To assist the reader to better understand this enigmatic figure and his contributions to contemporary educational philosophy, his life and thought are discussed briefly below. Following this discussion is a selection from Rousseau's *Émile,* a work characterized by Allan Bloom as "a truly great book," for it describes the education of democratic man.

Born in 1712 to a watchmaker in Geneva, Switzerland, Jean-Jacques Rousseau was not blessed with a stable childhood. When his mother died shortly after Rousseau was born, his father, with the aid of an incompetent aunt, assumed responsibility for raising him. He learned to read on his father's knee, but neither his father nor his aunt provided much discipline for the young child. While Rousseau was still an adolescent, his father abandoned him: Finding himself in trouble with a local patrician, the elder Rousseau left town never to return.

Rousseau was left with one of his uncles and over the next few years was apprenticed to a town clerk, to an engraver, and to a religious cleric. After failing miserably in each of these endeavors, Rousseau fled Geneva some three years later. For the next 20 years, Rousseau pursued many vocations, but achieved little success in any of them. He converted to Catholicism—only to renounce it later in life—even studying for the priesthood. He practiced music, worked as a secretary, and on occasion found work as a tutor.

There was little if any hint of genius until, at the age of 37, Rousseau entered and won an essay contest on the topic "Has the Progress of the Arts and Sciences Contributed More to the Corruption or Purification of Morals?" Emotionally unstable, often violating his own sense of duty and right, winning the prize for the best essay in this contest sponsored by the Academy of Dijon catapulted Rousseau into intellectual stardom. Though suffering from inadequacies in logic and historical accuracy, Rousseau's wild, impassioned rhetoric won the day. With the victory came entry into the intellectual salons of the time, and recognition, if not acceptance, by the *philosophes.* Following this initial success came the more significant and better known

Discourse on the Origin of Inequality, The Social Contract, and *Émile.* Rousseau completed what is arguably his most famous work, his autobiographical *Confessions,* just before his death in 1778.

In studying the ideas of Jean-Jacques Rousseau, one encounters what appear to be many contradictions or inconsistencies in his thought. Rousseau denies this possibility, arguing in his *Confessions* that his writings taken as a whole reveal a "consistent and coherent philosophy." As noted earlier and as we shall see in the brief discussion of his works that follows, the theme that binds all the many apparent discrepancies together is Rousseau's attempt to account for and resolve the conflict between the individual and the collectivity.

In the summer of 1749, while walking from Paris to Vincennes, Rousseau learned of the essay contest sponsored by the Academy of Dijon. Experiencing a vision in response to the question concerning the efficacy of the arts and sciences in promoting humankind's moral development, Rousseau responded in the negative, denying that progress in the arts and sciences translates into moral progress. His basic theme is perhaps best captured by a hypothetical prayer for the future of humankind:

> Almighty God! thou holdest in Thy hand the minds of men, deliver us from the fatal arts and sciences of our forefathers; give us back ignorance, innocence, and poverty, which alone can make us happy and precious in thy sight.

In short, Rousseau argued that human civilization, that is, the product of progress in the arts and sciences, had done little to advance the happiness of humankind. As such, he was attacking one of the basic tenets or faiths of the *philosophes* in particular and of the Enlightenment in general, that is, the equating of knowledge with goodness. Rousseau argued that increased knowledge in the arts and sciences, rather than contributing to the moral improvement of humankind, tended to corrupt humankind by taking away their natural innocence. In juxtaposing natural or primitive human beings with civilized or learned ones, Rousseau suggested that the primitive or natural human being is free and happy, not because of the absence of boundaries or constraints, but because primitive or natural human beings have learned to live in accordance with the limitations or constraints found in nature. For Rousseau, progress in the arts and sciences meant the creation of unnatural and evil boundaries and restraints on human freedom.

Herein lies the crucial point, or what Rousseau would subsequently identify as "the origin of inequality." Simply put, Rousseau believed that natural or primitive humankind has, through the impulses and instincts of nature, the ability to learn about and live within the world they inhabit. Rather than enhance or support this natural ability, advancements in the arts and sciences have tended to deny and thus alienate modern beings from this natural capacity.

Rousseau offers us more than just a lament over the lost innocence of the natural or primitive human beings. Realizing that we cannot "return again to the forests to live among bears," that we "can no longer subsist on plants or acorns," that we "must remain in society and respect the sacred bonds of the community, loving [our] fellow-citizens, obeying the laws, honoring the wise and good princes," the task becomes one of creating a human society that emulates the natural restraints primitive human beings once encountered. At the very least such a society must be grounded in what

Rousseau identified as the general will, which the members of the society knowingly defer to and accept.

It is at this point that Rousseau's *Social Contract* and *Émile* come into play. Rousseau introduces *The Social Contract* with the assertion that "Man is born free and everywhere he is in chains." Every and any society has chains for they are the necessary restraints or coercions that hold the separate parts together. As stated earlier, the problem becomes one of finding or creating some form of society so consistent with humankind's natural capacities that all will willingly accept its laws and restrictions. Establishing such a society requires negotiating a "social contract" in which the individual freely gives up natural freedom, but gains civil freedom in return. This means sublimating one's individual will to the will of the group or *general will.*

Rousseau's concept of the general will is different from and superior to the will of all in that it concerns common, as opposed to individual, interests. Rousseau's notion of the general will is elusive and apparently understandable only by those properly educated. Our only hope of developing individuals capable of sublimating their own private wills to the common or general will is to educate future generations in accordance with the laws or restraints of nature. To explain how this could and should be done, Rousseau wrote *Émile* and *The Social Contract* concurrently publishing *Émile* six months after publishing *The Social Contract.*

Reminiscent of *The Social Contract, Emile* begins by suggesting that "God makes all things good; man meddles with them and they become evil." Remember, from Rousseau's perspective, since his society—the one corrupted by the arts and sciences—is evil, for Émile to be properly educated he must be isolated from such a corrupt society. Such isolation is necessary if Émile is to recapture his natural state. Recapturing this natural state is necessary if Émile is to "see with his own eyes and feel with his own heart." Once this natural state has been recaptured and properly nurtured, Émile will, or so Rousseau suggests, make the right moral decision. Émile will knowingly and willingly subjugate himself to the general will and seek the common good.

Nature is the key to Rousseau's educational process. According to Rousseau, a young child is apolitical, asocial, and amoral. Initially the child knows only that she or he inhabits a physical world and quickly learns to abide by the law of necessity. Rousseau suggests that the young child should never act from obedience but only from necessity. In the early stages of her or his development, the child should be dependent only on things. As Émile develops under the skillful manipulation of his tutor (Rousseau himself), he internalizes the notion that restraints are natural and inevitable. Once this lesson is learned, and as Émile develops an appreciation for the moral, political, and social worlds he inhabits and the laws that govern these worlds, this properly educated individual comes to understand and appreciate the general will or common good. In short, what Rousseau offers us in *Émile* is the prototype of what human beings could and should be. Through an educational process that follows nature, Rousseau creates for us an exemplar, that is, a just human being in an unjust world. By emulating nature in the education of our children and youth, Rousseau is suggesting that it is possible to develop a society of Émiles who willingly sublimate their own desires to those of the common or general will. It is these individuals who will establish the just or good society by creating the social contract, in the process resolving once and for all the conflict between individual needs and societal demands.

FROM *ÉMILE* (1762)

Consistency is plainly impossible when we seek to educate a man for others, instead of for himself. If we have to combat either nature or society, we must choose between making a man or making a citizen. We cannot make both. There is an inevitable conflict of aims, from which come two opposing forms of education: the one communal and public, the other individual and domestic.

To get a good idea of communal education, read Plato's *Republic*. It is not a political treatise, as those who merely judge books by their titles think. It is the finest treatise on education ever written. Communal education in this sense, however, does not and can not now exist. There are no longer any real fatherlands and therefore no real citizens. The words "fatherland" and "citizen" should be expunged from modern languages. . . .

There remains then domestic education, the education of nature. But how will a man who has been educated entirely for himself get on with other people? If there were any way of combining in a single person the twofold aim, and removing the contradictions of life, a great obstacle to happiness would be removed. But before passing judgment on this kind of man it would be necessary to follow his development and see him fully formed. It would be necessary, in a word, to make the acquaintance of the natural man. This is the subject of our quest in this book. . . .

In the natural order where all men are equal, manhood is the common vocation. One who is well educated for that will not do badly in the duties that pertain to it. The fact that my pupil is intended for the army, the church or the bar does not greatly concern me. Before the vocation determined by his parents comes the call of nature to the life of human kind. Life is the business I would have him learn. When he leaves my hands, I admit he will not be a magistrate, or a soldier, or a priest. First and foremost, he will be a man. All that a man must be he will be when the need arises, as well as anyone else. Whatever the changes of fortune he will always be able to find a place for himself. . . .

Instead of the difficult task of educating a child, I now undertake the easier task of writing about it. To provide details and examples in illustration of my views and to avoid wandering off into airy speculations, I propose to set forth the education of Emile, an imaginary pupil, from birth to manhood. I take for granted that I am the right man for the duties in respect of age, health, knowledge and talents.

A tutor is not bound to his charge by the ties of nature as the father is, and so is entitled to choose his pupil, especially when as in this case he is providing a model for the education of other children. I assume that Emile is no genius, but a boy of ordinary ability; that he is the inhabitant of some temperate climate, since it is only in temperate climates that human beings develop completely; that he is rich, since it is only the rich who have need of the natural education that would fit them to live under all conditions; that he is to all intents and purposes an orphan, whose tutor having undertaken the parents' duties will also have their right to control all the circumstances of his upbringing; and, finally, that he is a vigorous, healthy, well-built child. . . .

True happiness comes with equality of power and will. The only man who gets his own way is the one who does not need another's help to get it: from which it follows that the supreme good is not authority, but freedom. The true free-man wants only what he can get, and does only what pleases him. This is my fundamental maxim. Apply it to childhood and all the rules of education follow.

There are two kinds of dependence: dependence on things, which is natural, and dependence on men, which is social. Dependence on things being non-moral is not prejudicial to freedom and engenders no vices: dependence on men being capricious engenders them all. The only cure for this evil in society would be to put the law in place of the individual, and to arm the general will with a real power that made it superior to every individual will.

Keep the child in sole dependence on things and you will follow the natural order in the course of his education. Put only physical obstacles in the way of indiscreet wishes and let his punishments spring from his own actions. Without forbidding wrong-doing, be content to prevent it. Experience or impotence apart from anything else should take the place of law for him. Satisfy his desires, not because of his demands but because of his needs. He should have no consciousness of obedience when he acts, nor of mastery when someone acts for him. Let him experience liberty equally in his actions and in yours. . . .

Let us lay it down as an incontestable principle that the first impulses of nature are always right. There is no original perversity in the human heart. Of every vice we can say how it entered and whence it came. The only passion natural to man is self-love, or self-esteem in a broad sense. This self-esteem has no necessary reference to other people. In so far as it relates to ourselves it is good and useful. It only becomes good or bad in the social application we make of it. Until reason, which is the guide of self-esteem, makes its appearance, the child should not do anything because he is seen or heard by other people, but only do what nature demands of him. Then he will do nothing but what is right. . . .

May I set forth at this point the most important and the most useful rule in all education? It is not to save time but to waste it. The most dangerous period in human life is that between birth and the age of twelve. This is the age when errors and vices sprout, before there is any instrument for their destruction. When the instrument is available the roots have gone too deep to be extracted. The mind should remain inactive till it has all its faculties.

It follows from this that the first education should be purely negative. It consists not in teaching virtue and truth, but in preserving the heart from vice and the mind from error. If you could do nothing and let nothing be done, so that your pupil came to the age of twelve strong and healthy but unable to distinguish his right hand from his left, the eyes of this understanding would be open to reason from your very first lessons. In the absence of both prejudices and habits there would be nothing in him to oppose the effects of your teaching and care. . . .

Assuming that my method is that of nature and that I have not made any mistakes in putting it into practice, I have now brought my pupil through the land of the sensations right up to the bounds of childish reason. The first step beyond this should take him towards manhood. But before entering on this new stage let us cast our eyes backward for a moment on the one we have traversed. Each age and state of life has its own proper perfection, its own distinctive maturity. People sometimes speak about a complete man. Let us think rather of a complete child. This vision will be new for us and perhaps not less agreeable.

When I picture to myself a boy of ten or twelve, healthy, strong and well built for his age, only pleasant thoughts arise in me, whether for his present or for his future. I see him bright, eager, vigorous, carefree, completely absorbed in the present, rejoicing in abounding vitality. I see him in the years ahead using senses, mind and power as they develop from day to day. I view him as a child and he pleases me. I think of him as a man and he pleases me still more. His warm blood seems to heat my own. I feel as if I were living in his life and am rejuvenated by his vivacity.

The clock strikes and all is changed. In an instant his eye grows dull and his merriment disappears. No more mirth, no more games! A severe, hard-faced man takes him by the hand, says gravely, "Come away, sir," and leads him off. In the room they enter I get a glimpse of books. Books! What a cheerless equipment for his age. As he is dragged away in silence, he casts a regretful look around him. His eyes are swollen with tears he dare not shed, his heart heavy with sighs he dare not utter.

Come, my happy pupil, and console us for the departure of the wretched boy. Here comes Emile, and at his approach I have a thrill of joy in which I see he shares. It is his friend and comrade, the companion of his games to whom he comes. His person, his bearing, his countenance reveal assurance and contentment. Health glows in his face. His firm step gives him an air of vigour. His complexion is refined without being effeminate; sun and wind have put on it the honourable imprint of his sex. His eyes are still unlighted by the fires of sentiment and have all their native serenity. His manner is open and free without the least insolence or vanity.

His ideas are limited but precise. If he knows nothing by heart, he knows a great deal by experience. If he is not as good a reader in books as other children, he reads better in the book of nature. His mind is not in his tongue but in his head. He has less memory but more judgment. He only knows one language, but he understands what he says and if he does not talk as well as other children he can do things better than they can.

Habit, routine and custom mean nothing to him. What he did yesterday has no effect on what he does today. He never follows a fixed rule and never accepts authority or example. He only does or says what seems good to himself. For this reason you must not expect stock speeches or studied manners from him but just the faithful expression of his ideas and the conduct that comes from his inclinations.

You will find in him a few moral notions relating to his own situation, but not being an active member of society he has none relating to manhood.

Talk to him about liberty, property and even convention, and he may understand you thus far. But speak to him about duty and obedience, and he will not know what you mean. Command him to do something, and he will pay no heed. But say to him: "If you will do me this favour, I will do the same for you another time," and immediately he will hasten to oblige. For his part, if he needs any help he will ask the first person he meets as a matter of course. If you grant his request he will not thank you, but will feel that he has contracted a debt. If you refuse, he will neither complain nor insist. He will only say: "It could not be done." He does not rebel against necessity once he recognizes it.

Work and play are all the same to him. His games are his occupations: he is not aware of any difference. He goes into everything he does with a pleasing interest and freedom. It is indeed a charming spectacle to see a nice boy of this age with open smiling countenance, doing the most serious things in his play or profoundly occupied with the most frivolous amusements.

Émile has lived a child's life and has arrived at the maturity of childhood, without any sacrifice of happiness in the achievement of his own perfection. He has acquired all the reason possible for his age, and in doing so has been as free and as happy as his nature allowed him to be. If by chance the fatal scythe were to cut down the flower of our hopes we would not have to bewail at the same time his life and his death, nor add to our griefs the memory of those we caused him. We would say that at any rate he had enjoyed his childhood and that nothing we had done had deprived him of what nature gave. . . .

The passions are the chief instruments for our preservation. The child's first sentiment is self-love, the only passion that is born with man. The second, which is derived from it, is the love he has for the people he sees ready to help him, and from this develops a kindly feeling for mankind. But with fresh needs and growing dependence on others comes the consciousness of social relations and with it the sense of duties and preference. It is at this point that the child may become domineering, jealous, deceitful, vindictive. Self-love being concerned only with ourselves is content when our real needs are satisfied, but self-esteem which involves comparisons with other people never is and never can be content because it makes the impossible demand that others should prefer us to themselves. That is how it comes that the gentle kindly passions issue from self-love, while hate and anger spring from self-esteem. Great care and skill are required to prevent the human heart being depraved by the new needs of social life. . . .

My readers, I foresee, will be surprised to see me take my pupil through the whole of the early years without mentioning religion. At fifteen he was not aware that he had a soul, and perhaps at eighteen it is not yet time for him to learn. For if he learns sooner than is necessary he runs the risk of never knowing.

My picture of hopeless stupidity is a pedant teaching the catechism to children. If I wanted to make a child dull I would compel him to explain what he says when he repeats his catechism. It may be objected that since most of the Christian doctrines are mysteries it would be necessary for the proper understanding of them to wait, not merely till the child becomes a man but till the man is no more. To that I reply, in the first place, that there are mysteries man can neither conceive nor believe and that I see no purpose in teaching them to children unless it be to teach them to lie. I say, further, that to admit there are mysteries one must understand that they are incomprehensible, and that this is an idea which is quite beyond children. For an age when all is mystery, there can be no mysteries, properly so-called.

Let us be on guard against presenting the truth to those unable to comprehend it. The effect of that is to substitute error for truth. It would be better to have no idea of the Divine Being than to have ideas that are mean, fantastic and unworthy. . . .

Sophie should be as typically woman as Emile is man. She must possess all the characteristics of humanity and of womanhood which she needs for playing her part in the physical and the moral order. Let us begin considering in what respects her sex and ours agree and differ.

In the mating of the sexes each contributes in equal measure to the common end but not in the same way. From the diversity comes the *first* difference which has to be noted in their personal relations. It is the part of the one to be active and strong, and of the other to be passive and weak. Accept this principle and it follows in the *second* place that woman is intended to please man. If the man requires to please the woman in turn the necessity is less direct. Masterfulness is his special attribute. He pleases by the very fact that he is strong. This is not the law of love, I admit. But it is the law of nature, which is more ancient than love.

The faculties common to the sexes are not equally shared between them; but take them all in all, they are well balanced. The more womanly a woman is, the better. Whenever she exercises her own proper powers she gains by it: when she tries to usurp ours she becomes our inferior. Believe me, wise mother, it is a mistake to bring up your daughter to be like a good man. Make her a good woman, and you can be sure that she will be worth more for herself and for us. This does not mean that she should be brought up in utter ignorance and confined to domestic tasks. A man does not want to make his companion a servant and deprive himself of the peculiar charms of her company. That is quite against the teaching of nature, which has endowed women with quick pleasing minds. Nature means them to think, to judge, to love, to know and to cultivate the mind as well as the countenance. This is the equipment nature has given them to compensate for their lack of strength and enable them to direct the strength of men.

As I see it, the special functions of women, their inclinations and their duties, combine to suggest the kind of education they require. Men and women are made for each other but they differ in the measure of their dependence on each other. We could get on better without women than women could get on without us. To play their part in life they must have our willing help, and for that they must earn our esteem. By the very law of nature women are at the mercy of men's judgments both for themselves and for their children. It is not enough that they should be estimable: they must be esteemed. It is not enough that they should be beautiful: they must be pleasing.

It is not enough that they should be wise: their wisdom must be recognised. Their honour does not rest on their conduct but on their reputation. Hence the kind of education they get should be the very opposite of men's in this respect. Public opinion is the tomb of a man's virtue but the throne of a woman's.

On the good constitution of the mothers depends that of the children and the early education of men is in their hands. On women too depend the morals, the passions, the tastes, the pleasures, aye and the happiness of men. For this reason their education must be wholly directed to their relations with men. To give them pleasure, to be useful to them, to win their love and esteem, to train them in their childhood, to care for them when they grow up, to give them counsel and consolation, to make life sweet and agreeable for them: these are the tasks of women in all times for which they should be trained from childhood.

Questions

1. Do you agree with Rousseau's position that the arts and sciences have done little to advance the happiness of humankind? Explain.

2. Why is Rousseau's view of education characterized as negative education?

3. From Rousseau's perspective, can human beings improve upon nature? Explain.

4. What is Rousseau's solution to the social malaise he sees all around him?

5. Émile's tutor clearly manipulates the environment to ensure that Émile responds properly or learns the desired principle. Is there anything morally wrong with such manipulation? In pedagogy, does the end justify the means? Explain.

6. Given what you know about Rousseau and his times, why do you think he was so openly critical of the harshness with which children were treated in his day?

7. How does Rousseau define freedom?

8. What, for Rousseau, should be the role of the teacher?

9. How does Rousseau suggest that we teach someone to read?

10. What does Rousseau have to say about competition in education?

11. What are Rousseau's views on the use of books in the education of our children?

12. Why was *Robinson Crusoe* Rousseau's favorite book?

13. Do you think that Rousseau succeeded in resolving the individual-collectivity dilemma? Explain.

14. Is the kind of education Rousseau advocates feasible in a democracy? Explain.

15. To what extent is the education advocated by Rousseau a kind of moral education?

16. Describe in your own words Rousseau's vision of the ideally educated individual.

17. How, for Rousseau, would an ideally educated woman be different from an ideally educated man?

5

Catharine Macaulay

Time Line for Macaulay

INTRODUCTION

As suggested by Jane Roland Martin in the 1982 article in the *Harvard Educational Review*, "Excluding Women from the Educational Realm," the contributions of women to the philosophy of education have largely been ignored. This is certainly true in the case of Catharine Macaulay—a contemporary of Rousseau—whose contribution to this field, *Letters on Education with Observations on Religious and Metaphysical*

Subjects, was published in 1790. Macaulay, well known for her eight-volume history of the English civil war and restoration, offers—in *Letters*—a feminist critique of eighteenth-century attitudes toward women. In *Letters,* she provides a counterpoint to Rousseau's commonly accepted view that there are essential differences in the nature of men and women and that these differences are complementary.

Catharine Sawbridge Macaulay Graham was born in Kent, England on March 23, 1731, the second daughter of John and Elizabeth Wanley Sawbridge. With the death of her mother at age two, Catharine spent much of her childhood and youth under the care of a governess hired by her father. Receiving an education typical of that given upper-class English girls of the period, Catharine's intellectual prowess resulted from sharing the educational experiences of her siblings—an older sister and an older and a younger brother—and from her own self-education. Growing tired of "fairy tales and romances," she discovered her father's library, and "history became her darling passion, and liberty the idol of her imagination."[1]

Catharine's marriage in 1760 to George Macaulay—a Scottish medical doctor fifteen years her senior—produced one daughter, Catharine Sophia. Widowed six years later, Catharine's scholarly reputation flourished with the publication of the first of eight volumes of her political history of seventeenth-century England in 1763. Some twelve years after George Macaulay's death, Catharine married William Graham, a twenty-one-year-old surgeon's mate. This unconventional marriage suggests that Catharine rebelled against the traditional marriage norms and that she refused to be restricted by the accepted roles for women in the eighteenth century.

In addition to her eight-volume *History of England* (1763–1783) and her *Letters on Education,* Macaulay commented on such past and contemporary philosophers as Plato, Hobbes, Locke, and Edmund Burke. Recognized for her work as a serious historian, Macaulay experienced both critics and admirers. Mary Wollstonecraft praised her as "the woman of the greatest abilities that this country ever produced"[2] and both Horace Walpole and Thomas Gray praised her work.

She supported the colonists in the American Revolution and participated in philosophical discussions on both sides of the Atlantic regarding the establishment of a republic in the New World. She journeyed to the former colonies in 1784, visiting nine of the original United States and concluding her visit by staying with George and Martha Washington at Mount Vernon. The visit with General Washington resulted in a continuing correspondence on various topics, including the establishment of the U.S. Constitution.

Macaulay wrote *Treatise on the Immutability of Moral Truth* in 1783, laying the metaphysical foundation for her last work, *Letters on Education with Observations on Religious and Metaphysical Subjects.* In *Letters on Education,* Macaulay counters Rousseau's claim that men and women possess different human natures and that these differences suggest complementary societal roles.

Macaulay argues that there is a single human essence and that the socially labeled feminine and masculine characteristics reside in both sexes. Painfully aware that this mistaken notion of essential differences in the nature of the sexes has been universally

---

[1]Gina Luria, "Introduction" to Catharine Macaulay's *Letters on Education with Observations on Religious and Metaphysical Subjects* (New York: Garland Publishing, Inc., 1974), p. 5.
[2]Ibid., p. 7.

accepted from the earliest times, Macaulay suggests that "the pride of one sex and the ignorance and vanity of the other, have helped to support an opinion which a close observation of Nature, and a more accurate way of reasoning, would disprove."[3]

Macaulay suggests that the education provided both sexes in her day and in days past reinforces the false premise that the sexes are essentially different and hence not equal. Since this false or miseducation has reinforced and continues to reinforce this erroneous view of human nature, Macaulay suggests that the first step is to expose the false premises upon which past and present education is based. Once these falsehoods are debunked—or in more contemporary language, deconstructed—then education can enable all human beings—men and women—to reach perfection.

In a description that is reminiscent of Plato's cosmic soul or of the absolute idealism of the next century, Macaulay equates perfection with the divine Being or divine mind—a disembodied and genderless entity. This cosmic or divine Being is her god, a god that is neither male nor female but one who is an omniscient, omnipotent, and benevolent parent. Possessing the so-called masculine characteristics of strength and reason as well as the "feminine" traits of tenderness and wisdom, Macaulay's divine Being integrates these characteristics and traits into harmonious perfection.

Again, much like Plato, Macaulay suggests that human nature is derivative of this divine or cosmic being and that in the nature of each human being is the potential to achieve perfection, that is, a mind or being that fully integrates feminine and masculine characteristics. Although perfection is a worthy goal and within reach of every human being, it has not yet been achieved by either sex. Macaulay suggests that this failure is due to the false or mis-education experienced by both sexes in the past and present. Such miseducation, or "blunders of art," results in imperfections in both sexes as both fall short of the ideal or perfect union of the feminine and masculine characteristics that defines the divine mind. Since such imperfections are the products of human errors and limited educational visions, Macaulay is optimistic that they can be corrected by ensuring that both men and women are properly and correctly educated.

Especially critical of the so called "arts of female allurement," Macaulay suggests that women accept much too quickly the roles assigned to them by society and too willingly engage in behavior designed to attract the male. In this way, females are complicit in a miseducation that denigrates the female mind. Such "feminine" attributes or arts of allurement not only demean women but also, and of more importance, contribute nothing to the development of the virtues associated with the divine being or mind.

A proper education should—suggests Macaulay—cultivate the genderless virtues that comprise the cosmic or divine mind and that are associated with perfection. Because of the similarity, if not inseparability, of Macaulay's human nature and that of the divine nature, humans—in striving for perfection—begin to feel sympathy and to embrace equity.

The ultimate virtue is benevolence, for it "contains the principle of every moral duty."[4] Using the Aristotelian concept that virtues occupy the middle ground between two extremes, benevolence resides in between greed—an unwillingness to share one's bounty with others—and a reckless extravagance—sharing or giving beyond what is needed or appropriate. As the premier virtue, benevolence is defined as a disposition

[3]Catharine Macaulay, *Letters on Education with Observations on Religious and Metaphysical Subjects* (London: Woodstock Books, 1790), pp. 203–204.
[4]Ibid., p. 112.

to do good so as to promote happiness in others. Critical of both the formal education and the informal socialization that minimize or deny the human tendency toward benevolence, Macaulay opposes such male and adolescent activities as "robbing birds of their young" and "hunting for sport." Such activities are vices that are "hostile to the principle of benevolence."[5]

For similar reasons, she criticizes the largely female pastime of reading novels because they often reinforce the false notion that there are essential and complementary differences between male and female natures. Macaulay argues that both formal education and socialization of both boys and girls work against and often counter the natural tendency toward sympathy and benevolence.

Macaulay has great faith in the power of education—properly conceived and executed—to foster benevolence and reason in each human being. She agrees with Rousseau that formal instruction should be delayed until early adolescence when the child's rational faculties are capable of identifying faulty reasoning and—if properly developed—are inclined to choose virtue over vice. For children at age ten or twelve and after carefully designed exposure to a wide variety of subjects, Macaulay outlines a rigorous classical curriculum for boys and girls designed to develop them into both good citizens—aware of and capable of obeying societal laws—and philosophers, capable of both understanding the principles behind these laws and assessing their utility in fostering human perfection.

In preparation for this rigorous classical curriculum, Macaulay suggests that the tutor or parent should carefully select the subject matter to be used with young children, making sure that it represents and fosters benevolence and reason as the ultimate human qualities. Macaulay's curricular recommendations are ambitious, but coverage and/or mastery of the content are not her goal. Macaulay believes that adolescents and young adults exposed to a wide range of material will use such diversity of content for self-development. Advocating a method of self-education remarkably similar to her own experience as a child and adolescent, Macaulay hoped to create critical and confident thinkers who draw upon this diverse content in forming their own opinions and in making decisions about the kind of person they want to be and the kind of life they want to lead. Macaulay goes beyond Rousseau's goal of educating a citizen and his mate to fostering the development of boys and girls into both citizens and philosophers.

Catharine Macaulay achieved significant notoriety in her day for her eight-volume *History of England, From the Succession of James I to the Elevation of the House of Hanover* and as an independent thinker who refused to accept society's limitation on women. As previously noted, her *Letters on Education* have largely been ignored by those studying educational thought even though it offers a compelling counterargument to her more famous contemporary's (Rousseau) call for the different, yet complementary, education of Émile and Sophie.

It is to correct this omission or oversight that Macaulay's work is included in this edition of *Philosophical Documents in Education*. As the selections here suggest, Macaulay was ahead of her time. In providing what is basically a feminist critique of the

---

[5]Ibid., pp. 64–65.

education of both men and women in her time and in suggesting that there is but a single human nature comprising both masculine and feminist traits, Macaulay anticipates the thought of Jane Roland Martin, a late-twentieth-century educational philosopher whose work is also included in this volume. As Connie Titone suggests in *Gender Equality in the Philosophy of Education: Catharine Macaulay's Forgotten Contribution,* Macaulay's contribution to educational philosophy is easily linked to Paulo Freire's—the modern-day Brazilian philosopher of education—advocacy of education for critical consciousness. Perhaps the most significant contemporary link to her educational thought is the similarities between Macaulay's belief in benevolence—that is, the integration of tenderness and reason—as the ultimate goal of education for all human beings and Nel Noddings's characterization of educational philosophy as an ethic of caring.

In the reading of the following selections from Macaulay's *Letters on Education,* a comparison with Rousseau's ideal of the educated individual is in order, but the reader must not stop there. To better understand and appreciate Macaulay's role in expanding our understanding of what it means to be an en educated individual, the reader should compare her ideas to those of Paulo Freire, Jane Roland Martin, and Nel Noddings. Selections from each of these educational philosophers are included later in this volume.

FROM *LETTERS ON EDUCATION* (1790)

Part I., Letter XXII

No Characteristic Difference in Sex The great difference that is observable in the characters of the sexes, Hortensia, as they display themselves in the scenes of social life, has given rise to much false speculation on the natural qualities of the female mind.—For though the doctrine of innate ideas, and innate affections, are in a great measure exploded by the learned, yet few persons reason so closely and so accurately on abstract subjects as, through a long chain of deductions, to bring forth a conclusion which in no respect militates with their premises.

It is a long time before the crowd give up opinions they have been taught to look upon with respect; and I know many persons who will follow you willingly through the course of your argument, till they perceive it tends to the overthrow of some fond prejudice; and then they will either sound a retreat, or begin a contest in which the contender for truth, though he cannot be overcome, is effectually silenced, from the mere weariness of answering positive assertions, reiterated without end. It is from such causes that the notion of a sexual difference in the human character has, with a very few exceptions, universally prevailed from the earliest times, and the pride of one sex, and the ignorance and vanity of the other, have helped to support an opinion which a close observation of Nature, and a more accurate way of reasoning, would disprove.

It must be confessed, that the virtues of the males among the human species, though mixed and blended with a variety of vices and errors, have displayed a bolder and a more consistent picture of excellence than female nature has hitherto done. It is on these reasons that, when we compliment the appearance of a more than ordinary energy in the female mind, we call it masculine; and hence it is, that Pope has elegantly said *a perfect woman's but a softer man*. And if we take in the consideration, that there can be but one rule of moral excellence for beings made of the same materials, organized after the same manner, and subjected to similar laws of Nature, we must either agree with Mr. Pope, or we must reverse the proposition, and say, that *a perfect man is a woman formed after a coarser mold*. The difference that actually does subsist between the sexes, is too flattering for men to be willingly imputed to accident; for what accident occasions, wisdom might correct; and it is better, says Pride, to give up the advantages we might derive from the perfection of our fellow associates, than to own that Nature has been just in the equal distribution of her favours. These are the sentiments of the men: but mark how readily they are yielded to by the women; not from humility I assure you, but merely to preserve with character those fond vanities on which they set their hearts. No; suffer them to idolize their persons, to throw away their life in the pursuit of trifles, and to indulge in the gratification of the meaner passions, and they will heartily join in the sentence of their degradation.

Among the most strenuous asserters of a sexual difference in character, Rousseau is the most conspicuous, both on account of that warmth of sentiment which distinguishes all his writings, and the eloquence of his compositions: but never did enthusiasm and the love of paradox, those enemies to philosophical disquisition, appear in more strong opposition to plain sense than in Rousseau's definition of this difference. He sets out with a supposition, that Nature intended the subjection of the one sex to the other; that consequently there must be an inferiority of intellect in the subjected party; but as man is a very imperfect being, and apt to play the capricious tyrant, Nature, to bring things nearer to an equality, bestowed on the woman such attractive graces, and such an insinuating address, as to turn the balance on the other scale. Thus Nature, in a giddy mood, recedes from her purposes, and subjects prerogative to an influence which must produce confusion and disorder in the system of human affairs. Rousseau saw this objection; and in order to obviate it, he has made up a moral person of the union of the two sexes, which, for contradiction and absurdity, outdoes every metaphysical riddle that was ever formed in the schools. In short, it is not reason, it is not wit; it is pride and sensuality that speak in Rousseau, and, in this instance, has lowered the man of genius to the licentious pedant.

But whatever might be the wise purpose intended by Providence in such a disposition of things, certain it is, that some degree of inferiority, in point of corporal strength, seems always to have existed between the two sexes; and this advantage, in the barbarous ages of mankind, was abused to such a degree, as to destroy all the natural rights of the female species, and reduce them to a state of abject slavery. What accidents have contributed in Europe to better their condition, would not be to my purpose to relate; for I do not intend to give you a history of women; I mean only to trace the sources of their peculiar foibles and vices; and these I firmly believe to originate in situation and education only: for so little did a wise and just Providence intend to make the condition of slavery an unalterable law of female nature, that in the same proportion as the male sex have consulted the interest of their own happiness, they have relaxed in their tyranny over women; and such is their use in the system of mundane creation, and such their natural influence over the male mind, that were these advantages properly exerted, they might carry every point of any importance to their honour and happiness. However, till that period arrives in which women will act wisely, we will amuse ourselves in talking of their follies.

The situation and education of women, Hortensia, is precisely that which must necessarily tend to corrupt and debilitate both the powers of mind and body. From a false notion of beauty and delicacy, their system of nerves is depraved before they come out of their nursery; and this kind of depravity has more influence over the mind, and consequently over morals, than is commonly apprehended. But it would be well if such causes only acted towards the debasement of the sex; their moral education is, if possible, more absurd than their physical. The principles and nature of virtue, which is never properly explained to boys, is kept quite a mystery to girls. They are told indeed, that they must abstain from those vices which are contrary to their personal happiness, or they will be regarded as criminals, both by God and man; but all the higher parts of rectitude, every thing that ennobles our being, and that renders us both innoxious and useful, is either not taught, or is taught in such a manner as to leave no proper impression on the mind. This is so obvious a truth, that the defects of female education have ever been a fruitful topic of declamation for the moralist; but not one of this class of writers have laid down any judicious rules for amendment. Whilst we still retain the absurd notion of a sexual excellence, it will militate against the perfecting a plan of education for either sex. The judicious Addison animadverts on the absurdity of bringing a young lady up with no higher idea of the end of education than to make her agreeable to a husband, and confining the necessary excellence for this happy acquisition to the mere graces of person.

Every parent and tutor may not express himself in the same manner as is marked out by Addison; yet certain it is, that the admiration of the other sex is held out to women as the highest honour they can attain; and whilst this is considered as their summum bonum, and the beauty of their persons the chief desideratum of men, Vanity, and its companion Envy, must taint, in their characters, every native and every acquired excellence. Nor can you, Hortensia, deny, that these qualities, when united to ignorance, are fully equal to the engendering and rivetting all those vices and foibles which are peculiar to the female sex; vices and foibles which have caused them to be considered, in ancient times, as beneath cultivation, and in modern days have subjected them to the censure and ridicule of writers of all descriptions, from the deep thinking philosopher to the man of ton and gallantry, who, by the bye, sometimes distinguishes himself by qualities which are not greatly superior to those he despises in women. Nor can I better illustrate the truth of this observation than by the following picture, to be found in the polite and gallant Chesterfield. "Women," says his Lordship, "are only children of a larger growth. They have an entertaining tattle, sometimes wit; but for solid reasoning, and good sense, I never in my life knew one that had it, or who acted or reasoned in consequence of it for four and twenty hours together. A man of sense only trifles with them, plays with them, humours and flatters them, as he does an engaging child; but he neither consults them, nor trusts them in serious matters."

Part I., Letter XXIII

Coquettry Though the situation of women in modern Europe, Hortensia, when compared with that condition of abject slavery in which they have always been held in the east, may be considered as brilliant; yet if we withhold comparison, and take the matter in a positive sense, we shall have no great reason to boast of our privileges, or of the candour and indulgence of the men towards us. For with a total and absolute exclusion of every political right to the sex in general, married women, whose situation demand a particular indulgence, have hardly a civil right to save them from the grossest injuries; and though the gallantry of some of the European societies have necessarily produced indulgence, yet in others the faults of women are treated with a severity and rancour which militates against every principle of religion and common sense. Faults, my friend, I hear you say; you take the matter in too general a sense; you know there is but one fault which a woman of honour may not commit with impunity; let her only take care that she is not caught in a love intrigue, and she may lie, she may deceive, she may defame, she may ruin her own family with gaming, and the peace of twenty others with her coquettry, and yet preserve both her reputation and her peace. These are glorious privileges indeed, Hortensia; but whilst plays and novels are the favourite study of the fair, whilst the admiration of men continues to be set forth as the chief honour of woman, whilst power is only acquired by personal charms, whilst continual dissipation banishes the hour of reflection, Nature and flattery will too often prevail; and when this is the case, self preservation will suggest to conscious weakness those methods which are the most likely to conceal the ruinous trespass, however base and criminal they may be in their nature. The crimes that women have committed, both to conceal and to indulge their natural failings, shock the feelings of moral sense; but indeed every love intrigue, though it does not terminate in such horrid catastrophes, must naturally tend to debase the female mind, from its violence to educational impressions, from the secrecy with which it must be conducted, and the debasing dependancy to which the intriguer, if she is a woman of reputation, is subjected. Lying, flattery, hypocrisy, bribery, and a long catalogue of the meanest of the human vices, must all be employed to preserve necessary appearances. Hence delicacy of sentiment gradually decreases; the warnings of virtue are no longer felt; the mind becomes corrupted, and lies open to every solicitation which appetite or passion presents. This must be the natural course of things in every being formed after the human plan; but it gives rise to the trite and foolish observation, that the first fault against chastity in woman has a radical power to deprave the character. But no such frail beings come out of the hands of Nature. The human mind is built of nobler materials than to be so easily corrupted; and with all the disadvantages of situation and education, women seldom become entirely abandoned till they are thrown into a state of desperation by the venomous rancour of their own sex.

The superiority of address peculiar to the female sex, says Rousseau, is a very equitable indemnification for their inferiority in point of strength. Without this, woman would not be the companion of man, but his slave; it is by her superior art and ingenuity that she preserves her equality, and governs him, whilst she affects to obey. Woman has every thing against her; as well our faults, as her own timidity and weakness. She has nothing in her favor but her subtlety and her beauty; is it not very reasonable therefore that she should cultivate both?

I am persuaded that Rousseau's understanding was too good to have led him into this error, had he not been blinded by his pride and his sensuality. The first was soothed by the opinion of superiority, lulled into acquiescence by cajolement; and the second was attracted by the idea of women playing off all the arts of coquettry to raise the passions of the sex. Indeed the author fully avows his sentiments, by acknowledging that he would have a young French woman cultivate her agreeable talents, in order to please her future husband, with as much care and assiduity as a young Circassian cultivates her's to fit her for the harem of an eastern bashaw.

These agreeable talents, as the author expresses it, are played off to great advantage by women in all the courts of Europe; who, for the arts of female allurement, do not give place to the Circassian. But it is the practice of these very arts, directed to enthral the men, which act in a peculiar manner to corrupting the female mind. Envy, malice, jealousy, a cruel delight in inspiring sentiments which at first perhaps were never intended to be reciprocal, are leading features in the character of the coquet, whose aim is to subject the whole world to her own humour; but in this vain attempt she commonly sacrifices both her decency and her virtue.

By the intrigues of women, and their rage for personal power and importance, the whole world has been filled with violence and injury; and their levity and influence have proved so hostile to the existence or permanence of rational manners, that it fully justifies the keenest of Mr. Pope's satire on the sex.

But I hear my Hortensia say, whither will this fit of moral anger carry you? I expected an apology, instead of a libel, on women; according to your description of the sex, the philosopher has more reason to regret the indulgence, than what you have sometimes termed the injustice of the men; and to look with greater complacency on the surly manners of the ancient Greeks, and the selfishness of Asiatic luxury, than on the gallantry of modern Europe.

Though you have often heard me express myself with warmth in the vindication of female nature, Hortensia, yet I never was an apologist for the conduct of women. But I cannot think the surliness of the Greek manners, or the selfishness of Asiatic luxury, a proper remedy to apply to the evil. If we could inspect narrowly into the domestic concerns of ancient and modern Asia, I dare say we should perceive that the first springs of the vast machine of society were set a going by women; and as to the Greeks, though it might be supposed that the peculiarity of their manners would have rendered them indifferent to the sex, yet they were avowedly governed by them. They only transferred that confidence which they ought to have given their wives, to their courtezans, in the same manner as our English husbands do their tenderness and their complaisance. They will sacrifice a wife of fortune and family to resentment, or the love of change, provided she give them opportunity, and bear with much Christian patience to be supplanted by their footman in the person of their mistress.

No; as Rousseau observes, it was ordained by Providence that women should govern some way or another; and all that reformation can do, is to take power out of the hands of vice and folly, and place it where it will not be liable to be abused.

To do the sex justice, it must be confessed that history does not set forth more instances of positive power abused by women, than by men; and when the sex has been taught wisdom by education, they will be glad to give up indirect influence for rational privileges; and the precarious sovereignty of an hour enjoyed with the meanest and most infamous of the species, for those established rights which, independent of accidental circumstances, may afford protection to the whole sex.

Part I., Letter XII

Benevolence The virtue of benevolence, Hortensia, is of so comprehensive a nature, that it contains the principle of every moral duty. It is true; there are some qualities of the heart, which we pass on ourselves and others for the virtue of benevolence; but they will be found on examination to want that which constitutes the very essence of this attribute. A great prince makes large donations to particular persons; he is called benevolent; but in the exercise of this benevolence he abuses his trust; he lays heavy burdens on the people for these donations; and thus the opulence of the few is purchased with the poverty of the many. A rich man, under the notion of liberality, becomes prodigally lavish of treasures, which, if well managed, would be the permanent source of enjoyment to himself, and to thousands of other beings; but as he is the dupe of all who deal with him, he spends what is justly his own like a fool; then imitating the knave, he either re-establishes his affairs by public robbery, or dies insolvent, and defrauds his creditors.

Donations, and other acts of kindness, are in general done in so partial a manner, and with so little judgment, that they seldom confer good on any being, without occasioning as much or more evil to others. The most important of all duties, says Rousseau, is not to do injury to any one. Who is there that does not do good? All the world, even the vicious man, does good to one party or another: he will often make one party happy at the expence of making others miserable. Hence arise, all our calamities. Oh how much good must that man necessarily do his fellow creatures, who never did any of them harm.

Though we should not confine benevolence merely to the not doing injury, yet it is certain that benevolence and injury are opposites, which can never unite; and if strict equity does in some points of view bear a distinction from benevolence, yet the distinction can only be seen in the inferior and superior degrees of the same virtue.

It has ever been the distinguishing mark of revelation, that its injunctions are to do good to others, and to bear injuries with patience. And experience, by the happiness annexed to a benevolent conduct, convinces the unprejudiced mind of the truths contained in the precepts of the gospel; for we never enjoy more mental felicity, than in the exercise of the benign affections; and we could by habit and cultivation give such a prevalence to the passion of benevolence, as to render all our inclinations subordinate to it, we might almost bid defiance to fortune, and vaunt the independence of stoicism.

But if the observations of the moralist are just, why does not education bend her whole care to produce a fruit thus advantageous to the possessor, and which when multiplied in private characters, would operate strongly in favour of public happiness.

The answer to this question is, that one can be acquainted with the happiness annexed to a truly benevolent mind, who is not in the possession of it. We are all partially good, and some are more extensively so than others; but there are few, very few of the sons of men, who are benevolent.

Those precepts of the gospel, which are adapted to the cultivation of this virtue, have ever been looked upon so difficult in practice, as in common to be totally disregarded. Revenge, which is only agreeable as it serves to allay the painful sensations of anger, is still sought after as the sweetest of all mental dainties. Envy, a passion nearly allied to revenge, and which owes its gratification to the same cause, infects every bosom with more or less of its malignancy, and universally breaks out into injuries, when it can be done with safety to reputation. Whilst Pride, the root of these passions, with its offspring, Vanity, gives birth to a variety of affections, hostile to the principle of benevolence, and which tend to render us capricious and partial in the favours we bestow.

The reason then, that education if found so deficient in producing benevolence is, that precept, without example, is of no use in the cultivation of this cardinal virtue. It is example only which can fire the mind to an emulation of disinterested actions, which can call its attention to distresses without itself; and by a retrospect of its own capabilities of misery, can teach it with the celerity of thought to transport itself into the situation of the suffering object.

Rousseau very justly censures all those methods which have been followed, and all those rules which have been laid down by writers, to teach the affections to flow in the channel of benevolence.

"To teach children charity, says Rousseau, we make them give alms, as if we were above giving it ourselves. It is the master, however, who should give alms, and not the scholar. Indeed, how fond so ever the former may be of his pupil, he ought to make him believe, that a child of his age is as yet unworthy of so great a privilege."

"To give alms, is the action of a man who may be supposed to know the value of what he bestows, and the want his fellow creatures have of it. A child who knows nothing of either, can have no merit in giving alms. What are to them the round pieces of metal they carry in their pocket, and which serve to no other purpose, but to give away? A child would sooner give a beggar a hundred guineas, than a cake; but require the little prodigal to give away his playthings, his sweetmeats, and other trifles he is fond of, and we shall presently see whether or not we have made him truly liberal."

The effects made by impressions on infants will be found to abide with them through life, and we shall find on observation, that every species of liberality we see practiced, except the sums extorted by sympathy, or by a religious sentiment from avarice, are but different modes of prodigality. There are thousands who will give their money, because they have been taught to set little store by it; but how few, how very few of those who make a figure in every public subscription for charitable purposes, would part with any trifle on which they set a value, or would bestow any of their time, or their attention, to meliorate the situation of sufferers, though such a sacrifice would in some cases better answer a benevolent end, than the most lavish donations? There are many miseries to which we are subjected, that money cannot remove. The sick man languishing under the tedium which accompanies his enervated state, wants the re-animating enjoyment of social intercourse. The afflicted mourner wants the consolations which flow from sympathy; and the weak and the giddy are often lost for the want of advice, which, if properly administered, would be gladly received. How much more good would be attained by the sums daily given, if they were distributed with economy, and with an attention to the situation of sufferers, and the degrees of misery endured. But these are duties which require time, attention, assiduity, and trouble; whereas the merely putting the hand in the pocket, is an action easily achieved, and if not, the offspring of vanity can only be considered as a tax paid for the quieting conscience, and those feelings which the sight of misery sometimes excites in the coldest bosom.

The parade with which children are commonly used to bestow alms, has a tendency to cherish the growth of pride, and a supercilious contempt for wretchedness. I have seen a beggar, bent down with age, standing for some minutes before a child, with his cap in his hand, and his knee bent, expecting in this humble and uneasy attitude the boon of a halfpenny, which was to be administered by little master or miss, on the opinion that the practice to bestowing alms was favourable to the acquiring habits of liberality.

Some tutors have endeavoured to induce these habits, by returning to children in a short time what they have given in presents; and the judicious Locke advises to manage, so as to convince children by experience, that the most liberal are always the best provided for; but the objections of Rousseau on this part of Locke's system, are undoubtedly founded in truth. You will by such methods, says he, only render children liberal in appearance, and covetous in fact. They will have the liberality of an usurer, who would give a penny for a pound. But, when they come to the point of giving things away in good earnest, adieu to habit; when they found things did not come back again, they would soon cease to give them away.

Part I., Letter XIII

The Same Subject Continued Yes, Hortensia; Rousseau is right in the opinion, that the virtues of children are of the negative kind; and that in endeavouring to produce the fruits of reason and experience at too early a season, we are deprived of the harvest of a riper age. Let it be then the principal care of tutors, to preserve the infant mind free from the malignant passions, and the benign affections will grow of themselves. Let it be their care to make their pupils feel the utility of benevolence, by being themselves the objects of it. Let no capricious partialities, no ill founded preference, growing from personal charms or accomplishments, or from the gifts of genius, set them the example of a departure from the strict principles of equity, and give them reason to complain both of the injustice of Nature and of man.

But it is not through the medium of self only, that children should be taught lessons of benevolence; they should see it dispensed to every object around them with such a constancy, as should keep them in perfect ignorance that vices of injustice and inhumanity have any existence. They ought not to be suffered to ridicule others, unreproved. Should they once take a pleasure in the pain they give the human mind, benevolence will never be the leading feature in their character. As children are not able to enter into any nice exam-ination on the different claims of wretchedness, it might be proper to avoid carrying them much in the way of objects of charity; but whenever accident presented such, they should never see them go away unrelieved.

You will perhaps say, that this indiscriminate liberality might lead them into enthusiasm or prodigality, and use them to bestow their alms without judgment or preference; but neither of these consequences would ensue. Enthusiasm is the offspring of speculation, never of habitual practice; and as I have said before, children are not able to enter into those distinctions, which experience can alone teach, it is sufficient for them, if their principles and habits are of the right kind; rules of prudence are to be left to after instruction, when a larger intercourse with the world sets forth a variety of examples to view. Prodigality, is a vice that either owes it rise to the little value we see put on money by those about us, or it proceeds from having our pockets loaded with coin before we can attain any knowledge of its worth. But to avoid giv-ing my pupils either habits of avarice or prodigality, or teazing them with pre-cepts, which would undoubtedly be misunderstood, I would never put them into the possession of any money, till they were of an age to be taught its value by the use they would be able to make of it.

If brutes were to draw a character of man, Hortensia, do you think they would call him a benevolent being? No; their presentations would be some-what of the same kind as the fabled furies and other infernals in ancient mythology. Fortunately, for the reputation of the species, the brutes can nei-ther talk nor write; and being our own panegyrists, we can give ourselves what attributes we please, and call our confined and partial sympathy, the sublime virtue of benevolence. Goodness to man, and mercy to brutes, is all that is taught by the moralist; and this mercy is of a nature which if properly defined, can only be distinguished by the inferiority of its degree from the vice of cruelty. Certainly every tutor not drawn from the dregs of the people, would prevent his pupil from partaking of Domitian's favorite amusement, and would rescue a miserable insect or other animal from the tortures inflict-ed by a wanton fancy; but would he not suffer him to extend evil in other modes? Would he prevent him from robbing birds of their young? Would he shut out all habits of cruelty by keeping him from the chace and other sports of the field, or from the hardened barbarity of putting worms on a hook as bait to catch fish? Would he set him the example both of a negative, and an ac-tive goodness in a total forbearance of every unnecessary injury, and in the seizing all opportunities to do acts of kindness to every feeling being?

There are very few of the insect or reptile tribes which belong to this coun-try, that can be said to be personally injurious to man; yet we are brought up with such prejudices, that they never escape our violence whenever they come within our reach. You will perhaps, call it a laughable weakness; but I do acknowledge to you, that I take a warm interest in the happiness of the brutes, as far as it is compatible with the nature of things. The stile of my amusements are quite opposite to that of Domitian's. I take a pleasure in restoring life; and though I do not give harbour to all animals, yet I never make them suffer for having taken shelter under my roof; and I am so persuaded of the advantages which attend the indulgence of such sensibilities, when not accompanied with caprice and partiality, that I would have all those who are about the persons of children act the same part, though their tempers should not be of the kind to receive pleasure from it.

I do not think that the poets in general are the best moralists; but the following lines of Miss Williams, raised the virtues of the author's heart high in my estimation.

> Eltruda o'er the distant mead,
>   Would haste at closing day;
> And to the bleating mother lead,
>   The lamb that chanced to stray.
>
> For the bruised insect on the waste,
>   A sigh would heave her breast,
> And oft her careful hand replaced,
>   The linnet's falling nest.
>
> To her, sensations calm as these
>   Could sweet delight impart,
> The simple pleasure most can please
>   The uncorrupted heart.
>
> Full oft with eager step she flies
>   To cheer the roofless cot,
> Where the lone widow breaths her sighs,
>   And wails her desperate lot.
>
> Their weeping mother's trembling knees,
>   Her lisping infants clasp;
> Their meek imploring look she sees,
>   She feels their tender grasp.
>
> Wild throbs her aching bosom swell,
>   They marked the bursting sigh;
> Nature has formed the soul to feel,
>   They weep, unknowing why.
>
> Her hands the liberal boon impart,
>   And much her tear avails,
> To raise the mourners drooping heart,
>   Where feeble utterance fails.
>
> On the pail cheek where hung the tear
>   Of agonizing woe,
> She bids the cheerful bloom appear,
>   The tear of rapture flow.
>
> Thus on soft wings the moments flew,
>   Tho' love implored their stay;
> While some new virtue rose to view,
>   And marked each fleeting day.

The soft and gentle satisfactions which flow from the practice of the benign virtues, are not of the fleeting kind; they afford pleasure on recollection, and they serve as a kind of store, on which the mind feeds, when in want of consolation from the pressure of present pain. But let us return to the subject of cultivating in children the virtue of benevolence.

Every child, from the pleasure which the exercise of power gives, is very fond of becoming the master of animals; but this inclination is often thwarted by parents, owing to prejudices arising from an undue contempt of the brutes, or from the apprehension of injury from them, or that they will meet with ill treatment from the caprice, or injudicious fondness of children.

The apprehension of injury from brute animals, is I believe totally without foundation; for their tempers are so generally good, that the wildest of them never injure those from whom they receive benefits; and tame animals extend their kindness to all whom they are used to see. The accident of madness, which sometimes attends dogs and cats, is indeed of the most dreadful kind; yet, as I believe it never happens to any animal who is well looked after and properly treated, the objection can never be regarded as material. The other objection of ill treatment to the brutes, from the caprice and injudicious fondness of children, has more weight; but can only affect those who do not know how to educate children properly.

I would therefore indulge my pupils in the keeping as many animals as they can properly attend. It will give them the practice of benevolence, it will serve as an agreeable and innocent amusement, and by the knowledge they will thus acquire of brute nature, they will be cured of prejudices founded on ignorance, and in the vanity and conceit of man.

From Catharine Macaulay (1790), *Letters on Education*. Banbury, England: Woodstock Books, pp. 112–125, 203–209, 210–215.

Questions

1. Why do you think that Catharine Macaulay's ideas on education were largely ignored by her contemporaries and by subsequent generations?

2. How does Macaulay distinguish between the education of a citizen and the education of a philosopher?

3. Compare Macaulay's educational ideas to those of her contemporary Jean-Jacques Rousseau.

4. Compare Macaulay's educational ideas to the educational ideas of Jane Roland Martin.

5. How does Macaulay explain the universal acceptance of the erroneous belief that there are differences in the nature of men and women?

6. Describe how, from Macaulay's point of view, women are complicit in perpetuating the idea that men and women have different and complementary natures.

7. In your own words, describe Macaulay's vision of the ideally educated individual.

8. What does Macaulay mean by "benevolence," and why does she characterize it as the supreme virtue?

9. Is Macaulay correct in characterizing Rousseau as both a "man of genius" and a "licentious pedant"?

10. In your own words, explain Macaulay's ideas on how to cultivate the virtue of benevolence in children.

Conflicting Educational Visions: The Puritans and Thomas Jefferson

Time Line for the Puritans

1629	Puritans settled Massachusetts Bay Colony
1635	Boston Latin Grammar School Boston established
1636	Founding of Harvard College
1642	Massachusetts School Law of 1642 enacted
1647	"ould deluder Satan" Act enacted

Time Line for Thomas Jefferson

1776	Wrote Declaration of Independence
1779	"Bill for Establishing Religious Freedom" proposed
1779	"Bill for the More General Diffusion of Knowledge" proposed

INTRODUCTION

As long as education remained a parental or familial responsibility, parents or guardians of means could significantly determine the nature of education to be offered to the children and youth under their charge. Once education became both a societal responsibility and a mass enterprise, conflicts between personal visions of what it means to be educated and more social or communal educational visions began to emerge.

To appreciate the impact such societal visions of the role that education can and should play in society, a comparison of Puritan educational ideas to those of Thomas Jefferson is illustrative.

The Puritans and Thomas Jefferson had similar yet conflicting visions of the role education should play in society. Although both considered education as a necessity for their respective visions of the ideal society, the theocracy (rule by religious men) of the Puritans is antithetical to the Jeffersonian ideal of a democratic republic.

Education for the City on the Hill

The Puritans came to the New World to practice their own religious beliefs, but were not tolerant of perspectives different from their own. Alarmed by the religious turmoil engulfing Europe at this time and especially opposed to the Anglican Church in their own country, the Puritans migrated to the New World to establish a true Biblical Commonwealth. Often referring to the settlement established on the Massachusetts Bay as the City on the Hill, this pure Biblical commonwealth was to serve as a beacon lighting the path toward ultimate salvation.

The concept of separation of church and state was alien to the Puritans due to their belief that the norms of society and the norms of the church were grounded in the same Biblical law. Embracing the teachings of John Calvin, Puritans believed that humankind was innately depraved and could be saved only through the grace of God. The Puritans created in the wilderness an entire society based on this premise, and their leaders were not above literally "beating the devil" out of those unwilling or unable to comply with the Biblical laws of society.

The Puritan theology was undeniably harsh and forbidding, but Puritans were not ignorant or anti-intellectual. As heirs to both the Renaissance and the Reformation, Puritans were convinced that reading the Bible was the Christian's sacred duty. For the Puritans, knowing how to read was an absolute necessity if their new commonwealth was to fulfill its destiny of lighting the path to salvation. Education—specifically literacy—was, for the Puritans, both a religious and civic necessity.

On the frontier of the New World, the daily struggle to survive often superseded the goal of transmitting God' transcendent truths to each new generation. Realizing that education was absolutely essential for their "city on a hill," the Puritans—some have suggested—created schools before "privies" or outhouses were built. Initially such schools were private or individual efforts, but, as the settlement expanded, leaders of the colony realized that education was too important to remain a familial, private, or individual concern.

In 1635—six years after the first settlers landed—the first Latin Grammar School was established in Boston. This secondary school—destined to become famous for the favorite sons it produced—prepared young men for the university. A year later, the Puritans established Harvard College. Establishing a college was an absolute necessity if their vision of creating a Biblical Commonwealth was to be achieved. The gnawing fear that some day their store of trained, learned leaders—both cleric and civilian— might run out led the Puritan fathers to stress secondary and higher education.

Fearing that the settlers on the fringes of the settlement might neglect their parental or societal duty, the General Court of the Massachusetts Bay Colony enacted a law in 1642 requiring all parents to provide for their offspring and apprentices instruction in the reading of Puritans tenets and the principle laws of the Colony. Though rarely enforced, this law planted the seed that bore fruit more than two centuries later with he passage of the first compulsory school law in the United States. This 1642 law established the precedent that education is more than a familial responsibility.

In 1647, the General Court of the Massachusetts Bay Colony took a more forceful step by enacting a law ordering every town of 50 or more households to offer instruction in reading and writing. Furthermore, for towns of 100 or more households, the law required that instruction in Latin grammar be provided so that students might be "fitted [prepared] for the university." In effect, this 1647 law mandated that towns of a specified size establish elementary and secondary schools. Known as the "ould sdeluder Satan" act, this legislation sought to ensure that the word of God and the laws derived from it would remain the birth right of every inhabitant of this Biblical commonwealth.

In these schools—first in Massachusetts and eventually throughout New England and beyond—the Bible was the primary text. Over time other works emerged to buttress the inspired Word. As their titles suggest, these texts were unabashedly religious. John Cotton's *Spiritual Milk for Babes Drawn from the Breasts of Testaments* is an early illustrative example. The most famous and most widely used text was *The New England Primer.*

Education as the Safeguard of Liberty

The religious perspective championed by the Puritans favored combining religious and secular authority in the hands of a select few. The select men of this Biblical Commonwealth were to govern with absolute authority in accordance with Puritans' understanding of the infallible word of God. From the Jeffersonian perspective, such a Puritan theocracy was tyranny of the highest order, for it denied the fundamental human right to the free exercise of religion.

The essence of Thomas Jefferson's educational legacy is captured in his own statement characterizing his life as a continuous struggle against "every form of tyranny against the mind of man." Jefferson is perhaps best known as the primary author of the Declaration of Independence. Of this achievement he was deservedly proud, for it exposed the tyranny of the British monarchy over the colonies. He is also well known for his authorship of the statutes of religious freedom in Virginia, freeing Virginians from the tyranny of organized religion. Unlike the Puritans, Jefferson believed that, in matters of religion, the state should neither promote nor impede the free exercise of religious beliefs. Although his statute applied only to the Colony of Virginia, it established the principle of separation of church and state that is the essence of the First Amendment to the U.S. Constitution.

Espousing a protectionist theory of government, Jefferson argued that "experience hath shown even under the best forms, those entrusted with power, have in time and by slow operation perverted it into tyranny." A government's only purpose is to protect the inalienable rights of life, liberty, and the pursuit of happiness. To perform this role, government officials must be properly educated and remain accountable to the people they serve.

According to Jefferson, only an educated people can create and maintain a government as a fortress against liberty. From this perspective, education is the ultimate safeguard of liberty. Education is so basic to the preservation of freedom that government itself must assume responsibility for educating its children. Though their visions of the ideal society are dramatically different, Jefferson and the Puritans share the belief that education is so important to the common good that it is more than just a familial responsibility.

For Americans to protect their new-found liberties, Jefferson believed that citizens had to be literate and able to appreciate the lessons of history. Awareness of history, Jefferson argues, enables citizens to recognize tyranny in all its forms. Historical understanding, literacy, and a free press are the essential ingredients of a democracy. In Jefferson's words, "When the press is free and every man able to read, all is safe."

A democratic republic presupposes an educated citizenry, but it also requires that the individuals assuming leadership roles receive an appropriate kind of education. Leaders should be men of character with both virtuous and intellectual abilities. According to Jefferson, leaders in a democracy must be drawn from the "natural aristocracy."

We must, Jefferson explains, encourage intellectual and virtuous talent wherever we find it. His "Bill for the More General Diffusion of Knowledge" called for the establishment of a state or colony-wide system of elementary schools offering three years of schooling free to every child. At the end of three years, scholarships would be available to those promising young geniuses to continue their education at state expense. In this way, Jefferson suggests, the "gems" can be raked "from the rubbish," identifying and preparing a "natural aristocracy" that a democratic republic requires. By creating such a state-supported educational pyramid, Jefferson hoped to develop the educated citizenry that a democracy requires and to cultivate the real or natural aristocracy that such a government needs. Though Jefferson's legislative colleagues rejected his proposal as too costly, Jefferson provided future generations with both a compelling rationale and blueprint for a comprehensive system of education.

In a sense, Jefferson embraced and secularized the Puritan notion that education is so important for the commonwealth that it must be a societal responsibility. When you combine this with his advocacy of education as the safeguard of liberty, the result is a very powerful educational legacy.

MASSACHUSETTS SCHOOL LAW OF 1642

This court, taking into consideration the great neglect of many parents and masters in training up their children in learning, and labor, and other imply-ments which may be proffitable to the common wealth, do hereupon order and decree, that in euery towne the chosen men appointed for managing the prudentiall affajres of the same shall henceforth stand charged with the care of the redresse of this evil, so as they shalbee sufficiently punished by fines for the neglect thereof, upon presentment of the grand jury, or other information or complaint in any Court within this jurisdiction; and for this end they, or the greater number of them, shall have power to take account from time to time of all parents and masters, and of their children, concerning their calling and implyment of their children, especially of their ability to read and understand the principles of religion and the capitall lawes of this country, and to impose fines upon such as shall refuse to render such accounts to them when they shall be required; and they shall have power, with consent of any Court or the magistrate, to put forth apprentices the children of such as they shall [find] not to be able and fitt to imploy and bring up . . . and they are to take care of such as are sett to keep cattle be set to some other imployment withall; as spinning upon the rock, knitting, weaving tape, etc. and that boyes and girles be not sufferd to converse together, so as may occasion any wanton, dishonest, or immodest behavior; and for their better performance of this trust committed to them, they may divide the towne amongst them, appointing to every of the said townesmen a certaine number of families to have special oversight of. They are also to provide that a sufficient quantity of materialls, as hemp, flaxe, etc., may be raised in their severall townes, and tooles and implements provided for working out the same; and for their assistance in this so needful and beneficiall imployment, if they meete with any difficulty or opposition which they cannot well master by their own power, they may have recourse to some of the magistrates, who shall take such course for their help and incouragment as the occasion shall require according to justice, and the said townsmen, at the next Court in those limits, after the end of their year, shall give a breife account in writing of their proceedings herein, provided that they have bene so required by some Court or magistrate a month at least before; and this order to continew for two yeares, and till the Court shall take further order.

From Nathaniel B. Shurtleff, ed., *Records of the Governor and Company of Massachusetts Bay in New England* (Boston, 1853–1854), vol. II. pp. 6–7.

MASSACHUSETTS SCHOOL LAW OF 1647

It being one chiefe project of that ould deluder Satan, to keepe men from the knowledge of the Scriptures, as in former times by keeping them in an unknowne tongue, so in these latter times by perswading from the used of tongues, that so at least the true sence and meaning of the originall might be clouded by false glosses of saint seeming deceivers, that learning may not be buried in the grave of our fathers in the church and commonwealth, the Lord assisting our endeavors,–

It is therefore ordered, that every towneship in this jurisdiction after the Lord hath increased them to the number of 50 housholders, shall then forthwith appoint one within their towne to teach all such children as shall resort to him to write and reade, whose wages shall be paid either by the parents or masters of such children, or by the inhabitants in generall, by way of supply, as the maior part of those that order the prudentials of the towne shall appoint; provided, those that send their children be not oppressed by paying much more than they can have them taught for in other townes; and it is further ordered, that where any towne shall increase to the number of 100 families or househoulders, they shall set up a grammer schoole, the master thereof being able to instruct youth so farr as they may be fited for the university, provided, that if any towne neglect the performance hereof above one yeare, that every such towne shall pay £5 to the next schoole till they shall performe this order.

From Nathaniel B. Shurtleff, ed., *Records of the Governor and Company of Massachusetts Bay in New England* (Boston, 1853–1854), vol. II, p. 203.

DESCRIPTION OF THE FOUNDING OF HARVARD COLLEGE (1636)

In Respect of the Colledge, and the Proceedings of Learning Therein

After God had carried us safe to *New-England*, and wee had builded our houses, provided necessaries for our liveli-hood, rear'd convenient places for Gods worship, and setled the Civill Government: One of the next things we longed for, and looked after was to advance Learning and perpetuate it to Posterity, dreading to leave an illiterate Ministery to the Churches, when our present Ministers shall lie in the Dust. And as wee were thinking and consulting how to effect this great Work; it pleased God to stir up the heart of one Mr. *Harvard* (a godly Gentleman, and a lover of Learning, there living amongst us) to give the one halfe of his Estate (it being in all about 1700.1.) towards the erecting of a Colledge, and all his Library; after him another gave 300.1., others after them cast in more, and the publique hand of the State added the rest: the Colledge was, by common consent, appointed to be at *Cambridge*, (a place very pleasant and accommodate) and is called (according to the name of the first founder) *Harvard Colledge*.

The Edifice is very faire and comely within and without, having in it a spacious Hall; (where they daily meet at Common Lectures) Exercises, and a large Library with some Bookes to it, the gifts of diverse of our friends their Chambers and studies also fitted for, and possessed by the Students, and all other roomes of Office necessary and convenient, with all needfull Offices thereto belonging: And by the side of the Colledge a faire *Grammar* Schoole, for the training up of young Schollars, and fitting of them for *Academicall Learning*, that still as they are judged ripe, they may be received into the Colledge of this Schoole: Master *Corlet* is the Mr., who hath very well approved himselfe for his abilities, dexterity and painfulnesse, in teaching and education of the youth under him.

Over the Colledge is master *Dunster* placed, as President, a learned conscionable and industrious man, who hath so trained up, his Pupills in the tongues and Arts, and so seasoned them with the principles of Divinity and Christianity, that we have to our great comfort, (and in truth) beyond our hopes, beheld their progresse in Learning and godlinesse also; the former of these hath appeared in their publique declamations in *Latine* and *Greeke*, and Disputations Logicall and Philosophicall, which they have beene wonted (besides their ordinary Exercises in the Colledge-Hall) in the audience of the Magistrates, Ministers, and other Schollars, for the probation of their growth in Learning upon set dayes, constantly once every moneth to make and uphold: The latter hath been manifested in sundry of them by the savoury breathings of their Spirits in their godly conversation. Insomuch that we are confident, if these early blossomes may be cherished and warmed with the influence of the friends of Learning and lovers of this pious worke, they will by the help of God, come to happy maturity in a short time.

Over the Colledge are twelve Overseers chosen by the generall Court, six of them are of the Magistrates, the other six of the Ministers, who are to promote the best good of it, and (having a power of influence into all persons in it) are to see that every one be diligent and proficient in his proper place.

From "New England's First Fruits," as quoted in Perry Miller and Thomas H. Johnson, eds., *The Puritans* (New York, 1938), pp. 701–702.

SELECTION FROM NOTES ON THE STATE OF VIRGINIA (1781)

Thomas Jefferson

Another object of the revisal is to diffuse knowledge more generally through a mass of the people. This bill proposes to lay off every county into small districts of five or six miles square, called hundreds, and in each of them to establish a school for teaching reading, writing, and arithmetic. The tutor to be supported by the hundred, and every person in it entitled to send their children three years gratis and as much longer as they please, paying for it. These schools to be under a visitor, who is annually to chuse the boy of best genius in the school, of those whose parents are too poor to give them further education, and to send him forward to one of the grammar schools, of which twenty are proposed to be erected in different parts of the country, for teaching Greek, Latin, geography, and the higher branches of numerical arithmetic. Of the boys thus sent in any one year, trial is to be made at the grammar schools one or two years, and the best genius of the whole selected, and continued six years, and the residue dismissed. By this means twenty of the best geniuses will be raked from the rubbish annually, and be instructed, at the public expense, so far as the grammar schools go. At the end of six years instruction, one half are to be discontinued (from among whom the grammar schools will probably be supplied with future masters); and the other half, who are to be chosen for the superiority of their parts and disposition, are to be sent and continued three years in the study of such sciences as they shall chuse, at William and Mary college, the plan of which is proposed to be enlarged, as will be hereafter explained, and extended to all the useful sciences. The ultimate result of the whole scheme of education would be the teaching all the children of the state reading, writing, and common arithmetic; turning out ten annually of superior genius, well taught in Greek, Latin, geography, and the higher branches of arithmetic; turning out ten others annually, of still superior parts, who, to those branches of learning, shall have added such of the sciences as their genius shall have led them to; the furnishing to the wealthier part of the people convenient schools, at which their children may be educated, at their own expence.

The general objects of this law are to provide an education adapted to the years, to the capacity, and the condition of every one, and directed to their freedom and happiness. Specific details were not proper for the law. These must be the business of the visitors entrusted with its execution. The first stage of this education being the schools of the hundreds, wherein the great mass of the people will receive their instruction, the principal foundations of future order will be laid here. Instead therefore of putting the Bible and Testament into the hands of the children, at an age when their judgments are not sufficiently matured for religious enquiries, their memories may here be stored with the most useful facts from Grecian, Roman, European and American history. The first elements of morality too may be instilled into their minds; such as, when further developed as their judgments advance in strength, may teach them how to work out their own greatest happiness, by shewing them that it does not depend on the condition of life in which chance has placed them, but it always the result of a good conscience, good health, occupation, and freedom in all just pursuits.

Those whom either the wealth of their parents or the adoption of the state shall destine to higher degrees of learning, will go on to the grammar schools, which constitute the next stage, there to be instructed in the languages. The learning Greek and Latin, I am told, is going into disuse in Europe. I know not what their manners and occupations may call for, but it would be very ill-judged in us to follow their example in this instance. There is a certain period of life, say from eight to fifteen or sixteen years of age, when the mind, like the body, is not yet firm enough for laborious and close operations. If applied to such, it falls an early victim to premature exertion, exhibiting indeed at first, in these young and tender subjects, the flattering appearance of their being men while they are yet children, but ending in reducing them to be children when they should be men. The memory is then most susceptible and tenacious of impressions, and the learning of languages being chiefly a work of memory, it seems precisely fitted to the powers of this period, which is long enough too for acquiring the most useful languages ancient and modern. I do not pretend that language is science. It is only an instrument for the attainment of science. But that time is not lost which is employed in providing tools for future operation; more especially as in this case the books put into the hands of the youth for this purpose may be such as will at the same time impress their minds with useful facts and good principles. If this period be suffered to pass in idleness, the mind becomes lethargic and impotent, as would the body it inhabits if unexercised during the same time. The sympathy between body and mind during their rise, progress, and decline is too strict and obvious to endanger our being misled while we reason from the one to the other.

As soon as they are of sufficient age, it is supposed they will be sent on from the grammar schools to the university, which constitutes our third and last stage, there to study those sciences which may be adapted to their views. By that part of our plan which prescribes the selection of the youths of genius from among the classes of the poor, we hope to avail the state of those talents which nature has sown as liberally among the poor as the rich, but which perish without use, if not sought for and cultivated.

But of all the view of this law none is more important, none more legitimate, than that of rendering the people safe, as they are the ultimate guardians of their own liberty. For this purpose the reading in the first stage, where *they* will receive their whole education, is proposed, as has been said, to be chiefly historical. History by apprising them of the past will enable them to judge of the future; it will avail them of the experience of other times and other nations; it will qualify them as judges of the actions and designs of men; it will enable them to know ambition under every disguise it may assume; and knowing it, to defeat its views. In every government on earth is some trace of human weakness, some germ of corruption and degeneracy, which cunning will discover, and wickedness insensibly open, cultivate, and improve. Every government degenerates when trusted to the rulers of the people alone. The people themselves therefore are its only safe depositories. And to render even them safe their minds must be improved to a certain degree. This indeed is not all that is necessary, though it be essentially necessary. An amendment of our constitution must here come in aid of the public education. The influence over government must be shared among all the people. If every individual which composes their mass participates of the ultimate authority, the government will be safe because the corrupting the whole mass will exceed any private resources of wealth; and public ones cannot be provided but by levies on the people. In this case every man would have to pay his own price. The government of Great-Britain has been corrupted, because but one man in ten has a right to vote for members of parliament. The sellers of the government therefore get nine-tenths of their price clear. It has been thought that corruption is restrained by confining the right of suffrage to a few of the wealthier of the people, but it would be more effectually restrained by an extension of that right to such numbers as would bid defiance to the means of corruption.

Lastly, it is proposed, by a bill in this revisal, to begin a public library and gallery, by laying out a certain sum annually in books, paintings, and statues.

From Jefferson, Thomas. 1781. *Notes on the State of Virginia*. Brooklyn, N.Y.: Historical Printing Club, 1894.

Questions

1. What is a theocracy?
2. What impact has the Puritan belief in the innate depravity of humankind had on educational beliefs in the United States?
3. Why was education so important for the Puritans?
4. Why was it necessary to establish Harvard College seven years after the Puritans settled in the Massachusetts Bay area?
5. What were the long-term consequences of the school laws passed by the Massachusetts General court in 1642 and 1647?
6. Is Jefferson correct in suggesting that education is the safeguard of liberty?
7. What did Jefferson mean by a "natural aristocracy"?
8. What is the role of education in developing such an aristocracy?
9. How are Jefferson's and the Puritans' vision of society alike? How are they different?
10. Describe in your own words, Jefferson's rationale for his "Bill for the More General Diffusion of Knowledge."
11. Does Jefferson's "natural aristocracy" include women?

7

Local versus Centralized Control of Schooling

INTRODUCTION

As noted in the previous chapter, Thomas Jefferson failed in his effort to develop a colony or statewide system of education. Indeed, education changed little in the decades following the American revolution. The lack of interest in Jefferson's plan for a centralized educational system suggests that citizens of the newly established United States were generally satisfied with the educational system inherited from the colonial era.

The District School: "Pure Little Democracies"

The district school, controlled by the local community, emerged as the dominant form of schooling in both the colonial and early national periods of American history. During these years, there was widespread suspicion of any form of centralized control. As a result, the village or neighborhood school often constituted the sole civic or public entity that people were willing to support. Towns or townships were established as legal entities for school purposes only. Absent state or federal involvement in education, these small political entities exercised total control over the school and the quality of education it provided.

In short, these district or village schools represent extreme examples of local or community control. They levied their own taxes, established a committee to hire and fire the schoolmaster, determined the length of the school term, and constructed and maintained a schoolhouse. Residents of the district took these activities seriously, resulting in—in the name of fairness and equity—placing the schoolhouse in the exact geographic center of the district. Sometimes this meant that schoolhouses stood in swamps or awkwardly perched on high ridges.

Often the only public facility in the district, the schoolhouse became a multipurpose facility, serving as the meeting place for political debates, social events, and even religious services. Functioning as the community center for the district, these "pure little democracies" often represented the pride and identity of these largely rural communities. The failure of a schoolmaster—often an outsider teaching school while preparing for a more lucrative career—to control the children and youth placed under his care often pleased the residents, for it suggested that outside world was no match for the local community. The quality of education offered in these district schools varied dramatically from district to district, though the level of instruction was often not high. District schools were often boring places where little was taught and learned.

American English: Language as Unifier

Even though local control—fueled by a fear of centralized government—dominated schooling during the early years of the republic, an educational solution to a significant political problem emerged during the early national period. Put simply, how is a sense of nationhood developed for a social order comprised of semiautonomous entities and cultures suspicious of centralization and nationalism? Rejecting the trappings of nationalism associated with the Old World (the monarch, the church, and the military establishment), the young country needed to create or manufacture its own sense of nationalism.

In what had recently become the United States of America, inhabitants of the original thirteen colonies were more likely to think of themselves as New Yorkers, Rhode Islanders, or Carolinians, or belonging to some other indigenous group (Cherokee or Iroquois) rather than consider themselves Americans. While citizens in such countries as France, England, or Spain had inherited their nationalism, Americans turned to education to foster a sense of unity in the new republic. In this regard, Noah Webster stands out in recognizing the importance of language for creating a sense of identity and national pride among former colonists.

In 1783, Noah Webster published what came to known as the "Blue Back Speller." Officially titled *A Grammatical Institute of the English Language, Part I,* this little spelling book met with immediate, if unexpected, success. Spanning both geographic and generational boundaries, Webster's spelling book became the standard for a uniquely American way of spelling. His speller conquered the land, travelling west in Conestoga wagons, leaping the mountains, and invading the south. Generations of young people from Maine to California learned the same words, the same pronunciations, and the same moral lessons from Noah Webster. Webster helped to liberate Americans from a sense of inferiority about their language. He helped break down regional differences in background, class, and religion. He provided Americans with something they all—New Yorkers as well as Carolinians—could be proud of: A common speech and language.

In his speller and dictionaries, Webster simplified the spelling of many words and explained their meaning using American, rather than British examples. Though no one anticipated the remarkable success of the blue back speller, Webster recognized the importance of education for promoting nationalism. First with his speller and later through his dictionaries, Webster's impact was both immediate and profound. At a time when the population feared and opposed centralization and nationalism, Webster fostered a sense of nationalism by creating a uniquely American version of the English language.

Webster contributed—albeit unwittingly—to mediating the deadening ethos of the district school. As his speller emerged as the authority or standard for the correct spelling of words in American English, district schools began conducting spelling "bees." Held once or twice a term on Friday afternoon, these spelling contests excited both students and adults. Similar to corn-husking or quilting bees, spelling bees became major social events as the whole community convened upon the schoolhouse for these special events. Analogous to the modern day Friday night high school football game, the young came to court, the politician to preen, and others to see and be seen.

The spelling bee not only transformed the drudgery of school work into a contest, but, for many Americans, "bees" suggested that genuine equality was within their grasp, based on the ability to read, write, and speak in the same way. In Europe, language was used to separate people but Webster envisioned it as a way to unify or bring people together. The spelling bee became a vehicle for fostering community pride and for creating a sense of unity as a uniquely American event. By making it possible for someone from a remote or rural district to demonstrate—by correctly spelling the last word on the last page of the blue back speller—that his or her village or hamlet was equal to or better than any other village in the country, the spelling bee fostered a sense of community or local pride while simultaneously promoting a national identity.

The Common School: A More Centralized School System

Proclaiming the common school as "the greatest discovery ever made by Man," Horace Mann and other common school crusaders offered a compelling rationale for an alternative to the district school and exhibited the will and skill necessary for creating statewide systems of schooling. A politician turned educator, Horace Mann succeeded where Jefferson failed in creating the first statewide system of schooling in the nation.

Born in 1796, Mann's life spanned a period in which Massachusetts changed dramatically. Throughout his youth and young manhood, more than two-thirds of the population lived in rural communities. Immigration was slow and had little effect on the homogenous nature of the population. Continuing the Puritan legacy, schools were created and supported for the common good. The economic base for such communities remained rooted in agriculture and commerce.

Mann saw all this change. During the 1830s and 1840s, he observed a mass Irish immigration pouring into this pure Yankee commonwealth. Mann experienced the transformation of Massachusetts from a rural, agrarian commonwealth into an urbanized, industrial and more culturally diverse society. To combat the evils associated with urbanization, industrialization, and immigration, Mann and others championed the revival of the public or common school.

Serving as a state senator from the Boston area, Mann expressed concern over the moral decay of society. Witnessing a spontaneous and senseless riot in the streets,

Mann became convinced that "the educated, the wealthy, the intelligent" had abdicated their roles as the moral stewards of society. Alarmed as many of his colleagues and others of the upper classes abandoned the common schools for private education, Mann feared that such segregation of education could only increase prejudice and hatred. To combat the apparent unraveling of the social fabric and the moral decline of American society, Mann and other school reformers sought to transform common or public schools into the best schools available.

In 1837, the Massachusetts legislature passed a bill establishing a state board of education. Appointed by the governor and intended to be advisory rather than a board of control, the legislation charged the board with gathering and disseminating information about education statewide. The governor made a wise choice in asking Horace Mann to serve as executive secretary for the first state board of education in the nation. Mann embraced this new position as an opportunity for changing future generations. Asserting that "men are cast iron, but children are wax," Mann enthusiastically embarked upon his new mission.

Embracing Daniel Webster's notion of education as "a wise and liberal system of police," Mann championed the virtues of common schooling to audiences big and small throughout the commonwealth. Though he possessed no formal authority, Mann wielded tremendous influence through the force of his own will and political acumen. For more than a decade, Mann recommended and the legislature passed a number of statutes that in effect created the first state system of public education in the country.

Not everyone agreed with Mann's vision. Champions of local control opposed Mann's attempt to dictate educational policy from the state capitol. Mann softened their opposition by convincing many of his opponents that an improved common school system could provide all children with the knowledge and skills necessary for success in this new, industrialized world of the nineteenth century.

Horace Mann began what became a national crusade for the revival of the common school in the United States. Along with other school reformers, Mann achieved a remarkable consensus regarding the nature and purpose of schooling. Following Massachusetts' lead, virtually every state produced a Mann-like crusader championing the virtues of the common or public school. By 1848, twenty-four of the thirty states in the union had named a chief state school officer and had begun establishing a statewide system of education. Through their collective skill, vision, and wisdom, these common school crusaders fashioned a centralized system of education in each state. Known as common or public schools, they were to be free (supported by tax dollars), open and attractive to all, teach basic skills (the three Rs) and inculcate into each new generation the significantly protestant values that were supposedly common to all Americans.

NOAH WEBSTER ON THE NECESSITY FOR AN AMERICAN LANGUAGE (1789)

A regular study of language has, in all civilized countries, formed a part of a liberal education. The Greeks, Romans, Italians and French successively improved their native tongues, taught them in Academies at home, and rendered them entertaining and useful to the foreign student.

The English tongue, tho later in its progress towards perfection, has attained to a considerable degree of purity, strength and elegance, and been employed, by an active and scientific nation, to record almost all the events and discoveries of ancient and modern times.

This language is the inheritance which the American have received from their British parents. To cultivate and adorn it, is a task reserved for men who shall understand the connection between language and logic, and form an adequate idea of the influence which a uniformity of speech may have on national attachments.

It will be readily admitted that the pleasures of reading and conversing, the advantage of accuracy in business, the necessity of clearness and precision in communicating ideas, require us to be able to speak and write our own tongue with ease and correctness. But there are more important reasons, why the language of this country should be reduced to such fixed principles, as may give its pronunciation and construction all the certainty and uniformity which any living tongue is capable of receiving.

The United States were settled by emigrants from different parts of Europe. But their descendants mostly speak the same tongue; and the intercourse among the learned of the different States, which the revolution has begun, and an American Court will perpetuate, must gradually destroy the differences of dialect which our ancestors brought from their native countries. This approximation of dialects will be certain; but without the operation of other causes than an intercourse at Court, it will be slow and partial. The body of the people, governed by habit, will still retain their respective peculiarities of speaking; and for want of schools and proper books, fall into many inaccuracies, which, incorporating with the language of the state where they live, may imperceptibly corrupt the national language. Nothing but the establishment of schools and some uniformity in the use of books, can annihilate differences in speaking and preserve the purity of the American tongue. A sameness of pronunciation is of considerable consequence in a political view; for provincial accents are disagreeable to strangers and sometimes have an unhappy effect upon the social affections. All men have local attachments, which lead them to believe their own practice to be the least exceptionable. Pride and prejudice incline men to treat the practice of their neighbors with some degree of contempt. Thus small differences in pronunciation at first excite ridicule—a habit of laughing at the singularities of strangers is followed by disrespect—and without respect friendship is a name, and social intercourse a mere ceremony.

These remarks hold equally true, with respect to individuals, to small societies, and to large communities. Small causes, such as a nicknames or a vulgar tone in speaking, have actually created a dissocial spirit between the inhabitants of the different states, which is often discoverable in private business and public deliberations. Our political harmony is therefore concerned in a uniformity of language.

As an independent nation, our honor requires us to have a system of our own, in language as well as government. Great Britain, whose children we are, and whose language we speak, should no longer be our standard; for the taste of her writers is already corrupted, and her language on the decline.

But if it were not so, she is at too great a distance to be our model, and to instruct us in the principles of our own tongue.

It must be considered further, that the English is the common root or stock from which our national language will be derived. All others will gradually waste away—and within a century and a half, North America will be peopled with a hundred millions of men, *all speaking the same language.* Place this idea in comparison with the present and possible future bounds of the language in Europe—consider the Eastern Continent as inhabited by nations, whose knowledge and intercourse are embarrassed by differences of language; then anticipate the period when the people of one quarter of the world, will be able to associate and converse together like children of the same family.[1] Compare this prospect, which is not visionary, with the state of the English language in Europe, almost confined to an Island and to a few millions of people; then let reason and reputation decide, how far America should be dependent on a transatlantic nation, for her standard and improvements in language.

Let me add, that whatever predilection the Americans may have for their native European tongues, and particularly, the British descendants for the English, yet several circumstances render a future separation of the American tongue from the English, necessary and unavoidable. The vicinity of the European nations, with the uninterrupted communication in peace, and the changes of dominion in war, are gradually assimilating their respective languages. The English with others is suffering continual alterations. America, placed at a distance from the those nations, will feel, in a much less degree, the influence of the assimilating causes; at the same time, numerous local causes, such as a new country, new associations of people, new combination of ideas in arts and science, and some intercourse with tribes wholly unknown in Europe, will introduce new words into the American tongue. These causes will produce, in a course of time, a language in North America, as different from the future language of England, as the modern Dutch, Danish and Swedish are from the German, or from one another: Like remote branches of a tree springing from the same stock; or rays of light, shot from the same center, and diverging from each other, in proportion to their distance from the point of separation.

Whether the inhabitants of America can be brought to a perfect uniformity in the pronunciation of words, it is not easy to predict; but it is certain that no attempt of the kind has been made, and an experiment, begun and pursued on the right principles, is the only way to decide the question. Schools in Great Britain have gone far towards demolishing local dialects—commerce has also had its influence—and in America these causes, operating more generally, must have a proportional effect.

In many parts of America, people at present attempt to copy the English phrases and pronunciation—an attempt that is favored by their habits, their prepossessions and the intercourse between the two countries. This attempt has, within the period of a few years, produced a multitude of changes in

[1]Even supposing that a number of republics, kingdoms or empires, should within a century arise and divide this vast territory; still the subjects of all will speak the same language, and the consequences of this uniformity will be an intimacy of social intercourse hitherto unknown, and a boundless diffusion of knowledge.

these particulars, especially among the leading classes of people. These changes make a difference between the language of the higher and common ranks, and indeed between the *same* ranks in *different* states; as the rage for copying the English, does not prevail equally in every part of North America.

But besides the reasons already assigned to prove this imitation absurd, there is a difficulty attending it, which will defeat the end proposed by its advocates; which is, that the English themselves have no standard of pronunciation, nor can they ever have one on the plan they propose. The Authors, who have attempted to give us a standard, make the practice of the court and stage in London the sole criterion of propriety in speaking. An attempt to establish a standard on this foundation is both *unjust* and *idle*. It is unjust, because it is abridging the nation of its rights: The *general practice* of a nation is the rule of propriety, and this practice should at least be consulted in so important a matter, as that of making laws for speaking. While all men are upon a footing and no singularities are accounted vulgar or ridiculous, every man enjoys perfect liberty. But when a particular set of men, in exalted stations, undertake to say, "we are the standards of propriety and elegance, and if all men do not conform to our practice, they shall be accounted vulgar and ignorant," they take a very great liberty with the rules of the language and the rights of civility.

But an attempt to fix a standard on the practice of any particular class of people is highly absurd: As a friend of mine once observed, it is like fixing a light house on a floating island. It is an attempt to *fix* that which is in itself *variable*; at least it must be variable so long as it is supposed that a local practice has no standard but a *local practice*; that is, no standards but *itself*. While this doctrine is believed, it will be impossible for a nation to follow as fast as the standard changes—for if the gentlemen at court constitute a standard, they are above it themselves, and their practice must shift with their passions and their whims.

But this is not all. If the practice of a few men in the capital is to be the standard, a knowledge of this must be communicated to the whole nation. Who shall do this? An able compiler perhaps attempts to give this practice in a dictionary; but it is probable that the pronunciation, even at court, or on the stage, is not uniform. The compiler therefore must follow his particular friends and patrons; in which case he is sure to be opposed and the authority of his standard called in question; or he must give two pronunciations as the standard, which leaves the student in the same uncertainty as it found him. Both these events have actually taken place in England, with respect to the most approved standards; and of course no one is unevenly followed.

Besides, if language must vary, like fashions at the caprice of a court, we must have our standard dictionaries republished, with the fashionable pronunciation, at least once in five years; otherwise a gentlemen in the country will become intolerably vulgar, by not being in a situation to adopt the fashion of the day. The *new* editions of them will supersede the *old* and we shall have our pronunciation to re-learn with the polite alterations, which are generally corruption.

Such are the consequences of attempting to make a local practice the *standard* of language in a *nation*. The attempt must keep the language in perpetual fluctuation, and the learner in uncertainty.

If a standard therefore cannot be fixed on local and variable custom, on what shall it be fixed? If the most eminent speakers are not to direct our practice, where shall we look for a guide? The answer is extremely easy; the *rules of the language itself,* and the *general practice of the nation*, constitute propriety in speaking. If we examine the structure of any language, we shall find a certain principle of analogy running through the whole. We shall find in English that similar combinations of letters have usually the same pronunciation, and that words, having the same terminating syllable, generally have the accent at the same distance from that termination. These principles of analogy were not the result of design—they must have been the effect of accident, or that tendency which all men feel towards uniformity. But the principles, when established, are productive of great convenience, and become an authority superior to the arbitrary decisions of any man or class of men. There is one exception only to this remark: When a deviation from analogy has become the universal practice of a nation, it then takes place of all rules and becomes the standard of propriety.

The two points therefore, which I conceive to be the basis of a standard in speaking, are these, *universal undisputed practice,* and the *principle of analogy. Universal practice* is generally, perhaps always, a rule of propriety; and in disputed points, where people differ in opinion and practice, *analogy* should always decide the controversy.

From Noah Webster, "An Essay on the Necessity, Advantages, and Practicality of Reforming the Mode of Spelling . . ." *Dissertations on the English Language . . .* (Boston, 1789), pp. 17–19, 288–90, 393–98.

SELECTIONS FROM REPORT NO. 12 OF THE MASSACHUSETTS SCHOOL BOARD (1848)

Horace Mann

Under the Providence of God, our means of education are the grand machinery by which the "raw material" of human nature can be worked up into inventors and discoverers, into skilled artisans and scientific farmers, into scholars and jurists, into the founders of benevolent institutions, and the great expounders of ethical and theological science. By means of early education, these embryos of talent may be quickened, which will solve the difficult problems of political and economical law; and by them too, the genius may be kindled which will blaze forth in the Poets of Humanity. Our schools, far more than they have done, may supply the Presidents and Professors of Colleges, and Superintendents of Public Instruction, all over the land; and send, not only into our sister states, but across the Atlantic, the men of practical science, to superintend the construction of the great works of art. Here, too, may those judicial powers be developed and invigorated, which will make legal principles so clear and convincing as to prevent appeals to force; and, should the clouds of war ever lower over our country, some hero may be found—the nursling of our schools, and ready to become the leader of our armies—that best of all heroes, who will secure the glories of a peace, unstained by the magnificent murders of the battle-field. . . .

Without undervaluing any other human agency, it may be safely affirmed that the Common School, improved and energized as it can easily be, may become the most effective and benignant of all the forces of civilization. Two reasons sustain this position. In the first place, there is a universality in its operation, which can be affirmed of no other institution whatever. If administered in the spirit of justice and conciliation, all the rising generation may be brought within the circle of its reformatory and elevating influences. And, in the second place, the materials upon which it operates are so pliant and ductile as to be susceptible of assuming a greater variety of forms than any other earthly work of the Creator. The inflexibility and ruggedness of the oak, when compared with the lithe sapling or the tender germ, are but feeble emblems to typify the docility of childhood, when contrasted with the obduracy and intractableness of man. It is these inherent advantages of the Common School, which, in our own State, have produced results so striking, from a system so imperfect, and an administration so feeble. In teaching the blind, and the deaf and dumb, in kindling the latent spark of intelligence that lurks in an idiot's mind, and in the more holy work of reforming abandoned and outcast children, education has proved what it can do, by glorious experiments. These wonders, it has done in its infancy, and with the lights of a limited experience; but, when its faculties shall be fully developed, when it shall be trained to wield its mighty energies for the protection of society against the giant vices which now invade and torment it—against intemperance, avarice, war, slavery, bigotry, the woes of want and the wickedness of waste—then, there will not be a height to which these enemies of the race can escape, which it will not scale, nor a Titan among them all, whom it will not slay.

I proceed, then, in endeavoring to show how the true business of the schoolroom connects itself, and becomes identical, with the great interests of society. The former is the infant, immature state of those interests; the latter, their developed, adult state. As "the child is father to the man," so may the training of the schoolroom expand into the institution and fortunes of the State . . .

Intellectual Education, as a Means of Removing Poverty, and Securing Abundance. Another cardinal object which the government of Massachusetts, and all the influential men in the State should propose to themselves, is the physical well-being of all the people—the sufficiency, comfort, competence of every individual, in regard to food, raiment, and shelter. And these necessaries and conveniences of life should be obtained by each individual for himself, or by each family for themselves, rather than accepted from the hand of charity, or extorted by poor-laws. It is not averred that this most desirable result can, in all instances, be obtained; but it is, nevertheless, the end to be aimed at. True statesmanship and true political economy, not less than true philanthropy, present this perfect theory as the goal, to be more and more closely approximated by our imperfect practice. The desire to achieve such a result cannot be regarded as an unreasonable ambition; for, though all mankind were well-fed, well-clothed, and well-housed, they might still be but half-civilized . . .

According to the European theory, men are divided into classes—some to toil and earn, others to seize and enjoy. According to the Massachusetts theory, all are to have an equal chance for earning, and equal security in the enjoyment of what they earn. The latter tends to equality of condition; the former to the grossest inequalities. Tried by any Christian standard of morals, or even by any of the better sort of heathen standards, can any one hesitate, for a moment, in declaring which of the two will produce the greater amount of human welfare; and which, therefore, is the more conformable to the Divine will? The European theory is blind to what constitutes the highest glory, as well as the highest duty, of a State . . .

I suppose it to be the universal sentiment of all those who mingle any ingredient of benevolence with their notions on Political Economy, that vast and overshadowing private fortunes are among the greatest dangers to which the happiness of the people in a republic can be subjected. Such fortunes would create a feudalism of a new kind, but one more oppressive and unrelenting than that of the Middle Ages. The feudal lords in England, and on the continent, never held their retainers in a more abject condition of servitude than the great majority of foreign manufacturers and capitalists hold their operatives and laborers at the present day. The means employed are different, but the similarity in results is striking. What force did then, money does now. The villein of the Middle Ages had no spot of earth on which he could live, unless one were granted to him by his lord. The operative or laborer of the present day has no employment, and therefore no bread, unless the capitalist will accept his services. The vassal had no shelter but such as his master provided for him. Not one in five thousand of English operatives, or farm laborers, is able to build or own even a hovel; and therefore they must accept such shelter as Capital offers them. The baron prescribed his own terms to his retainers; those terms were peremptory, and the serf must submit or perish. The British manufacturer or farmer prescribes the rate of wages he will give to his work-people; he reduces these wages under whatever pretext he pleases, and they too have no alternative but submission or starvation. In some respects, indeed, the condition of the modern dependent is more forlorn than that of the corresponding serf class in former times. Some attributes of the patriarchal relation did spring up between the lord and his lieges, to soften the harsh relations subsisting between them. Hence came some oversight of the condition of children, some relief in sickness, some protection and support in the decrepitude of age. But only in instances comparatively few have kindly offices smoothed the rugged relation between British Capital and British Labor. The children of the work-people are abandoned to their fate; and, notwithstanding the privations they suffer, and the danger they threaten, no power in the realm has yet been able to secure them an education; and when the adult laborer is prostrated by sickness, or eventually worn out by toil and age, the poor-house, which has all along been his destination, becomes his destiny.

Now two or three things will doubtless be admitted to be true, beyond all controversy, in regard to Massachusetts. By its industrial condition, and its business operations, it is exposed, far beyond any other state in the Union, to the fatal extremes of overgrown wealth and desperate poverty. Its population is more dense than that of any other state. It is four or five times more dense than the average of all the other states, taken together; and density of population has always been one of the proximate causes of social inequality. According to population and territorial extent, there is far more capital in Massachusetts—capital which is movable, and instantaneously available—than in any other state in the Union; and probably both these qualifications respecting population and territory could be omitted without endangering the truth of the assertion. It has been recently stated, in a very respectable public journal, on the authority of a writer conversant with the subject, that, from the last of June, 1846, to the 1st of August, 1848, the amount of money invested, by the citizens of Massachusetts, "in manufacturing cities, railroads, and other improvements," is "fifty-seven millions of dollars, of which more than fifty has been paid in and expended." The dividends to be received by the citizens of Massachusetts from June, 1848, to April, 1849, are estimated, by the same writer, at ten millions, and the annual increase of capital at "little short of twenty-two millions." If this be so, are we not in danger of naturalizing and domesticating among ourselves those hideous evils which are always engendered between Capital and Labor, when all the capital is in the hands of one class, and all the labor is thrown upon another?

Now, surely, nothing but Universal Education can counter-work this tendency to the domination of capital and the servility of labor. If one class possesses all the wealth and the education, while the residue of society is ignorant and poor, it matters not by what name the relation between them may be called; the latter, in fact and in truth, will be the servile dependents and subjects of the former. But if education be equably diffused, it will draw property after it, by the strongest of all attractions; for such a thing never did happen, and never can happen, as that an intelligent and practical body of men should be permanently poor. Property and labor, in different classes, are essentially antagonistic; but property and labor, in the same class, are essentially fraternal. The people of Massachusetts have, in some degree, appreciated the truth, that the unexampled prosperity of the State—its comfort, its competence, its general intelligence and virtue—is attributable to the education, more or less perfect, which all its people have received; but are they sensible of a fact equally important?—namely, that it is to this same education that two thirds of the people are indebted for not being, to-day, the vassals of as severe a tyranny, in the form of capital, as the lower classes of Europe are bound to in the form of brute force.

Education, then, beyond all other devices of human origin, is the great equalizer of the conditions of men—the balance-wheel of the social machinery. I do not here mean that it so elevates the moral nature as to make men disdain and abhor the oppression of their fellow men. This idea pertains to another of its attributes. But I mean that it gives each man the independence and the means by which he can resist the selfishness of other men. It does better than to disarm the poor of their hostility towards the rich; it prevents being poor. Agrarianism is the revenge of poverty against wealth. The wanton destruction of the property of others—the burning of hay-ricks and corn-ricks, the demolition of machinery, because it supersedes hand-labor, the sprinkling of vitriol on rich dresses—is only agrarianism run mad. Education prevents both the revenge and the madness. On the other hand, a fellow feeling for one's class or caste is the common instinct of hearts not wholly sunk in selfish regards for person, or for family. The spread of education, by enlarging the cultivated class or caste, will open a wider area over which the social feelings will expand; and, if this education should be universal and complete, it would do more than all things else to obliterate factitious distinctions in society.

The main idea set forth in the creeds of some political reformers, or revolutionizers, is that some people are poor because others are rich. This idea supposes a fixed amount of property in the community, which, by fraud or force, or arbitrary law, is unequally divided among men; and the problem presented for solution is how to transfer a portion of this property from those who are supposed to have too much to those who feel and know that they have too little. At this point, both their theory and their expectation of reform stop. But the beneficent power of education would not be exhausted, even though it should peaceably abolish all the miseries that spring from the coexistence, side by side, of enormous wealth and squalid want. It has a higher function. Beyond the power of diffusing old wealth, it has the prerogative of creating new. It is a thousand times more lucrative than fraud, and adds a thousandfold more to a nation's resources than the most successful conquests. Knaves and robbers can obtain only what was before possessed by others. Knaves and robbers can obtain only what was before possessed by others. But education creates or develops new treasures—treasures not before possessed or dreamed of by any one . . .

If a savage will learn how to swim, he can fasten a dozen pounds' weight to his back, and transport it across a narrow river, or other body of water of moderate width. If he will invent an axe, or other instrument, by which to cut down a tree, he can use the tree for a float, and one of its limbs for a paddle, and can thus transport many times the former weight, many times the former distance. Hollowing out his log, he will increase, what may be called, its tonnage—or, rather, its poundage—and, by sharpening its ends, it will cleave the water both more easily and more swiftly. Fastening several trees together, he makes a raft, and thus increases the buoyant power of his embryo water-craft. Turning up the ends of small poles, or using knees of timber instead of straight pieces, and grooving them together, or filling up the interstices between them, in some other way, so as to make them water-tight, he brings his rude raft literally into ship-shape. Improving upon hull below and rigging above, he makes a proud merchantman, to be wafted by the winds from continent to continent. But, even this does not content the adventurous naval architect. He frames iron arms for his ship; and, for oars, affixes iron wheels, capable of swift revolution, and stronger than the strong sea. Into iron-walled cavities in her bosom, he puts iron organs of massive structure and strength, and of cohesion insoluble by fire. Within these, he kindles a small volcano; and then, like a sentient and rational existence, this wonderful creation of his hands cleaves oceans, breast tides, defies tempests, and bears its living and jubilant freight around the globe. Now, take away intelligence from the ship-builder, and the steamship—that miracle of human art—falls back into a floating log; the log itself is lost; and the savage swimmer, bearing his dozen pounds on his back, alone remains.

And so it is, not in one department only, but in the whole circle of human labors. The annihilation of the sun would no more certainly be followed by darkness, than the extinction of human intelligence would plunge the race at once into the weakness and helplessness of barbarism. To have created such beings as we are, and to have placed them in this world, without the light of the sun, would be no more cruel than for a government to suffer its laboring classes to grow up without knowledge . . .

For the creation of wealth, then—for the existence of a wealthy people and a wealthy nation—intelligence is the grand condition. The number of improvers will increase, as the intellectual constituency, if I may so call it, increases. In former times, and in most parts of the world even at the present day, not one man in a million has ever had such a development of mind, as made it possible for him to become a contributor to art or science. Let this development precede, and contributions, numberless, and of inestimable value, will be sure to follow. That Political Economy, therefore, which busies itself about capital and labor, supply and demand, interest and rents, favorable and unfavorable balances of trade, but leaves out of account the element of a wide-spread mental development, is nought but stupendous folly. The greatest of all the arts in political economy is to change a consumer into a producer; and the next greatest is to increase the producer's producing power—an end to be directly attained, by increasing his intelligence . . .

Political Education. The necessity of general intelligence—that is, of education, (for I use the terms as substantially synonymous; because general intelligence can never exist without general education, and general education will be sure to produce general intelligence)—the necessity of general intelligence, under a republican form of government, like most other very important truths, has become a very trite one. It is so trite, indeed, as to have lost much of its force by its familiarity. Almost all the champions of education seize upon this argument, first of all, because it is so simple as to be understood by the ignorant, and so strong as to convince the skeptical. Nothing would be easier than to follow in the train of so many writers, and to demonstrate, by logic, by history, and by the nature of the case, that a republican form of government, without intelligence in the people, must be, on a vast scale, what a madhouse, without superintendent or keepers, would be on a small one—the despotism of a few succeeded by universal anarchy, and anarchy by despotism, with no change but from bad to worse. Want of space and time alike forbid me to attempt any full development of the merits of this theme; but yet, in the closing one of a series of reports, partaking somewhat of the nature of a summary of former arguments, an omission of this topic would suggest to the comprehensive mind the idea of incompleteness.

That the affairs of a great nation or state are exceedingly complicated and momentous, no one will dispute. Nor will it be questioned that the degree of intelligence that superintends, should be proportioned to the magnitude of the interests superintended. He who scoops out a wooden dish needs less skill than the maker of a steam-engine or a telescope. The dealer in small wares requires less knowledge than the merchant who exports and imports to and from all quarters of the globe. An ambassador cannot execute his functions with the stock of attainments or of talents sufficient for a parish clerk. Indeed, it is clear, that the want of adequate intelligence—of intelligence commensurate with the nature of the duties to be performed—will bring ruin or disaster upon any department. A merchant loses his intelligence, and he becomes a bankrupt. A lawyer loses his intelligence, and he forfeits all the interests of his clients. Intelligence abandons a physician, and his patients die, with more than the pains of natural dissolution. Should judges upon the bench be bereft of this guide, what havoc would be made of the property and the innocence of men! Let this counselor be taken from executive officers, and the penalties due to the wicked would be visited upon the righteous, while the rewards and immunities of the righteous would be bestowed upon the guilty. And so, should intelligence desert the halls of legislation, weakness, rashness, contradiction, and error would glare out from every page of the statute book. Now, as a republican government represents almost all interests, whether social, civil or military, the necessity of a degree of intelligence adequate to the due administration of them all is so self-evident that a bare statement is the best argument.

But in the possession of this attribute of intelligence, elective legislators will never far surpass their electors. By a natural law, like that which regulates the equilibrium of fluids, elector and elected, appointer and appointee, tend to the same level. It is not more certain that a wise and enlightened constituency will refuse to invest a reckless and profligate man with office, or discard him if accidentally chosen, than it is that a foolish or immoral constituency will discard or eject a wise man. This law of assimilation, between the choosers and the chosen, results, not only from the fact that the voter originally selects his representative according to the affinities of good or of ill, of wisdom or of folly, which exist between them; but if the legislator enacts or favors a law which is too wise for the constituent to understand, or too just for him to approve, the next election will set him aside as a certainly as if he had made open merchandise of the dearest interests of the people, by perjury and for a bribe. And if the infinitely Just and Good, in giving laws to the Jews, recognized the "hardness of their hearts," how much more will an earthly ruler recognize the baseness of wickedness of the people, when his heart is as hard as theirs! In a republican government, legislators are a mirror reflecting the moral countenance of their constituents. And hence it is, that the establishment of a republican government, without well-appointed and efficient means for the universal education of the people, is the most rash and fool-hardy experiment ever tried by man. Its fatal results may not be immediately developed—they may not follow as the thunder follows the lightning—for time is an element in maturing them, and the calamity is too great to be prepared in a day; but, like the slow-accumulating avalanche, they will grow more terrific by delay, and, at length, though it may be at a late hour, will overwhelm with ruin whatever lies athwart their path. It may be an easy thing to make a Republic; but it is a very laborious thing to make Republicans; and woe to the republic that rests upon no better foundation than ignorance, selfishness, and passion. Such a

Republic may grow in numbers and in wealth. As an avaricious man adds acres to his lands, so its rapacious government may increase its own darkness by annexing provinces and states to its ignorant domain. Its armies may be invincible, and its fleets may strike terror into nations on the opposite sides of the globe, at the same hour. Vast in its extent, and enriched with all the prodigality of nature, it may possess every capacity and opportunity of being great, and of doing good. But if such a Republic be devoid of intelligence, it will only the more closely resemble an obscene giant who has waxed strong in his youth, and grown wanton in his strength; whose brain has been developed only in the region of the appetites and passion, and not in the organs of reason and conscience; and who, therefore, is boastful of his bulk alone, and glories in the weight of his heel and in the destruction of his arm. Such a Republic, with all its noble capacities for beneficence, will rush with the speed of a whirlwind to an ignominious end; and all good men of after-times would be fain to weep over its downfall, did not their scorn and contempt at its folly and its wickedness repress all sorrow for its fate . . .

However elevated the moral character of a constituency may be, however well informed in matters of general science or history, yet they must, if citizens of a Republic, understand something of the true nature and functions of the government under which they live. That any one who is to participate in the government of a country, when he becomes a man, should receive no instruction respecting the nature and functions of the government he is afterwards to administer is a political solecism. In all nations, hardly excepting the most rude and barbarous, the future sovereign receives some training which is supposed to fit him for the exercise of the powers and duties of his anticipated station. Where, by force of law, the government devolves upon the heir, while yet in a state of legal infancy, some regency, or other substitute, is appointed, to act in his stead, until his arrival at mature age; and, in the meantime, he is subjected to such a course of study and discipline, as will tend to prepare him, according to the political theory of the time and the place, to assume the reins of authority at the appointed age. If, in England, or in the most enlightened European monarchies, it would be a proof of restored barbarism to permit the future sovereign to grow up without any knowledge of his duties—and who can doubt that it would be such a proof—then, surely, it would be not less a proof of restored, or of never-removed barbarism, amongst us, to empower any individual to use the elective franchise, without preparing him for so momentous a trust. Hence, the constitution of the United States, and of our own State, should be made a study in our Public Schools. The partition of the powers of government into the three co-ordinate branches—legislative, judicial, and executive—with the duties appropriately devolving upon each; the mode of electing or of appointing all officers, with the reason on which it was founded; and, especially, the duty of every citizen, in a government of laws, to appeal to the courts for redress, in all cases of alleged wrong, instead of undertaking to vindicate his own rights by his own arm; and, in a government where the people are the acknowledged sources of power, the duty of changing laws and rulers by an appeal to the ballot, and not by rebellion, should be taught to all the children until they are fully understood.

Had the obligations of the future citizen been sedulously inculcated upon all the children of this Republic, would the patriot have had to mourn over so many instances, where the voter, not being able to accomplish his purpose by voting, has proceeded to accomplish it by violence; where, agreeing with his fellow citizens, to use the machinery of the ballot, he makes a tacit reservation, that, if that machinery does not move according to his pleasure, he will wrest or break it? If the responsibleness and value of the elective franchise were duly appreciated, the day of our State and National elections would be among the most solemn and religious days in the calendar. Men would approach them, not only with preparation and solicitude, but with the sobriety and solemnity, with which discreet and religious-minded men meet the great crises of life. No man would throw away his vote, though caprice or wantonness, any more than he would throw away his estate, or sell his family into bondage. No man would cast his vote through malice or revenge, any more than a good surgeon would amputate a limp, or a good navigator sail through perilous straits, under the same criminal passions.

But, perhaps, it will be objected, that the constitution is subject to different readings, or that the policy of different administrations has become the subject of party strife; and, therefore, if any thing of constitutional or political law is introduced into our schools, there is danger that teachers will be chosen on account of their affinities to this or that political party; or that teachers will feign affinities which they do not feel, in order that they may be chosen; and so each schoolroom will at length become a miniature political club-room, exploding with political resolves, or flaming out with political addresses, prepared, by beardless boys, in scarcely legible hand-writing, and in worse grammar.

With the most limited exercise of discretion, all apprehensions of this kind are wholly groundless. There are different readings of the constitution, it is true; and there are partisan topics which agitate the country from side to side; but the controverted points, compared with those about which there is no dispute, do not bear the proportion of one to a hundred. And what is more, no man is qualified, or can be qualified, to discuss the disputable questions, unless previously and thoroughly versed in those questions, about which there is no dispute. In the terms and principles common to all, and recognized by all, is to be found the only common medium of language and of idea, by which the parties can become intelligible to each other; and there, too, is the only common ground, whence the arguments of the disputants can be drawn.

It is obvious, on the other hand, that if the tempest of political strife were to be let loose upon our Common Schools, they would be overwhelmed with sudden ruin. Let it be once understood, that the schoolroom is a legitimate theatre for party politics, and with what violence will hostile partisans struggle to gain possession of the stage, and to play their parts upon it! Nor will the stage be the only scene of gladiatorial contests. These will rage in all the avenues that lead to it. A preliminary advantage, indispensable to ultimate success, will be the appointment of a teacher of the true faith. As the great majority of the schools in the State are now organized, this can be done only by electing a prudential committee, who will make what he calls political soundness paramount to all other considerations of fitness. Thus, after petty skirmishings among neighbors, the fierce encounter will begin in the district's primary assembly—in the schoolroom itself. This contest being over, the election of the superintending, or town's committee, must be determined in the same way, and this will bring together the combustibles of each district, to burn with an intenser and a more devouring flame, in the town meeting. It is very possible, nay, not at all improbable, that the town may be of one political complexion, while a majority of the districts are of the opposite. Who shall moderate the fury of these conflicting elements when they rage against each other, and who shall save the dearest interests of the children from being consumed in the fierce combustion? If parents find that their children are indoctrinated into what they call political heresies, will they not withdraw them from the school; and, if they withdraw them from the school, will they not resist all appropriations to support a school from which they derive no benefit?

But, could the schools, themselves, survive these dangers for a single year, it would be only to encounter others still more perilous. Why should not the same infection that poisons all the relations of the schoolroom, spread itself abroad, and mingle with all questions of external organization and arrangement? Why should not political hostility cause the dismemberment of districts, already too small; or, what would work equal injury, prevent the union of districts, whose power of usefulness would be doubled by a combination of their resources? What better could be expected, than that one set of school books should be expelled, and another introduced, as they might be supposed, however remotely, to favor one party or the other; or, as the authors of the books might belong to one party or the other? And who could rely upon the reports, or even the statistics of a committee, chosen by partisan votes, goaded on by partisan impulses, and responsible to partisan domination; and this, too, without any opportunity of control or check from the minority? Nay, if the schools could survive long enough to meet the crisis, why should not any and every measure be taken, either to maintain an existing political ascendancy, or to recover a lost one, in a school district, or in a town, which has even been taken by unscrupulous politicians, to maintain or to recover an ascendancy at the polls? Into a district, or into a town, voters may be introduced from abroad, to turn the scale. An employer may dismiss the employed, for their refusal to submit to his dictation; or make the bread that is given to the poor man's children, perform the double office of payment for labor to be performed, and of a bribe for principle to be surrendered. And, beyond all this, if the imagination can conceive any thing more deplorable than this, what kind of political doctrines would be administered to the children, amid the vicissitudes of party domination—their alternations of triumph and defeat? This year, under the ascendancy of one side, the constitution declares one thing: and commentaries, glosses, and the authority of distinguished names, all ratify and confirm its decisions. But victory is a fickle goddess. Next year, the vanquished triumph; and constitution, gloss, and authority, make that sound doctrine, which was pestilent error before, and that false, which was true. Right and wrong have changed sides. The children must now join in chorus to denounce what they had been taught to reverence before, and to reverence what they had been taught to denounce. In the mean time, those great principles, which, according to Cicero, are the same at Rome and at Athens, the same now and forever—and which, according to Hooker, have their seat in the bosom of God, become the fittest emblems of chance and change.

Long, however, before this series of calamities would exhaust itself upon our schools, these schools themselves would cease to be. The plough-share would have turned up their foundations. Their history would have been brought to a close—a glorious and ascending history, until struck down by the hand of political parricide; then, suddenly falling with a double ruin—with death, and with ignominy. But to avoid such a catastrophe, shall all teaching, relative to the nature of our government, be banished from our schools; and shall our children be permitted to grow up in entire ignorance of the political history of their country? In the schools of a republic, shall the children be left without any distinct knowledge of the nature of a republican government; or only with such knowledge as they may pick up from angry political discussions, or from party newspapers; from caucus speeches, or Fourth of July orations—the Apocrypha of Apocrypha?

Surely, between these extremes, there must be a medium not difficult to be found. And is not this the middle course, which all sensible and judicious men, all patriots, and all genuine republicans, must approve?—namely, that those articles in the creed of republicanism, which are accepted by all, believed in by all, and which form the common basis of our political faith, shall be taught to all. But when the teacher, in the course of his lessons or lectures on the fundamental law, arrives at a controverted text, he is either to read it without comment or remark; or, at most, he is only to say that the passage is the subject of disputation, and that the schoolroom is neither the tribunal to adjudicate, nor the forum to discuss it.

Such being the rule established by common consent, and such the practice, observed with fidelity under it, it will come to be universally understood, that political proselytism is no function of the school; but that all indoctrination into matters of controversy between hostile political parties is to be elsewhere sought for, and elsewhere imparted. Thus, may all the children of the Commonwealth receive instruction in the great essentials of political knowledge—in those elementary ideas without which they will never be able to investigate more recondite and debatable questions—thus, will the only practicable method be adopted for discovering new truths, and for discarding—instead of perpetuating—old errors; and thus, too, will that pernicious race of intolerant zealots, whose whole faith may be summed up in two articles—that they, themselves, are always infallibly right, and that all dissenters are certainly wrong—be extinguished—extinguished, not by violence, nor by proscription, but by the more copious inflowing of the light of truth.

From Massachusetts Board of Education. 1948. *Twelfth Annual Report of the Board of Education,* 37–38, 42, 53, 55, 57–60, 76-80, 84–90. Boston: Dutton and Wentworth State Printers.

Questions

1. Why was there so little interest in a statewide system of education in post-Revolutionary War United States?

2. What is meant by the suggestion that Americans—citizens of the newly established United States—had to manufacture a sense of nationalism?

3. What role did Noah Webster's "Blue Back Speller" play in fostering community and national pride?

4. To what extent is the contemporary Friday night football game analogous to the spelling bee of the early nineteenth century district schools?

5. Describe in your own words how the evils associated with industrialization, urbanization, and immigration lead Mann and others to become champions of the common school.

6. Explain the meaning of the phrase "men are cast iron, but children are wax."

7. What are the characteristics of a common school? Why is it called or identified as common?

8. Explain what Mann means when he suggests that the common school—through the appropriate curriculum and instruction—can "reverse the ancient fable and transform swine into men."

9. Evaluate Mann's argument that education is the great equalizer of the conditions of men—the "balance-wheel" of the social machinery. Is his argument relevant today?

10. Describe in your own words the religious point of view—according to Mann—of the Massachusetts system of common schools. How would his views of Bible reading in the schools be viewed today?

8

John Dewey

Time Line for Dewey

1859	Is born October 20 in Burlington, Vermont.
1875	Enters the University of Vermont.
1879	Receives Bachelor's degree.
1879–1881	Teaches high school at Oil City, Pennsylvania.
1881	Studies philosophy with H. A. P. Torrey at Johns Hopkins University.
1882	Enters graduate school.
1884	Receives Ph.D. from Johns Hopkins.
1884–1894	Teaches philosophy at the University of Michigan.
1886	Marries Alice Chipman.
1894	Is appointed chairman of the Department of Philosophy, Psychology, and Pedagogy at the University of Chicago.
	Starts Lab School at University of Chicago.
1895	Suffers loss of son Morris from diphtheria while in Milan. The Deweys later return to Italy and adopt an orphan boy, Sabino.
1897	Publishes "My Pedagogic Creed."
1900	Publishes *The School and Society*.
1902	Publishes *The Child and the Curriculum*.
1904	Is appointed professor of philosophy at Columbia University.
1904	Suffers the loss of son Gordon from typhoid fever while vacationing in Ireland.
1910	Publishes *How We Think*.
1915	Establishes and is the first president of the American Association of University Professors.
1916	Publishes *Democracy and Education*.
1919–1928	Gives lectures in Japan, China, Turkey, Mexico, and Russia.
1920	Publishes *Reconstruction of Philosophy,* based on lectures given at the Imperial University, Japan.

1922	Publishes *Human Nature and Conduct.*
1925	Publishes *Experience and Nature.*
1927	Suffers loss of his wife, Alice.
1930	Is named professor emeritus at Columbia University.
1934	Publishes *Art as Experience* and *A Common Faith.*
1937	Serves as chairman of the commission of inquiry into the charges made against Leon Trotsky (Mexico City).
1938	Publishes *Experience and Education.*
1939	Publishes *Freedom and Culture.*
1946	Marries Roberta Lowitz Grant. They adopt two children. Publishes *Problems of Men.*
1949	Publishes, with Arthur Bentley, *Knowing and the Known.*
1952	Dies June 1 in New York City.

INTRODUCTION

Born in 1859—the same year that Horace Mann died and that saw the publication of Charles Darwin's *Origin of Species*—Dewey lived through the Civil War, two world wars, the Great Depression, and numerous lesser conflicts, and died as the cold war emerged full-blown on the global scene. During his lifetime, the United States was transformed from a largely agrarian, experimental republic into the major industrial and military power in the world. Growing up in Puritan New England, Dewey would gradually abandon his religious foundations, moving, as he explains, "from absolutism to experimentalism." Attaining his undergraduate degree from the University of Vermont and eventually his Ph.D. from Johns Hopkins University, Dewey retained his religious commitment through his professorship at the University of Michigan in the 1880s and 1890s. As a young man, Dewey embraced the Social Gospel movement in hopes of connecting his commitment to democracy to an absolutist metaphysics—Hegelian idealism.

His commitment to social justice and democratic principles never waned, but, by the early 1890s, Dewey had begun to distance himself from other worldly metaphysics. Upon moving to Chicago in 1894 to chair the Department of Philosophy, Psychology, and Pedagogy at the University of Chicago, Dewey stopped participating in religious activities. By this time he had transformed his metaphysical idealism into pragmatic naturalism. Finally, feeling comfortable that his commitment to democratic principles could be sustained by grounding them in experience, Dewey spent much of the remainder of his life working out the implications of this philosophical shift for his social, political, and educational ideas.

Leaving Chicago in 1904, Dewey assumed a professorship of philosophy at Columbia University in New York City, a position he held until his retirement in 1929. In addition to teaching, writing, and numerous other academic responsibilities, Dewey struggled to find ways to construct "the Great Community" and to make the world "safe for democracy." Initially supportive of Wilson's war policy—for which his former student, Randolph Bourne, criticized him for falling "prey to the very mistakes his philosophy was designed to prevent"[1]—Dewey participated in the quixotic Outlaw War movement during the postwar period. During these years and throughout his life, "Dewey was the most important advocate of participatory democracy, that is of the belief that democracy as an ethical ideal calls upon men and women to build communities in which the necessary opportunities and resources are available for every individual to fully realize his or her particular capacities and powers through participation in political, social, and cultural life."[2]

As suggested earlier, Dewey was a prolific scholar throughout his life; he published scores of books and pamphlets, hundreds of articles for scholarly and popular journals and magazines, and gave innumerable speeches and lectures—public as well as academic—on topics ranging from Hegelian metaphysics to woman's suffrage. Indeed, it is not an exaggeration to suggest that from 1900 to 1940, Dewey published more each year than many small college faculties produced during all of these years. Unfortunately, Dewey did not always write well. As Justice Oliver Wendell Holmes charges: "Dewey writes as the creator would write, if he were intent on explaining all of his creation but was hopelessly inarticulate." Dewey's works are often misunderstood, but more frequently Dewey is not read. As John Novak explains, "John Dewey is like the Bible—often alluded to (both by his supporters and detractors) but seldom read. . . ."[3]

Students who might be interested in Dewey's work, and who clearly could benefit from it, are often overwhelmed by the sheer volume of it. Those ambitious enough to dive into one of Dewey's works are likely to find his prose stiff and lacking in imagination. In addition, while there is an abundance of literature about Dewey, much of it treats him either as a saint or as a villain. In this secondary literature, Dewey has been reviled and praised, criticized and attacked, for being the father of progressive education, a communist dupe and a hopeless anticommunist, a pacifist and a turncoat to pacifist ideals, a secular humanist, and the founder of all things good (and bad) in American education.

A work like this one can do little to answer all the questions about Dewey and his influence on education other than to suggest that Dewey was a highly complex thinker whose thought could never be captured by any reductionist label. What this work can do—by introducing the reader to carefully selected excerpts from Dewey's works—is whet the reader's appetite for more information about this remarkable figure in American educational thought. If this work is successful, you will be motivated to further investigate both the man and his thought by reading Dewey's autobiographical essay "From Absolutism to Experimentalism"; George Dykhuizen's *The Life and Mind of John Dewey;* Robert B. Westbrook's *John Dewey and American Democracy;* as well as the many seminal works Dewey published during his long and distinguished life.

Here we focus on excerpts from *Democracy and Education* (1916), where, Dewey suggested, his philosophy was best developed, and *Experience and Education* (1938),

[1]Robert B. Westbrook, *John Dewey and American Democracy* (Ithaca: Cornell University Press, 1991), p. 203.
[2]Ibid., p. vi.
[3]This quotation as well as much of this information in this brief introduction is derived from John Novak's review (distributed by the John Dewey Society) of Westbrook's *John Dewey and American Democracy.*

which might be read as a corrective to Dewey's followers in the progressive education movement.

In what has been described as his magnum opus (*Democracy and Education*), Dewey unpacks what he means by education and relates education to democracy. In a move typical of Dewey, he suggests that as much as we educate for democracy, we should democratize for education.

Finally, it is hard to overstate Dewey's influence in American schooling from the turn of the twentieth century through the 1930s. During that period, all sorts of progressive educational experiments and programs were espoused and tried. In New York, people set up schools where children were allowed to do as they pleased and to devise their own curricula. At the same time, progressive educators like George S. Counts were urging teachers to indoctrinate children with proper social ideals and values. Everybody, however, claimed John Dewey as a special influence. This outcome led a somewhat exasperated Dewey to publish *Experience and Education,* making explicit what he meant by progressivism and correcting the excesses of many of his followers.

In *Experience and Education,* Dewey reiterates his opposition to either/or thinking. Specifically, Dewey rejects the either/or (Platonic/Aristotelian) worldview that dominated the Western world for so long. From this rather traditional perspective, knowledge is either innate—inside the individual at birth awaiting the right mnemonic device to bring it to consciousness—or external to human beings, awaiting our discovery. In either case, an absolute is implied, resulting in the imposition of knowledge and values upon each new generation. Such a worldview may be appropriate for a monarchy or some other form of autocracy, but it is antithetical to education in a democracy.

Dewey realizes that if the so-called new education is developed as a negative reaction to traditional beliefs, then its advocates have fallen into the trap of either/or thinking. All too often what occurred in Dewey's name and under the rubric of progressivism was nothing more than mere reaction to the authorities of the past, with little or no attempt to reconstruct that which had been torn down. Although such deconstruction may be necessary, it is not sufficient. For Dewey, there must be a vision of a better way, a more appropriate way for improving the individual within the collective, the human being in society.

Rather than just rebelling against the traditional version of either/or thinking, Dewey based his "new education" on experience. In distinguishing good or educative experiences from bad or miseducative experiences, Dewey suggests that good experience is characterized by both interaction and continuity. An educative experience is one in which an active mind interacts with a wide-open world to solve genuine problems that are continuous with, yet different from, previous experiences. Recognizing that we are creatures of habit, Dewey suggests that it is our unique ability to stop, reflect, and then act—that is, to respond intelligently to a problematic situation requiring more than a mere habitual reaction—that distinguishes humans from less intelligent animals.

A careful reading of both *Democracy and Education* and *Experience and Education* offers insights into Dewey's view of democracy. As already noted, Dewey championed democracy throughout his long life, but, for Dewey, democracy was more than opposition to authoritarian rule. Dewey was no anarchist. The basis for authority in a democracy is experience. Dewey suggests that in a true democracy, "it is not the will or desire of any one person (a philosopher-king or scientist) which establishes order but the moving spirit of the whole group." Creating and sustaining such a "moving spirit" is in Dewey's mind what education and philosophy should be about. The excerpts from *Democracy and Education* and *Experience and Education* are meant to be the first steps in helping the reader to better understand the connection between education and democracy.

FROM *DEMOCRACY AND EDUCATION* (1916)

For the most part, save incidentally, we have hitherto been concerned with education as it may exist in any social group. We have now to make explicit the differences in the spirit, material, and method of education as it operates in different types of community life. To say that education is a social function, securing direction and development in the immature through their participation in the life of the group to which they belong, is to say in effect that education will vary with the quality of life which prevails in a group. Particularly is it true that a society which not only changes but which has the ideal of such change as will improve it, will have different standards and methods of education from one which aims simply at the perpetuation of its own customs. To make the general ideas set forth applicable to our own educational practice, it is, therefore, necessary to come to closer quarters with the nature of present social life.

1. *The Implications of Human Association.* Society is one word, but many things. Men associate together in all kinds of ways and for all kinds of purposes. One man is concerned in a multitude of diverse groups, in which his associates may be quite different. It often seems as if they had nothing in common except that they are modes of associated life. Within every larger social organization there are numerous minor groups: not only political subdivisions, but industrial, scientific, religious associations. There are political parties with differing aims, social sets, cliques, gangs, corporations, partnerships, groups bound closely together by ties of blood, and so on in endless variety. In many modern states and in some ancient, there is great diversity of populations, of varying languages, religions, moral codes, and traditions. From this standpoint, many a minor political unit, one of our large cities, for example, is a congeries of loosely associated societies, rather than an inclusive and permeating community of action and thought.

The terms of society, community, are thus ambiguous. They have both a eulogistic or normative sense, and a descriptive sense; a meaning *de jure* and a meaning *de facto*. In social philosophy, the former connotation is almost always uppermost. Society is conceived as one by its very nature. The qualities which accompany this unity, praiseworthy community of purpose and welfare, loyalty to public ends, mutuality of sympathy, are emphasized. But when we look at the facts which the term *denotes* instead of confining our attention to its intrinsic *connotation,* we find not unity, but a plurality of societies, good and bad. Men banded together in a criminal conspiracy, business aggregations that prey upon the public while serving it, political machines held together by the interest of plunder, are included. If it is said that such organizations are not societies because they do not meet the ideal requirements of the notion of society, the answer, in part, is that the conception of society is then made so "ideal" as to be of no use, having no reference to facts; and in part, that each of these organizations, no matter how opposed to the interests of other groups, has some thing of the praiseworthy qualities of "Society" which hold it together. There is honor among thieves, and a band of robbers has a common interest as respects its members. Gangs are marked by fraternal feeling, and narrow cliques by intense loyalty to their own codes. Family life may be marked by exclusiveness, suspicion, and jealousy as to those without, and yet be a model of amity and mutual aid within. Any education given by a group tends to socialize its members, but the quality and value of the socialization depends upon the habits and aims of the group.

Hence, once more, the need of a measure for the worth of any given mode of social life. In seeking this measure, we have to avoid two extremes. We cannot set up, out of our heads, something we regard as an ideal society. We must base our conception upon societies which actually exist, in order to have any assurance that our ideal is a practicable one. But, as we have just seen, the ideal cannot simply repeat the traits which are actually found. The problem is to extract the desirable traits of forms of community life which actually exist, and employ them to criticize undesirable features and suggest improvement. Now in any social group whatever, even in a gang of thieves, we find some interest held in common, and we find a certain amount of interaction and coöperative intercourse with other groups. From these two traits we derive our standard. How numerous and varied are the interests which are consciously shared? How full and free is the interplay with other forms of association? If we apply these considerations to, say, a criminal band, we find that the ties which consciously hold the members together are few in number, reducible almost to a common interest in plunder; and that they are of such a nature as to isolate the group from other groups with respect to give and take of the values of life. Hence, the education such a society gives is partial and distorted. If we take, on the other hand, the kind of family life which illustrates the standard, we find that there are material, intellectual, aesthetic interests in which all participate and that the progress of one member has worth for the experience of other members—it is readily communicable—and that the family is not an isolated whole, but enters intimately into relationships with business groups, with schools, with all the agencies of culture, as well as with other similar groups, and that it plays a due part in the political organization and in return receives support from it. In short, there are many interests consciously communicated and shared; and there are varied and free points of contact with other modes of association.

I. Let us apply the first element in this criterion to a despotically governed state. It is not true there is no common interest in such an organization between governed and governors. The authorities in command must make some appeal to the native activities of the subjects, must call some of their powers into play. Talleyrand said that a government could do everything with bayonets except sit on them. This cynical declaration is at least a recognition that the bond of union is not merely one of coercive force. It may be said, however, that the activities appealed to are themselves unworthy and degrading—that such a government calls into functioning activity simply capacity for fear. In a way, this statement is true. But it overlooks the fact that fear need not be an undesirable factor in experience. Caution, circumspection, prudence, desire to foresee future events so as to avert what is harmful, these desirable traits are as much a product of calling the impulse of fear into play as is cowardice and abject submission. The real difficulty is that the appeal to fear is *isolated*. In evoking dread and hope of specific tangible reward—say comfort and ease—many other capacities are left untouched. Or rather, they are affected, but in such a way as to pervert them. Instead of operating on their own account they are reduced to mere servants of attaining pleasure and avoiding pain.

This is equivalent to saying that there is no extensive number of common interests; there is no free play back and forth among the members of the social group. Stimulation and response are exceedingly one-sided. In order to have a larger number of values in common, all the members of the group must have an equable opportunity to receive and to take from others. There must be a large variety of shared undertakings and experiences. Otherwise, the influences which educate some into masters, educate others into slaves. And the experience of each party loses in meaning, when the free interchange of varying modes of life-experience is arrested. A separation into a privileged and a subject-class prevents social endosmosis. The evils thereby affecting the superior class are less material and less perceptible, but equally real. Their culture tends to be sterile, to be turned back to feed on itself; their art becomes a showy display and artificial; their wealth luxurious; their knowledge overspecialized; their manners fastidious rather than humane.

Lack of the free and equitable intercourse which springs from a variety of shared interests makes intellectual stimulation unbalanced. Diversity of stimulation means novelty, and novelty means challenge to thought. The more activity is restricted to a few definite lines—as it is when there are rigid class lines preventing adequate interplay of experiences—the more action tends to become routine on the part of the class at a disadvantage, and capricious, aimless, and explosive on the part of the class having the materially fortunate position. Plato defined a slave as one who accepts from another the purposes which control his conduct. This condition obtains even where there is no slavery in the legal sense. It is found wherever men are engaged in activity which is socially serviceable, but whose service they do not understand and have no personal interest in. Much is said about scientific management of work. It is a narrow view which restricts the science which secures efficiency of operation to movements of the muscles. The chief opportunity for science is the discovery of the relations of a man to his work—including his relations to others who take part—which will enlist his intelligent interest in what he is doing. Efficiency in production often demands division of labor. But it is reduced to a mechanical routine unless workers see the technical, intellectual, and social relationships involved in what they do, and engage in their work because of the motivation furnished by such perceptions. The tendency to reduce such things as efficiency of activity and scientific management to purely technical externals is evidence of the one-sided stimulation of thought given to those in control of industry—those who supply its aims. Because of their lack of all-round and well-balanced social interest, there is not sufficient stimulus for attention to the human factors and relationships in industry. Intelligence is narrowed to the factors concerned with technical production and marketing of goods. No doubt, a very acute and intense intelligence in these narrow lines can be developed, but the failure to take into account the significant social factors means none the less an absence of mind, and a corresponding distortion of emotional life.

II. This illustration (whose point is to be extended to all associations lacking reciprocity of interest) brings us to our second point. The isolation and exclusiveness of a gang or clique brings its antisocial spirit into relief. But this same spirit is found wherever one group has interests "of its own" which shut it out from full interaction with other groups, so that its prevailing purpose is the protection of what it has got, instead of reorganization and progress through wider relationships. It marks nations in their isolation from one another; families which seclude their domestic concerns as if they had no connection with a larger life; schools when separated from the interest of home and community; the divisions of rich and poor; learned and unlearned. The essential point is that isolation makes for rigidity and formal institutionalizing of life, for static and selfish ideals within the group. That savage tribes regard aliens and enemies as synonymous is not accidental. It springs from the fact that they have identified their experience with rigid adherence to their past customs. On such a basis it is wholly logical to fear intercourse with others, for such contact might dissolve custom. It would certainly occasion reconstruction. It is a commonplace that an alert and expanding mental life depends upon an enlarging range of contact with the physical environment. But the principle applies even more significantly to the field where we are apt to ignore it—the sphere of social contacts.

Every expansive era in the history of mankind has coincided with the operation of factors which have tended to eliminate distance between peoples and classes previously hemmed off from one another. Even the alleged benefits of war, so far as more than alleged, spring from the fact that conflict of peoples at least enforces intercourse between them and thus accidentally enables them to learn from one another, and thereby to expand their horizons.

Travel, economic and commercial tendencies, have at present gone far to break down external barriers; to bring peoples and classes into closer and more perceptible connection with one another. It remains for the most part to secure the intellectual and emotional significance of this physical annihilation of space.

2. *The Democratic Ideal.* The two elements in our criterion both point to democracy. The first signifies not only more numerous and more varied points of shared common interest, but greater reliance upon the recognition of mutual interests as a factor in social control. The second means not only freer interaction between social groups (once isolated so far as intention could keep up a separation) but change in social habit—its continuous readjustment through meeting the new situations produced by varied intercourse. And these two traits are precisely what characterize the democratically constituted society.

Upon the educational side, we note first that the realization of a form of social life in which interests are mutually interpenetrating, and where progress, or readjustment, is an important consideration, makes a democratic community more interested than other communities have cause to be in deliberate and systematic education. The devotion of democracy to education is a familiar fact. The superficial explanation is that a government resting upon popular suffrage cannot be successful unless those who elect and who obey their governors are educated. Since a democratic society repudiates the principle of external authority, it must find a substitute in voluntary disposition and interest; these can be created only by education. But there is a deeper explanation. A democracy is more than a form of government; it is primarily a mode of associated living, of conjoint communicated experience. The extension in space of the number of individuals who participate in an interest so that each has to refer his own action to that of others, and to consider the action of others to give point and direction to his own, is equivalent to the breaking down of those barriers of class, race, and national territory which kept men from perceiving the full import of their activity. These more numerous and more varied points of contact denote a greater diversity of stimuli to which an individual has to respond; they consequently put a premium on variation in his action. They secure a liberation of powers which remain suppressed as long as the incitations to action are partial, as they must be in a group which in its exclusiveness shuts out many interests.

The widening of the area of shared concerns, and the liberation of a greater diversity of personal capacities which characterize a democracy, are not of course the product of deliberation and conscious effort. On the contrary, they were caused by the development of modes of manufacture and commerce, travel, migration, and intercommunication which flowed from the command of science over natural energy. But after greater individualization on one hand and a broader community of interest on the other have come into existence it is a matter of deliberate effort to sustain and extend them. Obviously a society to which stratification into separate classes would be fatal, must see to it that intellectual opportunities are accessible to all on equable and easy terms. A society marked off into classes need be specially attentive only to the education of its ruling elements. A society which is mobile, which is full of channels for the distribution of a change occurring anywhere, must see to it that its members are educated to personal initiative and adaptability. Otherwise they will be overwhelmed by the changes in which they are caught and whose significance or connections they do not perceive. The result will be a confusion in which a few will appropriate to themselves the results of the blind and externally directed activities of others.

FROM *EXPERIENCE AND EDUCATION* (1938)

If there is any truth in what has been said about the need of forming a theory of experience in order that education may be intelligently conducted upon the basis of experience, it is clear that the next thing in order in this discussion is to present the principles that are most significant in framing this theory. I shall not, therefore, apologize for engaging in a certain amount of philosophical analysis, which otherwise might be out of place. I may, however, reassure you to some degree by saying that this analysis is not an end in itself but is engaged in for the sake of obtaining criteria to be applied later in discussion of a number of concrete and, to most persons, more interesting issues.

I have already mentioned what I called the category of continuity, or the experiential continuum. This principle is involved, as I pointed out, in every attempt to discriminate between experiences that are worth while educationally and those that are not. It may seem superfluous to argue that this discrimination is necessary not only in criticizing the traditional type of education but also in initiating and conducting a different type. Nevertheless, it is advisable to pursue for a little while the idea that it is necessary. One may safely assume, I suppose, that one thing which has recommended the progressive movement is that it seems more in accord with the democratic ideal to which our people is committed than do the procedures of the traditional school, since the latter have so much of the autocratic about them. Another thing which has contributed to its favorable reception is that its methods are humane in comparison with the harshness so often attending the policies of the traditional school.

The question I would raise concerns why we prefer democratic and humane arrangements to those which are autocratic and harsh. And by "why," I mean the *reason* for preferring them, not just the *causes* which lead us to the preference. One *cause* may be that we have been taught not only in the schools but by the press, the pulpit, the platform, and our laws and law-making bodies that democracy is the best of all social institutions. We may have so assimilated this idea from our surroundings that it has become an habitual part of our mental and moral make-up. But similar causes have led other persons in different surroundings to widely varying conclusions—to prefer fascism, for example. The cause for our preference is not the same thing as the reason why we *should* prefer it.

It is not my purpose here to go in detail into the reason. But I would ask a single question: Can we find any reason that does not ultimately come down to the belief that democratic social arrangements promote a better quality of human experience, one which is more widely accessible and enjoyed, than do non-democratic and anti-democratic forms of social life? Does not the principle of re-gard for individual freedom and for decency and kindliness of human relations come back in the end to the conviction that these things are tributary to a higher quality of experience on the part of a greater number than are methods of repression and coercion or force? Is it not the reason for our preference that we believe that mutual consultation and convictions reached through persuasion make possible a better quality of experience than can otherwise be provided on any wide scale?

If the answer to these questions is in the affirmative (and personally I do not see how we can justify our preference for democracy and humanity on any other ground), the ultimate reason for hospitality to progressive educa-tion, because of its reliance upon and use of humane methods and its kinship to democracy, goes back to the fact that discrimination is made between the inherent values of different experiences. So I come back to the principle of continuity of experience as a criterion of discrimination.

At bottom, this principle rests upon the fact of habit, when *habit* is inter-preted biologically. The basic characteristic of habit is that every experience en-acted and undergone modifies the one who acts and undergoes, while this modification affects, whether we wish it or not, the quality of subsequent expe-riences. For it is a somewhat different person who enters into them. The princi-ple of habit so understood obviously goes deeper than the ordinary conception of *a* habit as a more or less fixed way of doing things, although it includes the latter as one of its special cases. It covers the formation of attitudes, attitudes that are emotional and intellectual; it covers our basic sensitivities and ways of meeting and responding to all the conditions which we meet in living. From this point of view, the principle of continuity of experience means that every expe-rience both takes up something from those which have gone before and modi-fies in some way the quality of those which come after. As the poet states it,

> . . . all experience is an arch wherethro'
> Gleams that untraveled world, whose margin fades
> For ever and for ever when I move.

So far, however, we have no ground for discrimination among experiences. For the principle is of universal application. There is *some* kind of continuity in every case. It is when we note the different forms in which continuity of experi-ence operates that we get the basis of discriminating among experiences. I may illustrate what is meant by an objection which has been brought against an idea which I once put forth—namely, that the educative process can be identified with growth when that is understood in terms of the active participle, *growing*.

Growth, or growing as developing, not only physically but intellectually and morally, is one exemplification of the principle of continuity. The objection made is that growth might take many different directions: a man, for example, who starts out on a career of burglary may grow in that direction, and by practice may grow into a highly expert burglar. Hence it is argued that "growth" is not enough; we must also specify the direction in which growth takes place, the end towards which it tends. Before, however, we decide that the objection is conclusive we must analyze the case a little further.

That a man may grow in efficiency as a burglar, as a gangster, or as a corrupt politician, cannot be doubted. But from the standpoint of growth as education and education as growth the question is whether growth in this direction promotes or retards growth in general. Does this form of growth create conditions for further growth, or does it set up conditions that shut off the person who has grown in this particular direction from the occasions, stimuli, and opportunities for continuing growth in new directions? What is the effect of growth in a special direction upon the attitudes and habits which alone open up avenues for development in other lines? I shall leave you to answer these questions, saying simply that when and *only* when development in a particular line conduces to continuing growth does it answer to the criterion of education as growing. For the conception is one that must find universal and not specialized limited application.

I return now to the question of continuity as a criterion by which to discriminate between experiences which are educative and those which are miseducative. As we have seen, there is some kind of continuity in any case since every experience affects for better or worse the attitudes which help decide the quality of further experiences, by setting up certain preference and aversion, and making it easier or harder to act for this or that end. Moreover, every experience influences in some degree the objective conditions under which further experiences are had. For example, a child who learns to speak has a new facility and new desire. But he has also widened the external conditions of subsequent learning. When he learns to read, he similarly opens up a new environment. If a person decides to become a teacher, lawyer, physician, or stockbroker, when he executes his intention he thereby necessarily determines to some extent the environment in which he will act in the future. He has rendered himself more sensitive and responsive to certain conditions, and relatively immune to those things about him that would have been stimuli if he had made another choice.

But, while the principle of continuity applies in some way in every case, the quality of the present experience influences the *way* in which the principle applies. We speak of spoiling a child and of the spoilt child. The effect of overindulging a child is a continuing one. It sets up an attitude which operates as an automatic demand that persons and objects cater to his desires and caprices in the future. It makes him seek the kind of situation that will enable him to do what he feels like doing at the time. It renders him averse to and comparatively incompetent in situations which require effort and perseverance in overcoming obstacles. There is no paradox in the fact that the principle of the continuity of experience may operate so as to leave a person arrested on a low plane of development, in a way which limits later capacity for growth.

On the other hand, if an experience arouses curiosity, strengthens initiative, and sets up desires and purposes that are sufficiently intense to carry a person over dead places in the future, continuity works in a very different way. Every experience is a moving force. Its value can be judged only on the ground of what it moves toward and into. The greater maturity of experience which should belong to the adult as educator puts him in a position to evaluate each experience of the young in a way in which the one having the less mature experience cannot do. It is then the business of the educator to see in what direction an experience is heading. There is no point in his being more mature if, instead of using his greater insight to help organize the conditions of the experience of the immature, he throws away his insight. Failure to take the moving force of an experience into account so as to judge and direct it on the ground of what it is moving into means disloyalty to the principle of experience itself. The disloyalty operates in two directions. The educator is false to the understanding that he should have obtained from his own past experience. He is also unfaithful to the fact that all human experience is ultimately social: that it involves contact and communication. The mature person, to put it in moral terms, has no right to withhold from the young on given occasions whatever capacity for sympathetic understanding his own experience has given him.

No sooner, however, are such things said than there is a tendency to react to the other extreme and take what has been said as a plea for some sort of disguised imposition from outside. It is worth while, accordingly, to say something about the way in which the adult can exercise the wisdom his own wider experience gives him without imposing a merely external control. On one side, it is his business to be on the alert to see what attitudes and habitual tendencies are being created. In this direction he must, if he is an educator, be able to judge what attitudes are actually conducive to continued growth and what are detrimental. He must, in addition, have that sympathetic understanding of individuals as individuals which gives him an idea of what is actually going on in the minds of those who are learning. It is, among other things, the need for these abilities on the part of the parent and teacher which makes a system of education based upon living experience a more difficult affair to conduct successfully than it is to follow the patterns of traditional education.

But there is another aspect of the matter. Experience does not go on simply inside a person. It does go on there, for it influences the formation of attitudes of desire and purpose. But this is not the whole of the story. Every genuine experience has an active side which changes in some degree the objective conditions under which experiences are had. The difference between civilization and savagery, to take an example on a large scale, is found in the degree in which previous experiences have changed the objective conditions under which subsequent experiences take place. The existence of roads, of means of rapid movement and transportation, tools, implements, furniture, electric light and power, are illustrations. Destroy the external conditions of present civilized experience, and for a time our experience would relapse into that of barbaric peoples.

In a word, we live from birth to death in a world of persons and things which in large measure is what it is because of what has been done and transmitted from previous human activities. When this fact is ignored, experience is treated as if it were something which goes on exclusively inside an individual's body and mind. It ought not to be necessary to say that experience does not occur in a vacuum. There are sources outside an individual which give rise to experience. It is constantly fed from these springs. No one would question that a child in a slum tenement has a different experience from that of a child in a cultured home; that the country lad has a different kind of experience from the city boy, or a boy on the seashore one different from the lad who is brought up on inland prairies. Ordinarily we take such facts for granted as too commonplace to record. But when their educational import is recognized, they indicate the second way in which the educator can direct the experience of the young without engaging in imposition. A primary responsibility of educators is that they not only be aware of the general principle of the shaping of actual experience by environing conditions, but that they also recognize in the concrete what surroundings are conducive to having experiences that lead to growth. Above all, they should know how to utilize the surroundings, physical and social, that exist so as to extract from them all that they have to contribute to building up experiences that are worth while.

Traditional education did not have to face this problem; it could systematically dodge this responsibility. The school environment of desks, blackboards, a small school yard, was supposed to suffice. There was no demand that the teacher should become intimately acquainted with the conditions of the local community, physical, historical, economic, occupational, etc., in order to utilize them as educational resources. A system of education based upon the necessary connection of education with experience must, on the contrary, if faithful to its principle, take these things constantly into account. This tax upon the educator is another reason why progressive education is more difficult to carry on than was ever the traditional system.

It is possible to frame schemes of education that pretty systematically subordinate objective conditions to those which reside in the individuals being educated. This happens whenever the place and function of the teacher, of books, of apparatus and equipment, of everything which represents the products of the more mature experience of elders, is systematically subordinated to the immediate inclinations and feelings of the young. Every theory which assumes that importance can be attached to these objective factors only at the expense of imposing external control and of limiting the freedom of individuals rests finally upon the notion that experience is truly experience only when objective conditions are subordinated to what goes on within the individuals having the experience.

I do not mean that it is supposed that objective conditions can be shut out. It is recognized that they must enter in: so much concession is made to the inescapable fact that we live in a world of things and persons. But I think that observation of what goes on in some families and some schools would disclose that some parents and some teachers are acting upon the idea of *subordinating* objective conditions to internal ones. In that case, it is assumed not only that the latter are primary, which in one sense they are, but that just as they temporarily exist they fix the whole educational process.

Let me illustrate from the case of an infant. The needs of a baby for food, rest, and activity are certainly primary and decisive in one respect. Nourishment must be provided; provision must be made for comfortable sleep, and so on. But these facts do not mean that a parent shall feed the baby at any time when the baby is cross or irritable, that there shall not be a program of regular hours of feeding and sleeping, etc. The wise mother takes account of the needs of the infant but not in a way which dispenses with her own responsibility for regulating the objective conditions under which the needs are satisfied. And if she is a wise mother in this respect, she draws upon past experiences of experts as well as her own for the light that these shed upon what experiences are in general most conducive to the normal development of infants. Instead of these conditions being subordinated to the immediate internal condition of the baby, they are definitely ordered so that a particular kind of *interaction* with these immediate internal states may be brought about.

The word "interaction," which has just been used, expresses the second chief principle for interpreting an experience in its educational function and force. It assigns equal rights to both factors in experience—objective and internal conditions. Any normal experience is an interplay of these two sets of conditions. Taken together, or in their interaction, they form what we call a *situation*. The trouble with traditional education was not that it emphasized the external conditions that enter into the control of the experiences but that it paid so little attention to the internal factors which also decide what kind of experience is had. It violated the principle of interaction from one side. But this violation is no reason why the new education should violate the principle from the other side—except upon the basis of the extreme *Either-Or* educational philosophy which has been mentioned.

The illustration drawn from the need for regulation of the objective conditions of a baby's development indicates, first, that the parent has responsibility for arranging the conditions under which an infant's experience of food, sleep, etc., occurs, and, secondly, that the responsibility is fulfilled by utilizing the funded experience of the past, as this is represented, say, by the advice of competent physicians and others who have made a special study of normal physical growth. Does it limit the freedom of the mother when she uses the body of knowledge thus provided to regulate the objective conditions of nourishment and sleep? Or does the enlargement of her intelligence in fulfilling her parental function widen her freedom? Doubtless if a fetish were made of the advice and directions so that they came to be inflexible dictates to be followed under every possible condition, then restriction of freedom of both parent and child would occur. But this restriction would also be a limitation of the intelligence that is exercised in personal judgment.

In what respect does regulation of objective conditions limit the freedom of the baby? Some limitation is certainly placed upon its immediate movements and inclinations when it is put in its crib, at a time when it wants to continue playing, or does not get food at the moment it would like it, or when it isn't picked up and dandled when it cries for attention. Restriction also occurs when mother or nurse snatches a child away from an open fire into which it is about to fall. I shall have more to say later about freedom. Here it is enough to ask whether freedom is to be thought of and adjudged on the basis of relatively momentary incidents or whether its meaning is found in the continuity of developing experience.

The statement that individuals live in a world means, in the concrete, that they live in a series of situations. And when it is said that they live *in* these situations, the meaning of the word "in" is different from its meaning when it is said that pennies are "in" a pocket or paint is "in" a can. It means, once more, that interaction is going on between an individual and objects and other persons. The conceptions of *situation* and of *interaction* are inseparable from each other. An experience is always what it is because of a transaction taking place between an individual and what, at the time, constitutes his environment, whether the latter consists of persons with whom he is talking about some topic or event, the subject talked about being also a part of the situation; or the toys with which he is playing; the book he is reading (in which his environing conditions at the time may be England or ancient Greece or an imaginary region); or the materials of an experiment he is performing. The environment, in other words, is whatever conditions interact with personal needs, desires, purposes, and capacities to create the experience which is had. Even when a person builds a castle in the air he is interacting with the objects which he constructs in fancy.

The two principles of continuity and interaction are not separate from each other. They intercept and unite. They are, so to speak, the longitudinal and lateral aspects of experience. Different situations succeed one another. But because of the principle of continuity something is carried over from the earlier to the later ones. As an individual passes from one situation to another, his world, his environment, expands or contracts. He does not find himself living in another world but in a different part or aspect of one and the same world. What he has learned in the way of knowledge and skill in one situation becomes an instrument of understanding and dealing effectively with the situations which follow. The process goes on as long as life and learning continue. Otherwise the course of experience is disorderly, since the individual factor that enters into making an experience is split. A divided world, a world whose parts and aspects do not hang together, is at once a sign and a cause of a divided personality. When the splitting-up reaches a certain point we call the person insane. A fully integrated personality, on the other hand, exists only when successive experiences are integrated with one another. It can be built up only as a world of related objects is constructed.

Continuity and interaction in their active union with each other provide the measure of the educative significance and value of an experience. The immediate and direct concern of an educator is then with the situations in which interaction takes place. The individual, who enters as a factor into it, is what he is at a given time. It is the other factor, that of objective conditions, which lies to some extent within the possibility of regulation by the educator. As has already been noted, the phrase "objective conditions" covers a wide range. It includes what is done by the educator and the way in which it is done, not only words spoken but the tone of voice in which they are spoken. It includes equipment, books, apparatus, toys, games played. It includes the materials with which an individual interacts, and, most important of all, the total *social* set-up of the situations in which a person is engaged.

When it is said that the objective conditions are those which are within the power of the educator to regulate, it is meant, of course, that his ability to influence directly the experience of others and thereby the education they obtain places upon him the duty of determining that environment which will interact with the existing capacities and needs of those taught to create a worth-while experience. The trouble with traditional education was not that educators took upon themselves the responsibility for providing an environment. The trouble was that they did not consider the other factor in creating an experience; namely, the powers and purposes of those taught. It was assumed that a certain set of conditions was intrinsically desirable, apart from its ability to evoke a certain quality of response in individuals. This lack of mutual adaptation made the process of teaching and learning accidental. Those to whom the provided conditions were suitable managed to learn. Others got on as best they could. Responsibility for selecting objective conditions carries with it, then, the responsibility for understanding the needs and capacities of the individuals who are learning at a given time. It is not enough that certain materials and methods have proved effective with other individuals at other times. There must be a reason for thinking that they will function in generating an experience that has educative quality with particular individuals at a particular time.

It is no reflection upon the nutritive quality of beefsteak that it is not fed to infants. It is not an invidious reflection upon trigonometry that we do not teach it in the first or fifth grade of school. It is not the subject *per se* that is educative or that is conducive to growth. There is no subject that is in and of itself, or without regard to the stage of growth attained by the learner, such that inherent educational value can be attributed to it. Failure to take into account adaptation to the needs and capacities of individuals was the source of the idea that certain subjects and certain methods are intrinsically cultural or intrinsically good for mental discipline. There is no such thing as educational value in the abstract. The notion that some subjects and methods and that acquaintance with certain facts and truths possess educational value in and of themselves is the reason why traditional education reduced the material of education so largely to a diet of predigested materials. According to this notion, it was enough to regulate the quantity and difficulty of the material provided, in a scheme of quantitative grading, from month to month and from year to year. Otherwise a pupil was expected to take it in the doses that were prescribed from without. If the pupil left it instead of taking it, if he engaged in physical truancy, or in the mental truancy of mind-wandering and finally built up an emotional revulsion against the subject, he was held to be at fault. No question was raised as to whether the trouble might not lie in the subject-matter or in the way in which it was offered. The principle of interaction makes it clear that failure of adaptation of material to needs and capacities of individuals may cause an experience to be non-educative quite as much as failure of an individual to adapt himself to the material.

The principle of continuity in its educational application means, nevertheless, that the future has to be taken into account at every stage of the educational process. This idea is easily misunderstood and is badly distorted in traditional education. Its assumption is, that by acquiring certain skills and by learning certain subjects which would be needed later (perhaps in college or perhaps in adult life) pupils are as a matter of course made ready for the needs and circumstances of the future. Now "preparation" is a treacherous idea. In a certain sense every experience should do something to prepare a person for later experiences of a deeper and more expansive quality. That is the very meaning of growth, continuity, reconstruction of experience. But it is a mistake to suppose that the mere acquisition of a certain amount of arithmetic, geography, history, etc., which is taught and studied because it may be useful at some time in the future, has this effect, and it is a mistake to suppose that acquisition of skills in reading and figuring will automatically constitute preparation for their right and effective use under conditions very unlike those in which they were acquired.

Almost everyone has had occasion to look back upon his school days and wonder what has become of the knowledge he was supposed to have amassed during his years of schooling, and why it is that the technical skills he acquired have to be learned over again in changed form in order to stand him in good stead. Indeed, he is lucky who does not find that in order to make progress, in order to go ahead intellectually, he does not have to unlearn much of what he learned in school. These questions cannot be disposed of by saying that the subjects were not actually learned, for they were learned at least sufficiently to enable a pupil to pass examinations in them. One trouble is that the subject-matter in question was learned in isolation; it was put, as it were, in a water-tight compartment. When the question is asked, then, what has become of it, where has it gone to, the right answer is that it is still there in the special compartment in which it was originally stowed away. If exactly the same conditions recurred as those under which it was acquired, it would also recur and be available. But it was segregated when it was acquired and hence is so disconnected from the rest of experience that it is not available under the actual conditions of life. It is contrary to the laws of experience that learning of this kind, no matter how thoroughly engrained at the time, should give genuine preparation.

Nor does failure in preparation end at this point. Perhaps the greatest of all pedagogical fallacies is the notion that a person learns only the particular thing he is studying at the time. Collateral learning in the way of formation of enduring attitudes, of likes and dislikes, may be and often is much more important than the spelling lesson or lesson in geography or history that is learned. For these attitudes are fundamentally what count in the future. The most important attitude that can be formed is that of desire to go on learning. If impetus in this direction is weakened instead of being intensified, something much more than mere lack of preparation takes place. The pupil is actually robbed of native capacities which otherwise would enable him to cope with the circumstances that he meets in the course of his life. We often see persons who have had little schooling and in whose case the absence of set schooling proves to be a positive asset. They have at least retained their native common sense and power of judgment, and its exercise in the actual conditions of living has given them the precious gift of ability to learn from the experiences they have. What avail is it to win prescribed amounts of information about geography and history, to win ability to read and write, if in the process the individual loses his own soul: loses his appreciation of things worth while, of the values to which these things are relative; if he loses desire to apply what he has learned and, above all, loses the ability to extract meaning from his future experiences as they occur?

What, then, is the true meaning of preparation in the educational scheme? In the first place, it means that a person, young or old, gets out of his present experience all that there is in it for him at the time in which he has it. When preparation is made the controlling end, then the potentialities of the present are sacrificed to a suppositious future. When this happens, the actual preparation for the future is missed or distorted. The ideal of using the present simply to get ready for the future contradicts itself. It omits, and even shuts out, the very conditions by which a person can be prepared for his future. We always live at the time we live and not at some other time, and only by extracting at each present time the full meaning of each present experience are we prepared for doing the same thing in the future. This is the only preparation which in the long run amounts to anything.

All this means that attentive care must be devoted to the conditions which give each present experience a worth-while meaning. Instead of inferring that it doesn't make much difference what the present experience is as long as it is enjoyed, the conclusion is the exact opposite. Here is another matter where it is easy to react from one extreme to the other. Because traditional schools tended to sacrifice the present to a remote and more or less unknown future, therefore it comes to be believed that the educator has little responsibility for the kind of present experiences the young undergo. But the relation of the present and the future is not an *Either-Or* affair. The present affects the future anyway. The persons who should have some idea of the connection between the two are those who have achieved maturity. Accordingly, upon them devolves the responsibility for instituting the conditions for the kind of present experience which has a favorable effect upon the future. Education as growth or maturity should be an ever-present process.

From *Experience and Education* by John Dewey (Indianapolis, IN: Kappa Delta Pi, © 1938), pp. 33–50. Reprinted by permission of Kappa Delta Pi, International Honor Society in Education.

Questions

1. Is Dewey in favor of a child-centered curriculum? Explain.
2. In a time like ours, in which many homes and many families seem to be in disarray, would Dewey continue to argue that the school should exist on a continuum with the home? Explain.
3. Explain "reconstruction of experience."
4. If Dewey is right about reconstruction of experience, would you say that American schools today are trying to educate children? Explain.
5. What is the difference between an aggregate and a community?
6. State "the democratic ideal" in your own words.
7. What is the relationship of democracy to education?
8. What are the two principles Dewey uses to evaluate experience?
9. How might you use those criteria in determining a curriculum or in determining how to treat your students?

9

Traditional versus Progressive Education: The Great Debate

INTRODUCTION

Mortimer J. Adler's dedication of *The Paideia Proposal* (1982) to John Dewey, along with Robert Maynard Hutchins and Horace Mann, is surprising. It is surprising because Adler joined Hutchins and other classicists in the 1930s and 1940s in attacking Dewey and other progressive educators. As Diane Ravitch notes, John Dewey and Robert M. Hutchins "did not disagree about whether children needed to read, or needed to understand the past, or needed to experience literature,"[1] but they did disagree over the appropriate means for achieving these common goals.

In January 1943, Hutchins published *Education for Freedom.* This little book aroused the ire of progressive educators. Responding in the May 1943 issue of *Teachers College Record*, Abraham Citron agrees that our nation requires an "education for freedom," but suggests that Hutchins's means of achieving such a desirable goal gives "aid and comfort to the forces of social and educational reaction." For Citron and other progressives, Hutchins's view suggested that human freedom could best be achieved through the recognition and understanding of the immutable truths which defined the universe. In contrast, the experimentalists considered the

---

[1]Diane Ravitch, "The Proposal in Perspective," *Harvard Educational Review,* 53. (November 1983), 383.

world to be developing with no predetermined pattern. According to Citron, "any quest for the absolute certainty can only be a search for a will of the wisp."[2] Recognizing that Hutchins and others profess a concern for human freedom, Citron and other progressives suggest that their adherence to a traditional metaphysics is more likely to produce a benevolent dictatorship than the "education for freedom" a democracy requires.

Heated rhetoric characterized this conflict. Since both traditionalists and progressives agreed that human civilization was at stake, each side was quick to condemn one another. Hutchins criticized the progressives for fostering "the cult of skepticism," lamenting that such phrases as "I don't know because nobody can," or "everything is a matter of opinion," or "I will take no position because I am tolerant and open-minded," had become the prevalent attitude of the day. Translated into educational practice, Hutchins contends that such moral relativism suggests that tours of the stockyard and steel plants are better suited to prepare students for the modern world than are traditional historical and literary studies. Critical of the progressives for reducing education to a crude vocationalism concerned only with developing producers and consumers, Hutchins feared the collapse of human civilization since "gold" had replaced salvation as the ultimate goal. The world is in need of a moral, intellectual, and spiritual reformation, but, suggests Hutchins, progressives are not capable of leading such a transformation since they believe "that men are no different from the brutes, that morals are another name for mores, that freedom is doing what you please, that everything is a matter of opinion, and that the test of truth is immediate practical success."[3]

Such views were anathema to John Dewey. Writing in the August 1944 issue of *Fortune,* Dewey contends that "the attempt to reestablish linguistic skills and material as the center of education and to do it under the guise of 'education for freedom' is directly opposed to all that democracies cherish as freedom." It is laughable, suggests Dewey, to assert that a true liberal education consists of the study of one hundred great books, for such an educational theory or philosophy lends support to authoritarian control. Dewey suggests that the traditionalists' glorification of "the gulf between the 'material' and the 'spiritual,' between immutable principles and social conditions," is a step backward, rather than progress toward a genuine liberal education. According to Dewey, the major fallacy of the traditionalists is the belief "that the subject matter of a liberal education is fixed in itself."[4]

Dewey agrees with the traditionalists that education should aim at the development of thinking skills, but thinking means a restructuring of experiences, not the discovery of the immutable truths that govern the universe. Dewey also agrees that thinking distinguishes humans from brutes, but thinking "does naturally what Kantian forms and schematizations do only supernaturally."[5] Finally, Dewey describes the

[2]Abraham F. Citron, "Experimentalism and the Classicism of President Hutchins," *Teachers College Record,* 44:8 (May 1943), 545, 548.

[3]Robert Maynard Hutchins, *Education for Freedom* (Baton Rouge: Louisiana State University Press, 1943), pp. 32, 47.

[4]John Dewey, "Challenge to Liberal Thought," *Fortune,* 30:2 (August 1944), 157, 156.

[5]John Dewey, *The Influence of Darwin on Philosophy and Other Essays in Contemporary Thought* (New York: Peter Smith, 1910), p.211.

attempt by Hutchins, Adler, and other traditionalists to revive classical liberal arts as reactionary. Though Hutchins offers his "education for freedom" as a cure for the evils of the modern world, Dewey admonishes us to recognize it as the "moral quackery it actually is."

Though most of the actors in this twentieth century drama are gone, the conflict continues. Adler, an associate of Hutchins, continued to vigorously promote the traditionalist position until his death in 2001. Of his numerous publications in support of a classical liberal arts education, none more forcibly outlines the major themes than his essay "Everybody's Business," first published in 1979. Here he reiterates his modified Aristotelian position that a "basic and common schooling . . . should be given to all without exception." Here, too, he reasserts the fundamental Aristotelian notion that all people by nature desire to know and possess the inherent potential to be actualized as rational human beings. This inherent rational potential requires nurturing, which is best accomplished through humanistic or philosophic learning, "the learning of the generalist, which is everybody's business."

Philosophic or humanistic learning offers the kind of education everybody needs, because such content appeals to the common experience of humanity. It serves as catalyst, stimulating each human being's rational powers to reflect upon universal problems. Through this process, each individual is able to glean glimpses of the immutable, universal truths. According to Adler,

> The core of common experience is the universal experience that is the same for all human beings at all times and places. Some parts of the common experience may vary with the circumstances of particular environments or the particular times, but there is always a common core that is universal—the same at all times and places regardless of circumstances.[6]

This statement—along with Adler's reaffirmation in *The Paideia Proposal* of Hutchins's belief that the best education is the best education for all—demonstrates that Adler is not interested in a truce with the followers of Dewey. *The Paideia Proposal* is essentially an Aristotelian or traditionalist blueprint for educational reform. Later in life, Adler discovered common ground in Dewey's assertion that "What the best and wisest parent wants for his own child, that must the community want for all of it its children" (*School and Society,* 1900). Adler also finds comfort in Dewey's criticism of other progressive educators for misunderstanding and misrepresenting his views. Adler, after reading Dewey's little book—*Experience and Education*—concludes that Dewey's views were more compatible to his and Hutchins's than to the tenets of progressivism often attributed to Dewey.

Adler justifies his dedication of *The Paideia Proposal* to Dewey after his reassessment of Dewey's contribution to progressive education. It is impossible to know whether Adler's reassessment of Dewey's contribution is genuine or one final strategy for persuading the average citizen that his traditional version of liberal education is what America needs. In either case, *The Paideia Proposal* is Hutchins's *Education for Freedom* revisited. Less strident than Hutchins, *The Paideia Proposal* is a political document designed to persuade school board members, superintendents,

---

[6]Mortimer J. Adler, "Everybody's Business," in Seymour Fox, ed., *Philosophy for Education* (Jerusalem: The Van Leer Jerusalem Foundation), 1983, pp. 2, 11.

principals, teachers, and parents to adopt a traditional educational program. Simply, but eloquently, *The Paideia Proposal* makes the case for a traditional education in service of a democratic ideal. Keenly aware of the political climate of the late twentieth century, Adler seized this one last opportunity to champion traditional educational ideas. Having outlived his major antagonist, Mortimer Adler emerged as one of the main architects of education reform in the late twentieth century.

EVERYBODY'S BUSINESS

Mortimer J. Adler

I

In our educational institutions and in our culture, there is a great deal of current concern about the humanities in relation to the sciences. The problem raised by that concern is stated in a number of different ways, depending on how we define the scope of the humanities and the sciences. As currently stated in this century, and in most academic circles, the problem—in my judgment—has no good solution. The choice we are offered—the alternatives we are asked to consider and evaluate—confront us with equally undesirable options: on the one hand, the academic departments currently classified as the humanities (literature, languages and philology, history, philosophy, and the fine arts); on the other hand, a set of academic departments currently classified as the sciences (the social or behavioral sciences, and sometimes with them history as a social science, together with the natural sciences and mathematics). And in both cases, we have the highly specialized techniques of research associated with these disciplines.

Confronted with these options, my response is: *a plague on both your houses!* This is a choice between tweedledum and tweedledee. What is represented here is not, as C.P. Snow would have it, two cultures, but one culture, or, as I think it is more accurate to say, no culture at all—but a multiplicity of fragments that do not constitute a culture.

I would, therefore, like to propose another set of alternatives. When stated in the terms I propose, there is no problem to be solved, for the choice to be made is dictated by the alternatives as stated. The dividing line that I would draw is between what is everybody's business, on the one hand, and what is the business only of the specialist, the expert, or the professional, on the other.

Another way of stating this division is as follows: the learning of the generalist, together with the general skills or arts appropriate to the acquirement of such learning, as against the knowledge of the specialist, together with the specialized skills or techniques appropriate to the development of such knowledge.

To the first of these—the learning of the generalist—I would give the name "humanities," or, if you will, humanistic and philosophical learning, together with the liberal arts—everybody's business. To the second of these— the knowledge of the specialist—I would give the name "sciences," including here not only the academic departments ordinarily classified as the physical, biological, and social or behavioral sciences, but also the academic departments that represent specialized or professionally expert scholarship in literature and philology, history, philosophy, and the fine arts.

Please note that the current academic names for the disciplines do not by themselves indicate on which side of the dividing line a particular subject matter falls. Taught or pursued in a certain way—the way that makes them everybody's business—the sciences and mathematics fall on the side of humanistic or philosophical learning. Taught or pursued in a different way—the way that makes them not everybody's business, but only the business of this or that branch of highly specialized, expert, or professional scholarship—literature and the other arts, history, and philosophy belong with the sciences rather than with the humanities.

With this clarification of the terms in which I think the problem should be stated, let me now state the three theses that I wish to defend. The first is that the basic and common schooling that should be given to all without exception, because it is the kind of schooling appropriate to their common humanity, should aim to cultivate their minds with the learning of the generalist, humanistic or philosophical learning, and with the liberal arts needed for the acquirement of such learning. It is the initial acquirement of such learning, in the years of basic schooling, that should be certified by the degree of Bachelor of Arts.

My second thesis is that there is only one culture in which all human beings can and should participate or share—as communicating members of a single cultural community—and that is the culture which results from the cultivation of the mind by humanistic or philosophical learning—the learning of the generalist, which is everybody's business.

My third and final thesis is that the acquirement of such learning cannot be accomplished during the years of schooling. It can be begun there: the Bachelor of Arts is initiated into it, but he is only an initiate. It remains to be completed, in a lifetime of learning, by those who remain in the academy to become experts or professionals in the specialized fields of science or scholarship, as well as by those who leave the academy for other pursuits or occupations. For the members of either group to realize in some degree the ideal of the educated human being, they must continue to pursue the learning of the generalist throughout their lives.

I have stated my theses as bluntly and succinctly as possible. Since the terms of reference in which I have stated them may seem somewhat strange, paradoxical, or puzzling within the context of current academic discussions, let me provide some further clarifications and explanations: first, by briefly reviewing the historical background of the problem we are considering; second, by explaining why what I have called humanistic or philosophical learning is everybody's business, and why what I have called the sciences and specialized scholarship are not everybody's business. When I have done these two things, I will present a number of conclusions—about our colleges and universities, about our culture, and about education—that follow from the theses as stated, clarified, and explained.

II

From the Greeks until modern times—in fact, until the 19th century, when the modern university with its professional departments and its professors of this or that, its Ph.D.'s, began to dominate both the educational scene and the culture of our society—the distinction between the learning of the generalist and the knowledge of the specialist was understood and acknowledged, though not always with the same degree of clarity or with a full recognition of its significance.

We owe the first clear statement of this distinction, as we owe most of our fundamental insights, to Aristotle. The distinction is made in the opening chapter of the first book of his treatise *On the Parts of Animals*.

The Greek words that Aristotle used to make the distinction, and the meanings he assigned to them, are as follows: On the one hand, *episteme* (which in Latin becomes *scientia*, and in English "science")—this Aristotle regarded as the knowledge of the specialist, together with the special methods or techniques required for pursuing such knowledge. On the other hand, *paideia* (which in Latin becomes *humanitas*, and in English "learning")—this Aristotle regarded as the learning of the generalist, the learning appropriate to an educated man, one who has acquaintance with all branches of knowledge, but an acquaintance that does not make him an expert, a specialist, or a professor of any one of them. As my paraphrase of Aristotle's text indicates, he is presenting us with the distinction between the kind of learning that is everybody's business and the kind of knowledge that is not.

This basic distinction is preserved in the centuries that follow: in Roman culture, by such orators or rhetoricians as Cicero and Quintillian (who, by the way, thought that the ideal orator had also to be philosopher); in the high Middle Ages, by the distinction between the kind of learning that made a man a master of the arts and the kind of professional competence that made him a doctor of medicine, law, or theology. Please note, in passing, that there were no doctors of philosophy. The masters of the arts were all philosophers, all generalists. The Ph.D. degree was first created in the German universities to signify professional competence in a specialized branch knowledge (*episteme* or *scientia*, not *paedeia* or *humanitas*). It misuses the word "philosophy," which should be associated with the humanistic learning of the generalist, not with the scientific knowledge or professional scholarship of the specialist. The degree should have been Sc.D.—doctor of science or scholarship. So named, it would have clearly indicated that the bearers of this degree, most of whom become university professors, are men of specialized knowledge, not generalists, not humanists, least of all philosophers.

After the Middle Ages and at the beginning of modern times, the so-called "renaissance of learning" was a return to the Roman version of Aristotle's distinction. It placed emphasis on literature and the languages—on humane letters—rather than on the sciences. It failed to see, as the Romans failed to see, that, according to Aristotle's way of making the distinction, the sciences and even mathematics, approached in a certain way, could be included in the learning of the generalist—in humanistic or philosophical learning.

What I am saying, in other words, is that with the Romans and the Renaissance, the humanities, or humanistic learning, became too restricted, with the major or almost exclusive emphasis on humane letters—language, literature, and rhetoric—and with too sharp a distinction between humane letters, on the one hand, and the special sciences, on the other.

Beginning in the 17th century, we have the modern development of the experimental and investigative sciences, but it was not until the end of the 18th century and the middle or end of the 19th century that all these specialized disciplines broke away from the parent stem of philosophy and became independent or autonomous branches of specialized knowledge.

The first modern statements of the opposition or conflict between the sciences (the knowledge of the specialist) and the humanities (the humanistic or philosophical learning of the generalist) are to be found in the writings of three 19th-century educators. One, himself a scientist and philosopher of science, William Whewell, Master of Trinity College, Cambridge; another, himself a philosopher, John Stuart Mill, in his Inaugural Address as Rector of St. Andrews University; the third, himself a theologian, John Henry Cardinal Newman, in his *Idea of a University*.

Let me first summarize briefly the central educational theses advanced by these three writers, and then comment on them. Whewell distinguished between permanent and progressive studies, the permanent studies being the main substance or core of everyone's education, to which should be added some acquaintance with, but not expert or specialized proficiency in, the sphere of progressive studies. J.S. Mill distinguished between the kind of learning that should be the property of all educated human beings and the kind that should be reserved for particular professions or occupations.

Here I cannot refrain from quoting two passages from Mill that sum up his basic insight. In the first, Mill, using the word "university" where we would use the phrase "undergraduate college," declares, without qualification, that the university should not be concerned with professional education. He says:

> It is not a place of professional education. Universities are not intended to teach the knowledge required to fit men for some special mode of gaining their livelihood. Their object is not to make skilful lawyers, or physicians, or engineers, but capable and cultivated human beings. It is very right that there should be public facilities for the study of professions. It is well that there should be Schools of Law, and of Medicine, and it would be well if there were schools of engineering, and the industrial arts.

Rephrasing this point in our vernacular, Mill is here saying that specialized or professional knowledge of all sorts—scientific knowledge and specialized scholarship—belong in what we would call the graduate school, which is built on the 19th-century model of the German university, not in the undergraduate college which should be devoted to initiating the young into the humanistic or philosophical learning of the generalist.

The second quotation from his Address gives his reason for saying this:

Men are men before they are lawyers, or physicians, or merchants, or manufacturers; and if you make them capable and sensible men, they will make themselves capable and sensible lawyers or physicians. What professional men should carry away with them from an University, is not professional knowledge, but that which should direct the use of their professional knowledge, and bring the light of general culture to illuminate the technicalities of a special pursuit. Men may be competent lawyers without general education, but it depends on general education to make them philosophic lawyers—who demand, and are capable of apprehending, principles, instead of merely cramming their memory with details. And so of all other useful pursuits, mechanical included. Education makes a man a more intelligent shoemaker, if that be his occupation, but not by teaching him how to make shoes; it does so by the mental exercise it gives, and the habits it impresses.

Cardinal Newman distinguished between liberal or philosophical learning, on the one hand, and specialized scientific knowledge having technological or useful applications, on the other. Again, I must call your attention to the fact that for Newman, as for Mill, what is meant by "university" is what we man by "undergraduate college." Though their language differs in other respects, both are saying that the basic schooling of the young, up to the Bachelor of Arts degree, should be devoted entirely to general learning, at once philosophical and humanistic, not to highly specialized knowledge, however useful that may be.

To this summary of the views of Whewell, Mill, and Newman, I need add only the following brief comments: Whewell, unfortunately, placed too much emphasis on language, literature, and ancient philosophy in his conception of the permanent studies (the subjects then constituting the main substance of the classical curriculum at Oxford and Cambridge). Mill and Newman had a broader conception of the learning of the generalist, as contrasted with the knowledge of the specialist. They both included the whole range of subject matters, but only through the kind of acquaintance with them that results from approaching them philosophically and humanistically—in a way that makes them everybody's business. Even though the German universities of the 19th century imposed the misnamed Ph.D. upon us and glorified the accomplishments of the research specialist, not only in the natural sciences, but also in history, in philology, and in philosophy, it must also be pointed out that those who became professors of specialized knowledge in the university were all men trained in the humanistic gymnasium (devoted mainly to the classical languages and literature—Whewell's permanent studies), not in the technical high school. (The German humanistic gymnasium thus paralleled the classical curriculum at an Oxford college.)

Turning now to the 20th century (in order to complete this brief statement of the historical background relevant to the theses I have proposed), let me call your attention to and comment briefly on four things.

First, the protracted controversy that followed C. P. Snow's essay on the two cultures is one source of our present confusion about the relation of the humanities to the sciences. The two cultures referred to in Snow's essay and in the many responses it evoked are not two cultures at all, but separate fragments of one and the same culture—the culture of the specialist. Snow's main point turned on the failure of communication between the literary man and the scientist, the failure of each to understand the language or the contribution of the other. The explanation of that failure lies in the extraordinary degree to which specialization has advanced in all academic disciplines, not just in the natural and social sciences, but in historical research, in literary scholarship, in philology and philosophy as well.

The real point that Snow should have made is not that we are now confronted with two cultures that cannot communicate with one another, but rather that we are confronted with a vast multiplicity of specialized disciplines (some of them classified as sciences, some as non-scientific scholarship), none of which can communicate with any other. The annual meetings of A.A.A.S. bear witness to this. Even the mathematicians meet in fifteen or twenty different sections, divided by the intense degree of specialization that now exists in mathematics. Communication and understanding has now been narrowed down to the minute sectional subdivisions of each specialized academic discipline. What is true of mathematics is equally true of historical research, of philosophy, of psychology, and so on.

In other words, what we are confronted with, as a result of the ever more intense specialization of knowledge in all academic fields, is not two cultures, but no culture at all—if a culture is understood as the common learning in which all human beings should be able to participate and in terms of which they should be able to communicate and understand one another.

Second, as further evidence of this deplorable state of affairs, let me mention briefly my own experience in the work of producing the new *Britannica,* the 15th edition, which appeared in 1974. At the initiation of this work 10 years earlier, I proposed that the 15th edition should differ from all earlier editions, especially from the famous 11th, in making all its articles intelligible to the intelligent layman. Nothing less than that deserves the name "encyclo-pedia"—the circle of general learning, of *paideia* in Aristotle's sense of that term. In both the 11th and the subsequent 14th edition, the articles were written by specialists as if they were intended to be read by other specialists in the same field. The encyclopaedia had become an anthology of specialized knowledge, rather than a compendium of generalized learning. How far did we succeed in achieving our objective? I wish I could say one hundred percent, but we fell a little short of that. It is remarkable that we did succeed eighty or eighty-five percent of the way. That is a remarkable improvement on earlier editions of *Britannica.*

We should have been able to succeed one hundred percent if we could have solicited articles from men of general learning that includes an acquaintance with and understanding of mathematics and the sciences, as well as history, literature, philosophy, religion, and the arts. One measure of the degree to which we can no longer call upon such general learning is the amount of editing we had to do to make the scholarly contributions as readable as they should be. Another indication of the same is the number of instances in which scholars refused to comply with our request for generally intelligible writing, or refused to accept editorial revisions we felt compelled to make in order to remove technical and specialized jargon and to render their articles more intelligible and appropriate for a general encyclopaedia.

Third, when about twenty-five years ago I worked with Father John Cavanaugh, then President of Notre Dame, to create at that university a Program of General Studies that would, like the program at St. John's College in Annapolis, have a completely required curriculum devoted to humanistic and philosophical learning, the learning of the generalist, the opposition came from the professors of English and other languages and literature, from professors of history, and even from professors of philosophy, as much as it came from professors of mathematics and of the natural and social sciences.

Why? Because all these men had been trained as specialists in the fields in which they had earned their Ph.D.'s. None was himself a generalist, none was a man of humanistic or philosophical learning. As professors of specialized knowledge, they wished to impart it to the young in the college courses they taught, even though, in most cases, they were mainly interested in their own ongoing research and its effect on their advancement in the graduate school. A completely required curriculum of general studies would have prevented that and would, in addition, have been uncongenial to their professional interests if they had been asked to participate in it as teachers.

In this connection, it is worth recalling that the introduction of the elective system by President Eliot at Harvard at the end of the last century was similarly motivated. It was intended to allow the specialized disciplines of the graduate schools, modelled after the German university, to gain a foothold in the undergraduate college; and, through the insidious system of majors and minors, to draw the undergraduate student into specialized study and away from general learning.

Fourth, examine the catalogue of any undergraduate college today, not only colleges that belong to universities with graduate schools that control the college curriculum, but also colleges separate from universities but which imitate the pattern set by colleges in universities. What do you find? A vast assemblage of variegated courses from A to Z representing branches of specialized knowledge, both scientific and non-scientific, that constitute the multiplicity of fragmented departments in the graduate school. In a great many instances, the courses offered got into the catalogue in the first place because of the highly specialized research interest of some professor in the graduate school. The catalogue, with its system of majors and minors, presents no program of general learning. On the contrary, it prevents the evolvement of such a program. The competition for the student's attention is not a competition between humanistic learning, on the one hand, and scientific knowledge, on the other. It is only a competition between one set of specialized disciplines, currently classified as sciences, and another set of specialized disciplines such as history, literature, and philosophy, currently classified as humanities, where that word does not signify that they are truly humanistic, but only that they are non-scientific.

At the University of Chicago in the thirties and forties, President Hutchins tried to reverse the picture by instituting a complete required curriculum which would give all the students in the college the humanistic learning of the generalist, through the reading of great books and through discipline in the liberal arts. His *Higher Learning in America*, published in 1936, was an eloquent appeal for a reform of undergraduate education by emancipating the college from the graduate school and by reconstituting it in line with the vision of general humanistic learning set forth by Whewell, Mill, and Newman. He succeeded in establishing this reform at the University of Chicago, but never as fully as he wished, and his success was short-lived. Within a few years of his departure from the university, the graduate departments reasserted themselves and dismantled the Hutchins college. To my knowledge, the Hutchins reform persists only in two places—at St. John's College and in the Program of General Studies at Notre Dame, which, it must be added, enrolls only a handful of the undergraduates at that university; the rest are exposed to the elective system with its majors and minors in highly specialized knowledge.

III

Up to this point, I have repeatedly insisted upon and employed the distinction between what is everybody's business and what is not—between the learning of the generalist and the knowledge of the specialist. I have presented the historical background relevant to understanding this distinction, especially as it bears on education, on our colleges and universities, and on our culture. But I have not explained the distinction itself. I have not explained what makes a certain kind of learning everybody's business, and how it differs from the kind of knowledge that is not everybody's business. The quickest and most effective way of doing that is to explain why philosophy is everybody's business and why the sciences are not.

My understanding of the difference between philosophy and science developed over many years and finally emerged in mature form in a book, *The Conditions of Philosophy*, which I wrote and published in the early sixties. For the controlling insights in that book, I am indebted to what Jacques Maritain taught me about the grounding of philosophy in common experience and about its relation to common sense.

First let me be sure you understand that if we use the term "knowledge" to stand for some hold on the truth about reality, philosophy no less than science can claim to be knowledge. Both achieve some truth in their effort to answer questions about the nature of the world in which we live, about the nature of man and human behavior, and about society and its institutions. In both cases, the truth they achieve involves reliance upon experience and involves processes of thought reflecting upon and analyzing that experience. But the scientist cannot answer the kind of questions that the philosopher asks by the method that makes him a scientist. Similarly, the philosopher cannot answer the kind of questions that the scientist asks by the method that makes him a philosopher.

The pivotal and crucial difference in their methods lies in the kind of experience to which they appeal, and then, consequently, in the kind of thinking they must do to interpret that experience. The philosopher appeals only to the common experience of mankind, the experience that all human beings have simply by being awake, without the slightest effort of deliberate and methodic investigation, without having in mind any prior questions to answer by means of investigation.

In sharp contrast, the scientist is, first and foremost, an investigator, a man who devises special methods of observation in order to answer questions he has formulated. As a result of his methodically carried out observations, whether in laboratories or not, whether with instrumentation or not, the experience on which the scientist relies is the very special experience produced by his methodical observations. Like philosophical knowledge, our common sense knowledge is also based on common experience. That is why philosophy is an extension and refinement of common sense and that is why both differ sharply from the scientific knowledge that is based entirely on special experience.

Common experience, I repeat, is the everyday experience of the ordinary man—experience he has without any effort or plan of investigation on his part. It may give rise to the asking of questions and once it does, he begins to philosophize about it, but it does not originate from the asking of questions, as the special experience of the investigative scientist does. The core of common experience is the universal experience that is the same for all human beings at all times and places. Some parts of common experience may vary with the circumstances of particular environments or of particular times; but there is always a common core that is universal—the same at all times and places regardless of circumstances.

Let me read you a statement by George Santayana which conveys most eloquently what I mean by the universal core of common experience.

> For good or ill, I am an ignorant man, almost a poet, and I can only spread a feast of what everybody knows. Fortunately, exact science and the books of the learned are not necessary to establish my essential doctrine, nor can any of them claim a higher warrant than it has in itself: for it rests on public experience. It needs, to prove it, only the stars, the seasons, the swarm of animals, the spectacle of birth and death, of cities and wars. My philosophy is justified, and has been justified in all ages and countries, by the facts before every man's eyes . . . In the past or in the future, my language and my borrowed knowledge would have been different, but under whatever sky I had been born, since it is the same sky, I should have had the same philosophy.

Precisely because it is based, as common sense is, on common experience, and because it is an extension of common sense, elucidating and illuminating insights that belong to common sense in a rudimentary form, philosophy is everybody's business. And precisely because they are based on one or another highly specialized method of investigation, the sciences are not everybody's business, neither their special techniques of investigation nor the specialized knowledge that these techniques produce.

Like philosophy, the liberal arts are also everybody's business, at least to the extent that they are skills the mind employs in reflecting upon the common experience of mankind and upon the communication of that experience or of reflections about it in language. Imaginative literature—epic, dramatic, and lyric poetry, novels and plays—is also like philosophy in that it too draws upon the common experience of mankind and represents reflections about it. Nothing but common experience and reflection about it is needed for the understanding of such literature. Even the literature of the sciences and of mathematics can be read and understood in a way that brings them within the grasp of the generalist who, in the light of his common sense and his common experience, asks philosophical questions about them and uses the liberal arts to pursue the answers.

When John Erskine introduced the reading of the great books at Columbia in the early twenties, he—a professor of English literature and a specialist in the scholarship of the Elizabethan period—read and discussed all the books on the list: the historical, scientific, and theological books as well as the poetry, the novels, and the plays. He read them all as literature which any intelligent person should be able to discuss in the light of his common experience and his common sense and with whatever philosophical insights he could bring to bear. Subsequently, when the great books course at Columbia expanded its enrollment and many seminar sections had to be formed, to be conducted by other members of the faculty, the professors of sociology or of economics, of history or of literature, who were then drawn into the picture, abstained from reading and discussing the books on the list that did not fall within their sphere of special scholarly competence. They obtained substitutes for themselves by asking other professors to discuss the books that fell in their special fields.

I tell this story in order to indicate the difference between Erskine's humanistic and philosophical approach to the reading and discussion of books, which made all of them the province of the generalist, and the non-humanistic, non-philosophical approach of his colleagues who assigned the books to one or another of the academic specialties they professed and in which they claimed scholarly competence.

I hope I have now made clear why philosophy is everybody's business and why the sciences are not. In addition, I hope that what I have said about the relation of philosophy to common experience and common sense also explains why the learning of the generalist includes a humanistic and philosophical approach to all subject matters—to the kind of philosophical reading and discussion of books that treat all of them as humane letters, whether they are books written by poets or philosophers, by historians or scientists, or by physicians, lawyers, or theologians.

To this, I must add one very important qualification. Until the last hundred and fifty years or so, great books in every field were written for the intelligent layman. This is true of Galileo, Newton, and Darwin, of Augustine and Aquinas, of Herodotus, Thucydides, Tacitus, and Gibbon, of Plato, Aristotle, Locke, and Mill, of Machiavelli and Hobbes, as well as of Homer, Virgil, Dante, and Shakespeare. But since the rise of specialization in almost all fields of research and scholarship, since the crushing of the generalist in the coils of what Williams James called "the Ph.D. octopus," since the modern university has outlawed generalists from its faculties by demanding of its professors highly specialized competence in some narrowly restricted field of special knowledge, it is no longer true. In 1902, Alfred North Whitehead wrote an *Introduction to Mathematics* that could be read and understood by the intelligent layman. No book like that has been written since then. In the early years of this century, Bergson, Santayana, James, Dewey, and Russell wrote philosophical books intended for the intelligent layman, not just for the eyes of their colleagues in departments of philosophy. In the last twenty-five years, few, if any, books like that have appeared. Philosophers are now as much specialists as their scientific colleagues in the university: they write, whether books or periodical articles, only for their peers—other professors of philosophy.

What I have just said holds comparably in the fields of literary criticism, the study of literature, so-called scientific or sociological history, the history of the arts, and so on. In other words, almost all subject matters have now become the exclusive province of one or another form of specialized scholarship or technique of research. That is why there is no good choice, either with respect to education or to culture, if one has to choose between the present academic disciplines that are misnamed "humanities" and the academic disciplines that are classified as the sciences. For both groups of disciplines are essentially alike in being highly specialized branches of expert knowledge, fragmented into minute subdivisions and rendered incommunicable to one another by the technical jargons that each employs.

Let me repeat what I said at the beginning—that the only good, the only meaningful choice, is one that permits us to choose the humanistic and philosophical learning of the generalist, learning which belongs to everybody and should be the common culture in which everybody participates; and, having made that choice, we would assign a secondary and subordinate place—in education and in culture—to the non-humanistic, non-philosophical knowledge that should be reserved for scholars, researchers, or professionals in special fields.

IV

In the light of what has happened before, the conclusions to which we are led by the analysis I have presented should be obvious. Let me state them with maximum brevity.

First, we regard to basic education—the schooling that, in a democracy such as ours, should cultivate the kind of learning that is everybody's business. Such schooling should terminate with the Bachelor of Arts degree. The curriculum should be a completely required one. It should involve the reading of the great books in all fields of subject matter, approached in the manner that I have described as humanistic and philosophical, not in the manner that I have attributed to professors of narrowly specialized professional competence. To ensure that the learning which an undergraduate college cultivates is the humanistic and philosophical learning of the generalist, the members of a college faculty should not be professors of this or that subject matter, or members of this or that academic department. If possible, they should not be disabled for college teaching by having formed the wrong habits inculcated by working for a Ph.D. Their competence should be the competence of generalists, not the competence of specialists. The acquirement of specialized scientific knowledge or of specialized scholarly knowledge in non-scientific fields—the kind of knowledge that is not everybody's business—should be reserved for the graduate school, where it is proper to have academic departments and professors of this or that. And, most important of all, the college faculty should be completely autonomous, completely emancipated from the influence of the departments in the graduate school.

Second, even though the university is the place for the cultivation of specialized knowledge and specialized scholarship, it, too, needs the leaven of the generalist. Without the presence, to some extent and in some way, of humanistic and philosophical learning, the university cannot be a community of scholars, for a community of specialists is a community in name only, and not in fact. How to achieve this is extremely difficult to devise. My only suggestion, which falls far short of a proposal of detailed measures to adopt, is that philosophy as everybody's business—not philosophy as it is now taught in philosophy departments—should somehow pervade the university and serve to provide a universe of discourse in which all the specialists can participate and talk to one another about their specialties.

Third, and finally, I must say that only if these reforms are accomplished in our educational institutions—in our undergraduate and in our graduate schools, and only if human beings thus properly schooled continue throughout their adult life to pursue the humanistic and philosophical learning of the generalist, is there any hope for the restoration of a truly human culture in which all can participate—one culture, not two, and certainly not the multiplicity of cultural fragments which constitute the cultural chaos that now confronts and bewilders us.

"Everybody's Business" by Mortimer Adler (© 1979 University of Kansas) taken from Seymour Fox, ed., Philosophy for Education (Jerusalem: The Van Leer Jerusalem Foundation, 1983), used by permission from University of Kansas.

Questions

1. Why is it surprising that Adler dedicated *The Paideia Proposal* to John Dewey?
2. Distinguish between traditional and progressive educational ideas.
3. How does Dewey's characterization of "thinking" differ from that of the traditionalists?
4. Compare Adler's educational ideas to those of Aristotle discussed in an earlier chapter.
5. What does Adler mean when he suggests that the choice between the humanities and the sciences is a choice between tweedledum and tweedledee?
6. Explain Adler's distinction between the learning of the generalist and knowledge of the specialist.
7. Explain Adler's assertion that philosophy is an extension and refinement of common sense.

10

The Panacea for African Americans: The Educational Ideas of Washington, Du Bois, and King

Time Line

1872	Booker T. Washington enrolls in Hampton Normal and Agricultural Institute.
1881	Washington named head of Tuskegee Institute.
1895	Washington delivers "Atlanta Compromise" speech at Atlanta Exposition.
1896	Supreme Court legalizes "separate but equal" doctrine.
1903	Washington publishes "Industrial Education for Negroes."
1903	William E. B. Du Bois publishes "The Talented Tenth."
1954	Supreme Court declares "separate but equal" to be unconstitutional.
1955	Montgomery Bus Strike ushers in Civil Rights movement.
1963	Martin Luther King, Jr. writes "Letter from Birmingham Jail."

INTRODUCTION

As noted earlier, the common school crusade originated in New England, spread rapidly through the Mid-Atlantic and Mid-western states, and even established a foothold in the West before the Civil War. As the Civil War came to an end, some northern school reformers suggested that the common school movement could peacefully heal the wounds produced by this conflict and could help reunite the wayward South back into the fold of the United States of America.

Such an inflated sense of the power of the common school movement produced a flurry of activity in the aftermath of the war as common school teachers flocked to the

South to imbue the newly freed slaves and other uneducated southerners with the common values and knowledge that had been so successful throughout much of the North and Mid-west. This missionary effort failed miserably as these naïve, albeit well-intentioned, school teachers quickly learned that South Carolina was different from Massachusetts. Rather than realizing that their goal was beyond the means of common schooling to achieve, these enthusiastic reformers began to accept the idea that the former slave was not capable of leaning and benefitting from the kind of schooling that worked so well in other environments. Reformers lost faith in the efficacy of common schooling for all children and gradually embraced "industrial training" as the appropriate education for the so-called child races.

Booker T. Washington emerged in the late nineteenth century as the most famous advocate of industrial training. Born a slave in Virginia, Washington encountered the roots or foundation of industrial training as an adolescent in Malden, West Virginia. Working as a house boy for Mrs. Viola Ruffner, a Vermont-bred, Yankee woman, Washington experienced and embraced the Puritan ethic as his own. According to this ethic, the good Christian merited salvation, and—as secularized by Benjamin Franklin and others—came to mean that material or worldly success came only to those who earned it. In short, God rewards industry, perseverance, and thrift with material wealth.

Like the religious and secularized Puritans that preceded him, Washington believed the universe to be a just order. Just as the good Christian merited salvation and the good capitalist merited wealth, the good Negro merited the status of a full-fledged human being. Entering the Hampton Normal and Agricultural Institute in 1872, Washington experienced a curriculum grounded in these principles. Designed primarily to prepare Negro elementary teachers, the Hampton Institute emphasized the Puritan virtues. According to General Samuel Chapman Armstrong, the founder and head of Hampton Institute, the Negro teacher must serve as a model of moral character for his or her students. From this perspective, industrial education is the salvation of the Negro race. Supposedly, it roots out their natural tendencies toward laziness, improvidence, and sensuality.

Washington became Armstrong's most famous student. Selected as the principal of the newly established Tuskegee Institute in Alabama in 1881, Washington's voice became increasingly influential in both white and black communities. Aware of the repression of and animosity toward Negroes sweeping the country in the closing decades of the nineteenth century, Washington argued that industrial education ensured both the survival of the blacks and secured the cooperation of the whites.

Washington is best known for his speech to a largely white audience at the Atlanta Exposition of 1895. In suggesting that a racially segregated, caste society is compatible with the economic well being of both races, Washington—arguably the most prominent black leader in the nation—seemed to sanction Jim Crow practices and policies (*Jim Crow* is the term associated with segregated facilities for the white and "colored " races).

Washington's accomodationist tendencies had its critics. Foremost among them was William E. B. Du Bois. Raised a free man in Great Barrington, Massachusetts, Du Bois received an education second to none, including a classical program in high school, baccalaureate and doctoral degrees form Fisk and Harvard Universities, and study abroad at the University of Berlin. Initially supportive of Washington and his commitment to improving the conditions of Negroes in America, Du Bois grew increasingly critical of Washington's acquiescence to the white power structure. According to Du Bois, Washington asked the Negro to give up—at least temporarily—three things: political power, insistence on civil rights, and the opportunity for genuine higher education. With

Washington championing industrial training as the education most appropriate for Negroes, Du Bois argued that philanthropy that could have supported high quality college education for Negro youth went to industrial training institutes like Hampton and Tuskegee.

Du Bois argued that all races have a talented tenth that could and should become doctors, lawyers, ministers, business, and community leaders. With the majority of the available resources then targeted toward industrial training institutes, Du Bois asserted that the talented tenth of the Negro race were being denied the opportunity to achieve their potential and to serve as role models for future generations. Though Du Bois gained recognition for his role in founding the National Association for the Advancement of Colored People (NAACP), his haughty, arrogant demeanor eventually alienated many of his own race as well as members of the white power structure. Recognized as the leading black intellectual of his day, Du Bois never achieved the stature or influence of Booker T. Washington.

Though Du Bois rejected Washington's advocacy of industrial education as the solution for the Negro race, he remained committed to the power of genuine higher education as the great equalizer. Du Bois reasoned that even white America could not deny equal rights once that talented tenth of the Negro population achieved a higher education. While his personal authority and influence waned in the early decades of the twentieth century, the NAACP picked up his banner, arguing that once Negroes obtained a good education, discrimination would evaporate.

It is more than coincidence that a year after Washington's famous Atlanta Compromise speech, the United States Supreme Court legalized the segregation of the races. In what was to become a very familiar phrase, the *Plessy v. Ferguson* decision provided legal sanction for "separate but equal" facilities for *colored* and whites. For more than fifty years, states throughout the south used this "separate but equal" doctrine to justify dual systems of education for white and *colored* children and youth.

Embracing Du Bois's belief that an educated black elite was the necessary first step toward securing equal rights for Negroes, the NAACP focused on higher and professional education, attacking clear violations of the "separate but equal" doctrine. By the mid-twentieth century, the NAACP's strategy of stressing the "equal" half of this doctrine was beginning to bear fruit. Building upon their successes in stressing that education, if separate, must be equal, the NAACP established the foundation for a subsequent challenge to the constitutionality of the "separate but equal" doctrine.

In what came to be know as the Brown decisions, the United States Supreme Court ruled in 1954 that "separate but equal" had no place in public education. A year later the Court instructed state and local governments to move "with all deliberate speed" to eliminate all segregated educational facilities. For many blacks, the long-awaited integrated society was at hand. If blacks were euphoric, many southerners were outraged. But as schools opened their doors each fall with little or no change in the makeup of their student body, neither the jubilation of the blacks nor the anger of whites was justified.

The hope denied due to the failure of the Brown decisions to deliver an integrated society added fuel to the civil rights movement that surfaced with the Montgomery bus strike of 1955. In addition to establishing Rosa Parks as the international icon of the civil rights movement, Americans—both black and white—discovered a new charismatic leader committed to unmasking the horror of racism in the United States. Unlike his predecessors, the Reverend Martin Luther King, Jr. rejected schooling as the solution to the Negro problem. Instead of focusing on formal education as the path forward for Negroes, King's strategy of nonviolent protest against discrimination sought to educate the white population to the inhumanity and absurdity of racial discrimination in America. A charismatic leader and eloquent champion of equality for blacks, King skillfully used the media, especially television, to illustrate the moral evil of racism in America. As white Americans viewed from the comfort of their own homes televised accounts of the violent responses—exemplified by the actions of Eugene (Bull) Connor of Birmingham—to King's nonviolent demonstrations, the incongruity of such racism and the American creed of "liberty and justice for all" became all too obvious.

In an essentially moral crusade to educate the American population about the pervasiveness of racial prejudice in the United States, King employed considerable oratorical skill and uncommon political acumen in uniting Negroes and many whites in support of such nonviolent protests. In the selection included below, King responds to complaints that he is moving too fast by eloquently explaining why his race can wait no longer.

"INDUSTRIAL EDUCATION FOR THE NEGRO" (1903)

Booker T. Washington

In what I say here I would not by any means have it understood that I would limit or circumscribe the mental development of the Negro student. No race can be lifted until its mind is awakened and strengthened. By the side of industrial training should always go mental and moral training, but the pushing of mere abstract knowledge into head means little. We want more than the mere performance of mental gymnastics. Our knowledge must be harnessed to the things of real life. I would encourage the Negro to secure all the mental strength, all the mental culture—whether gleaned from science, mathematics, history, language, or literature that his circumstances will allow, but I believe most earnestly that for years to come the education of the people of my race should be so directed that the greatest proportion of the mental strength of the masses will be brought to bear upon the every-day practical things of life, upon something that is needed to be done, and something which they will be permitted to do in the community in which they reside . . .

I would teach the race that in industry the foundation must be laid—that the very best service which any one can render to what is called the higher education is to teach the present generation to provide a material or industrial foundation. On such a foundation as this will grow habits of thrift, a love of economy, ownership of property, bank accounts. Out of it in the future will grow practical education, professional education, positions of public responsibility. Out of it will grow moral and religious strength. Out of it will grow wealth from which alone can come leisure and the opportunity for the enjoyment of literature and the fine arts. . . .

I would set no limits to the attainments of the Negro in arts, in letters or statesmanship, but I believe the surest way to reach those ends is by laying the foundation in the little things of life that lie immediately about one's door. I plead for industrial education and development for the Negro not because I want to cramp him, but because I want to free him. I want to see him enter the all-powerful business and commercial world. . . .

Early in the history of the Tuskegee Institute we began to combine industrial training with mental and moral culture. Our first efforts were in the direction of agriculture, and we began teaching this with no appliances except one hoe and blind mule. From this small beginning we have grown until now the Institute owns two thousand acres of land, eight hundred of which are cultivated each year by the young men of the school. We began teaching wheel wrighting and blacksmithing in a small way to the men, and laundry work, cooking and sewing and housekeeping to the young women. The fourteen hundred and over young men and women who attended the school during the last school year received instruction—in addition to academic and religious training—in thirty-three trades and industries, including carpentry, blacksmithing, printing, wheelwrighting, harnessmaking, painting, machinery, founding, shoemaking, brickmasonry and brickmaking, plastering, sawmilling, tinsmithing, tailoring, mechanical and architectural drawing, electrical and steam engineering, canning, sewing, dressmaking, millinery, cooking, laundering, housekeeping, mattress making, basketry, nursing, agriculture, dairying and stock raising, horticulture.

Not only do the students receive instruction in these trades, but they do actual work, by means of which more than half of them pay some part or all of their expenses while remaining at the school. Of the sixty buildings belonging to the school all but four were almost wholly erected by the students as a part of their industrial education. Even the bricks which go into the walls are made by students in the school's brick yard, in which, last year, they manufactured two million bricks. . . .

I close, then, as I began, by saying that as a slave the Negro was worked, and that as a freeman he must learn to work. There is still doubt in many quarters as to the ability of the Negro unguided, unsupported, to hew his own path and put into visible, tangible, indisputable form, products and signs of civilization. This doubt cannot be much affected by abstract arguments, no matter how delicately and convincingly woven together. Patiently, quietly, doggedly, persistently, through summer and winter, sunshine and shadow, by self-sacrifice, by foresight, by honesty and industry, we must re-enforce argument with results. One farm bought, one house built, one home sweetly and intelligently kept, one man who is the largest tax payer or has the largest bank account, one school or church maintained, one factory running successfully, one truck garden profitably cultivated, one patient cured by a Negro doctor, one sermon well preached, one office well filled, one life cleanly lived—these will tell more in our favor than all the abstract eloquence that can be summoned to plead our cause. Our pathway must be up through the soil, up through swamps, up through forests, up through the streams, the rocks, up through commerce, education, and religion!

From Booker T. Washington, 1903. "Industrial Education for the Negro." *The Negro Problem: A Series of Articles by Representative American Negroes of Today*, edited by Booker T. Washington et al., 16–23, 28–29. New York: James Pott.

"THE TALENTED TENTH" (1903)

W. E. B. Du Bois

The Negro race, like all races, is going to be saved by its exceptional men. The problem of education, then, among Negroes must first of all deal with the Talented Tenth; it is the problem of developing the Best of this race that they may guide the Mass away from the contamination and death of the Worst, in their own and other races. Now the training of men is a difficult and intricate task. Its technique is a matter for educational experts, but its object is for the vision of seers. If we make money the object of man-training, we shall develop money-makers but not necessarily men; if we make technical skill the object of education, we may possess artisans but not, in nature, men. Men we shall have only as we make manhood the object of the work of the schools—intelligence, broad sympathy, knowledge of the world that was and is, and of the relation of men to it—this is the curriculum of that Higher Education which must underlie true life. On this foundation we may build bread winning, skill of hand and quickness of brain, with never a fear lest the child and man mistake the means of living for the object of life.

If this be true—and who can deny it—three tasks lay before me; first to show from the past that the Talented Tenth as they have risen among American Negroes have been worthy of leadership; secondly to show how these men may be educated and developed; and thirdly to show their relation to the Negro problem.

You misjudge us because you do not know us. From the very first it has been the educated and intelligent of the Negro people that have led and elevated the mass, and the sole obstacles that nullified and retarded their efforts were slavery and race prejudice; for what is slavery but the legalized survival of the unfit and the nullification of the work of natural internal leadership? Negro leadership therefore sought from the first to rid the race of this awful incubus that is might make way for natural selection and the survival of the fittest. . . .

How then shall the leaders of a struggling people be trained and the hands of the risen few strengthened? There can be but one answer: The best and most capable of their youth must be schooled in the colleges and universities of the land. We will not quarrel as to just what the university of the Negro should teach or how it should teach it—I willingly admit that each soul and each race-soul needs its own peculiar curriculum. But this is true: A university is a human invention for the transmission of knowledge and culture from generation to generation, through the training of quick minds and pure hearts, and for this work no other human invention will suffice, not even trade and industrial schools.

All men cannot go to college but some men must; every isolated group or nation must have its yeast, must have for the talented few centers of training where men are not so mystified and befuddled by the hard and necessary toil of earning a living, as to have no aims higher than their bellies, and no God greater than Gold. This is true training, and thus in the beginning were the favored sons of the freedmen trained. Out of the colleges of the North came, after the blood of war, Ware, Cravath, Chase, Andrews, Bumstead, and

Spence to build the foundations of knowledge and civilization in the black South. Where ought they to have begun to build? At the bottom, of course, quibbles the mole with his eyes in the earth. Aye! truly at the bottom, at the very bottom; at the bottom of knowledge, down in the very depths of knowledge there where the roots of justice strike into the lowest soil of Truth. And so they did begin; they founded colleges, and up from the colleges shot normal schools, and out from the normal schools went teachers, and around the normal teachers clustered other teachers to teach the public schools; the college trained in Greek and Latin and mathematics, 2,000 men; and these men trained full 50,000 others in morals and manners, and they in turn taught thrift and the alphabet to nine millions of men, who today hold $300,000,000 of property. It was a miracle—the most wonderful peace-battle of the 19th century, and yet today men smile at it, and in fine superiority tell us that it was all a strange mistake; that a proper way to found a system of education is first to gather the children and buy them spelling books and hoes; afterward men may look about for teachers, if haply they may find them; or again they would teach men Work, but as for Life—why, what has Work to do with Life, they ask vacantly. . . .

The problem of training the Negro is today immensely complicated by the fact that the whole question of the efficiency and appropriateness of our present systems of education, for any kind of child, is a matter of active debate, in which final settlement seems still afar off. Consequently it often happens that persons arguing for or against certain systems of education for Negroes have these controversies in mind and miss the real question at issue. The main question, so far as the Southern Negro is concerned, is: What under the present circumstance must a system of education do in order to raise the Negro as quickly as possible in the scale of civilization? The answer to this question seems to me clear: It must strengthen the Negro's character, increase his knowledge, and teach him to earn a living. Now it goes without saying that it is hard to do all these things simultaneously or suddenly and that at the same time it will not do to give all the attention to one and neglect the others; we could give black boys trades, but that alone will not civilize a race of ex-slaves; we might simply increase their knowledge of the world, but this would not necessarily make them wish to use this knowledge honestly; we might seek to strengthen character and purpose, but to what end if these people have nothing to eat or to wear? A system of education is not one thing, nor does it have a single definite object, nor is it a mere matter of schools. Education is that whole system of human training within and without the school house walls, which molds and develops men. If then we start out to train an ignorant and unskilled people with a heritage of bad habits, our system of training must set before itself two great aims—the one dealing with knowledge and character, the other part seeking to give the child the technical knowledge necessary for him to earn a living under the present circumstances. These objects are accomplished in part by the opening of the common schools on the one, and of the industrial schools on the other. But only in part, for there must also be trained those who are to teach these schools—men and women of knowledge and culture and technical skill who understand modern civilization, and have the training and aptitude to impart it to the children under them. There must be teachers, and teachers of teachers, and to attempt to establish any sort of a system of common and industrial school training, without *first* (and I say *first* advisedly) providing for the higher training of the very best teachers, is simply throwing your money to the winds. School houses do not teach themselves—piles of brick and mortar and machinery do not send out *men*. It is the trained, living human soul, cultivated and strengthened by long study and thought, that breathes the real breath of life into boys and girls and makes them human, whether they be black or white, Greek, Russian, or American. Nothing, in these latter days, has so dampened the faith of thinking Negroes in recent educational movements, as the fact that such movements have been accompanied by ridicule and denouncement and decrying of those very institutions of higher training which made the Negro public school possible, and make Negro industrial schools thinkable. It was: Fisk, Atlanta, Howard, and Straight, those colleges born of the faith and sacrifice of the abolitionists, that placed in the black schools of the South the 30,000 teachers and more, which some, who depreciate the work of these higher schools, are using to teach their own new experiments. If Hampton, Tuskegee, and the hundred other industrial schools prove in the future to be as successful as they deserve to be, then their success in training black artisans for the South will be due primarily to the white colleges of the North and the black colleges of the South, which trained the teachers who today conduct these institutions. There was a time when the American people believed pretty devoutly that a log of wood with a boy at one end and Mark Hopkins at the other represented the highest ideal of human training. But in these eager days it would seem that we have changed all that and think it necessary to add a couple of saw-mills and a hammer to this outfit, and, at a pinch, to dispense with the services of Mark Hopkins. I would not deny, or for a money seem to deny, the paramount necessity of teaching the Negro to work, and to work steadily and skillfully; or seem to depreciate in the slightest degree the important part industrial schools must play in the accomplishment of these ends, but I *do* say, and insist upon it, that it is industrialism drunk with its vision of success to imagine that its own work can be accomplished without providing for the training of broadly cultured men and women to teach its own teachers and to teach the teachers of the public schools.

But I have already said that human education is not simply a matter of schools; it is much more a matter of family and group life—the training of one's home, of one's daily companions, of one's social class. Now the black boy of the South moves in a black world—a world with its own leaders, it own thoughts, its own ideals. In this world he gets by far the larger part of his life training, and through the eyes of this dark world he peers into the veiled world beyond. Who guides and determines the education which he receives in his world? His teachers here are the group-leaders of the Negro people— the physicians and clergymen, the trained fathers and mothers, the influential and forceful men about him of all kinds; here it is, if at all, that the culture of the surrounding world trickles through and is handed on by the graduates of the higher schools. Can such culture training of group leaders be neglected? Can we afford to ignore it? Do you think that if the leaders of thought among Negroes are not trained and educated thinkers, that they will have no leaders? On the contrary a hundred half-trained demagogues will still hold the places they so largely occupy now, and hundreds of vociferous busy-bodies will multiply. You have no choice; either you must help furnish this race from within its own ranks with thoughtful men or trained leadership, or you must suffer the evil consequences of a headless misguided rabble.

I am an earnest advocate of manual training and trade teaching for black boys, and for white boys, too. I believe that next to the founding of Negro colleges the most valuable addition to Negro education since the war has been industrial training for black boys. Nevertheless, I insist that the object of all true education is not to make men carpenters, it is to make carpenters men; there are two means of making the carpenter a man, each equally important: the first is to give the group and community in which he works liberally trained teachers and leaders to teach him and his family what life means; the second is to give him sufficient intelligence and technical skill to make him an efficient workman; the first object demands the Negro college and college-bred men—not a quantity of such colleges, but a few of excellent quality; not too many college-bred men, but enough to leaven the lump, to inspire the masses, to raise the Talented Tenth to leadership; the second object demands a good system of common schools, well-taught, conveniently located and properly equipped. . . .

Men of America, the problem is plain before you. Here is a race transplanted through the criminal foolishness of your fathers. Whether you like it or not the millions are here, and here they will remain. If you do not lift them up, they will pull you down. Education and work are the levers to uplift a people. Work alone will not do it unless inspired by the right ideals and guided by intelligence. Education must not simply teach work—it must teach life. The Talented Tenth of the Negro race must be made leaders of thought and missionaries of culture among their people. No others can do this work and Negro colleges must train men for it. The Negro race, like all other races, is going to be saved by its exceptional men.

Du bois, W.W.B. 1903. "The Talented Tenth." *The Negro Problem: A Series of Articles by Representative American Negroes of Today,* edited by Booker T. Washington, et.al., Chap. 2. New York: James Potts.

LETTER FROM BIRMINGHAM JAIL

April 16, 1963
Martin Luther King, Jr.

My Dear Fellow Clergymen:

While confined here in the Birmingham city jail, I came across your recent statement calling my present activities "unwise and untimely." Seldom do I pause to answer criticism of my work and ideas. If I sought to answer all the criticisms that cross my desk, my secretaries would have little time for anything other than such correspondence in the course of the day, and I would have no time for constructive work. But since I feel that you are men of genuine good will and that your criticisms are sincerely set forth, I want to try to answer your statement in what I hope will be patient and reasonable terms.

I think I should indicate why I am here in Birmingham, since you have been influenced by the view which argues against "outsiders coming in." I have the honor of serving as president of the Southern Christian Leadership Conference, an organization operating in every southern state, with headquarters in Atlanta, Georgia. We have some eighty-five affiliated organizations across the South, and one of them is the Alabama Christian Movement for Human Rights. Frequently we share staff, educational and financial resources with our affiliates. Several months ago the affiliate here in Birmingham asked us to be on call to engage in a nonviolent direct-action program if such were deemed necessary. We readily consented, and when the hour came we lived up to our promise. So I, along with several members of my staff, am here because I was invited here. I am here because I have organizational ties here.

But more basically, I am in Birmingham because injustice is here. Just as the prophets of the eighth century B.C. left their villages and carried their "thus saith the Lord" far beyond the boundaries of their home towns, and just as the Apostle Paul left his village of Tarsus and carried the gospel of Jesus Christ to the far corners of the Greco-Roman world, so am I compelled to carry the gospel of freedom beyond my own home town. Like Paul, I must constantly respond to the Macedonian call for aid.

Moreover, I am cognizant of the interrelatedness of all communities and states. I cannot sit idly by in Atlanta and not be concerned about what happens in Birmingham. Injustice anywhere is a threat to justice everywhere. We are caught in an inescapable network of mutuality, tied in a single garment of destiny. Whatever affects one directly, affects all indirectly. Never again can we afford to live with the narrow, provincial "outside agitator" idea. Anyone who lives inside the United States can never be considered an outsider anywhere within its bounds.

You deplore the demonstrations taking place in Birmingham. But your statement, I am sorry to say, fails to express a similar concern for the conditions that brought about the demonstrations. I am sure that none of you would want to rest content with the superficial kind of social analysis that deals merely with effects and does not grapple with underlying causes. It is unfortunate that demonstrations are taking place in Birmingham, but it is even more unfortunate that the city's white power structure left the Negro community with no alternative.

In any nonviolent campaign there are four basic steps: collection of the facts to determine whether injustices exist; negotiation; self-purification; and direct action. We have gone through all these steps in Birmingham. There can be no gainsaying the fact that racial injustice engulfs this community. Birmingham is probably the most thoroughly segregated city in the United States. Its ugly record of brutality is widely known. Negroes have experienced grossly unjust treatment in the courts. There have been more unsolved bombings of Negro homes and churches in Birmingham than in any other city in the nation. These are the hard, brutal facts of the case. On the basis of these conditions, Negro leaders sought to negotiate with the city fathers. But the latter consistently refused to engage in good-faith negotiation.

Then, last September, came the opportunity to talk with leaders of Birmingham's economic community. In the course of the negotiations, certain promises where made by the merchants—for example, to remove the stores' humiliating racial signs. On the basis of these promises, the Reverend Fred Shuttlesworth and the leaders of the Alabama Christian Movement for Human Rights agreed to a moratorium on all demonstrations. As the weeks and months went by, we realized that we were the victims of a broken promise. A few signs, briefly removed, returned; the others remained.

As in so many past experiences, our hopes had been blasted, and the shadow of deep disappointment settled upon us. We had no alternative except to prepare for direct action, whereby we would present our very bodies as a means of laying our case before the conscience of the local and the national community. Mindful of the difficulties involved, we decided to undertake a process of self-purification. We began a series of workshops on nonviolence, and we repeatedly asked ourselves: "Are you able to accept blows without retaliating?" "Are you able to endure the ordeal of jail?" We decided to schedule our direct-action program for the Easter season, realizing that except for Christmas, this is the main shopping period of the year. Knowing that a strong economic-withdrawal program would be the by-product of direct action, we felt that this would be the best time to bring pressure to bear on the merchants for the needed change.

Then it occurred to us that Birmingham's mayoralty election was coming up in March, and we speedily decided to postpone action until after election day. When we discovered that the Commissioner of Public Safety, Eugene "Bull" Connor, had piled up enough votes to be in the run-off, we decided again to postpone action until the day after the run-off so that the demonstrations could not be used to cloud the issues. Like many others, we waited to see Mr. Connor defeated, and to this end we endured postponement after postponement. Having aided in this community need, we felt that our direct-action program could be delayed no longer.

You may well ask: "Why direct action? Why sit-inns, marches and so forth? Isn't negotiation a better path?" You are quite right in calling for negotiation. Indeed, this is the very purpose of direct action. Nonviolent direct action seeks to create such a crisis and foster such a tension that a community which has constantly refused to negotiate is forced to confront the issue. It seeks so to dramatize the issue that it can no longer be ignored. My citing the creation of tension as part of the work of the nonviolent-resister may sound rather shocking. But I must confess that I am not afraid of the word "tension." I have earnestly opposed violent tension, but there is a type of constructive, nonviolent tension which is necessary for growth. Just as Socrates felt that it was necessary to create a tension in the mind so that individuals could rise from the bondage of myths and half-truths to the unfettered realm of creative analysis and objective appraisal, so must we see the need for nonviolent gadflies to create the kind of tension in society that will help men rise from the dark depths of prejudice and racism to the majestic heights of understanding and brotherhood.

The purpose of our direct-action program is to create a situation so crisis-packed that it will inevitably open the door to negotiation. I therefore concur with you in your call for negotiation. Too long has our beloved Southland been bogged down in a tragic effort to live in monologue rather than dialogue.

One of the basic points in your statement is that the action that I and my associates have taken in Birmingham is untimely. Some have asked: "Why didn't you give the new city administration time to act?" The only answer that I can give to this query is that the new Birmingham administration must be prodded about as much as the outgoing one, before it will act. We are sadly mistaken if we feel that the election of Albert Boutwell as mayor will bring the millennium to Birmingham. While Mr. Boutwell is a much more gentle person than Mr. Connor, they are both segregationists, dedicated to maintenance of the status quo. I have hope that Mr. Boutwell will be reasonable enough to see the futility of massive resistance to desegregation. But he will not see this without pressure from devotees of civil rights. My friends, I must say to you that we have not made a single gain in civil rights without determined legal and nonviolent pressure. Lamentably, it is an historical fact that privileged groups seldom give up their privileges voluntarily. Individuals may see the moral light and voluntarily give up their unjust posture; but, as Reinhold Niebuhr has reminded us, groups tend to be more immoral than individuals.

We know through painful experience that freedom is never voluntarily given by the oppressor; it must be demanded by the oppressed. Frankly, I have yet to engage in a direct-action campaign that was "well timed" in the view of those who have not suffered unduly from the disease of segregation. For years now I have heard the word "Wait!" It rings in the ear of every Negro with piercing familiarity. This "Wait" has almost always meant "Never." We must come to see, with one of our distinguished jurists, that "justice too long delayed is justice denied."

We have waited for more than 340 years for our constitutional and God-given rights. The nations of Asia and Africa are moving with jetlike speed toward gaining political independence, but we still creep at horse-and-buggy pace toward gaining a cup of coffee at a lunch counter. Perhaps it is easy for those who have never felt the stinging darts of segregation to say, "Wait." But when you have seen vicious mobs lynch your mothers and fathers at will and drown your sisters and brothers at whim; when you have seen hate-filled policemen curse, kick and even kill your black brothers and sisters; when you see the vast majority of your twenty million Negro brothers smothering in an airtight cage of poverty in the midst of an affluent society; when you suddenly find your tongue twisted and your speech stammering as you seek to explain to your six-year-old daughter whey she can't go to the public amusement park that has just been advertised on television, and see tears welling up in her eyes when she is told that Funtown is closed to colored children, and see ominous clouds of inferiority beginning to form in her little mental sky, and see her beginning to distort her personality by developing an unconscious bitterness toward white people; when you have to concoct an answer for a five-year-old son who is asking: "Daddy, why do white people treat colored people so mean?"; when you take a cross-country drive and find it necessary to sleep night after night in the uncomfortable corners of your automobile because no motel will accept you; when you are humiliated day in and day out by nagging signs reading "white" and "colored"; when your first name becomes "nigger," your middle name becomes "boy" (however old you are) and your last name becomes "John," and your wife and mother are never given the respected titles "Mrs."; when you are harried by day and haunted by night by the fact that you are a Negro, living constantly at tiptoe stance, never quite knowing what to expect next, and are plagued with inner fears and outer resentments; when you are forever fighting a degenerating sense of "nobodiness"—then you will understand why we find it difficult to wait. There comes a time when the cup of endurance runs over, and men are no longer willing to be plunged into the abyss of despair. I hope, sirs, you can understand our legitimate and unavoidable impatience.

You express a great deal of anxiety over our willingness to break laws. This is certainly a legitimate concern. Since we so diligently urge people to obey the Supreme Court's decision of 1954 outlawing segregation in the public schools, at first glance it may seem rather paradoxical for us consciously to break laws. One may well ask: "How can you advocate breaking some laws and obeying others?" The answer lies in the fact that there are two types of laws: just and unjust. I would be the first to advocate obeying just laws. One has not only a legal but a moral responsibility to obey just laws. Conversely, one has moral responsibility to disobey unjust laws. I would agree with St. Augustine that "an unjust law is no law at all."

Now, what is the difference between the two? How does one determine whether a law is just or unjust? A just law is a man-made code that squares with the moral law or the law of God. An unjust law is a code that is out of harmony with the moral law. To put it in the terms of St. Thomas Aquinas: An unjust law is a human law that is not rooted in eternal law and natural law. Any law that uplifts human personality is just. Any law that degrades human personality is unjust. All segregation statues are unjust because segregation distorts the soul and damages the personality. It gives the segregator a false sense of superiority and the segregated a false sense of inferiority. Segregation, to use the terminology of the Jewish philosopher Martin Buber, substitutes an "I-it" relationship for an "I-thou" relationship and ends up relegating persons to the status of things. Hence segregation is not only politically, economically and sociologically unsound, it is morally wrong and sinful. Paul Tillich has said that sin is separation. Is not segregation an existential expression of man's tragic separation, his awful estrangement, his terrible sinfulness? Thus it is that I can urge men to obey the 1954 decision of the Supreme Court, for it is morally right; and I can urge them to disobey segregation ordinances, for they are morally wrong.

Let us consider a more concrete example of just and unjust laws. An unjust law is a code that a numerical or power majority group compels a minority group to obey but does not make binding on itself. This is difference made legal. By the same token, a just law is a code that a majority compels a minority to follow and that it is willing to follow itself. This is sameness made legal.

Let me give another explanation. A law is unjust if it is inflicted on a minority that, as a result of being denied the right to vote, had no part in enacting or devising the law. Who can say that the legislature of Alabama which set up that state's segregation laws was democratically elected? Throughout Alabama all sorts of devious methods are used to prevent Negroes from becoming registered voters, and there are some counties in which, even though Negroes constitute a majority of the population, not a single Negro is registered. Can any law enacted under such circumstances be considered democratically structured?

Sometimes a law is just on its face and unjust in its application. For instance, I have been arrested on a charge of parading without a permit. Now, there is nothing wrong in having an ordinance which requires a permit for a parade. But such an ordinance becomes unjust when it is used to maintain segregation and to deny citizens the First-Amendment privilege of peaceful assembly and protest.

I hope you are able to see the distinction I am trying to point out. In no sense do I advocate evading or defying the law, as would the rabid segregationist. That would lead to anarchy. One who breaks an unjust law must do so openly, lovingly, and with a willingness to accept the penalty. I submit that an individual who breaks a law that conscience tells him is unjust, and who willingly accepts the penalty of imprisonment in order to arouse the conscience of the community over its injustice, is in reality expressing the highest respect for law.

Of course, there is nothing new about this kind of civil disobedience. It was evidenced sublimely in the refusal of Shadrach, Meshach and Abednego to obey the laws of Nebuchadnezzar, on the ground that a higher moral law was at stake. It was practiced superbly by the early Christians, who were willing to face hungry lions and the excruciating pain of chopping blocks rather than submit to certain unjust laws of the Roman Empire. To a degree, academic freedom is a reality today because Socrates practiced civil disobedience. In our own nation, the Boston Tea Party represented a massive act of civil disobedience.

We should never forget that everything Adolf Hitler did in Germany was "legal" and everything the Hungarian freedom fighters did in Hungary was "illegal." It was "illegal" to aid and comfort a Jew in Hilter's Germany. Even so, I am sure that, had I lived in Germany at the time, I would have aided and comforted my Jewish brothers. If today I lived in a Communist country where certain principles dear to the Christian faith are suppressed, I would openly advocate disobeying that country's antireligious laws.

I must make two honest confessions to you, my Christian and Jewish brothers. First, I must confess that over the past few years I have been gravely disappointed with the white moderate. I have almost reached the regrettable conclusion that the Negro's great stumbling block in his stride toward freedom is not the White Citizen's Counciler or the Ku Klux Klanner, but the white moderate, who is more devoted to "order" than to justice; who prefers a negative peace which is the absence of tension to a positive peace which is the presence of justice; who constantly says: "I agree with you in the goal you seek, but I cannot agree with your methods of direct action"; who paternalistically believes he can set the timetable for another man's freedom; who lives by a mythical concept of time and who constantly advises the Negro to wait for a "more convenient season." Shallow understanding from people of good will is more frustrating than absolute misunderstanding from people of ill will. Lukewarm acceptance is much more bewildering than outright rejection.

I had hoped that the white moderate would understand that law and order exist for the purpose of establishing justice and that when they fail in this purpose they become the dangerously structured dams that block the flow of social progress. I had hoped that the white moderate would understand that the present tension in the South is a necessary phase of the transition from an obnoxious negative peace, in which the Negro passively accepted his unjust plight, to a substantive and positive peace, in which all men will respect the dignity and worth of human personality. Actually, we who engaged in nonviolent direct action are not the creators of tension. We merely bring to the surface the hidden tension *that is already alive. We bring it out in the open, where it can be seen and dealt with. Like a boil that can never be cured so long as it is covered up but must be opened with all its ugliness to the natural medicines of air and light, injustice must be exposed, with all the tension its exposure creates, to the light of human conscience and the air of national opinion before it can be cured.*

In your statement you assert that our actions, even though peaceful, must be condemned because they precipitate violence. But is this a logical assertion? Isn't this like condemning a robbed man because his possession of money precipitated the evil act of robbery? Isn't this like condemning Socrates because his unswerving commitment to truth and his philosophical inquires precipitated the act by the misguided populace in which they made him drink hemlock? Isn't this like condemning Jesus because his unique God-consciousness and never-ceasing devotion to God's will precipitated the evil act of crucifixion? We must come to see that, as the federal courts have consistently affirmed, it is wrong to urge an individual to cease his efforts to gain his basic constitutional rights because the quest may be precipitate violence. Society must protect the robbed and punish the robber.

I had also hoped that the white moderate would reject the myth concerning time in relation to the struggle for freedom. I have just received a letter from a white brother in Texas. He writes: "All Christians know that the colored people will receive equal rights eventually, but it is possible that you are in too great a religious hurry. It has taken Christianity almost two thousand years to accomplish what it has. The teachings of Christ take time to come to earth." Such an attitude stems from a tragic misconception of time, from the strangely irrational notion that there is something in the very flow of time that will inevitably cure all ills. Actually, time itself is neutral; it can be used either destructively or constructively. More and more I feel that the people of ill will have used time much more effectively than have the people of good will. We will have to repent in this generation not merely for the hateful words and actions of the bad people but for the appalling silence of the good people. Human progress never rolls in on wheels of inevitability; it comes through the tireless efforts of men willing to be co-workers with God, and without this hard work, time itself becomes an ally of the forces of social stagnation. We must use time creatively, in the knowledge that the time is always ripe to do right. Now is the time to make real the promise of democracy and transform our pending national elegy into a creative psalm of brotherhood. Now is the time to lift our national policy from the quicksand of racial injustice to the solid rock of human dignity.

You speak of our activity in Birmingham as extreme. At first I was rather disappointed that fellow clergymen would see my nonviolent efforts as those of an extremist. I began thinking about the fact that I stand in the middle of two opposing forces in the Negro community. One is a force of complacency, made up in part of Negroes who, as a result of long years of oppression, are so drained of self-respect and a sense of "somebodiness" that they have adjusted to segregation; and in part of a few middle-class Negros who, because of a degree of academic and economic security and because in some ways they profit by segregation, have become insensitive to the problems of the masses. The other force is one of bitterness and hatred, and it comes perilously close to advocating violence. It is expressed in the various black nationalist groups that are springing up across the nation, the largest and best-known being Elijah Muhammad's Muslim movement. Nourished by the Negro's frustration over the continued existence of racial discrimination, this movement is made up of people who have lost faith in America, who have absolutely repudiated Christianity, and who have concluded that the white man is an incorrigible "devil."

I have tried to stand between these two forces, saying that we need emulate neither the "do nothingism" of the complacent nor the hatred and despair of the black nationalist. For there is the more excellent way of love and nonviolent protest. I am grateful to God that, through the influence of the Negro church, the way of nonviolence became an integral part of our struggle.

If this philosophy had not emerged, by now many streets of the South would, I am convinced, be flowing with blood. And I am further convinced that if our white brothers dismiss as "rabble-rousers" and "outside agitators" those of us who employ nonviolent direct action, and if they refuse to support our nonviolent efforts, millions of Negros will, out of frustration and despair, seek solace and security in black-nationalist ideologies—a development that would inevitable lead to a frightening racial nightmare.

Oppressed people cannot remain oppressed forever. The yearning for freedom eventually manifests itself, and that is what has happened to the American Negro. Something within has reminded him of his birthright of freedom, and something without has reminded him that it can be gained. Consciously or unconsciously, he has been caught up by the Zeigeist, and with his black brothers of Africa and his brown and yellow brothers of Asia, South America and the Caribbean, the United States Negro is moving with a sense of great urgency toward the promised land of racial justice. If one recognizes this vital urge that has engulfed the Negro community, one should readily understand why public demonstrations are taking place. The Negro has many pent-up resentments and latent frustrations, and he must release them. So let him march; let him make prayer pilgrimages to the city hall; let him go on freedom rides—and try to understand why he must do so. If his repressed emotions are not released in nonviolent ways, they will seek expression through violence; this is not a threat but a fact of history. So I have not said to my people: "Get rid of your discontent." Rather, I have tried to say that this normal and healthy discontent can be channeled into the creative outlet of nonviolent direct action. And now this approach is being termed extremist.

But though I was initially disappointed at being categorized as an extremist, as I continued to think about the matter I gradually gained a measure of satisfaction from the label. Was not Jesus an extremist for love: "Love your enemies, bless them that curse you, do good to them that hate you, and pray for them which despitefully use you, and persecute you." Was not Amos an extremist for justice: "Let justice roll down like waters and righteousness like an ever-flowing stream." Was not Paul an extremist for the Christian gospel: "I bear in my body the marks of the Lord Jesus." Was not Martin Luther an extremist: "Here I stand; I cannot do otherwise, so help me God." And John Bunyan: "I will stay in jail to the end of my days before I make a butchery of my conscience." And Abraham Lincoln: "This nation cannot survive half slave and half free." And Thomas Jefferson: "We hold these truths to be self-evident, that all men are created equal . . . " So the question is not whether we will be extremists, but what kind of extremists we will be. Will we be extremists for hate or for love? Will we be extremists for the preservation of injustice or for the extension of justice? In that dramatic scene on Calvary's hill three men were crucified. We must never forget that all three were crucified for the same crime—the crime of extremism. Two were extremists for immorality, and thus fell below their environment. The other, Jesus Christ, was an extremist for love, truth and goodness, and thereby rose above his environment. Perhaps the South, the nation and the world are in dire need of creative extremists.

I had hoped that the white moderate would see this need. Perhaps I was too optimistic; perhaps I expected too much. I suppose I should have realized that few members of the oppressor race can understand the deep groans and passionate yearnings of the oppressed race, and still fewer have the vision to see that injustice must be rooted out by strong, persistent and determined action. I am thankful, however, that some of our white brothers in the South have grasped the meaning of this social revolution and committed themselves to it. They are still all too few in quantity, but they are big in quality. Some—such as Ralph McGill, Lillian Smith, Harry Golden, James McBride Dabbs, Ann Braden and Sara Patton Boyle—have written about our struggle in eloquent and prophetic terms. Others have marched with us down nameless streets of the South. They have languished in filthy, roach-infested jails, suffering the abuse and brutality of policemen who view them as "dirty nigger-lovers." Unlike so many of their moderate brothers and sisters, they have recognized the urgency of the moment and sensed the need for powerful "action" antidotes to combat the disease of segregation.

Let me take note of my other major disappointment. I have been so greatly disappointed with the white church and its leadership. Of course, there are some notable exceptions. I am not unmindful of the fact that each of you has taken some significant stands on this issue. I commend you, Reverend Stallings, for your Christian stand on this past Sunday, in welcoming Negroes to your worship service on a nonsegregated basis. I commend the Catholic leaders of this state for integrating Spring Hill College several years ago.

But despite these notable exceptions, I must honestly reiterate that I have been disappointed with the church. I do not say this as one of those negative critics who can always find something wrong with the church. I say this as a minister of the gospel, who loves the church; who was nurtured in its bosom; who has been sustained by its spiritual blessings and who will remain true to it as long as the cord of life shall lengthen.

When I was suddenly catapulted into the leadership of the bus protest in Montgomery, Alabama, a few years ago, I felt we would be supported by the white church. I felt that the white ministers, priests and rabbis of the South would be among our strongest allies. Instead, some have been outright opponents, refusing to understand the freedom movement and misrepresenting its leaders; all too many others have been more cautious than courageous and have remained silent behind the anesthetizing security of stained-glass windows.

In spite of my shattered dreams, I came to Birmingham with the hope that the white religious leadership of this community would see the justice of our cause and, with deep moral concern, would serve as the channel through which our just grievances could reach the power structure. I had hoped that each of you would understand. But again I have been disappointed.

I have heard numerous southern religious leaders admonish their worshipers to comply with a desegregation decision because it is the law; but I have longed to hear white ministers declare: "Follow this decree because integration is morally right and because the Negro is your brother." In the midst of blatant injustices inflicted upon the Negro, I have watched white churchmen stand on the sideline and mouth pious irrelevancies and sanctimonious trivialities. In the midst of a mighty struggle to rid our nation of facial and economic injustice, I have heard many ministers say: "Those are social issues, with which the gospel has no real concern." And I have watched many churches commit themselves to a completely other-worldly religion which makes a strange, un-Biblical distinction between body and soul, between the sacred and the secular.

I have traveled the length and breadth of Alabama, Mississippi and all the other southern states. On sweltering summer days and crisp autumn mornings I have looked at the South's beautiful churches with their lofty spires pointing heavenward. I have beheld the impressive outlines of her massive religious-education buildings. Over and over I have found myself asking: "What kind of people worship here? Who is their God? Where were their voices when the lips of Governor Barnett dripped with words of interposition and nullification? Where were they when

Governor Wallace gave a clarion call for defiance and hatred? Where were their voices of support when bruised and weary Negro men and women decided to rise from the dark dungeons of complacency to the bright hills of creative protest?"

Yes, these questions are still in my mind. In deep disappointment I have wept over the laxity of the church. But be assured that my tears have been tears of love. There can be no deep disappointment where there is not deep love. Yes, I love the church. How could I do otherwise? I am in the rather unique position of being the son, the grandson and the great-grandson of preachers. Yes, I see the church as the body of Christ. But, oh! How we have blemished and scarred that body through social neglect and through fear of being nonconformists.

There was a time when the church was very powerful—in the time when the early Christians rejoiced at being deemed worthy to suffer for what they believed. In those days the church was not merely a thermometer that recorded the ideas and principles of popular opinion; it was a thermostat that transformed the mores of society. Whenever the early Christians entered a town, the people in power became disturbed and immediately sought to convict the Christians for being "disturbers of the peace" and "outside agitators." But the Christians pressed on, in the conviction that they were "a colony of heaven," called to obey God rather than man. Small in number, they were big in commitment. They were too God-intoxicated to be "astronomically intimidated." By their effort and example they brought an end to such ancient evils as infanticide and gladiatorial contests.

Things are different now. So often the contemporary church is a weak, ineffectual voice with an uncertain sound. So often it is an archdefender of the status quo. Far from being disturbed by the presence of the church, the power structure of the average community is consoled by the church's silent—and often even vocal—sanction of things as they are.

But the judgment of God is upon the church as never before. If today's church does not recapture the sacrificial spirit of the early church, it will lose its authenticity, forfeit the loyalty of millions, and be dismissed as an irrelevant social club with no meaning for the twentieth century. Every day I meet young people whose disappointment with the church has turned into outright disgust.

Perhaps I have once again been too optimistic. Is organized religion too inextricably bound to the status quo to save our nation and the world? Perhaps I must turn my faith to the inner spiritual church, the church within the church, as the true ekklesia and the hope of the world. But again I am thankful to God that some noble souls from the ranks of organized religion have broken loose from the paralyzing chains of conformity and joined us as active partners in the struggle for freedom. They have left their secure congregations and walked the streets of Albany, Georgia, with us. They have gone down the highways of the South on tortuous rides for freedom. Yes, they have gone to jail with us. Some have been dismissed from their churches, have lost the support of their bishops and fellow ministers. But they have acted in the faith that right defeated is stronger than evil triumphant. Their witness has been the spiritual salt that has preserved the true meaning of the gospel in these troubled times. They have carved a tunnel of hope through the dark mountain of disappointment.

I hope the church as a whole will meet the challenge of this decisive hour. But even if the church does not come to the aid of justice, I have no despair about the future. I have no fear about the outcome of our struggle in Birmingham, even if our motives are at present misunderstood. We will reach the goal of freedom in Birmingham and all over the nation, because the goal of America is freedom. Abused and scorned though we may be, our destiny is tied up with America's destiny. Before the pilgrims landed at Plymouth, we were here. Before the pen of Jefferson etched the majestic words of the Declaration of Independence across the pages of history, we were here. For more than two centuries our forebears labored in this country without wages; they made cotton king; they built the homes of their masters while suffering gross injustice and shameful humiliation—and yet out of a bottomless vitality they continued to thrive and develop. If the inexpressible cruelties of slavery could not stop us, the opposition we now face will surely fail. We will win our freedom because the sacred heritage of our nation and the eternal will of God are embodied in our echoing demands.

Before closing I feel impelled to mention one other point in your statement that has troubled me profoundly. You warmly commended the Birmingham police force for keeping "order" and "preventing violence." I doubt that you would have so warmly commended the police force if you had seen its dogs sinking their teeth into unarmed, nonviolent Negroes. I doubt that you would so quickly commend the policemen if you were to observe their ugly and inhumane treatment of Negroes here in the city jail; if you were to watch them push and curse old Negro women and young Negro girls; if you were to see them slap and kick old Negro men and young boys; if you were to observe them, as they did on two occasions, refuse to give us food because we wanted to sing our grace together. I cannot join you in your praise of the Birmingham police department.

It is true that the police have exercised a degree of discipline in handling the demonstrators. In this sense they have conducted themselves rather "nonviolently" in public. But for what purpose? To preserve the evil system of segregation. Over the past few years I have consistently preached that nonviolence demands that the means we use must be as pure as the ends we seek. I have tried to make clear that it is wrong to use immoral means to attain moral ends. But now I must affirm that it is just as wrong, or perhaps even more so, to use moral means to preserve immoral ends. Perhaps Mr. Connor and his policemen have been rather nonviolent in public, as was Chief Pritchett in Albany, Georgia, but they have used the moral means of nonviolence to maintain the immoral end of racial injustice. As T. S. Eliot has said: "The last temptation is the greatest treason: To do the right deed for the wrong reason."

I wish you had commended the Negro sit-inners and demonstrators of Birmingham for their sublime courage, their willingness to suffer and their amazing discipline in the midst of great provocation. One day the South will recognize its real heroes. They will be the James Merediths, with the noble sense of purpose that enables them to face jeering and hostile mobs, and with the agonizing loneliness that characterizes the life of the pioneer. They will be old, oppressed, battered Negro women, symbolized in a seventy-two-year-old woman in Montgomery, Alabama, who rose up with a sense of dignity and with her people decided not to ride segregated buses, and who responded with ungrammatical profundity to one who inquired about her weariness: "My feets is tired, but my soul is at rest." They will be the young high school and college students, the young ministers of the gospel and a host of their elders, courageously and nonviolently sitting in at lunch counters and willingly going to jail for conscience' sake. One day the South will know that when these disinherited children of God sat down at lunch counters, they were in reality standing up for what is best in the American dream and for the most sacred values in our Judaeo-Christian heritage, thereby bringing our nation back to those great wells of democracy which were dug deep by the founding fathers in their formulation of the Constitution and the Declaration of Independence.

Never before have I written so long a letter. I'm afraid it is much too long to take your precious time. I can assure you that it would have been much shorter if I had been writing from a comfortable desk, but what else can one do when he is alone in a narrow jail cell, other than write long letters, think long thoughts and pray long prayers?

If I have said anything in this letter that overstates the truth and indicates an unreasonable impatience, I beg you to forgive me. If I have said anything that understates the truth and indicates my having a patience that allows me to settle for anything less than brotherhood, I beg God to forgive me.

I hope this letter finds you strong in the faith. I also hope the circumstances will soon make it possible for me to meet each of you, not as an integrationist or a civil-rights leader but as a fellow clergyman and a Christian brother. Let us all hope that the dark clouds of racial prejudice will soon pass away and the deep fog of misunderstanding will be lifted from our fear-drenched communities, and in some not too distant tomorrow the radiant stars of love and brotherhood will shine over our great nation with all their scintillating beauty.

Yours for the cause of Peace and Brotherhood,

Martin Luther King, Jr.

Author's Note: This response to a published statement by eight fellow clergymen from Alabama (Bishop C. C. J. Carpenter, Bishop Joseph A. Durick, Rabbi Hilton L. Grafman, Bishop Pual Hardin, Bishop Holan B. Harmon, the Reverend George M. Murray, the Reverend Edward V. Ramage and the Reverend Earl Stallings) was composed under somewhat constricting circumstances. Begun on the margins of the newspaper in which the statement appeared while I was in jail, the letter was continued on scraps of writing paper supplied by a friendly Negro trusty, and concluded on a pad my attorneys were eventually permitted to leave me. Although the text remains in substance unaltered, I have indulged in the author's prerogative of polishing it for publication.

Questions

1. What is the relationship of industrial training to the Puritan ethic?
2. Why do you think that Washington's Atlanta compromise was so well received?
3. Describe in your own words what Du Bois meant by the phrase "the talented tenth."
4. Describe in your own words Du Bois's criticism of Booker T. Washington.
5. Explain why Du Bois suggests that it is the duty of black men in the United States to oppose the work of Washington, their greatest leader.
6. Distinguish between King's just and unjust laws.
7. Why was King disappointed with the white moderates?
8. Explain the connection between Socrates and the contemporary proactive of academic freedom.
9. Was King an extremist? Explain your answer.
10. Explain King's assertion that the destiny of the Negro is America's destiny.
11. Who, according to King, are the real heroes of the south?

11

Maxine Greene

Time Line for Greene

1917	Is born December 23 in New York City.
1938	Receives B.A. from Barnard College.
1949	Receives M.A. from New York University.
1955	Receives Ph.D. from New York University.
1956–1957	Is assistant professor of English at Montclair State College, New Jersey.
1957	Is named assistant professor at New York University.
1962	Is named assistant professor at Brooklyn College.
1965	Is named associate professor at Teachers College/Columbia University. Publishes *Public School and the Private Vision*.
1967	Is named professor at Teachers College. Publishes *Existential Encounters for Teachers*.
1973	Publishes *Teacher as Stranger: Educational Philosophy for a Modern Age*.
1975	Publishes *Education, Freedom, and Possibility*.
1978	Publishes *Landscapes of Learning*.
1988	Publishes *The Dialectic of Freedom*.
1994	Publishes *Composing a Culture: Inside a Summer Writing Program with High School Teachers*.
1995	Publishes *Releasing the Imagination*.
2002	Publishes *Variations on a Blue Guitar*.
2003	Maxine Greene Foundation is established as a private foundation. Receives an honorary doctorate from Long Island University.
2004	The Maxine Greene Chair for Distinguished Contributions to Education is established for outstanding educators and researchers on Teachers College's faculty.
2005	Wins a Lifelong Learning Award from the Center for Education Outreach & Innovation (CEO&I) of Teachers College at Columbia University. Receives a Lifetime Achievement Award at the First Annual Learning Prize Ceremony.

INTRODUCTION

A theme permeating much of Maxine Greene's work is her unyielding faith in humankind's willingness and ability to build on and transcend their lived worlds. Her own life exemplifies this human characteristic in that as one who loves literature and the ideas embodied there, Greene grew up in a world in which "intellectual adventure" was not encouraged. Having grown up in New York City, Greene describes "the opera and the Sunday concerts in the Brooklyn Museum Sculpture Court and the outdoor concerts in the summer" as "rebellions, breakthroughs, secret gardens." As a child Greene took refuge in her journal writing, using it "as a way of ridding myself of my perplexities and confusions, instead of really dealing with them."[1]

Consistent with her advocacy of multiple ways of knowing for much of her academic career, Greene experienced life from a variety of perspectives. Before graduating from Barnard with a degree in history and a minor in philosophy, Greene visited Europe in her late teens, becoming involved in the antifascist activities in support of Republican Spain. While still quite young, she married a medical doctor, worked in his office, and had a child. She remained active in politics, serving as legislative director of the American Labor Party in Brooklyn. Though she wrote "two and a half novels" and numerous articles as a young woman, little of this work was published. At this time, there was little to suggest that Greene's future lay in academia or that she would gain prominence for her unique contribution to the educational thought of the twentieth century. Following World War II and after a divorce and remarriage, Greene decided to go back to school and pursue a master's degree. With this move, she embarked on a journey that led to her becoming the William F. Russell Professor in the Foundations of Education at Teachers College, Columbia University.

As is true for many of us, Greene's professional development resulted from discovering and creating a match between rather fortuitous circumstances and her own personal talents and interests. Her decision to attend graduate school at New York University proved to be one such fortuitous circumstance. She chose NYU not for academic reasons but because she could attend classes there on her own time as a special student. Here she encountered a philosophy of education course team-taught by Adolphe Meyer, George Axtelle, and Theodore Brameld, offered at a time when her daughter was in school. She was fascinated by this first real exposure to educational thought and was suddenly and totally hooked. This professional troika recognized her talent and potential and asked her to assist in the teaching of the course the next time around. Greene's affiliation with NYU continued for several years as she earned there both her master's and her doctorate in philosophy of education. As a graduate assistant, she taught philosophy of education courses and began developing courses in what has become her unique trademark: the union of educational philosophy and literature.

As a doctoral student at NYU, Greene taught for both the English and the education foundations departments. Once she received her Ph.D., she accepted a position in English at Montclair State College in New Jersey, commuting there from

---

[1] Maxine Greene, "Curriculum and Consciousness," in William Pinar, ed., *Curriculum Theorizing: The Reconceptualists* (Berkeley , CA: McCutchan Publishing Corporation, 1975), p. 295.

Queens each day. She soon returned to NYU to teach courses in literature and educational theory. As her work began to be recognized, she moved on to Brooklyn College to teach philosophy of education courses. To her credit and surprise, the analytically oriented Philosophy of Education Society appreciated her work, and she eventually served as president of that professional association. Invited to Teachers College, Columbia University, in 1965 to edit *The Teachers College Record,* Greene found her academic home, remaining there for the remainder of her career and becoming the leading light among Teachers College's prominent social foundations of education faculty.[2]

More interested in the artistic or aesthetic mode of inquiry, Greene uses characters and ideas from both traditional and contemporary literature to help the reader connect with and personalize the philosophical question or issue under scrutiny. Her blurring of the fields of philosophy and literature characterizes her major works, which include *The Public School and the Private Vision, Existential Encounters for Teachers, Teacher as Stranger,* and *Landscapes of Learning.* This unique, signature way of doing educational philosophy is also present in a more recent work, *The Dialectic of Freedom.* Here, Greene explains how for most of her life she has been preoccupied with both a personal and a professional pilgrimage:

> On the one hand, the quest has been deeply personal: that of a woman striving to affirm the feminine as wife, mother, and friend, while reaching, always reaching beyond the limits imposed by the obligations of a woman's life. On the other hand, it has been in some sense deeply public as well: that of a person struggling to connect the undertaking of education, with which she has been so long involved, to the making and remaking of a public space, a space of dialogue and possibility.[3]

As this personal statement suggests, to be free means to be engaged in searching for or creating "an authentic public space" where "diverse human beings can appear before one another as, to quote Hannah Arendt, 'the best they know how to be.'"[4] Freedom means the overcoming of obstacles or barriers that one encounters that impede or obstruct our struggle to define ourselves and fulfill our potential. If one does not understand the obstacle or recognize it as an impediment, or if one simply does not care, then genuine freedom is not possible. As Greene explains, such an individual is like the indifferent gentleman traveler in Dostoevsky's *Notes from Underground* who simply stops when he encounters a stone wall.[5]

Greene joins both the existentialists and the pragmatists in suggesting that the obstacles or "walls" we encounter are human constructs subject to mediation or removal and not objective, universal realities impervious to human action. From this perspective, the educator has the formidable task of promoting freedom in each individual. Since embracing it is a matter of choice, freedom—like virtue—cannot be taught. Still, by creating an atmosphere conducive to the development of freedom, students can be awakened to the realities of their lived worlds, and their belief that

---

[2]Ibid., pp. 295–298.
[3]Maxine Greene, *The Dialectic of Freedom* (New York: Teachers College Press, 1988), p. xi.
[4]Ibid.
[5]Ibid., p. 5.

things do not have to remain as they are can be rekindled. Through education, individuals

> can be provoked to reach beyond themselves in their intersubjective space. It is through and by means of education that they may be empowered to think about what they are doing, to become mindful, to share meanings, to conceptualize, to make varied sense of their lived worlds.[6]

This, according to Greene, is the role that education must play in any just and free social order. From her perspective the ideally educated person is one who cares, that is, one who both recognizes the "wall" as an obstacle and chooses to intelligently and persistently attack it. To foster the development of such individuals, Greene turns to literature. For example, she suggests encouraging students to experience vicariously the refusal of Tom Joad and other Okies to accept their "wall"—manifested in *The Grapes of Wrath* by "the banks and the monstrous shapes of tractors levelling the fields." As students identify with Tom Joad—or some equally poignant fictional or historical character—as "he moves out to what may be a new frontier of collective action, a people's movement that may (or may not) bring about the desperately needed change," they may be motivated to resist the tendency of our increasingly technocratic and bureaucratic societies to lull us into passivity.[7]

For Greene, the educated individual is one who poses critical questions about the worlds we inhabit, one who is engaged with others in dialogue about their shared worlds and how to improve them, and one who seeks and scrutinizes the explanations of the human condition offered by others. If freedom is to characterize the human condition, we all need to become more wide awake, but, as suggested in the essay that follows, it is a necessary prerequisite for those who have chosen teaching as their "fundamental project" in life.

FROM *THE DIALECTIC OF FREEDOM* (1988)

Our exploration began in an awareness of a taken-for-grantedness and a void where present-day thinking is concerned, of a lassitude and a lack of care. The void exists with regard to the question of freedom, the givenness of which is taken for granted. We have, in the course of this inquiry, distinguished freedom from liberty for the purpose of highlighting the tension and the drama of personal choosing in an intersubjective field—choosing among others in a conditioned world. Liberty may be conceived of in social or political terms: Embodied in laws or contracts or formulations of human rights, it carves out a domain where free choices can be made. For Isaiah Berlin, the sense of freedom entails "the absence of obstacles to possible choices and activities—absence of obstructions on roads along which a man can decide to walk" (1970, p. xxxix). We recognize, as he did, that among the obstructions

---

[6]Ibid., p. 12.
[7]Ibid., p. 49.

to be removed (and preferably through social action) are those raised by poverty, sickness, even ignorance. We recognize as well that the removal of obstacles to "possible choices and activities" may, in many cases, lead to domination by the few and the closing off of opportunities for the many. We know too that, even given conditions of liberty, many people do not act on their freedom; they do not risk becoming different; they accede; often, they submit.

The problems for education, therefore, are manifold. Certain ones cluster around the presumed connection between freedom and autonomy; certain ones have to do with the relation between freedom and community, most significantly moral community. Autonomy, many believe, is a prime characteristic of the educated person. To be autonomous is to be self-directed and responsible; it is to be capable of acting in accord with internalized norms and principles; it is to be insightful enough to know and understand one's impulses, one's motives, and the influences of one's past. There are those who ascribe to the autonomous person a free rational will, capable of making rational sense of an extended objective world. Values like independence, self-sufficiency, and authenticity are associated with autonomy, because the truly autonomous person is not supposed to be susceptible to outside manipulations and compulsions. Indeed, he/she can, by maintaining a calm and rational stance, transcend compulsions and complexes that might otherwise interfere with judgment and clarity.

As is well known, the attainment of autonomy characterizes the highest state in the developmental patterns devised by Jean Piaget (1977) and, later, by Lawrence Kohlberg (1971). Piaget saw autonomy as emergent from experience of mutual reciprocity and regard. A life plan, he wrote, is "an affirmation of autonomy"; and "a life plan is above all a scale of values which puts some ideals above others and subordinates the middle-range values to goals thought of as permanent" (p. 443). For Kohlberg, whose primary interest was in moral development, people who reach a high-enough cognitive stage of development become autonomous enough to guide their choices by universalizable principles of justice and benevolence. "That welfare and justice," he said, "are guiding principles of legislation as well as of individual moral action points to the fact that a principle is always a maxim or a rule for making rules or laws as well as a maxim of individual situational conduct" (p. 60). If the presumption is that autonomy is associated with "higher order" thinking and with the ability to conceptualize abstractions like human rights and justice, and if indeed such principles become maxims of individual conduct, many conclude that autonomous persons can be considered free persons. To abide by internalized principles, after all, is to acknowledge the rule of "ought" or "should." R. M. Hare has written that it is because we *can* act in this way or that, that we ask whether we ought to do this or that (1965, p. 51ff.). Granting the various usages of words like "ought" and "should," we can still understand why persons who are capable of principled action and who are responsive to ideals they have incarnated for themselves are considered self-determining and therefore free.

The implications for education have had to do with cognition—with logical thinking, the resolution of moral dilemmas, the mastery of interpersonal rules. For R. S. Peters, this kind of education involves the nurture of a "rational passion" associated with commitment to the worthwhile. Peters wrote: "Respect for truth is intimately connected with fairness, and respect for persons, which together with freedom, are fundamental principles which underlie our moral life and which are personalized in the form of the rational passions" (1970, p. 55). The problem with this highly cognitive focus in the classroom has in part to do with what it excludes. Also, it has to do with whether or not reasoning is enough when it comes to acting in a resistant world, or opening fields of possibilities among which people may choose to choose. There have been many reports on classroom discussions of issues ostensibly of moment to the students: cheating, betraying confidences, nonviolent resistance, sexual relations, discrimination. Not only has there been little evidence that the participants take such issues personally; there has been little sign of any transfer to situations in the "real world," even when there were opportunities (say, in a peace demonstration) to act on what were affirmed as guiding principles. We will touch, before long, on the importance of imagination and the exploration of alternative possibilities. It seems clear, as Oliver and Bane have said, that young people "need the opportunity to project themselves in rich hypothetical worlds created by their own imagination or those of dramatic artists. More important, they need the opportunity to test out new forms of social order—and only then to reason about their moral implications" (1971, p. 270).

Most of the writers to whom we have referred in these paragraphs are, of course, interested primarily in moral commitments, not freedom *per se*. It does appear, as has been said, that there is a presupposition linking autonomy to personal freedom, autonomy in the sense of rational and principled self-government. For many, a movement out of heteronomous existence, with all its conditioning and shaping factors, cannot but be a movement in the direction of a kind of rule-governed self-sufficiency and independence. And this (at least where qualified students are concerned) is viewed by numbers of educators as the most desirable end of pedagogy, to be achieved by liberal education and commitment to the worthwhile.

Such inquiries into women's moral development as Carol Gilligan's *In a Different Voice* (1981) and into women's distinctive modes of reflection as *Women's Ways of Knowing* by Mary Field Belenky and her colleagues (1986) have, at the very least, made problematic the focal emphasis on separateness and responsiveness to purely formal principle. Gilligan has pointed time and time again to the neglect of the patterns of women's development, whose "elusive mystery . . . lies in its recognition of the continuing importance of attachment in the human life cycle. Woman's place in man's life cycle is to protect this recognition while the developmental litany intones the celebration of separation, autonomy, individuation, and natural rights" (p. 23). Belenky's work emphasizes the relational thinking and the integration of voices that characterize women's life stories. Where freedom is concerned (and it is rarely mentioned in contemporary women's literature), it is taken to signify either liberation from domination or the provision of spaces where choices can be made. There is a general acknowledgment that the opening of such spaces depends on support and connectedness. "Connected teaching," for example, involves what Nel Noddings describes as "care" (1984, pp. 15–16). Rather than posing dilemmas to students or presenting models of expertise, the caring teacher tries to look through students' eyes, to struggle *with* them as subjects in search of their own projects, their own ways of making sense of the world. Reflectiveness, even logical thinking remain important; but the *point* of cognitive development is not to gain an increasingly complete grasp of abstract principles. It is to interpret from as many vantage points as possible lived experience, the ways there are of being in the world.

This recent attentiveness to mutuality and to responsiveness to others' wants and concerns cannot but recall the contextual thinking of Dewey, Merleau-Ponty, Hannah Arendt, Michel Foucault, and others. Dewey wrote of the habit of viewing sociality as a trait of an individual "isolated by nature, quite as much as, say, a tendency to combine with others in order to get protection against something threatening one's own private self" (1938/1963, p. 22). He believed it essential to consider the problem of freedom within the context of culture, surely within a context of multiple transactions and relationships. Part of the difficulty for him and those who followed him had to do with the positing of a "free will" associated with a mysterious interiority, even as it had to do with a decontextualization that denied the influences of associated life. Hannah Arendt found some of the century's worst contradictions in the distinction made between "inner" freedom and the kind of outward "unfreedom" or causality described by Immanuel Kant and his successors. The search for a freedom within, she said, denied notions of *praxis* and the public space. For her, as we have seen, freedom was identified with a space that provided room for human action and interaction. She believed that freedom was the major reason persons came together in political orders; it is, she wrote, "the *raison d'être* of politics" and the opposite of "inner freedom," which she called "the inward space into which we may escape from external coercion and *feel* free" (1961, pp. 141–146).

The relationships and responsibilities stressed by women inquirers are not to be identified entirely with the cultural matrix of such importance to Dewey; nor is either emphasis precisely the same as Arendt's concern with the public space. Nonetheless, all these strains of thought are significant responses to present calls, in philosophy and the human sciences, for some reconstitution of core values, some rebuilding of community today. Attention is being repeatedly called to the crucial good of "friendship" in the Aristotelian qualitative-moral sense (see *Nichomachean Ethics,* Bk. VIII)—the relation between those who desire the good of friends for their friends' sake, no matter how different that "good" may be from what a companion chooses and pursues. In some degree, this is a way of acknowledging and respecting another's freedom to choose among possibilities, as it involves a desire to foster that choosing, because the other is a friend. There is talk of "solidarity" as well, as in the case of Richard Rorty talking about human beings giving sense to their lives by placing them in a larger context. There are two ways of doing this, he says: "by telling the story of their contribution to a community" or "by describing themselves as standing in immediate relation to a nonhuman reality." He calls the first story an example of the desire for solidarity, the second an example of the desire for objectivity. "Insofar as a person is seeking solidarity, he or she does not ask about the relation between the practices of the chosen community and something outside that community" (1985, p. 3). Rorty associates the notion of solidarity with pragmatism, especially when the suggestion is made that the only foundation for the sense of community is "shared hope and the trust created by such sharing." This removes not only objectivism but absoluteness; it returns us to the ideas of relatedness, communication, and disclosure, which provide the context in which (according to the viewpoint of this book) freedom must be pursued.

It is because of people's embeddedness in memory and history, because of their incipient sense of community, that freedom in education cannot be conceived either as an autonomous achievement or as merely one of the principles underlying our moral life, personalized (as R. S. Peters said) "in the form of rational passions." It is because of the apparent normality, the givenness of young people's everyday lives, that intentional actions ought to be undertaken to bring things within the scope of students' attention, to make situations more palpable and visible. Only when they are visible and "at hand" are they likely to cry out for interpretation. And only when individuals are empowered to interpret the situations they live together do they become able to mediate between the object-world and their own consciousness, to locate themselves so that freedom can appear.

Aware of how living persons are enmeshed, engaged with what surrounds them, Merleau-Ponty wrote:

> It is because we are through and through compounded of relationships with the world that for us the only way to become aware of the fact is to suspend the resultant activity . . . to put it out of play. Not because we reject the certainties of common sense and a natural attitude to things—they are, on the contrary, the consistent theme of philosophy—but because, being the presupposed basis of any thought, they are taken for granted and go unnoticed, and because in order to arouse them and bring them into view we have to suspend for a moment our recognition of them. (1962/1967, p. xiii)

He was not talking about withdrawing into some interior domain. Nor was he calling for a deflection of attention from ordinary life. Rather, he was exploring the possibilities of seeing what was ordinarily obscured by the familiar, so much part of the accustomed and the everyday that it escaped notice entirely. We might think about the clocks that play such important parts in schoolrooms, or school bells, or loudspeakers blaring at the beginning and end of the day; about calling individual children "third graders" or "lower track"; about threats to summon the remote principal; even about the Pledge of Allegiance, and about the flags drooping in the public rooms. Why *should* these phenomena be presupposed as a "basis" for thought and self-identification? We might think of the way the chalkboard is placed, of the peculiar distancing of the teacher at the front desk, of books firmly shut before the reading is done. The point is to find a means of making all this an object of thought, of critical attention. And we may be reminded again of Foucault's remark that "thought is freedom in relation to what one does." Part of the effort might be to defamiliarize things, to make them strange. How would a Martian view what was there, a "boat person" newly arrived? What would happen if the hands were removed from the clock? (No one, for instance, who has read William Faulkner's *The Sound and the Fury* is likely to forget the strangeness of what happens when Quentin pulls the hands off his watch on the day of his suicide. "Hearing it, that is," thinks Quentin, "I don't suppose anybody ever deliberately listens to a watch or a clock. You don't have to. You can be oblivious to the sound for a long while, then in a second of ticking it can create in the mind unbroken the long diminishing parade of time you didn't hear" [1946, p. 96]. Later, he remembers that "Father said clocks slay time. He said time is dead as long as it is being clicked off by little wheels; only when the clock stops does time come to life" [p. 104]. Reading that, one cannot but find the clock-field, the clock-world, expanding. And the possibilities of thinking multiply.) What of paper? Why is there so much paper? So many files? (George Konrad's novel about a Hungarian social worker, called *The Caseworker,* also makes a reader see—and ask, and question. "I question, explain, prove, disprove, comfort, threaten, grant, deny, demand, approve. . . . The order I defend is brutal though fragile, it is unpleasant and austere; its ideas are impoverished and its style is lacking in grace. . . . I repudiate the high priests of individual salvation and the sob sisters of altruism, who exchange commonplace partial responsibility for the aesthetic transports of cosmohistorical guilt or the gratuitous slogans of universal love. I refuse to emulate these Sunday-school clowns and prefer—I know my limitations—to be the sceptical bureaucrat that I am. My highest aspiration is that a medium-rank, utterly insignificant civil servant should, as far as possible, live with his eyes open" [1974, p. 168]. Again, familiar bureaucratic orders in one's own world thrust themselves into visibility. Seeing more, feeling more, one reaches out for more to do.)

Walker Percy's narrator in *The Moviegoer* says it in another way. He is trying to relieve his own boredom, a boredom verging on despair; and the idea of a search suddenly occurs to him.

> What is the nature of the search? you ask.
>
> Really, it is very simple, at least for a fellow like me; so simple that it is easily overlooked.
>
> The search is what anyone would undertake if he were not sunk in the everydayness of his own life. This morning, for example, I felt as if I had come to myself on a strange island. And what does such a castaway do? Why, he pokes around the neighborhood and he doesn't miss a trick.
>
> To become aware of the possibility of the search is to be onto something. Not to be onto something is to be in despair. (1979, p. 13)

To undertake a search is, of course, to take an initiative, to refuse stasis and the flatness of ordinary life. Since the narrator says he was "sunk in everydayness," his search is clearly for another perspective, one that will disclose what he has never seen. Even to realize that he can be "onto something" is to begin perceiving lacks in his own life. The question as to what the "neighborhood" holds and implies remains open. He may be moved to "poke around" because others have taken heed of him, because he has appeared in the open for almost the first time. If this is so, he may acquire the space that will free him from his environment of everydayness. The experience may be one denoting a willingness "to learn again to see the world"—and to restore "a power to signify, a birth of meaning, or a wild meaning, an expression of experience by experience" (Merleau-Ponty, 1962/1967, p. 60). I am suggesting that there may be an integral relationship between reaching out to learn to learn and the "search" that involves a pursuit of freedom. Without being "onto something," young people feel little pressure, little challenge. There are no mountains they particularly want to climb, so there are few obstacles with which they feel they need to engage. They may take no heed of neighborhood shapes and events once they have become used to them—even the figures of homelessness, the wanderers who are mentally ill, the garbage-strewn lots, the burned-out buildings. It may be that no one communicates the importance of thinking about them or suggests the need to play with hypothetical alternatives. There may be no sense of identification with people sitting on the benches, with children hanging around the street corners after dark. There may be no ability to take it seriously, to take it personally. Visible or invisible, the world may not be problematized; no one aches to break through a horizon, aches in the presence of the question itself. So there are no tensions, no desires to reach beyond.

There is an analogy here for the passivity and the disinterest that prevent discoveries in classrooms, that discourage inquiries, that make even reading seem irrelevant. It is not simply a matter of motivation or interest. In this context, we can call it a question having to do with freedom or, perhaps, the absence of freedom in our schools. By that I do not necessarily mean the ordinary limits and constraints, or even the rules established to ensure order. I mean, in part, the apparent absence of concern for the ways in which young people feel conditioned, determined, even *fated* by prevailing circumstances. Members of minority groups, we are repeatedly informed, do not see the uses of commitment to schooling and studying. No matter how they yearn for success in society, they are convinced of inimical forces all around them, barricades that cannot be overcome. Poor children and others often experience the weight of what is called "cultural reproduction," although they cannot name it or resist it. By that is meant not only the reproduction of ways of knowing, believing, and valuing, but the maintenance of social patternings and stratifications as well. The young people may not chafe under the inequities being kept alive through schools, as inequities often are; they are likely to treat them as wholly "normal," as predictable as natural laws. The same might be said about advantaged children who grow up with a sense of entitlement and privilege, but still feel they have no choice.

The challenge is to engage as many young people as possible in the thought that is freedom—the mode of thought that moved Sarah Grimké,

Elizabeth Cady Stanton, Septima Clark, Leonard Covello, the Reverend King, and so many others into action. Submergence and the inability to name what lies around interfere with questioning and learning. Dewey had something much like this in mind when he emphasized the dangers of "recurrence, complete uniformity," "the routine and mechanical" (1934, p. 272). What he sometimes called the "anaesthetic" in experience is what numbs people and prevents them from reaching out, from launching inquiries. For Dewey, experience becomes fully conscious only when meanings derived from earlier experience enter in through the exercise of the imaginative capacity, since imagination "is the only gateway through which these meanings can find their way into a present interaction; or rather . . . the conscious adjustment of the new and the old *is* imagination" (p. 272). The word, the concept "conscious" must be emphasized. Experience, for Dewey, becomes "human and conscious" only when what is "given here and now is extended by meanings and values drawn from what is absent in fact and present only imaginatively." Conscious thinking always involves a risk, a "venture into the unknown"; and it occurs against a background of funded or sedimented meanings that must themselves be tapped and articulated, so that the mind can continue dealing consciously and solicitously with lived situations, those situations (as Dewey put it) "in which we find ourselves" (p. 263).

Education for freedom must clearly focus on the range of human intelligences, the multiple languages and symbol systems available for ordering experience and making sense of the lived world. Dewey was bitterly opposed to the anti-intellectual tendencies in the culture and frequently gave voice to what he called "a plea for casting off that intellectual timidity which hampers the wings of imagination, a plea for speculative audacity, for more faith in ideas, sloughing off a cowardly reliance upon those partial ideas to which we are wont to give the name facts" (1931, p. 12). He spoke often as well about the kinds of inquiry that deliberately challenge desires for certainty, for fixity. He would undoubtedly have agreed with John Passmore's more recent call for "critico-creative thinking," the kind that is consciously norm-governed but at once willing to challenge rules that become irrelevant or stultifying. No principle, Passmore wrote, no person or text or work of art should be kept beyond the reach of rational criticism. There should nonetheless be a continuing initiation into the great traditions in which we are all, whether we are aware of it or not, embedded. Passmore went on:

> Critical thinking as it is exhibited in the great traditions conjoins imagination and criticism in a single form of thinking; in literature, science, history, philosophy or technology, the free flow of the imagination is controlled by criticism and criticisms are transformed into a new way of looking at things. Not that either the free exercise of the imagination or the raising of objections is in itself to be despised; the first can be suggestive of new ideas, the second can show the need for them. But certainly education tries to develop the two in combination. The educator is interested in encouraging critical discussion as distinct from the mere raising of objections; and discussion is an exercise of the imagination. (1975, p. 33)

A concern for the critical and the imaginative, for the opening of new ways of "looking at things," is wholly at odds with the technicist and behaviorist emphases we still find in American schools. It represents a challenge, not yet met, to the hollow formulations, the mystifications so characteristic of our time. We have taken note of the forms of evangelism and fundamentalism, the confused uneasiness with modernism that so often finds expression in anti-intellectualism or an arid focus on "Great Books." Given the dangers of small-mindedness and privatism, however, I do not think it sufficient to develop even the most variegated, most critical, most imaginative, most "liberal" approach to the education of the young. If we are seriously interested in education for freedom as well as for the opening of cognitive perspectives, it is also important to find a way of developing a *praxis* of educational consequence that opens the spaces necessary for the remaking of a democratic community. For this to happen, there must of course be a new commitment to intelligence, a new fidelity in communication, a new regard for imagination. It would mean fresh and sometimes startling winds blowing through the classrooms of the nation. It would mean the granting of audibility to numerous voices seldom heard before and, at once, an involvement with all sorts of young people being provoked to make their own the multilinguality needed for structuring of contemporary experience and thematizing lived worlds. The languages required include many of the traditional modes of sensemaking: the academic disciplines, the fields of study. But none of them must ever be thought of as complete or all-encompassing, developed as they have been to respond to particular kinds of questions posed at particular moments in time. Turned, as lenses or perspectives, on the shared world of actualities, they cannot but continue resonating and reforming in the light of new undercurrents, new questions, new uncertainties.

Let us say young high school students are studying history. Clearly, they require some understanding of the rules of evidence where the historical record is concerned. They need to distinguish among sources, to single out among multiple determinants those forces that can be identified as causal, to find the places where chance cuts across necessity, to recognize when calculations are appropriate and when they are not. All this takes reflective comprehension of the norms governing the discipline of history. But this does not end or exhaust such study. There is a consciousness now, as there was not in time past, of the significance of doing history "from the ground up," of penetrating the so-called "cultures of silence" in order to discover what ordinary farmers and storekeepers and elementary schoolteachers and street children and Asian newcomers think and have thought about an event like the Holocaust or the Vietnam War or the bombing of Hiroshima or the repression in South Africa that continues to affect them directly or indirectly even as it recedes into the visualizable past. They need to be empowered to reflect on and talk about what happened in its varying connections with other events in the present as well as the past. And they may be brought to find out that a range of informed viewpoints may be just as important when it comes to understanding the Civil War, or the industrial revolution, or the slave trade, or the Children's Crusade. Clearly, if the voices of participants or near-participants (front-line soldiers, factory workers, slaves, crusaders) could be heard, whole dimensions of new understanding (and perplexity and uncertainty) would be disclosed. The same is true with respect to demographic studies, studies based on census rolls or tax collections, studies that include diaries and newspaper stories and old photographs. Turning the tools and techniques of history to resources of this kind often means opening up new spaces for study, metaphorical spaces sometimes, places for "speculative audacity." Such efforts may provide experiences of freedom in the study of history, because they unleash imagination in unexpected ways. They draw the mind to what lies beyond the accustomed boundaries and often to what is not yet. They do so as persons become more and more aware of the unanswered questions, the unexplored corners, the nameless faces behind the forgotten windows. These are the obstacles to be transcended if understanding is to be gained. And it is in the transcending, as we have seen, that freedom is often achieved.

The same can be said for the other disciplines and fields of study in the social and natural sciences; and, even among the exact sciences, a heightened curiosity may accompany the growth of feelings of connection between human hands and minds and the objects of study, whether they are rocks or stars or memory cores. Again, it is a matter of questioning and sense-making from a grounded vantage point, an interpretive vantage point, in a way that eventually sheds some light on the commonsense world, in a way that is always perspectival and therefore forever incomplete. The most potent metaphor for this can be found at the end of Melville's chapter called "Cetology" in the novel *Moby Dick*. The chapter deals with the essentially futile effort to provide a "systematized exhibition of the whale in his broad genera," or to classify the constituents of a chaos. And finally:

> It was stated at the outset, that this system would not be here, and at once, perfected. You cannot but plainly see that I have kept my word. But now I leave my cetological System standing thus unfinished, even as the great Cathedral of Cologne was left, with the crane still standing upon the top of the uncompleted tower. For small erections may be finished by their first architects; grand ones, true ones, ever leave the copestone to posterity. God keep me from ever completing anything. This whole book is but a draught—nay, but the draught of a draught. Oh, Time, Strength, Cash, and patience! (1851/1981, p. 148)

To recognize the role of perspective and vantage point, to recognize at the same time that there are always multiple perspectives and multiple vantage points, is to recognize that no accounting, disciplinary or other-wise, can ever be finished or complete. There is always more. There is always possibility. And this is where the space opens for the pursuit of freedom. Much the same can be said about experiences with art objects—not only literary texts, but music, painting, dance. They have the capacity, when authentically attended to, to enable persons to hear and to see what they would not ordinarily hear and see, to offer visions of consonance and dissonance that are unfamiliar and indeed abnormal, to disclose the incomplete profiles of the world. As importantly, in this context, they have the capacity to defamiliarize experience: to begin with the overly familiar and transfigure it into something different enough to make those who are awakened hear and see.

Generalizations with regard to what forms possess such potential for different people are tempting, but they must be set aside. Jazz and the blues have long had a transformative, often liberating effect on many populations, for example. We have only to read the musical history of our country, recall the stories of our great black musicians, heed such novels as *Invisible Man* (constructed, its author said, according to the patterns of the blues), take note of the importance of jazz in European art forms throughout the century, see how the Jazz Section of the Czech dissident movement has become the live center of dissent. The ways in which the blues have given rise to rock music and what are called "raps" testify as well to a power, not merely to embody and express the suffering of oppressed and constricted lives, but to name them somehow, to identify the gaps between what is and what is longed for, what (if the sphere of freedom is ever developed) will some day come to be.

Recent discoveries of women's novels, like discoveries of black literature, have certainly affected the vision of those reared in the traditions of so-called "great" literature, as they have the constricted visions of those still confined by outmoded ideas of gender. The growing ability to look at even classical works through new critical lenses has enabled numerous readers, of both genders, to apprehend previously unknown renderings of their lived worlds. Not only have many begun coming to literature with the intent of *achieving* it as meaningful through realization by means of perspectival readings. Many have begun engaging in what Mikhail Bakhtin called "dialogism," viewing literary texts as spaces where multiple voices and multiple discourses intersect and interact (1981, pp. 259–422). Even to confront what Bakhtin calls "heteroglossia" in a novel is to enlarge one's experience with multiplicity of perspectives and, at once, with the spheres that can open in the midst of pluralities.

With *Invisible Man* in mind, we might recall the point that invisibility represents a condition in the mind of the one who encounters the black person and draw implications for the ways we have looked at other strangers, and even for the ways we have looked at those posited as "other" or as enemies. We can find ourselves reading so-called canonical works like *Jane Eyre* and become astonished by a newly grasped interpretation of the "madwoman" imprisoned upstairs in Mr. Rochester's house. Shocked into a new kind of awareness, we find ourselves pushing back the boundaries again, hearing new voices, exploring new discourses, unearthing new possibilities. We can ponder such works as Tillie Olsen's "I Stand There Ironing" or "Tell Me a Riddle" and uncover dimensions of oppression, dream, and possibility never suspected before. We can look again at Gabriel Garcia Márquez's *One Hundred Years of Solitude* and find ourselves opening windows in our experience to startling renderings of time, death, and history that subvert more of our certainties. It is not only, however, in the domains of the hitherto "silent" cultures that transformations of our experience can take place. There is a sense in which the history of any art form carries with it a history of occasions for new visions, new modes of defamiliarization, at least in cases where artists thrust away the auras, and broke in some way with the past.

It has been clear in music, pushing back the horizons of silence for at least a century, opening new frequencies for ears willing to risk new sounds. It has been true of dance, as pioneers of movement and visual metaphor uncover new possibilities in the human body and therefore for embodied consciousnesses in the world. In painting, it has been dramatically the case. An example can be found in the work of the painter John Constable, who abandoned old paradigms of studio painting and studio light and began sketching his subjects in the open air. Breaking through "horizons of expectation," as the critic Ernst Gombrich writes (1965, p. 34), Constable enabled spectators to perceive green in the landscape, rather than rendering it in the traditional manner in gradations of brown. He defamiliarized the visible world, in effect, making accessible shadings and nuances never suspected before. We can say similar things about numerous visual artists, if we are enabled, say, to see them against their forerunners; moving through the "museums without walls," listening to those Merleau-Ponty called the "voices of silence," we can discover ourselves variously on an always-changing place on earth. Giotto, della Francesca, Botticelli, Michelangelo, Raphael, Poussin: The names sound, the doors open to vista after vista. Exemplary for moderns may be Claude Monet making visible the modelling effects of light on objects once seen as solidly and objectively *there*. Some can recall the multiple studies of haystacks in his garden at different seasons of the year or of Rouen Cathedral at different times of day. Recalling, we are reminded again how visions of fixity can be transformed, how time itself can take on new meanings for the perceiver, for the one choosing to journey through works of visual art. And we can (we ought to) recall Pablo Picasso's abrupt expansion of Western observers' conceptions of humanity and space with his "Demoiselles d'Avignon" and its African and Iberian visages, or his imaging of unendurable pain in the "Guernica."

Of course, such visions are unknown in most of our classrooms; and relatively few people are informed enough or even courageous enough actually to "see." And it must be acknowledged that, for all their emancipatory potential, the arts cannot be counted on to liberate, to ensure an education for freedom. Nonetheless, for those authentically concerned about the "birth of meaning," about breaking through the surfaces, about teaching others to "read" their own worlds, art forms must be conceived of as ever-present possibility. They ought not to be treated as decorative, as frivolous. They ought to be, if transformative teaching is our concern, a central part of curriculum, wherever it is devised. How can it be irrelevant, for example, to include such images as those of William Blake, with contraries and paradoxes that make it forever impossible to place the "lamb" and the "tiger" in distinctive universes, to separate the "marriage" from the "hearse"? How can it be of only extracurricular interest to turn to Emily Dickinson, for instance, and find normal views of experience disrupted and transformed? She wrote:

I stepped from plank to plank
  So slow and cautiously;
The stars about my head I felt,
  About my feet the sea.
I knew not but the next
  Would be my final inch,—
This gave me that precarious gait
  Some call experience.

(1890/1959, p. 166)

The spaces widen in the poem—from plank to plank under an open sky. She identifies experience itself with a "precarious gait"; and the risk involved is emphasized. Reading such a work, we cannot but find our own world somehow defamiliarized. Defamiliarized, it discloses aspects of experience ordinarily never seen. Critical awareness may be somehow enhanced, as new possibilities open for reflection. Poetry does not offer us empirical or documentary truth, but it enables us to "know" in unique ways. So many poems come to mind, among them W. H. Auden's "Surgical Ward," which may emerge from memory because of the AIDS epidemic, or because of a concern about distancing and lack of care. He wrote of the remoteness of those who "are and suffer; that is all they do" and of the isolation of the sufferers compared with those who believe "in the common world of the uninjured and cannot imagine isolation—" (1970, pp. 44–45). Any one of a hundred others might have come to mind: the choice is arbitrary. A writer, like the writer of this book, can only hope to activate the memories of *her* readers, to awaken, to strike sparks.

The same is true, even more true, when it comes to novels and plays: The occasions for revelation and disclosure are beyond counting. In my train of thought (and readers will locate themselves in their own), I find Antigone, committed to her sense of what is moral and dying for her cause; King Lear, with all artifice and "superfluity" abandoned on the heath in the raging storm. I somehow see Lucifer falling in *Paradise Lost* and continually falling, reappearing at the end of James Joyce's *A Portrait of the Artist as a Young Man* when Stephen Dedalus says, "I will not serve." And then, remembering Joyce, I hear that resounding "Yes" at the end of Molly Bloom's soliloquy in *Ulysses*. In the background, softly, stubbornly, there is Bartleby's "I prefer not to" in the Melville story; there is the dying Ivan Ilyitch in the Tolstoy story, speaking of himself as "little Vanya" to the peasant holding his legs; there is the shadow of the little girl who hung herself in Dostoevsky's *The Possessed*. There are the soldiers described in Malraux's *Man's Fate,* young soldiers about to be executed on the Lithuanian front and forced to take off their trousers in the snow. They begin to sneeze, "and those sneezes were so intensely human in that dawn of execution, that the machine-gunners, instead of firing, waited—waited for life to become less indiscreet" (1936, p. 76). Indiscreet—and I see the house beaten by the storms and the dilapidations of time in the "Time Passes" section of Virginia Woolf's *To the Lighthouse;* Willa Cather's Paul (in "Paul's Case") and the winter roses and a boy's death on the railroad tracks. There are the spare, lace-curtained bedrooms and the slave women in red in Margaret Atwood's *The Handmaid's Tale;* and, in another future, there is the stark transcendence of the rocket in *Gravity's Rainbow* by Thomas Pynchon. There is Mark Helprin's white horse in the snow-bound city in *Winter's Tale,* the "air-borne toxic event" in Don DeLillo's *White Noise.*

Any reader might go on to recall how, as Herbert Marcuse has put it, "art is committed to that perception of the world which alienates individuals from their functional existence and performance in society" (1978, p. 9). An education for freedom must move beyond function, beyond the subordination of persons to external ends. It must move beyond mere performance to action, which entails the taking of initiatives. This is not meant to imply that aesthetic engagements, because they take place in domains of freedom, separate or alienate learners so fully from the tasks of the world that they become incapacitated for belonging or for membership or for work itself. Marcuse also spoke of an aesthetic transformation as a "vehicle of recognition," drawing the perceiver away from "the mystifying power of the given" (1978, p. 72). He was pointing to an emancipatory possibility of relevance for an education in and for freedom. Encounters with the arts alone will not realize it; but the arts will help open the situations that require interpretation, will help disrupt the walls that obscure the spaces, the spheres of freedom to which educators might some day attend.

With situations opening, students may become empowered to engage in some sort of *praxis,* engaged enough to name the obstacles in the way of their shared becoming. They may at first be identified with the school itself, with the neighborhood, with the family, with fellow-beings in the endangered world. They may be identified with prejudices, rigidities, suppressed violence: All these can petrify or impinge on the sphere of freedom. As Foucault would have it, persons may be made into subjects, docile bodies to be "subjected, used, transformed, and improved" (1977, p. 136). It is not merely the structures of class, race, and gender relations that embody such power and make it felt in classrooms. Much the same can happen through the differential distribution of knowledge, through a breaking of what is distributed into discrete particles, through an unwarranted classification of a "chaos."

Having attended to women's lives and the lives of many strangers, we are aware of the relation between the subjugation of voices and the silencing of memories. All these have often been due to the insidious workings of power or the maintenance of what has been called "hegemony" (Entwhistle, 1979, pp. 12–14). Hegemony, as explained by the Italian philosopher Antonio Gramsci, means direction by moral and intellectual persuasion, not by physical coercion. That is what makes it a matter of such concern for those interested in education for freedom. The persuasion is often so quiet, so seductive, so disguised that it renders young people acquiescent to power without their realizing it. The persuasion becomes most effective when the method used obscures what is happening in the learners' minds. Strangely, the acquiescence, the acceptance, may find expression through dropping out or other modes of alienation, as much as through a bland compliance to what is taken to be the given. This may be because the message or the direction emphasizes an opportunity system or a stratification system offering a limited range of possibilities, apparently attentive to but a few modes of being. This becomes most drastically clear in the case of youngsters whose IQs, according to current testing practices, are low. Ours is not a society that ponders fulfilling options for people with low IQs. Lacking an awareness of alternatives, lacking a vision of realizable possibilities, the young (left unaware of the messages they are given) have no hope of achieving freedom.

In the classroom opened to possibility and at once concerned with inquiry, critiques must be developed that uncover what masquerade as neutral frameworks, or what Rorty calls "a set of rules which will tell us how rational agreement can be reached on what would settle the issue on every point where statements seem to conflict" (1979, p. 315). Teachers, like their students, have to learn to love the questions, as they come to realize that there can be no final agreements or answers, no final commensurability. And we have been talking about stories that open perspectives on communities grounded in trust, flowering by means of dialogue, kept alive in open spaces where freedom can find a place.

Looking back, we can discern individuals in their we-relations with others, inserting themselves in the world by means of projects, embarking on new beginnings in spaces they open themselves. We can recall them—Thomas Jefferson, the Grimké sisters, Susan B. Anthony, Jane Addams, Frederick Douglass, W. E. B. DuBois, Martin Luther King, John Dewey, Carol Gilligan, Nel Noddings, Mary Daly—opening public spaces where freedom is the mainspring, where people create themselves by acting in concert. For Hannah Arendt, "power corresponds to the human ability . . . to act in concert. Power is never the property of an individual; it belongs to a group and remains in existence only so long as the group keeps together" (1972, p. 143). Power may be thought of, then, as "empowerment," a condition of possibility for human and political life and, yes, for education as well. But spaces have to be opened in the schools and around the schools; the windows have to let in the fresh air. The poet Mark Strand writes:

> It is all in the mind, you say, and has
> nothing to do with happiness. The coming of cold,
> The coming of heat, the mind has all the time in the world.
> You take my arm and say something will happen,
> something unusual for which we were always prepared,
> like the sun arriving after a day in Asia,
> like the moon departing after a night with us.
>
> (1984, p. 126)

And Adrienne Rich, calling a poem "Integrity" and beginning, "A wild patience has taken me this far" (1981, p. 8). There is a need for a wild patience. And, when freedom is the question, it is always a time to begin.

Questions

1. What is the difference between liberty and freedom?
2. What is the relationship between autonomy and freedom?
3. How are freedom and autonomy related to women's ways of knowing?
4. What does Greene mean by suggesting that freedom must be pursued through relatedness, communication, and disclosure?
5. What does Greene mean by the statement that "freedom in education cannot be conceived . . . as an autonomous achievement . . . "?
6. How does being "onto something" connect with the "search" that involves a pursuit of freedom?
7. What is meant by places for "speculative audacity," and how does speculative audacity relate to achieving freedom?
8. Why is it important to enable or empower persons to hear and see what they would not ordinarily see and hear?
9. Why is it important to "identify the gaps between what is and what is longed for, what will someday come to be?"
10. Why should the arts be a central, rather than frivolous, part of a curriculum?
11. How does a work of art, literature, music, and the like enhance our critical awareness?
12. Why are encounters with the arts insufficient for an education in and for freedom?
13. What is meant by *praxis,* and how does it relate to freedom?
14. What does education have to do with unmasking neutral frameworks?

12

Jane Roland Martin

Time Line for Martin

1929	Is born July 20 in New York City. Her father, Charles, is a journalist, and her mother, Sarah, is a teacher.
1951	Receives A.B. from Radcliffe College.
1956	Receives Ed.M. from Harvard University.
1961	Receives Ph.D. from Radcliffe College.
1962	Marries Michael Martin on June 15. They have two sons.
1972–1981	Is associate professor of philosophy at University of Massachusetts, Boston.
1981–1994	Is professor of philosophy at University of Massachusetts, Boston.
1983–1984	Is Visiting Woman Scholar at the University of New Hampshire.
1985	Publishes *Reclaiming a Conversation: The Ideal of the Educated Woman.*
1992	Publishes *The Schoolhome.*
1994	Publishes *Changing the Educational Landscape: Philosophy, Women, and Curriculum.*
	Is named professor emerita of philosophy at the University of Massachusetts, Boston.
1995	Publishes *The Schoolhome* (paperback).
1999	Publishes *Coming of Age in Academe: Rekindling Women's Hopes and Reforming the Academy.*
2000	Publishes *Transforming Critical Thinking: Constructive Thinking.*
2002	Publishes *Cultural Miseducation: In Search of a Democratic Solution.*
2007	Publishes *Educational Metamorphoses: Reflections on Identity and Culture.*

For more analysis of Martin's thought, see: D. G. Mulcahy, *Knowledge, Gender, and Schooling: The Feminist Educational Thought of Jane Roland Martin* (2002) and *The Educated Person: Toward a New Paradigm for Liberal Education* (2008)

INTRODUCTION

Today it is hard to recapture the feeling of a vast theoretical shift that seemed to be taking place in philosophy, psychology, and education in the 1980s. Carol Gilligan's deceptively slim but monumental *In a Different Voice* published in 1982, suggested that women's ways of knowing might be radically different from men's, that a woman's hierarchy of values might be substantively distinct from a man's, and that previous ways of understanding persons, most notably the psychologist Lawrence Kohlberg's, might be seriously biased in favor of males and against females. Then, in 1984, appeared an equally slim but just as revolutionary work—Jane Roland Martin's *Reclaiming a Conversation.*

In many ways, Martin's work was the educational analogue to the work of art historians of the 1970s whose work, in turn, was precipitated by a deceptively "simple" question, namely, Why are there so few great women artists? Those historians responded in a number of different but related ways. They suggested that there are a number of great women artists but, for various reasons, the art forms they work in are considered "marginal," that is, more decorative than serious, producing pleasing designs rather than high art. They also suggested that many women are not allowed the same sort of access to the art world as men; for example, a woman first would have to meet obligations to family and hearth before she could take up the brush, while her male counterpart could ignore familial obligations. Finally, they suggested that there are a number of serious women painters whose works are largely ignored by the tradition precisely because the artists are women. The art historian's role became then, in large part, recovering those forgotten women artists.

In *Reclaiming a Conversation,* Martin suggests that, historically, women have typically been excluded from the "conversation" that constitutes the history of Western educational thought. There are three aspects to that exclusion. First, there has been very little written about the education of women. Either it was assumed that what was said about the education of men could, with equal justice, be said about the education of women and, hence, there was no real need to speak about the education of women, or it was assumed that issues surrounding the education of women were not as critical as those surrounding the education of men.

Second, what little writing there has been regarding the education of women by the important philosophers has been largely ignored, consigned, in effect, to the margins of their writing. Plato's writing about the education of women has been treated, within the history of philosophy, almost like Aristotle's views on various physical laws— quaint, of antiquarian interest, but hardly at the center of his philosophic discourse.

Finally, when women have written about the education of women, their work has quickly found a place on the edges of scholarship, where it can be safely ignored. By a curious stroke of logic, the argument goes something like this: Important philosophers do not write about the education of women. X wrote about the education of women. X was not an important philosopher and, so, can be safely ignored.

In *Reclaiming a Conversation,* Martin shows that the education of women is truly problematic and that questions regarding the education of women cannot be answered by simply reworking the answers to questions regarding the education of men. She does this, in large part, by unearthing a tradition of inquiry regarding the education of women that stretches back to Plato, leaps ahead to Jean-Jacques Rousseau, especially to his writing about the education of Émile and Sophie, and weaves through the works of Mary Wollstonecraft, Catherine Beecher, and Charlotte Perkins Gilman.

In addition to recovering a tradition of scholarship that was lost and/or trivialized, Martin recalls to mind one of the earliest understandings of the educated person available in the Western tradition. If one looks at the early dialogues of Plato, dialogues like the *Apology,* the *Crito,* and the *Phaedo,* one finds an implicit model of education as one of reasoned discourse, that is, intelligent, decent, well-meaning people, people of good faith, people who trust and like each other, people who might even be called friends, getting together and trying to talk themselves to a reasonable conclusion. They engage in a conversation, learn something from one another and from the conversation itself, and, if the gods smile on them, may even become wise.

For Martin, to be educated is to engage in a conversation that stretches back in time, that enables the student today to converse with previous scholars. In the words of Michael Oakeshott:

> We are all inheritors neither of an inquiry about ourselves and the world nor of an accumulating body of information, but of a conversation begun in the primeval forest and extended and made more articulate in the course of centuries. It is a conversation which goes on both in public and within each of ourselves. Of course there is argument and inquiry and information, but wherever these are profitable they are recognized as passages in this conversation. Education, properly speaking, is an initiation into the skill and partnership of this conversation in which we learn to recognize the voices, to distinguish the proper occasions of utterance, and in which we acquire the intellectual and moral habits appropriate to conversation. And it is this conversation which, in the end, gives place and character to every human activity and utterance.[1]

It does not hurt to underscore the significance of education for both Oakeshott and Martin. Education is not simply something that occurs in a specific building at a given time in one's life. It is not simply training in basic skills or the learning of essential elements. And it is not simply training or preparation for the next stage in one's life. For Martin and Oakeshott, education *is* the development of intellectual and moral habits through the give-and-take of the conversation that ultimately gives "place and character to every human activity and utterance." Education—the conversation—is the place where one comes to learn what it is to be a person.

Cast in that light, the seriousness of Martin's charge is obvious. If the conversation, this discourse stretching back to the primeval forest, is the place in which personhood is defined, to exclude women, or any group for that matter, from the conversation is to deny members of that group the right to become persons. It is to treat them as something less than human.

Finally, if the educational conversation is like more prosaic ones, it will depend for energy and vivacity on a multiplicity of perspectives and a diversity of voices. In ordinary conversations, if we all see things from the same vantage point, if we all look and sound and think alike, eventually the conversation will wind down to where we say

[1]Michael Oakeshott, *Rationalism in Politics and Other Essays* (London: Methuen, 1962), p. 199.

the same old things in the same old ways, where, rather than learning from one another, we simply reaffirm our beliefs. As much as she is talking about who should have a voice in the conversation, Martin is talking about the health of the educational conversation itself.

FROM *RECLAIMING A CONVERSATION: THE IDEAL OF THE EDUCATED WOMAN* (1985)

Contemporary philosophers of education ignore the subject of women. In the technical writings of the academy, as in popular polemical works, questions of gender simply do not arise. These theorists analyze the concept of education, discuss the nature and structure of liberal education, construct theories of teaching and learning, set forth criteria of excellence, and debate educational aims and methods without attending to the difference of sex. It has not always been this way. Plato—perhaps the greatest educational philosopher in the history of Western thought and certainly the first systematic one—wrote specifically about the education of females. So did Jean-Jacques Rousseau, one of the few Western philosophers whose educational thought rivals Plato's both in its depth of understanding and in its far-reaching influence. Indeed, throughout Western history both men and women have taken the subject of women's education sufficiently seriously to have written countless treatises about it.

The question arises, then, why educational theorists in our day take no notice of gender and why feminist theorists, in their turn, pay so little attention to questions of educational philosophy. Studies of sex differences in learning and sex bias in educational practices abound, research in the history of women's education flourishes, discussions of feminist pedagogy are numerous, and debates on the best way to incorporate the study of women into the liberal curriculum are commonplace. An examination of educational ideals, however, is seldom found in contemporary literature on women, and the construction of an adequate philosophy of women's education is rarely seen as relevant to the task of developing a comprehensive feminist theory.[2]

Feminist theory has not always been divorced from educational philosophy. Mary Wollstonecraft's *A Vindication of the Rights of Woman* (1792) is a treatise both on woman's place and on woman's education, and Charlotte Perkins Gilman's utopian novel *Herland* (1915) joins a well-developed theory of education to a feminist social vision. But that women now are receiving an education very much like the one Wollstonecraft urged for her daughters does not mean it is the one women *should* be receiving. Indeed, as Adrienne Rich,

---

[2]I realize that although individual feminist thinkers have tended to neglect questions of educational philosophy, the women's studies movement is directly concerned with just such issues. The extent to which this movement has explored alternative educational *ideals* is a question that requires further investigation.

one of the few contemporary feminists who has written incisively and evocatively on the education of women, has pointed out, that women continue to *receive* an education is itself a matter of concern.

Addressing a group of female college students in 1977, Rich asked them to think of themselves as *claiming* rather than *receiving* an education. The difference between the two verbs is the difference between acting and being acted upon, she said, "and for women it can literally mean the difference between life and death."[3] Why is passivity toward learning a potentially fatal attitude? Rich was not merely echoing the psychologists who tell us that learning must be active if it is to be effective, although she might well accept the validity of the argument. Perceiving the extent to which education can promote or stunt women's growth and development, Rich grounded her thesis on a feminist vision of what women's lives can and should be. She was saying that in becoming mere receptacles for a university learning that excludes their experience and thought, women's lives can be damaged beyond repair.

Rich urged her audience to take charge not just of the manner in which they learn but of the content of their learning: "What you can learn here (and I mean not only at Douglass but any college in any university) is how *men* have perceived and organized their experience, their history, their ideas about social relationships, good and evil, sickness and health, etc. When you read or hear about 'great issues,' 'major texts,' 'the mainstream of Western thought,' you are hearing about what men, above all white men, in their male subjectivity, have decided is important."[4] She might have added that one should not expect to find included among those great issues or in the major texts her topic—the education of women. For although conversation on women's education began centuries before the birth of Christ and has continued into the present time, it has simply been ignored by the standard texts and anthologies in the history of educational thought.[5]

Does it matter that this conversation over time and space is missing? If females today have access to the same education as males—and in the United States to a great extent they do—what difference does it make that historians of educational thought neglect the topic of women, that Plato's, Rousseau's, Wollstonecraft's, and Gilman's discussions of women's education have not been incorporated into the mainstream of Western thought? Does the discovery in educational history of epistemological inequality—by which I mean inequality in knowledge itself: in this instance, in the representation of women in historical narratives and philosophical interpretations—have any practical significance for those who would follow Rich's advice and claim an education for and about themselves?[6]

---

[3]Adrienne Rich, "Claiming an Education," in *On Lies, Secrets and Silence* (New York: W. W. Norton & Co., 1979), p. 231.

[4]Ibid., p. 232.

[5]Jane Roland Martin, "Excluding Women from the Educational Realm," *Harvard Educational Review 52* (1982):133–48.

[6]To say that a discipline such as the history of educational thought has not achieved epistemological equality is to comment on the nature of the knowledge produced by that discipline, not on the nature of practitioners of the discipline and not on, for example, the hiring practices within the profession.

Since the early 1970s research has documented the ways in which such intellectual disciplines as history and psychology, literature and the fine arts, sociology and biology are biased according to sex.[7] This work has revealed that on at least three counts the disciplines fall short of the ideal of epistemological equality for women: they exclude women from their subject matter, distort the female according to the male image of her, and deny value to characteristics the society considers feminine. When a discipline does not meet the standard of epistemological equality, not only women but the tasks and functions society associates with them are denigrated. The problem is compounded when the history of educational thought falls short of this ideal because so many parties to the ongoing conversation about female education are women.

To the extent that the major historical texts overlook Plato's female guardians and Rousseau's Sophie, women's lives and experiences are devalued. When the voices of Wollstonecraft and Gilman are unrecorded, students are denied contact with some of the great female minds of the past; the implicit message is that women have never thought systematically about education, that indeed, they may be incapable of serious philosophical reflection on the topic.

I do not mean to suggest that every female educational theorist has been interested primarily in the education of her own sex. Maria Montessori is a notable example of a woman who developed a philosophy of education without reference to sex or gender. Yet many women have focused on female education. For example, with *A Vindication of the Rights of Woman* Mary Wollstonecraft entered the ongoing conversation by questioning Rousseau's theory of the education of girls and women and presenting one of her own. She, in turn, was influenced by the contribution Catherine Macaulay had made to this conversation in her *Letters on Education* (1790). In numerous books and articles written at a later date in another country, Catharine Beecher set forth a philosophy of the education of girls and women that presents interesting contrasts to Wollstonecraft's. And Beecher's grandniece, Charlotte Perkins Gilman, wove into her utopian novel, *Herland,* her educational philosophy for women.

Although these theorists of female education were well known in their own day, it is likely that until recently even Wollstonecraft's name would have been unfamiliar to historians of educational thought. I am able to cite them here because contemporary research on women is in the process of recovering the lives and works of so many who had been lost to history. Yet even if blame does not attach to the authors of the texts that silence women's voices, the fate of the contributions of Plato and Rousseau suggests that had the writings on female education of Macauley, Wollstonecraft, Beecher, and Gilman been known to exist, they too would have been ignored.

---

[7] This new scholarship on women is too extensive to be cited in its entirety here. For reviews of it, see the journal *Signs*. See also anthologies such as Julia A. Sherman and Evelyn Torton Beck, eds., *The Prism of Sex* (Madison: University of Wisconsin Press, 1979); Elizabeth Langland and Walter Gove, eds., *A Feminist Perspective in the Academy* (Chicago: University of Chicago Press, 1983); Sandra Harding and Merill B. Hintikka, eds., *Discovering Reality* (Dordrecht: D. Reidel Publishing Co., 1983).

The devaluation of women is not the only unhappy consequence of the exclusion from the history of educational thought of all conversation about female education. The noted philosopher of education Israel Scheffler has said that the function of philosophy is to enlighten policy "by pressing its traditional questions of value, virtue, veracity, and validity."[8] These questions need to be pressed in relation to policies concerning the education of girls and women; yet as long as the conversation to which they belong is considered to fall outside the province of philosophy, they cannot be.

In inviting students to take responsibility for their own education, Rich beseeched them to reject those models of feminine weakness, self-denial, and subservience the culture holds up to them:

> Responsibility to yourself means that you don't fall for shallow and easy solutions—predigested books and ideas, weekend encounters guaranteed to change your life, taking 'gut' courses instead of ones you know will challenge you, bluffing at school and life instead of doing solid work, marrying early as an escape from real decisions, getting pregnant as an evasion of already existing problems. It means that you refuse to sell your talents and aspirations short, simply to avoid conflict and confrontation. And this, in turn, means resisting forces in society which say that women should be nice, play safe, have low professional expectations, drown in love and forget about work, live through others, and stay in the places assigned to us.[9]

Every woman has felt the pull of one or more of these negative models. She who is not attracted to the ideal of the self-denying wife and mother may become a woman who denies her intelligence; she who disdains the ideal of silent passivity may find the model of "the slapdash dilettante who never commits herself to anything the whole way" irresistible. Each of us will see mother or daughter, sister or friend, if not oneself, represented on Rich's list. Unfortunately, if a woman does what Rich asks—if she takes responsibility for her own education—she will find herself at a disadvantage. How can a woman avoid shallow solutions to the problems education poses if she never hears what has been said by those who have thought deeply on the subject? How can she know what education to claim if she has never entered into philosophical conversation about this education herself, indeed never even realized that such conversation existed?[10]

Not only women are led astray in this circumstance; men also suffer when they are denied knowledge of the range of educational ideals past

---

[8]Israel Scheffler, "Philosophy of Education: Some Recent Contributions," *Harvard Educational Review 50* (1980):402–06.

[9]Rich, "Claiming an Education," pp. 233–34.

[10]Dale Spender says: "While men take it for granted that they can build on what has gone before, selecting, refining, adapting the knowledge they have inherited to meet their needs, women are constantly required to begin with a blank sheet" (*Invisible Women: The Schooling Scandal* [London: Writers and Readers Publishing Cooperative Society, 1982], p. 17).

philosophers have held up for half the population. In *A Vindication* Wollstonecraft makes clear the disastrous consequences for the man, Emile, of the faulty education Rousseau designs for Sophie. Sophie's case can be generalized. So long as men and women inhabit the same society and live overlapping lives, each sex will be affected by the education of the other. Unenlightened policies of female education will inevitably redound on males.

There is another reason men suffer when past conversation about women's education is ignored. Historians of educational thought are not antiquarians whose sole concern is to preserve the ideas of the past. They justify their inquiries by reference to the insights into contemporary education yielded by a study of past philosophies. "Philosophy, unlike the sciences, never fully outgrows its history," says Scheffler. "The arguments and conceptions of past thinkers retain a fundamental relevance for contemporary philosophy even as it struggles to find new ways for itself."[11] Historical study, then, illuminates educational practice today and guides the development, clarification, and testing of new theories about what education should be.[12]

How much illumination can be shed on the education of boys and men by a historical narrative that ignores girls and women? Philosophers do not construct theories of education in a vacuum. Viewing education as preparation for carrying on societal roles, they tie their proposals to some vision of the good society. And insofar as the society the philosopher pictures is peopled by both sexes, we cannot evaluate the educational ideal it holds up for males unless we know its expectations for females. We will not even know the right questions to ask. Do men and women in the envisioned society have reciprocal roles, with men carrying out the functions of citizenship and women those of domesticity? If so, we must ask not only if the education claimed for males will equip them to be good citizens but also if it will promote or frustrate the efforts of women to perform their own functions effectively. Alternatively, do men and women in this society share roles and the tasks and functions associated with them? If so, we must ask if the full complement of significant social roles is reflected in the education claimed for both men and women.

When history neglects past philosophical conversations about women's education, it follows that the tasks, functions, institutions, and traits of character that philosophy, as a part of our culture, has associated with women are neglected. Discussions about marriage, home, family are missing as are discussions about society's *reproductive* processes—a category I define broadly to include not simply conception and birth but the rearing of children to more or less maturity and associated activities such as tending the sick, taking care of family needs, and running a household.

We look to the history of educational thought for guidance. Because its narrative does not record conversation about female education, it is implied

[11]Israel Scheffler, Preface to *Three Historical Philosophies of Education,* by William E. Frankena (Chicago: Scott, Foresman & Co., 1965).
[12]Paul Nash, *Models of Man* (New York: John Wiley & Sons, 1968), p. vii; Henry J. Perkinson, *Since Socrates: Studies in the History of Western Educational Thought* (New York: Longman, 1980), p. xi.

that the only valid questions about education have to do with its adequacy as preparation for citizenship and the workplace.[13] No one would deny the importance of education for society's *productive* processes—in which category I include political and cultural activities as well as economic ones—but other tasks and functions are just as compelling. In the United States in the late twentieth century, we may reject a sex-based division of labor, but we must not forget that many of the tasks and functions that have traditionally been assigned to women are essential to the existence of society and must be carried on well if we are to have any chance of creating a better world.[14]

The statistics on child abuse and domestic violence in our society today[15] belie the assumption that the knowledge, skills, attitudes, and traits of character necessary for effectively carrying out the reproductive processes of society occur naturally in people. Education for these processes is not only as essential as education for society's productive processes but also has an overarching political, social, and moral significance. Jonathan Schell has said that "the nuclear peril makes all of us, whether we happen to have children of our own or not, the parents of all future generations"; he has called the will to save the human species a form of love resembling "the generative love of parents."[16] A historical narrative that neglects conversation about the education of women has little, if anything, to say about this kind of love and cannot serve either sex well.

Men and women need to claim the best possible education for themselves and their sons and daughters. All must listen to and participate in conversation about the ideals governing the education of both sexes. Only then will we understand that the education most of us receive today is too narrow. Only then can we begin to construct theories of education that give the reproductive as well as the productive processes of society their due, and only then can we press our questions of "value, virtue, veracity, and validity" in relation to the whole range of educational concerns. Is education for rearing children and caring for home and family desirable? If so, for whom? Should this education be placed on a par with citizenship education and become a universal requirement or should it be considered a specialty? If it is a specialty, does it properly belong to vocational or professional education? These are a few of the submerged questions that rise to the surface when conversation about women's education is incorporated into public learning. . . .

[13]Recent reports on American education reflect this same focus. See, for example, Mortimer J. Adler, *The Paideia Proposal* (New York: Macmillan, 1982); Ernest L. Boyer, *High School* (New York: Harper & Row, 1983); John I. Goodlad, *A Place Called School* (New York: McGraw-Hill Book Co., 1984); Theodore R. Sizer, *Horace's Compromise* (Boston: Houghton Mifflin Co., 1984).

[14]For more on the distinction between productive and reproductive societal processes, see Lorenne Clark, "The Rights of Women: The Theory and Practice of the Ideology of Male Supremacy," in *Contemporary Issues in Political Philosophy,* ed. William R. Shea and John King-Farlow (New York: Science History Publications, 1976), pp. 49–65.

[15]For a thorough discussion of these topics, see Wini Breines and Linda Gordon, "The New Scholarship on Family Violence," *Signs 8* (1983):493–507.

[16]Jonathan Schell, *The Fate of the Earth* (New York: Avon, 1982), p. 175.

Educating Our Sons

"What do we want for our sons?" asks Adrienne Rich in *Of Woman Born.* "We want them to remain, in the deepest sense, sons of the mother, yet also to grow into themselves, to discover new ways of being men even as we are discovering new ways of being women."[17] If she could have one wish for her own sons, Rich continues, it is that they should have the courage of women: "I mean by this something very concrete and precise: the courage I have seen in women who, in their private and public lives, both in the interior world of their dreaming, thinking, and creating, and the outer world of patriarchy, are taking greater and greater risks, both psychic and physical, in the evolution of a new vision" (p. 215).

Rich's new vision includes the assimilation of males into a full-time, universal system of child care that would change not only the expectations of both sexes about gender roles but "the entire community's relationship to children." A latter-day Charlotte Perkins Gilman in her insistence that "the mother-child relationship is the essential human relationship" and simultaneously that "the myth that motherhood is 'private and personal' is the deadliest myth we have to destroy,"[18] Rich makes clear the need men will have for "a kind of compensatory education in the things about which their education as males has left them illiterate."[19]

The realm of illiteracy Rich has in mind is populated by the virtues of Sophie and Sarah: a well-developed capacity for sympathetic identification, a denial of the separation between love and work, a desire and an ability to nurture children. One need not adopt Rich's social vision—in which children are no longer "mine" and "thine," the mother-child relationship is placed at the very center of society, and child rearing is a universal responsibility—to agree that in the late twentieth century men should be claiming for themselves an education in Sophie's and Sarah's virtues as well as Emile's. Family living and child rearing are not today, if they ever were, solely in the hands of women. Males and females alike have responsibility for making the reproductive processes of society work well. Thus, men must claim an education that does justice to those processes even as they claim one that gives the productive processes their due.

The reproductive processes are of central importance to any society. It is no small matter, then, to insist that men as well as women be educated to carry them on. It would be a terrible mistake, however, to suppose that in our own society the virtues of Sophie and Sarah have no relevance beyond marriage, home, family, and child rearing. Ours is a country in which one out of four women is raped at some time in her life, one out of four girls and one out of ten boys is sexually abused before the age of eighteen, and some $4–6 billion per year are grossed by the pornography industry.[20] Our country belongs to

---

[17]Adrienne Rich, *Of Woman Born* (New York: Bantam, 1977), p. 210.

[18]Adrienne Rich, "The Contemporary Emergency and the Quantum Leap," in *On Lies, Secrets, and Silence* (New York: Norton, 1979), p. 271.

[19]Rich, *Of Woman Born,* p. 216.

[20]Allen Griswold Johnson, "On the Prevalence of Rape in the United States," *Signs* 6 (1980):136–46; Bernice Lott, Mary Ellen Reilly, and Dale R. Howard, "Sexual Assault and Harassment: A Campus Community Case Study," *Signs* 8 (1982):296–319; Jack Thomas, "Subject: Child Abuse," *Boston Globe,* September 15, 1984, p. 18; "The Pornographic Industry," *Boston Globe,* February 13–18, 1983.

a world on the brink of nuclear and/or ecological disaster. Efforts to overcome these problems, as well as the related ones of poverty, economic scarcity, and racial injustice, flounder today under the direction of people who do not know how to sustain human relationships or respond directly to human needs, indeed, do not even see the value of trying to do so. We should not suppose that education can solve the world's problems. Yet if there is to be any hope of the continuation of life on earth, let alone of a good life for all, those who carry on society's productive processes must acquire the nurturing capacities and ethics of care Rousseau attributes to Sophie's nature.

Unfortunately, easy as it is to say that men's education must take Sophie and Sarah into account, and convincing as it may sound, our Platonic heritage stands between us and this goal. A case study of what almost everyone today would consider American education at its best reveals the extent to which Plato's educational vision persists in our own time and the damage it does.

In his educational autobiography *Hunger of Memory,* Richard Rodriguez tells of growing up in Sacramento, California, the third of four children in a Spanish speaking family.[21] Upon entering first grade he could understand perhaps fifty English words. For half a year he resisted his teachers' demands that he speak English. When asked questions, he mumbled; otherwise he sat waiting for the bell to ring. One Saturday morning three nuns descended upon his house: "Do your children speak only Spanish at home?" they asked his mother. "Is it possible for you and your husband to encourage your children to practice their English when they are at home?" In an instant, Rodriguez's parents agreed, in his words, "to give up the language (the sounds) that had revealed and accentuated our family's closeness." An astounding resolve, but it bore fruit. Within a year Rodriguez was a fluent speaker of English; a short while later he graduated from elementary school with citations galore and entered high school having read hundreds of books; he next attended Stanford University; and, twenty years after the nuns' visit, he sat in the British Museum working on a Ph.D. dissertation in English literature.

Rodriguez, having learned to speak English, went on to acquire a liberal education in history, literature, science, mathematics, philosophy. His is a story of the cultural assimilation of a Mexican-American, but it is more than this, for by no means do all assimilated Americans conform to our image of a well-educated person. Rodriguez does because, to use the terms philosopher R. S. Peters employs in his analysis of the concept of the educated man, he did not simply acquire knowledge and skill.[22] He acquired conceptual schemes to raise his knowledge beyond the level of a collection of disjointed facts and to enable him to understand the reason for things; moreover, the knowledge he acquired is not inert, but characterizes the way he looks at the world and involves the kind of commitment to the standards of evidence and canons of

[21]Richard Rodriguez, *Hunger of Memory: The Education of Richard Rodriguez* (Boston: David B. Godine, 1982).

[22]R. S. Peters, *Ethics and Education* (London: Allen & Unwin, 1966); "Education and the Educated Man" in *A Critique of Current Educational Aims,* ed. R. F. Dearden, P. H. Hirst, and R. S. Peters (London: Routledge & Kegan Paul, 1972).

proof of the various disciplines that comes from "getting on the inside of a form of thought and awareness."

Quite a success story; yet *Hunger of Memory* is notable primarily for being a narrative of loss. In the process of becoming an educated man Rodriguez loses his fluency in Spanish, but that is the least of it. As soon as English becomes the language of the Rodriguez family, the special feeling of closeness at home is diminished. As his days are devoted more and more to understanding the meaning of words, it becomes increasingly difficult for Rodriguez to hear intimate family voices. When it is Spanish-speaking, his home is a noisy, playful, warm, emotionally charged environment; with the advent of English the atmosphere becomes quiet and restrained. There is no acrimony. The family remains loving. But the experience of "feeling individualized" by family members is now rare, and occasions for intimacy are infrequent.

Thus, Rodriguez tells a story of alienation: from his parents, for whom he soon has no names; from the Spanish language, in which he loses his childhood fluency; from his Mexican roots, in which he loses interest; from his own feelings and emotions, which all but disappear in the process of his learning to control them; from his body itself, as he discovers when, after his senior year in college, he takes a construction job.

John Dewey spent his life trying to combat the tendency of educators to divorce mind from body and reason from emotion. Rodriguez's educational autobiography documents these divorces and another that Dewey deplored, that of self from other. *Hunger of Memory,* above all, depicts a journey from intimacy to isolation. Close ties with family members are dissolved as public anonymity replaces private attention. Rodriguez becomes a spectator in his own home as noise gives way to silence and connection to distance. School, says Rodriguez, bade him trust "lonely" reason primarily. And there is enough time and "silence," he adds, "to think about ideas (big ideas)."

What is the significance of this narrative of loss for those who want to claim the best possible education for their sons? Not every American has Rodriguez's good fortune of being born into a loving home filled with the warm sounds of intimacy; yet the separation and distance he ultimately experienced are by no means unique to him. On the contrary, they represent the natural end point of the educational journey Rodriguez took.

Dewey repeatedly pointed out that the distinction educators draw between liberal and vocational education represents a separation of mind from body, head from hand, thought from action. Since we define an educated person as one who has profited from a liberal education, these splits are built into our ideal of the educated person. Since most definitions of excellence in education derive from that ideal, these splits are built into them as well. A split between reason and emotion is built into our definitions of excellence, too, for we take the aim of a liberal education to be the development not of mind as a whole but of rational mind. We define this in terms of the acquisition of knowledge and understanding, construed very narrowly. It is not surprising that Rodriguez acquires habits of quiet reflection rather than noisy activity, reasoned deliberation rather than spontaneous reaction, dispassionate inquiry rather than emotional response, abstract analytic theorizing rather than concrete storytelling. These are integral to our ideal of the educated person, an ideal familiar to readers of the *Republic*.

Upon completion of his educational journey Rodriguez bears an uncanny resemblance to the guardians of the Just State. Granted, not one of Plato's guardians will be the "disembodied mind" Rodriguez says he became. Yet Plato designs for his guardians an education of heads, not hands. (Presumably the artisans of the Just State will serve as their hands.) Furthermore, holding up for the guardians an ideal of self-discipline and self-government he emphasizes inner harmony at the expense of outward connection. If his guardians do not begin their lives in intimacy, as Rodriguez did, their education, like his, is intended to confirm in them a sense of self in isolation from others.

Do the separations bequeathed to us by Plato matter? The great irony of the liberal education that comes down to us from Plato and still today is the mark of an educated man or woman is that it is neither tolerant nor generous. As Richard Rodriguez discovered, there is no place in it for education of the body, and since most action involves bodily movement, this means there is little room in it for education of action. Nor is there room for education of other-regarding feelings and emotions. The liberally educated man or woman will be provided with knowledge about others but will not be taught to care about their welfare or to act kindly toward them. That person will be given some understanding of society, but will not be taught to feel its injustices or even to be concerned over its fate. The liberally educated person will be an ivory-tower person—one who can reason but has no desire to solve real problems in the real world—or a technical person—one who likes to solve real problems but does not care about the solutions' consequences for real people and for the earth itself.

The case of Rodriguez illuminates several unhappy aspects of our Platonic heritage while concealing another. No one who has seen Fred Wiseman's film *High School* can forget the woman who reads to the assembled students a letter she has received from a pupil in Vietnam. But for a few teachers who cared, she tells her audience, Bob Walters, a subaverage student academically, "might have been a nobody." Instead, while awaiting a plane that is to drop him behind the DMZ, he has written her to say that he has made the school the beneficiary of his life insurance policy. "I am a little jittery right now," she reads. She is not to worry about him, however, because "I am only a body doing a job." Measuring his worth as a human being by his monetary provision for the school, she overlooks the fact that Bob Walters was not merely participating in a war of dubious morality but was taking pride in being an automaton.

High School was made in 1968, but Bob Walters's words were echoed many times over by eighteen- and nineteen-year-old Marine recruits in the days immediately following the Grenada invasion. Readers of *Hunger of Memory* will not be surprised. The underside of a liberal education devoted to the development of "disembodied minds" is a vocational education whose business is the production of "mindless bodies." In Plato's Just State, where, because of their rational powers, the specially educated few will rule the many, a young man's image of himself as "only a body doing a job" is desirable. That the educational theory and practice of a democracy derives from Plato's explicitly undemocratic philosophical vision is disturbing. We are not supposed to have two classes of people, those who think and those who do not. We are not supposed to have two kinds of people, those who rule and those who obey.

The Council for Basic Education has long recommended and some people concerned with excellence in education now suggest that a liberal education at least through high school be extended to all.[23] For the sake of argument, let us suppose that this program can be carried out without making more acute the inequities it is meant to erase. We would then presumably have a world in which no one thinks of him- or herself as simply a body doing a job. We would, however, have a world filled with unconnected, uncaring, emotionally impoverished people. Even if it were egalitarian, it would be a sorry place in which to live. Nor would the world be better if somehow we combined Rodriguez's liberal education with a vocational one. For assuming our world were then peopled by individuals who joined "head" and "hand," reason would still be divorced from feeling and emotion, and each individual cut off from others.

The Platonic divorce of reason from feeling and emotion and of self from other is built into our prevailing theories of liberal and vocational education as well as into our very definition of the function of education. For Rodriguez, the English language was a metaphor. In the literal sense of the term he had to learn English to become an educated *American,* yet in his narrative the learning of English represents the acquisition not so much of a new natural language as of new ways of thinking, acting, and being, which he associates with the public world. Rodriguez makes it clear that the transition from Spanish to English for him represented the transition almost every child in our society makes from the "private world" of home to the "public world" of business, politics, and culture. He realizes that Spanish is not intrinsically a private language and English a public one, although his own experience made it seem this way. He knows that the larger significance of his story lies in the fact that whether English is one's first or second language, education inducts one into new activities and processes. His autobiography thus reveals that it is not just historians of educational thought and philosophers who define education as preparation solely for carrying on the productive processes of society.

Needless to say, the liberal education Rodriguez received did not fit him to carry on *all* productive processes of society. Aiming as it did at the development of a rational mind, his liberal education prepared him to be a consumer and creator of ideas, not an auto mechanic or factory worker. A vocational education—had he received one—would have prepared him to work with his hands and use procedures designed by others. Very different

---

[23]See, for example, Mortimer J. Adler, *The Paideia Proposal* (New York: Macmillan Co., 1982); Ernest J. Boyer, *High School* (New York: Harper & Row, 1983).

kinds of education, yet both kinds are designed to fit students to carry on productive, not reproductive, societal processes.[24]

Rodriguez's perception that the function of education is to induct us into the public world and its productive processes is of great consequence. Yet although this function harks back to Plato and constitutes an implicit presupposition of almost all educational thought in our own time, it has never been explicitly acknowledged and so its implications have not been traced. *Hunger of Memory* contains a wonderful account of Rodriguez's grandmother taking him to her room and telling him stories of her life. He is moved by the sounds she makes and by the message of intimacy her person transmits. The words themselves are not important to him, for, as he makes clear, he perceives the private world in which she moves—the world of child rearing and homemaking—to be one of feeling and emotion, intimacy and connection, and hence a realm of the nonrational. In contrast, he sees the public world—the world of productive processes for which his education fit him—as the realm of the rational. Feeling and emotion have no place in it, and neither do intimacy and connection. Instead, analysis, critical thinking, and self-sufficiency are the dominant values.

Rodriguez's assumption that feeling and emotion, intimacy and connection are naturally related to the home and society's reproductive processes and that these qualities are irrelevant to carrying on the productive processes is commonly accepted. But then, it is to be expected that their development is ignored by education in general and by liberal education in particular. Since education is supposed to equip people for carrying on productive societal processes, from a practical standpoint would it not be foolhardy for liberal *or* vocational studies to foster these traits?

Only in light of the fact that education turns its back on the reproductive processes of society and the private world of the home can Rodriguez's story of alienation be properly understood. His alienation from his body will reoccur as long as we equate being an educated person with having a liberal education. His journey of isolation and divorce from his emotions will be repeated as long as we define education exclusively in relation to the productive processes of society. But the assumption of inevitability underlying *Hunger of Memory* is mistaken. Education need not separate mind from body and thought from action, for it need not draw a sharp line between liberal and vocational education. More to the point, it need not separate reason from emotion and self from other. The reproductive processes *can* be brought into the educational realm, thereby overriding the theoretical and practical grounds for ignoring feeling and emotion, intimacy and connection.

If we define education in relation to *both* kinds of societal processes and then act upon our redefinition, future generations will not have to experience Rodriguez's pain. The dichotomies upon which his education rested—and

---

[24]Home economics is the exception to this generalization. However, the chances that Rodriguez would have studied this subject are slight.

which he never questions—must be questioned if we want our sons to be educated well. We must recognize, however, that to challenge the productive/reproductive dichotomy is to call for a basic rethinking of education.

From *Reclaiming a Conversation: The Ideal of the Educated Woman* by Jane Roland Martin (New Haven, CT: Yale University Press, © 1985 by Jane Roland Martin), pp. 1–7, 178–199. Reprinted by permission of Yale University Press.

Questions

1. What does Jane Roland Martin mean by suggesting that education should be viewed as a sort of "conversation"?
2. Do you think the kinds of conversation Socrates engaged his students in would have been different if the students were girls? If they had included girls? If Socrates had been a woman?
3. What is a separate-strand approach to the history of educational thought, and why, according to Martin, is it self-defeating?
4. What does Martin mean by a gender-sensitive ideal of education?
5. How is *gender-sensitive* different from *gender-biased?*
6. What does it mean, in terms of education, for a person or a group to be marginal?

13

Paulo Freire

Time Line for Freire

1921	Is born in Recife, Brazil.
1959	Receives Ph.D. from University of Recife.
	Is named professor of philosophy and education.
1962	Is named director of the university's Cultural Extension Service.
	Begins a literacy program for peasants and workers.
1964	Is arrested and imprisoned (for seventy days). He is then forced into exile with his wife, Elza, and their five children.
	Travels from Brazil to Bolivia to Chile to Massachusetts and then to Switzerland.
1970	Works for the World Council of Churches in Geneva.
1972	Publishes *Pedagogy of the Oppressed*.
1974	Publishes *Education for Critical Consciousness*.
1976	Publishes *Educational Practice of Freedom*.
1980	Returns with his family to Brazil.
1985	Is appointed minister of education, Rio de Janeiro.
1986	Receives the UNESCO Prize for Education award.
1994	Publishes *Pedagogy of Hope*.
1996	Publishes *Letters to Cristina*.
1997	Publishes *Pedagogy of the Heart*.
	Dies of heart failure in Brazil
1997	Publishes *Teachers as Cultural Workers*.

INTRODUCTION

It can be said of Paulo Freire that he practices what he preaches. Freire offers us a utopian vision of what life should be and articulates a progressive pedagogy for attaining this desired goal. Though utopian, his democratic vision is grounded in the poverty and oppression that characterized his native area of Recife, Brazil. As Richard

Shaull suggests in his foreword to *Pedagogy of the Oppressed,* "Freire's thought represents the response of a creative mind and sensitive conscience to the extraordinary misery and suffering of the oppressed around him."[1] Living in abject poverty as a child, Freire experienced and understood what he later named the "culture of silence" that characterizes the dispossessed. Victimized by the economic, social, and political paternalism of the dominant classes, the poor and dispossessed are not equipped, suggests Freire, to respond to the world's realities in a critical fashion. According to Freire, the dominant classes devised an educational system for the purpose of keeping the masses "submerged" and contained in a "culture of silence."

Perhaps because he shared the plight of the "wretched of the earth"—his family lost its middle-class status during the worldwide depression of the 1930s—Freire realized that the "culture of silence" could and should be overcome. Aware that the extant educational system fostered and sustained this culture of silence, Freire retained his faith in the power of a genuine education to enable and empower even the most wretched to first recognize their oppressed condition and then participate in its transformation. To assist those submerged in this culture of silence, Freire combined theory and practice into what is best known as a "pedagogy of the oppressed." It is important to note that this pedagogy did not emerge full-blown out of the mind of Freire but evolved as he worked with the dispossessed of his own country. In developing a pedagogy that centers on dialogue, that is, "the encounter between men, mediated by the world, in order to name the world," Freire remained true to his basic beliefs that all human beings merit our respect and are capable of understanding and transforming the world of which they are a part.

Experiencing firsthand the hunger and poverty that characterized Recife during the 1930s, Freire fell behind in school and was thought by some to be mentally retarded. Though he suffered no serious or permanent damage from his malnourishment, the experience affected him greatly. While still an adolescent, Freire devoted himself to working among the poor to assist them in improving their lot in life. This led to the study of law and to working as a labor union lawyer "among the people of the slums." In trying to help the poor understand their legal rights, Freire became involved in adult literacy programs during the late 1940s. Working with such programs for more than a decade, Freire rejected traditional methods of instruction, finding them much too authoritarian to be effective in teaching adults to read.

As he began doctoral study at the University of Recife, Freire read and made use of the insights of such great minds as "Sartre and Mounier, Eric Fromm and Lois Althusser, Ortega y Gassett and Mao, Martin Luther King and Che Guevara, Unamuno and Marcuse,"[2] but his educational philosophy remained grounded in these experiences of working with the dispossessed of Brazil. Though he first articulated his philosophy of education in his doctoral dissertation, Freire continued to advocate for a "problem-posing" approach to teaching as a member of the faculty of the University of Recife and of Harvard University.

In contrast to the "banking" method of education—where one privileged to know the truth deposits it in the appropriate amount and form into the empty and limited

---

[1]Paulo Freire, *Pedagogy of the Oppressed* (New York: the Seabury Press, 1972) p.10.
[2]Ibid., p. 11.

minds of the unwashed or dispossessed—Freire advocates an education or pedagogy that enhances and expands every human being's ability to understand and transform the world of which she or he is a part. For example, in teaching Brazilian peasants to read, Freire did not lecture to them. Instead, by beginning with a concept or concepts with which they were already familiar, Freire helped the peasants understand that they too were makers of culture and that they could contribute to the transformation of their own reality.

Beginning with a series of pictures "designed to demonstrate the fundamental differences between *nature* (the natural world) and *culture* (all that is created or transformed by men and women),"[3] Freire was able to assist illiterates in developing rudimentary literacy skills within thirty hours. As the peasants begin to learn the symbols for the words that name concepts familiar to them, their view of their world gradually expands. Through this process they begin to understand that "their world is not fixed and immutable," but is a reality in process that can be transformed.

Clearly, Freire's "pedagogy of the oppressed" is more than just literacy training. It is nothing less than a liberating process that enables and empowers each human being to achieve humankind's ontological vocation, that is, "to be a Subject who acts upon and transforms his world. . . ."[4] As human beings regain the right to rename their worlds, individually and collectively, they consciously engage in the uniquely human activity of constructing and reconstructing their own worlds.

Though Freire's ideas are grounded in the poverty and oppression of his earlier years, the utility of his approach transcends national, class, and ethnic boundaries. According to Freire, the transforming power of words enables all of us to live fuller, more humane lives. As Peter J. Caulfield explains, "words," for Freire, "have meaning only in relation to their effect on human beings and the world in which we live." For example, the word *Chernobyl* connotes much more than merely a geographic location in what was once the Soviet Union. Many of us probably correctly associate the word with the worst nuclear accident in human history, but to appreciate the richness of such a statement, its many layers of meaning need to be connected to each person's personal reality. In short, for those who relate it to the dropping of atomic bombs during World War II and to the effects of radiation exposure produced by continued testing of nuclear weapons during the 1950s and 1960s, *Chernobyl* connotes more than it does for today's youth whose knowledge is limited to textbook accounts of the disaster. From Freire's point of view, it is the educator's task to assist individuals in expanding the connection between concepts or issues of importance to them to a larger evolving reality. As Caulfield suggests:

> In order for students to comprehend truly the meaning of Chernobyl, they would probably need to discuss among themselves (with the teacher's help) the effects of radiation on neighboring grasses, vegetables, animals, and people, perhaps through generations. Indeed, how could they grasp the threat suggested by Chernobyl unless they researched Hiroshima and Nagasaki; they

[3]Peter J. Caulfield, "From Brazil to Buncombe County: Freire and Posing Problems," *Educational Forum* 55:4(Summer 1991), p. 312.
[4]Freire, *Pedagogy of the Oppressed*, p. 12

might also inquire into the long-term effects of radiation exposure to Americans living near atomic testing sites in Nevada in the 1950s. Only then would students begin to comprehend the significance of a statement like "Chernobyl was the site of the first serious nuclear accident."[5]

Such a progressive approach to pedagogy is a far cry from the "banking" education so prevalent in educational institutions throughout the world. In the selection that follows, Freire, in addition to critiquing such traditional pedagogies, explains his "problem-posing" approach to education.

FROM *PEDAGOGY OF THE OPPRESSED* (1972)

A careful analysis of the teacher-student relationship at any level, inside or outside the school, reveals its fundamentally *narrative* character. This relationship involves a narrating Subject (the teacher) and patient, listening objects (the students). The contents, whether values or empirical dimensions of reality, tend in the process of being narrated to become lifeless and petrified. Education is suffering from narration sickness.

The teacher talks about reality as if it were motionless, static, compartmentalized, and predictable. Or else he expounds on a topic completely alien to the existential experience of the students. His task is to "fill" the students with the contents of his narration—contents which are detached from reality, disconnected from the totality that engendered them and could give them significance. Words are emptied of their concreteness and become a hollow, alienated, and alienating verbosity.

The outstanding characteristic of this narrative education, then, is the sonority of words, not their transforming power. "Four times four is sixteen; the capital of Pará is Belém." The student records, memorizes, and repeats these phrases without perceiving what four times four really means, or realizing the true significance of "capital" in the affirmation "the capital of Pará is Belém," that is, what Belém means for Pará and what Pará means for Brazil.

Narration (with the teacher as narrator) leads the students to memorize mechanically the narrated content. Worse yet, it turns them into "containers," into "receptacles" to be "filled" by the teacher. The more completely he fills the receptacles, the better a teacher he is. The more meekly the receptacles permit themselves to be filled, the better students they are.

Education thus becomes an act of depositing, in which the students are the depositories and the teacher is the depositor. Instead of communicating, the teacher issues communiqués and makes deposits which the students patiently receive, memorize, and repeat. This is the "banking" concept of education, in which the scope of action allowed to the students extends only as far as receiving, filing, and storing the deposits. They do, it is true, have the opportunity to become collectors or cataloguers of the things they store. But in the last analysis, it is men themselves who are filed away through the lack

[5]Caulfield, "From Brazil to Buncombe County," pp. 309–310

of creativity, transformation, and knowledge in this (at best) misguided system. For apart from inquiry, apart from the praxis, men cannot be truly human. Knowledge emerges only through invention and re-invention, through the restless, impatient, continuing, hopeful inquiry men pursue in the world, with the world, and with each other.

In the banking concept of education, knowledge is a gift bestowed by those who consider themselves knowledgeable upon those whom they consider to know nothing. Projecting an absolute ignorance onto others, a characteristic of the ideology of oppression, negates education and knowledge as processes of inquiry. The teacher presents himself to his students as their necessary opposite; by considering their ignorance absolute, he justifies his own existence. The students, alienated like the slave in the Hegelian dialectic, accept their ignorance as justifying the teacher's existence—but, unlike the slave, they never discover that they educate the teacher.

The *raison d'être* of libertarian education, on the other hand, lies in its drive towards reconciliation. Education must begin with the solution of the teacher-student contradiction, by reconciling the poles of the contradiction so that both are simultaneously teachers *and* students.

This solution is not (nor can it be) found in the banking concept. On the contrary, banking education maintains and even stimulates the contradiction through the following attitudes and practices, which mirror oppressive society as a whole:

a. the teacher teaches and the students are taught;

b. the teacher knows everything and the students know nothing;

c. the teacher thinks and the students are thought about;

d. the teacher talks and the students listen—meekly;

e. the teacher disciplines and the students are disciplined;

f. the teacher chooses and enforces his choice, and the students comply;

g. the teacher acts and the students have the illusion of acting through the action of the teacher;

h. the teacher chooses the program content, and the students (who were not consulted) adapt to it;

i. the teacher confuses the authority of knowledge with his own professional authority, which he sets in opposition to the freedom of the students;

j. the teacher is the Subject of the learning process, while the pupils are mere objects.

It is not surprising that the banking concept of education regards men as adaptable, manageable beings. The more students work at storing the deposits entrusted to them, the less they develop the critical consciousness which would result from their intervention in the world as transformers of that world. The more completely they accept the passive role imposed on them, the more they tend simply to adapt to the world as it is and to the fragmented view of reality deposited in them.

The capability of banking education to minimize or annul the students' creative power and to stimulate their credulity serves the interests of the oppressors, who care neither to have the world revealed nor to see it transformed. The oppressors use their "humanitarianism" to preserve a profitable situation. Thus they react almost instinctively against any experiment in education which stimulates the critical faculties and is not content with a partial view of reality but always seeks out the ties which link one point to another and one problem to another.

Indeed, the interests of the oppressors lie in "changing the consciousness of the oppressed, not the situation which oppresses them"[6] for the more the oppressed can be led to adapt to that situation, the more easily they can be dominated. To achieve this end, the oppressors use the banking concept of education in conjunction with a paternalistic social action apparatus, within which the oppressed receive the euphemistic title of "welfare recipients." They are treated as individual cases, as marginal men who deviate from the general configuration of a "good, organized, and just" society. The oppressed are regarded as the pathology of the healthy society, which must therefore adjust these "incompetent and lazy" folk to its own patterns by changing their mentality. These marginals need to be "integrated," "incorporated" into the healthy society that they have "forsaken."

The truth is, however, that the oppressed are not "marginals," are not men living "outside" society. They have always been "inside"—inside the structure which made them "beings for others." The solution is not to "integrate" them into the structure of oppression, but to transform that structure so that they can become "beings for themselves." Such transformation, of course, would undermine the oppressors' purposes; hence their utilization of the banking concept of education to avoid the threat of student *conscientização*.

The banking approach to adult education, for example, will never propose to students that they critically consider reality. It will deal instead with such vital questions as whether Roger gave green grass to the goat, and insist upon the importance of learning that, on the contrary, *R*oger gave green grass to the *r*abbit. The "humanism" of the banking approach masks the effort to turn men into automatons—the very negation of their ontological vocation to be more fully human.

Those who use the banking approach, knowingly or unknowingly (for there are innumerable well-intentioned bank-clerk teachers who do not realize that they are serving only to dehumanize), fail to perceive that the deposits themselves contain contradictions about reality. But, sooner or later, these contradictions may lead formerly passive students to turn against their domestication and the attempt to domesticate reality. They may discover through existential experience that their present way of life is irreconcilable with their vocation to become fully human. They may perceive through their relations with reality that reality is really a *process,* undergoing constant transformation. If men are searchers and their ontological vocation is humanization, sooner or later they may perceive the contradiction in which banking education seeks to maintain them, and then engage themselves in the struggle for their liberation.

[6]Simone de Beauvoir, *La Pensée de Droite, Aujord'hui* (Paris); ST, *El Pensamiento político de la Derecha* (Buenos Aires, 1963), p. 34.

But the humanist, revolutionary educator cannot wait for this possibility to materialize. From the outset, his efforts must coincide with those of the students to engage in critical thinking and the quest for mutual humanization. His efforts must be imbued with a profound trust in men and their creative power. To achieve this, he must be a partner of the students in his relations with them.

The banking concept does not admit to such partnership—and necessarily so. To resolve the teacher-student contradiction, to exchange the role of depositor, prescriber, domesticator, for the role of student among students would be to undermine the power of oppression and serve the cause of liberation.

Implicit in the banking concept is the assumption of a dichotomy between man and the world: man is merely *in* the world, not *with* the world or with others; man is spectator, not re-creator. In this view, man is not a conscious being *(corpo consciente);* he is rather the possessor of *a* consciousness: an empty "mind" passively open to the reception of deposits of reality from the world outside. For example, my desk, my books, my coffee cup, all the objects before me—as bits of the world which surrounds me—would be "inside" me, exactly as I am inside my study right now. This view makes no distinction between being accessible to consciousness and entering consciousness. The distinction, however, is essential: the objects which surround me are simply accessible to my consciousness, not located within it. I am aware of them, but they are not inside me.

It follows logically from the banking notion of consciousness that the educator's role is to regulate the way the world "enters into" the students. His task is to organize a process which already occurs spontaneously, to "fill" the students by making deposits of information which he considers to constitute true knowledge.[7] And since men "receive" the world as passive entities, education should make them more passive still, and adapt them to the world. The educated man is the adapted man, because he is better "fit" for the world. Translated into practice, this concept is well suited to the purposes of the oppressors, whose tranquility rests on how well men fit the world the oppressors have created, and how little they question it.

The more completely the majority adapt to the purposes which the dominant minority prescribe for them (thereby depriving them of the right to their own purposes), the more easily the minority can continue to prescribe. The theory and practice of banking education serve this end quite efficiently. Verbalistic lessons, reading requirements,[8] the methods for evaluating "knowledge," the distance between the teacher and the taught, the criteria for promotion: everything in this ready-to-wear approach serves to obviate thinking.

---

[7]This concept corresponds to what Sartre calls the "digestive" or "nutritive" concept of education, in which knowledge is "fed" by the teacher to the students to "fill them out." See Jean-Paul Sartre, "Une idée fundamentale de la phénoménologie de Husserl: L'intentionalité," *Situations I* (Paris, 1947).

[8]For example, some professors specify in their reading lists that a book should be read from pages 10 to 15—and do this to "help" their students!

The bank-clerk educator does not realize that there is no true security in his hypertrophied role, that one must seek to live *with* others in solidarity. One cannot impose oneself, nor even merely co-exist with one's students. Solidarity requires true communication, and the concept by which such an educator is guided fears and proscribes communication.

Yet only through communication can human life hold meaning. The teacher's thinking is authenticated only by the authenticity of the students' thinking. The teacher cannot think for his students, nor can he impose his thought on them. Authentic thinking, thinking that is concerned about *reality*, does not take place in ivory tower isolation, but only in communication. If it is true that thought has meaning only when generated by action upon the world, the subordination of students to teachers becomes impossible.

Because banking education begins with a false understanding of men as objects, it cannot promote the development of what Fromm calls "biophily," but instead produces its opposite: "necrophily."

> While life is characterized by growth in a structured, functional manner, the necrophilous person loves all that does not grow, all that is mechanical. The necrophilous person is driven by the desire to transform the organic into the inorganic, to approach life mechanically, as if all living persons were things. . . . Memory, rather than experience; having, rather than being, is what counts. The necrophilous person can relate to an object—a flower or a person—only if he possesses it; hence a threat to his possession is a threat to himself; if he loses possession he loses contact with the world. . . . He loves control, and in the act of controlling he kills life.[9]

Oppression—overwhelming control—is necrophilic; it is nourished by love of death, not life. The banking concept of education, which serves the interests of oppression, is also necrophilic. Based on a mechanistic, static, naturalistic, spatialized view of consciousness, it transforms students into receiving objects. It attempts to control thinking and action, leads men to adjust to the world, and inhibits their creative power.

When their efforts to act responsibly are frustrated, when they find themselves unable to use their faculties, men suffer. "This suffering due to impotence is rooted in the very fact that the human equilibrium has been disturbed."[10] But the inability to act which causes men's anguish also causes them to reject their impotence, by attempting

> . . . to restore [their] capacity to act. But can [they], and how? One way is to submit to and identify with a person or group having power. By this symbolic participation in another person's life, [men have] the illusion of acting, when in reality [they] only submit to and become a part of those who act.[11]

[9]Eric Fromm, *The Heart of Man* (New York 1966), p. 41.
[10]Ibid., p. 31.
[11]Ibid.

Populist manifestations perhaps best exemplify this type of behavior by the oppressed, who, by identifying with charismatic leaders, come to feel that they themselves are active and effective. The rebellion they express as they emerge in the historical process is motivated by that desire to act effectively. The dominant elites consider the remedy to be more domination and repression, carried out in the name of freedom, order, and social peace (that is, the peace of the elites). Thus they can condemn—logically, from their point of view—"the violence of a strike by workers and [can] call upon the state in the same breath to use violence in putting down the strike."[12]

Education as the exercise of domination stimulates the credulity of students, with the ideological intent (often not perceived by educators) of indoctrinating them to adapt to the world of oppression. This accusation is not made in the naïve hope that the dominant elites will thereby simply abandon the practice. Its objective is to call the attention of true humanists to the fact that they cannot use banking educational methods in the pursuit of liberation, for they would only negate that very pursuit. Nor may a revolutionary society inherit these methods from an oppressor society. The revolutionary society which practices banking education is either misguided or mistrusting of men. In either event, it is threatened by the specter of reaction.

Unfortunately, those who espouse the cause of liberation are themselves surrounded and influenced by the climate which generates the banking concept, and often do not perceive its true significance or its dehumanizing power. Paradoxically, then, they utilize this same instrument of alienation in what they consider an effort to liberate. Indeed, some "revolutionaries" brand as "innocents," "dreamers," or even "reactionaries" those who would challenge this educational practice. But one does not liberate men by alienating them. Authentic liberation—the process of humanization—is not another deposit to be made in men. Liberation is a praxis: the action and reflection of men upon their world in order to transform it. Those truly committed to the cause of liberation can accept neither the mechanistic concept of consciousness as an empty vessel to be filled, nor the use of banking methods of domination (propaganda, slogans—deposits) in the name of liberation.

Those truly committed to liberation must reject the banking concept in its entirety, adopting instead a concept of men as conscious beings, and consciousness as consciousness intent upon the world. They must abandon the educational goal of deposit-making and replace it with the posing of the problems of men in their relations with the world. "Problem-posing" education, responding to the essence of consciousness—*intentionality*—rejects communiqués and embodies communication. It epitomizes the special characteristic of consciousness: being *conscious of,* not only as intent on objects but as turned in upon itself in a Jasperian "split"—consciousness as consciousness *of* consciousness.

Liberating education consists in acts of cognition, not transferrals of information. It is a learning situation in which the cognizable object (far from being the end of the cognitive act) intermediates the cognitive actors—teacher

[12]Reinhold Niebuhr, *Moral Man and Immoral Society* (New York, 1960), p. 130.

on the one hand and students on the other. Accordingly, the practice of problem-posing education entails at the outset that the teacher-student contradiction be resolved. Dialogical relations—indispensable to the capacity of cognitive actors to cooperate in perceiving the same cognizable object—are otherwise impossible.

Indeed, problem-posing education, which breaks with the vertical patterns characteristic of banking education, can fulfill its function as the practice of freedom only if it can overcome the above contradiction. Through dialogue, the teacher-of-the-students and the students-of-the-teacher cease to exist and a new term emerges: teacher-student with students-teachers. The teacher is no longer merely the-one-who-teaches, but one who is himself taught in dialogue with the students, who in turn while being taught also teach. They become jointly responsible for a process in which all grow. In this process, arguments based on "authority" are no longer valid; in order to function, authority must be *on the side of* freedom, not *against* it. Here, no one teaches another, nor is anyone self-taught. Men teach each other, mediated by the world, by the cognizable objects which in banking education are "owned" by the teacher.

The banking concept (with its tendency to dichotomize everything) distinguishes two stages in the action of the educator. During the first, he cognizes a cognizable object while he prepares his lessons in his study or his laboratory; during the second, he expounds to his students about that object. The students are not called upon to know, but to memorize the contents narrated by the teacher. Nor do the students practice any act of cognition, since the object towards which that act should be directed is the property of the teacher rather than a medium evoking the critical reflection of both teacher and students. Hence in the name of the "preservation of culture and knowledge" we have a system which achieves neither true knowledge nor true culture.

The problem-posing method does not dichotomize the activity of the teacher-student: he is not "cognitive" at one point and "narrative" at another. He is always "cognitive," whether preparing a project or engaging in dialogue with the students. He does not regard cognizable objects as his private property, but as the object of reflection by himself and the students. In this way, the problem-posing educator constantly re-forms his reflections in the reflection of the students. The students—no longer docile listeners—are now critical co-investigators in dialogue with the teacher. The teacher presents the material to the students for their consideration, and reconsiders his earlier considerations as the students express their own. The role of the problem-posing educator is to create, together with the students, the conditions under which knowledge at the level of the *doxa* is superseded by the true knowledge, at the level of the *logos*.

Whereas banking education anesthetizes and inhibits creative power, problem-posing education involves a constant unveiling of reality. The former attempts to maintain the *submersion* of consciousness; the latter strives for the *emergence* of consciousness and *critical intervention* in reality.

Students, as they are increasingly posed with problems relating to themselves in the world and with the world, will feel increasingly challenged and obliged to respond to that challenge. Because they apprehend the challenge as interrelated to other problems within a total context, not as a theoretical question, the resulting comprehension tends to be increasingly critical and thus constantly less alienated. Their response to the challenge evokes new challenges, followed by new understandings; and gradually the students come to regard themselves as committed.

Education as the practice of freedom—as opposed to education as the practice of domination—denies that man is abstract, isolated, independent, and unattached to the world; it also denies that the world exists as a reality apart from men. Authentic reflection considers neither abstract man nor the world without men, but men in their relations with the world. In these relations consciousness and world are simultaneous; consciousness neither precedes the world nor follows it.

La conscience et le monde sont dormés d'un même coup: extérieur par essence à la conscience, le monde est, par essence relatif à elle.[13]

In one of our culture circles in Chile, the group was discussing . . . the anthropological concept of culture. In the midst of the discussion, a peasant who by banking standards was completely ignorant said: "Now I see that without man there is no world." When the educator responded: "Let's say, for the sake of argument, that all the men on earth were to die, but that the earth itself remained, together with trees, birds, animals, rivers, seas, the stars . . . wouldn't all this be a world?" "Oh no," the peasant replied emphatically. "There would be no one to say: 'This is a world.'"

The peasant wished to express the idea that there would be lacking the consciousness of the world which necessarily implies the world of consciousness. *I* cannot exist without a *not-I*. In turn, the *not-I* depends on that existence. The world which brings consciousness into existence becomes the world *of* that consciousness. Hence, the previously cited affirmation of Sartre: *"La conscience et le monde sont dormés d'un même coup."*

As men, simultaneously reflecting on themselves and on the world, increase the scope of their perception, they begin to direct their observations towards previously inconspicuous phenomena:

In perception properly so-called, as an explicit awareness [*Gewahren*], I am turned towards the object, to the paper, for instance. I apprehend it as being this here and now. The apprehension is a singling out, every object having a background in experience. Around and about the paper lie books, pencils, ink-well, and so forth, and these in a certain sense are also "perceived," perceptually there, in the "field of intuition" but whilst I was turned towards the paper there was no turning in their direction, nor any apprehending of them, not even in a secondary sense. They appeared

---

[13]Sartre, *Une idée fundamentale,* p. 32.

and yet were not singled out, were not posited on their own account. Every perception of a thing has such a zone of background intuitions or background awareness, if "intuiting" already includes the state of being turned towards, and this also is "conscious experience," or more briefly a "consciousness of" all indeed that in point of fact lies in the co-perceived objective background.[14]

That which had existed objectively but had not been perceived in its deeper implications (if indeed it was perceived at all) begins to "stand out," assuming the character of a problem and therefore of challenge. Thus, men begin to single out elements from their "background awarenesses" and to reflect upon them. These elements are now objects of men's consideration, and, as such, objects of their action and cognition.

In problem-posing education, men develop their power to perceive critically *the way they exist* in the world *with which* and *in which* they find themselves; they come to see the world not as a static reality, but as a reality in process, in transformation. Although the dialectical relations of men with the world exist independently of how these relations are perceived (or whether or not they are perceived at all), it is also true that the form of action men adopt is to a large extent a function of how they perceive themselves in the world. Hence, the teacher-student and the students-teachers reflect simultaneously on themselves and the world without dichotomizing this reflection from action, and thus establish an authentic form of thought and action.

Once again, the two educational concepts and practices under analysis come into conflict. Banking education (for obvious reasons) attempts, by mythicizing reality, to conceal certain facts which explain the way men exist in the world; problem-posing education sets itself the task of demythologizing. Banking education resists dialogue; problem-posing education regards dialogue as indispensable to the act of cognition which unveils reality. Banking education treats students as objects of assistance; problem-posing education makes them critical thinkers. Banking education inhibits creativity and domesticates (although it cannot completely destroy) the *intentionality* of consciousness by isolating consciousness from the world, thereby denying men their ontological and historical vocation of becoming more fully human. Problem-posing education bases itself on creativity and stimulates true reflection and action upon reality, thereby responding to the vocation of men as beings who are authentic only when engaged in inquiry and creative transformation. In sum: banking theory and practice, as immobilizing and fixating forces, fail to acknowledge men as historical beings; problem-posing theory and practice take man's historicity as their starting point.

Problem-posing education affirms men as beings in the process of *becoming*—as unfinished, uncompleted beings in and with a likewise unfinished reality. Indeed, in contrast to other animals who are unfinished, but not historical, men know themselves to be unfinished; they are aware of their

---

[14] Edmund Husserl, *Ideas—General Introduction to Pure Phenomenology* (London, 1969), pp. 105–106.

incompletion. In this incompletion and this awareness lie the very roots of education as an exclusively human manifestation. The unfinished character of men and the transformational character of reality necessitate that education be an ongoing activity.

Education is thus constantly remade in the praxis. In order to *be,* it must *become.* Its "duration" (in the Bergsonian meaning of the word) is found in the interplay of the opposites *permanence* and *change.* The banking method emphasizes permanence and becomes reactionary; problem-posing education—which accepts neither a "well-behaved" present nor a predetermined future—roots itself in the dynamic present and becomes revolutionary.

Problem-posing education is revolutionary futurity. Hence, it is prophetic (and, as such, hopeful). Hence, it corresponds to the historical nature of man. Hence, it affirms men as beings who transcend themselves, who move forward and look ahead, for whom immobility represents a fatal threat, for whom looking at the past must only be a means of understanding more clearly what and who they are so that they can more wisely build the future. Hence, it identifies with the movement which engages men as beings aware of their incompletion—an historical movement which has its point of departure, its Subjects and its objective.

The point of departure of the movement lies in men themselves. But since men do not exist apart from the world, apart from reality, the movement must begin with the men-world relationship. Accordingly, the point of departure must always be with men in the "here and now," which constitutes the situation within which they are submerged, from which they emerge, and in which they intervene. Only by starting from this situation—which determines their perception of it—can they begin to move. To do this authentically they must perceive their state not as fated and unalterable, but merely as limiting—and therefore challenging.

Whereas the banking method directly or indirectly reinforces men's fatalistic perception of their situation, the problem-posing method presents this very situation to them as a problem. As the situation becomes the object of their cognition, the naïve or magical perception which produced their fatalism gives way to perception which is able to perceive itself even as it perceives reality, and can thus be critically objective about that reality.

A deepened consciousness of their situation leads men to apprehend that situation as an historical reality susceptible of transformation. Resignation gives way to the drive for transformation and inquiry, over which men feel themselves to be in control. If men, as historical beings necessarily engaged with other men in a movement of inquiry, did not control that movement, it would be (and is) a violation of men's humanity. Any situation in which some men prevent others from engaging in the process of inquiry is one of violence. The means used are not important; to alienate men from their own decision-making is to change them into objects.

This movement of inquiry must be directed towards humanization—man's historical vocation. The pursuit of full humanity, however, cannot be carried out in isolation or individualism, but only in fellowship and solidarity; therefore it cannot unfold in the antagonistic relations between oppressors and oppressed. No one can be authentically human while he prevents others from being so. Attempting *to be more* human, individualistically, leads to *having more,* egotistically: a form of dehumanization. Not that it is not fundamental *to have* in order *to be* human. Precisely because it *is* necessary, some men's *having* must not be allowed to constitute an obstacle to others' *having,* must not consolidate the power of the former to crush the latter.

Problem-posing education, as a humanist and liberating praxis, posits as fundamental that men subjected to domination must fight for their emancipation. To that end, it enables teachers and students to become Subjects of the educational process by overcoming authoritarianism and an alienating intellectualism; it also enables men to overcome their false perception of reality. The world—no longer something to be described with deceptive words— becomes the object of that transforming action by men which results in their humanization.

Problem-posing education does not and cannot serve the interests of the oppressor. No oppressive order could permit the oppressed to begin to question: Why? While only a revolutionary society can carry out this education in systematic terms, the revolutionary leaders need not take full power before they can employ the method. In the revolutionary process, the leaders cannot utilize the banking method as an interim measure, justified on grounds of expediency, with the intention of *later* behaving in a genuinely revolutionary fashion. They must be revolutionary—that is to say, dialogical—from the outset.

Questions

1. What is a "culture of silence"?
2. How has our traditional education system submerged the masses in a "culture of silence"?
3. How did Freire develop a pedagogy of the oppressed?
4. Explain Freire's assertion that "education is suffering from narration sickness."
5. What is the "banking" concept of education?
6. What does Freire mean by the phrase "humankind's ontological vocation"?
7. How does this view of humankind differ from the perspective of humankind associated with "banking" education?
8. How do "bank-clerk" teachers dehumanize themselves and their students?
9. What is the difference between being *in* the world rather than *with* the world?
10. What does Freire mean by praxis?
11. Describe in your own words the problem-posing education advocated by Freire.
12. What role does dialogue play in problem-posing education?
13. If one embraces teaching as a problem-posing activity, what does one teach? What is the curriculum? Where does one begin?
14. What is humanization, and why is this a goal worthy of Freire's pedagogy?
15. How might economic class determine classroom practice?
16. In your own words, describe the ideally educated individual from Freire's point of view.

14

Nel Noddings

Time Line for Noddings

1929	Is born in Irvington, New Jersey, on January 19.
1949	Receives B.A. in Mathematics and Physical Science from Montclair State College.
1949–1972	Teacher of mathematics and other subjects in schools of New Jersey; Department Chair, Curriculum Supervisor, and Assistant Principal.
1964	Receives M.A. in Mathematics from Rutgers University.
1972	Assistant Professor of Education at Pennsylvania State University.
1973	Receives Ph.D. in Educational Philosophy and Theory from Stanford University.
1975–1976	Director of Pre-Collegiate Education, The University of Chicago.
1977–1983	Assistant Professor of Education, Stanford University.
1983–1986	Associate Professor and Director of Teacher Education, Stanford University.
1984	Publishes *Caring: A Feminine Approach to Ethics and Moral Education* and, with Paul Shore, *Awakening the Inner Eye: Intuition in Education*.
1986–1992	Professor and Associate Dean of Academic Affairs, Stanford University.
1989	Publishes *Women and Evil*.
1990	Publishes *Constructivist Views on the Teaching and Learning of Mathematics*.
1991	Publishes *Stories Lives Tell: Narrative and Dialogue in Education*.
1992	Lee L. Jacks Professor of Education at Stanford University.
	Publishes *The Challenge to Care in Schools*.
1993	Publishes *Educating for Intelligent Belief or Unbelief*.
1994	Visiting Professor, Teachers College, Columbia University.
1995	Publishes *Philosophy of Education*.
1996	Publishes *Caregiving*.
1997	Lee L. Jacks Professor of Education, Stanford University, and Professor of Philosophy and Education, Teachers College, Columbia University.
1998	Publishes *Justice and Care in Education*.

2001	Publishes *Uncertain Lives: Children of Promise, Teachers of Hope.*
2002	Publishes *Educating Moral People* and *Starting at Home: Caring and Social Policy.*
	Appointed to the A. Lindsay O'Connor Professorship of American Institutions at Colgate University.
2003	Publishes *Happiness and Education.*
2006	Publishes *Moral Matters: Five Ways to Develop the Moral Life of Schools* and *Critical Issues: What Our Schools Should Teach.*
2007	Publishes *When School Reform Goes Wrong.*
2010	Publishes *The Maternal Factor: Two Paths to Morality.*

INTRODUCTION

Nel Noddings is the Lee L. Jacks Professor of Education at Stanford University and Professor of Philosophy and Education at Teachers College, Columbia University. She is perhaps best known for *Caring: A Feminine Approach to Ethics and Moral Education* and for *The Challenge to Care in Schools.* Beginning with the "first wonderful accident" that "happened in the second grade," Noddings suggests that her professional life, like that of many other women, developed largely as a result of "various accidents and an awareness of opportunity." As a young child, Noddings remembers moving to a new town and finding herself in a "strange and much more demanding academic environment." Thanks to being placed into the top reading group by Miss Christ, her second-grade teacher, school became her second home and provided her with emotional and intellectual support. Another such accident occurred in the seventh grade when, after another move, Noddings experienced another teacher who cared enough about her to attend her valedictorian speech upon graduation from high school. Noddings provides us with numerous life-shaping "accidents" that contributed to her becoming a secondary math teacher and later an academic and philosopher. As she explains, "all of these accidents . . . involve love, or led to love, and these loves, like bits of colored sea glass, are the elements from which my life has been composed."[1]

Such accidents and the awareness and willingness to take advantage of the opportunities provided by them has enabled Noddings to reach the pinnacle of the academic world. While her academic and professional accomplishments are many, including serving as President of the Philosophy of Education Society, Noddings' success remains rooted in the caring relationships alluded to before and discussed in more depth in her "Accident, Awareness, and Actualization." In emphasizing the importance of caring relationships for teaching and learning, Noddings integrates her lived experiences with her academic and professional pursuits. In suggesting that children will work hard for people they like and trust, Noddings is both describing her own educational experiences and positing a significant educational principle.

[1] Nel Noddings, "Accident, Awareness, and Actualization" in Ann Newmann and Penelope L. Peters, eds., *Learning from Our Lives: Women, Research, and Autobiography in Education* (New York: Teachers College Press, 1997), p. 166.

Professor Noddings suggests that caring and courage are required to initiate the changes that our schools so desperately need. Noting that the social context has changed dramatically since she taught math in the public school, Professor Noddings contends that the established curriculum is not providing today's students with what they really need. To further illustrate this point, Noddings suggests that the outstanding curriculum projects developed in the aftermath of the "Sputnik" crisis were praiseworthy, but, as Jerome Bruner concluded in 1971, curriculum reform is not the answer. Bruner's MACOS (Man, A Course of Study) and many other outstanding curriculum projects represent significant achievements, but they are not capable of solving the malaise that grips our society.

If such outstanding curriculum projects as these were not the solution to our problems, it is not surprising, suggests Noddings, that our current disciplined and standards-based approach is failing. As an alternative, Noddings suggests incorporating themes of caring into our traditional subjects. Based on her work in the ethics of caring and from *The Challenge to Care in Schools,* Noddings offers examples of caring for the spiritual self, for intimate others, for strangers, and for plants and animals.

Professor Noddings explains that, even in math, we can acknowledge that children care about spiritual questions. To illustrate, she suggests that a high school geometry class could critique Descarte's proof for the existence of God, while Pascal's wager on God's existence could serve as a problem for a probability class. The value of infusing these and other examples into our curriculum is to help students understand that even the "great minds" struggled with spiritual questions.

Noting that responses to such questions as "What does it mean to be educated?" have, until recently, been largely male voices, Noddings suggests that had women developed the disciplines, the curriculum would have been organized around the stages of life. For example, philosophy—until recently, a male dominated field—focuses on questions of death and an afterlife. Noddings suggests that questions of birth would be more prominent in a feminist-oriented philosophy and education. In language similar to that of Jane Roland Martin, Noddings suggests that a rigorous and challenging curriculum could be developed around the question. What does it mean to make a home? Noddings reminds us that John Dewey admonishes us to think of geography as the study of earth as humankind's home.

In short, Noddings suggests that an education grounded in caring is incompatible with the idea that there is *the* one or *same* curriculum for all. Noting that a mechanically oriented curriculum can be as intellectually rigorous as any other, Noddings admonishes us to treasure the child who will become a plumber just as much as the child who will become a philosopher.[2]

Noddings argues that "liberal education (defined as a set of traditional disciplines) is an outmoded and dangerous model of education for today's young." Restating and updating the position John Dewey presented more than half a century ago, Noddings has no quarrel with literature, history, the physical sciences, or her own teaching field (mathematics), until and unless these subjects are used as weapons of an "ideology of control that forces students to study a particular, narrowly prescribed curriculum

[2]Information provided by Professor Noddings during a presentation at the University of North Carolina at Greensboro on March 17, 1994.

devoid of content they might really care about."[3] Noddings is particularly incensed by Mortimer Adler's recent attempt in *The Paideia Proposal* to revive Robert Maynard Hutchins's argument that "the best education is the best education for all." Reminiscent of Dewey's opposition to Hutchins's argument that to be free human beings means mastering the traditional content that constitutes the best that humankind has to offer, Noddings suggests that Adler and Hutchins confuse equality with sameness.

Noddings objects to Adler's statement that "there are no unteachable children," only teachers, parents, and schools that fail to teach them. On the basis of her own experience teaching elementary and secondary students, Noddings asserts "that no matter how fine the teaching, there will be considerable differences between what is achieved in, say geometry, by students most and least interested in mathematics." Realizing that not everyone—including many bright and good citizens—shares her passion for mathematics, Noddings understands that some students "will never understand the logic of mathematical proof or the power and generality of its greatest products."[4] While it is important, perhaps essential, that tomorrow's citizens "understand what it means to live in a mathematicized world," Noddings doubts that mastery of algebra is required for such understanding. She suggests that students could better achieve this necessary understanding of mathematics "through the study of social problems that really interest them."[5]

Extending her argument one step further, Noddings suggests that a traditional liberal education is the best education for no one. By focusing almost exclusively on linguistic and logical-mathematical reasoning, liberal education limits rather than liberates the human mind and spirit. By neglecting, if not ignoring, "feeling, concrete thinking, practical activity, and even moral action," an educational scheme grounded in the traditional liberal arts values the education of a philosopher more than the education of a plumber. In addition, such a traditional curriculum perpetuates a sexist society by largely omitting the "activities, attitudes, and values historically associated with women. . . ."[6]

Noddings proposes an alternative educational scheme based on caring. Her concept of "caring" is more fully developed in the selection that follows, but for now it is enough to suggest that it "speaks to the existential heart of life— . . . that draws attention to our passions, attitudes, connections, concerns, and experienced responsibilities." Rather than the traditional disciplines, the organization of this alternative vision for education focuses on kinds or domains of caring. Noddings' educational scheme is multidimensional and includes the domains of caring that all humans share: for self; for intimate others; for associates and distant others; for nonhuman life; for the human-made environment of objects and instruments; and for ideas.[7] She envisions schools where children and youth are grouped together in centers of care, actively exploring and discussing topics of interest to them. In such an

---

[3]Nel Noddings, *The Challenge to Care in Schools: An Alternative Approach to Education* (New York: Teachers College Press, 1992), p. xii.

[4]Ibid., p. 29.

[5]"Accident, Awareness, and Actualization," p. 177.

[6]*The Challenge to Care in Schools,* p. 43.

[7]Ibid., p. 47.

environment, individuals are encouraged to pursue that which interests them but since there are centers of care that all humans share, students learn to work collaboratively in developing their unique capacities or intelligences. Noddings argues that an educational scheme that builds upon what students care about will more likely develop adults capable of caring for themselves and the world they inhabit than will a revival of a discredited liberal arts tradition.

FROM *THE CHALLENGE TO CARE IN SCHOOLS: AN ALTERNATIVE APPROACH TO EDUCATION* (1992)

The German philosopher Martin Heidegger (1962) described care as the very Being of human life. His use of the term is very broad, covering an attitude of solicitousness toward other living beings, a concern to do things meticulously, the deepest existential longings, fleeting moments of concern, and all the burdens and woes that belong to human life. From his perspective, we are immersed in care; it is the ultimate reality of life.

Heidegger's full range of meanings will be of interest as this exploration continues, but the meaning that will be primary here is relational. A *caring relation* is, in its most basic form, a connection or encounter between two human beings—a carer and a recipient of care, or cared-for. In order for the relation to be properly called caring, both parties must contribute to it in characteristic ways. A failure on the part of either carer or cared-for blocks completion of caring and, although there may still be a relation—that is, an encounter or connection in which each party feels something toward the other—it is not a *caring* relation. Even before I describe the contributions of carer and cared-for, one can see how useful this relational definition is. No matter how hard teachers try to care, if the caring is not received by students, the claim "they don't care" has some validity. It suggests strongly that something is very wrong.

In *Caring* (1984), I described the state of consciousness of the carer (or "one-caring") as characterized by engrossment and motivational displacement. By engrossment I mean an open, nonselective receptivity to the cared-for. Other writers have used the word "attention" to describe this characteristic. Iris Murdoch (1970), for example, discussed attention as essential in moral life, and she traced the concept to Simone Weil. Weil placed attention at the center of love for our neighbors. It is what characterizes our consciousness when we ask another (explicitly or implicitly), "What are you going through?" Weil wrote:

> This way of looking is first of all attentive. The soul empties itself of all its own contents in order to receive into itself the being it is looking at, just as he is, in all his truth. Only he who is capable of attention can do this. (1951, p. 115)

To say that the soul empties itself of all its own contents in order to receive the other describes well what I mean by engrossment. I do not mean infatuation, enchantment, or obsession but a full receptivity. When I care, I really hear, see, or feel what the other tries to convey. The engrossment or attention may last only a few moments and it may or may not be repeated in future encounters, but it is full and essential in any caring encounter. For example, if a stranger stops me to ask directions, the encounter may produce a caring relation, albeit a brief one. I listen attentively to his need, and I respond in a way that he receives and recognizes. The caring relation is completed when he receives my efforts at caring.

As carer in the brief encounter just described, I was attentive, but I also felt the desire to help the stranger in his need. My consciousness was characterized by motivational displacement. Where a moment earlier I had my own projects in mind, I was now concerned with his project—finding his way on campus. When we watch a small child trying to tie her shoes, we often feel our own fingers moving in sympathetic reaction. This is motivational displacement, the sense that our motive energy is flowing toward others and their projects. I receive what the other conveys, and I want to respond in a way that furthers the other's purpose or project.

Experiencing motivational displacement, one begins to think. Just as we consider, plan, and reflect on our own projects, we now think what we can do to help another. Engrossment and motivational displacement do not tell us what to do; they merely characterize our consciousness when we care. But the thinking that we do will now be as careful as it is in our own service. We are seized by the needs of another.

What characterizes the consciousness of one who is cared for? Reception, recognition, and response seem to be primary. The cared-for receives the caring and shows that it has been received. This recognition now becomes part of what the carer receives in his or her engrossment, and the caring is completed.

Some critics worry that my account puts a tremendous burden on the carer and very little on the recipient of care. But we must keep in mind that the basic caring relation is an encounter. My description of a caring relation does not entail that carer and cared-for are permanent labels for individuals. Mature relationships are characterized by mutuality. They are made up of strings of encounters in which the parties exchange places; both members are carers and cared-fors as opportunities arise.

Even in the basic situation, however, the contribution of the cared-for is not negligible. Consider the mother-infant relationship. In every caring encounter, the mother is necessarily carer and the infant cared-for. But the infant responds—he or she coos, wriggles, stares attentively, smiles, reaches out, and cuddles. These responses are heartwarming; they make caregiving a rewarding experience. To see just how vital the infant's response is to the caring relation, one should observe what happens when infants cannot respond normally to care. Mothers and other caregivers in such situations are worn down by the lack of completion—burned out by the constant outward flow of energy that is not replenished by the response of the cared-for. Teachers, too, suffer this dreadful loss of energy when their students do not respond. Thus, even when the second party in a relation cannot assume the status of carer, there is a genuine form of reciprocity that is essential to the relation.

The desire to be cared for is almost certainly a universal human characteristic. Not everyone wants to be cuddled or fussed over. But everyone wants to be received, to elicit a response that is congruent with an underlying need or desire. Cool and formal people want others to respond to them with respect and a touch of deference. Warm, informal people often appreciate smiles and hugs. Everyone appreciates a person who knows when to hug and when to stand apart. In schools, all kids want to be cared for in this sense. They do not want to be treated "like numbers," by recipe—no matter how sweet the recipe may be for some consumers. When we understand that everyone wants to be cared for and that there is no recipe for caring, we see how important engrossment (or attention) is. In order to respond as a genuine carer, one does have to empty the soul of its own contents. One cannot say, "Aha! This fellow needs care. Now, let's see—here are the seven steps I must follow." Caring is a way of being in relation, not a set of specific behaviors.

I have put great emphasis on caring as relation, because our temptation is to think of caring as a virtue, an individual attribute. We do talk this way at times. We say, "He is a caring person," or even, "She is really a caring person, but she has trouble showing it." Both of these comments capture something of our broad notion of care, but both are misleading because of their emphasis on caring as an individual virtue. As we explore caring in the context of caregiving—any long-term unequal relation in which one person is carer and the other cared-for—we will ask about the virtues that support caring. But for now, it is important not to detach carers from caring relations. No matter how much a person professes to care, the result that concerns us is the caring relation. Lots of self-righteous, "caring" people induce the response, "she doesn't really care about me at all."

Even though I will often use the word *caring* to apply to relations, I will also need to apply it to capacities. The uses should be clear in context. I want to avoid a concentration on judgment or evaluation that accompanies an interpretation of caring as an individual virtue, but I also want to acknowledge that people have various capacities for caring—that is, for entering into caring relations as well as for attending to objects and ideas.

When we discuss teaching and teacher-learner relationships in depth, we will see that teachers not only have to create caring relations in which they are the carers, but that they also have a responsibility to help their students develop the capacity to care. What can this mean? For Heidegger care is inevitable; all aware human beings care. It is the mark of being human. But not everyone develops the capacity to care for others in the way described above. Perhaps very few learn to care for ideas, for nonhuman life, for objects. And often we confuse the forms of caring and suppose caring to be a unitary capacity that transfers easily from one domain to another.

Simone Weil is a good example of an outstanding thinker who seems to have believed that intellectual caring and interpersonal caring are closely related. In the essay from which the earlier passage was extracted, Weil observed that the study of geometry requires attention and that attention so learned could increase students' concentration in prayer. Thence, we may suppose, Weil concluded that closer connection in prayer would produce more sensitive interpersonal relations; that is, she believed that intellectual attention could be transferred to interpersonal attention. This is doubtful. Evidence abounds that people can attain high levels of intellectuality and remain insensitive to human beings and other living things. Consider the Nazi high command or the fictional Professor Moriarty (Sherlock Holmes's nemesis) who attended lovingly to his orchids but was evil incarnate in the human domain. So the varieties of care need analysis.

Unequal caring relations are interesting not only in the human domain but also in the realm of nonhuman animals. It is doubtful whether any animal can be a carer with respect to humans (although there are those who have argued the case for dogs), but many animals are responsive cared-fors, and taking care of animals can be a wonderful way to learn caring. In our interaction with animals, we also have an opportunity to study the forms of response that we value. Some animals respond with intelligence, and we usually value that. Some respond with affection; they like to be stroked, cuddled, held, or scratched. Still others respond vocally. All of these responses affect us and call forth a caring attitude. Further, certain physical characteristics that suggest the possibility of a valued response also affect us. Most of us feel sympathy for baby seals threatened by hunters, because they look as though they might respond in the ways mentioned. Creatures that are slimy, scaly, or spiny rarely evoke a sympathetic response in us. The nature of our responses will be seen as important when we consider the roots of ethical life.

In another sense of care, human beings can care about ideas or objects. An approach to education that begins with care is not, as I pointed out earlier, anti-intellectual. Part of what we receive from others is a sense of their interests, including intellectual passions. To enhance a student's understanding and skill in a given subject is an important task for teachers, but current educational practices are riddled with slogans and myths that are not very helpful.

Often we begin with the innocent-sounding slogan mentioned earlier, "All children can learn." The slogan was created by people who mean well. They want teachers to have high expectations for all their students and not to decide on the basis of race, ethnicity, sex, or economic status that some groups of children simply cannot learn the subject at hand. With that much I agree.

But I will argue that not all individual children can learn everything we might like to teach them. Further, the good intentions captured in the slogan can lead to highly manipulative and dictatorial methods that disregard the interests and purposes of students. Teachers these days are expected to induce a desire to learn in all students. But all students already want to learn; it is a question of *what* they want to learn. John Dewey (1963) argued years ago that teachers had to start with the experience and interests of students and patiently forge connections between that experience and whatever subject matter was prescribed. I would go further. There are few things that all students need to know, and it ought to be acceptable for students to reject some material in order to pursue other topics with enthusiasm. Caring teachers listen and respond differentially to their students. Much more will be said on this highly controversial issue in later chapters. For now it is enough to note that our schools are not intellectually stimulating places, even for many students who are intellectually oriented.

Few students learn to care for ideas in school. Perhaps even fewer learn to care for objects. I am not talking about mere acquisitiveness; this seems to be learned all too well. I am talking about what Harry Broudy (1972) called "enlightened cherishing" and what the novelist and essayist John Galsworthy (1948) called "quality." This kind of caring produces fine objects and takes care of them. In a society apparently devoted to planned obsolescence, our children have few opportunities to care lovingly for old furniture, dishes, carpets, or even new bicycles, radios, cassette players, and the like. It can be argued that the care of many tools and instruments is a waste of time because they are so easily replaced. But one wonders how long a throwaway society can live harmoniously with the natural environment and also how closely this form of carelessness is related to the gross desire for more and more acquisitions. Is there a role for schools to play in teaching care of buildings, books, computers, furniture, and laboratory equipment?

Caring for ideas and objects is different from caring for people and other living things. Strictly speaking, one cannot form a relation with mathematics or music or a food processor. The cared-for cannot feel anything for us; there is no affect in the second party. But, oddly, people do report a form of responsiveness from ideas and objects. The mathematician Gauss was "seized" by mathematics. The poet Robert Frost insisted that "a poem finds its own way" (see the accounts in Noddings & Shore, 1984). And we know that well-tended engines purr, polished instruments gleam, and fine glassware glistens. The care we exert induces something like a response from fields of ideas and from inanimate objects. Do our students hear enough—or anything at all—about these wondrous events?

Finally, we must consider Heidegger's deepest sense of care. As human beings, we care what happens to us. We wonder whether there is life after death, whether there is a deity who cares about us, whether we are loved by those we love, whether we belong anywhere; we wonder what we will become, who we are, how much control we have over our own fate. For adolescents these are among the most pressing questions: Who am I? What kind of person will I be? Who will love me? How do others see me? Yet schools spend more time on the quadratic formula than on any of these existential questions.

In reviewing the forms of care, it becomes clear that there is a challenge to care in schools. The structures of current schooling work against care, and at the same time, the need for care is perhaps greater than ever.

The Debate in Ethics

No discussion of caring today could be adequate without some attention to the ethic of care. In 1982, Carol Gilligan published her now famous *In a Different Voice,* describing an alternative approach to moral problems. This approach was identified in the voices of women, but Gilligan did not claim that the approach is exclusively female, nor did she claim that all women use it. Still, the avalanche of response from women who recognized themselves in Gilligan's description is an impressive phenomenon. "This is me," many women said. "Finally someone has articulated the way I come at moral problems."

Gilligan described a morality based on the recognition of needs, relation, and response. Women who speak in the different voice refuse to leave themselves, their loved ones, and connections out of their moral reasoning. They speak from and to a situation, and their reasoning is contextual. Those of us who write about an ethic of care have emphasized affective factors, but this is not to say that caring is irrational or even nonrational. It has its own rationality or reasonableness, and in appropriate situations carers draw freely on standard linear rationality as well. But its emphasis is on living together, on creating, maintaining, and enhancing positive relations—not on decision making in moments of high moral conflict, nor on justification.

An ethic of care—a needs-and response-based ethic—challenges many premises of traditional ethics and moral education. First, there is the difference of focus already mentioned. There is also a rejection of universalizability, the notion that anything that is morally justifiable is necessarily something that anyone else in a similar situation is obligated to do. Universalizability suggests that who we are, to whom we are related, and how we are situated should have nothing to do with our moral decision making. An ethic of caring rejects this. Next, although an ethic of care puts great emphasis on consequences in the sense that it always asks what happens to the relation, it is not a form of utilitarianism; it does not posit one greatest good to be optimized, nor does it separate means and ends. Finally, it is not properly labeled an ethic of virtue. Although it calls on people to be carers and to develop the virtues and capacities to care, it does not regard caring solely as an individual attribute. It recognizes the part played by the cared-for. It is an ethic of relation.

In moral education, an ethic of care's great emphasis on motivation challenges the primacy of moral reasoning. We concentrate on developing the attitudes and skills required to sustain caring relations and the desire to do so, not nearly so much on the reasoning used to arrive at a decision. Lawrence Kohlberg (1981) and his associates, following Plato and Socrates, have focused on moral reasoning. The supposition here is that moral knowledge is sufficient for moral behavior. From this perspective, wrongdoing is always equated with ignorance. Gilligan explicitly challenged Kohlberg's scale or hierarchy of moral reasoning (suggesting a powerful alternative developmental model), but others of us have challenged the whole idea of a developmental model, arguing that moral responses in a given individual may vary contextually at almost any age. (The language used to discuss what one is doing and why may, of course, depend on intellectual development, but moral behavior and its intellectual articulation are not synonymous.)

Moral education from the perspective of an ethic of caring has four major components: modeling, dialogue, practice, and confirmation (Noddings, 1984). Modeling is important in most schemes of moral education, but in caring it is vital. In this framework we are not trying to teach students principles and ways of applying them to problems through chains of mathematical reasoning. Rather, we have to show how to care in our own relations with cared-fors. For example, professors of education and school administrators cannot be sarcastic and dictatorial with teachers in the hope that coercion will make them care for students. I have heard administrators use this excuse for "being tough" with teachers—"because I care about the kids of this state"—but, of course, the likely outcome is that teachers will then turn attention protectively to themselves rather than lovingly to their students. So we do not tell our students to care; we show them how to care by creating caring relations with them.

There is a second reason why modeling is so vital. The capacity to care may be dependent on adequate experience in being cared for. Even while a child is too young to be a carer, he or she can learn how to be a responsive cared-for. Thus our role as carer is more important than our role as model, but we fill both simultaneously. We remind ourselves when we are tempted to take short cuts in moral education that we are, inevitably, models. But otherwise, in our daily activities we simply respond as carers when the need arises. The function of modeling gets special attention when we try to explain what we are doing and why in moral education. But the primary reason for responding as carers to our students' needs is that we are called to such response by our moral orientation.

Dialogue is the second essential component of moral education. My use of the term *dialogue* is similar to that of Paulo Freire (1970). It is not just talk or conversation—certainly not an oral presentation of argument in which the second party is merely allowed to ask an occasional question. Dialogue is open-ended; that is, in a genuine dialogue, neither party knows at the outset what the outcome or decision will be. As parents and teachers, we cannot enter into dialogue with children when we know that our decision is already made. It is maddening to young people (or any people) to engage in "dialogue" with a sweetly reasonable adult who cannot be persuaded and who, in the end, will say, "Here's how it's going to be. I tried to reason with you. . . ." We do have to talk this way at times, but we should not pretend that this is dialogue. Dialogue is a common search for understanding, empathy, or appreciation. It can be playful or serious, logical or imaginative, goal or process oriented, but it is always a genuine quest for something undetermined at the beginning.

Dialogue permits us to talk about what we try to show. It gives learners opportunities to question "why," and it helps both parties to arrive at well-informed decisions. Although I do not believe that all wrongdoing can be equated with ignorance, I do believe that many moral errors are ill-informed decisions, particularly in the very young. Thus dialogue serves not only to inform the decision under consideration; it also contributes to a habit of mind—that of seeking adequate information on which to make decisions.

Dialogue serves another purpose in moral education. It connects us to each other and helps to maintain caring relations. It also provides us with the knowledge of each other that forms a foundation for response in caring. Caring (acting as carer) requires knowledge and skill as well as characteristic attitudes. We respond most effectively as carers when we understand what the other needs and the history of this need. Dialogue is implied in the criterion of engrossment. To receive the other is to attend fully and openly. Continuing dialogue builds up a substantial knowledge of one another that serves to guide our responses.

A third component of moral education is practice. Attitudes and "mentalities" are shaped, at least in part, by experience. Most of us speak regularly of a "military mind," a "police mentality," "business thinking," and the like. Although some of this talk is a product of stereotyping, it seems clear that it also captures some truth about human behavior. All disciplines and institutional organizations have training programs designed not only to teach specific skills but also to "shape minds," that is, to induce certain attitudes and ways of looking at the world. If we want people to approach moral life prepared to care, we need to provide opportunities for them to gain skills in caregiving and, more important, to develop the characteristic attitudes described earlier.

Some of the most fascinating work in contemporary feminist theory is devoted to the study of women's experience and its articulation. It seems likely that women's traditional experience is closely related to the moral approach described in ethics of care. Women, more often than men, have been charged with the direct care of young children, the ill, and the aged. They have been expected to maintain a pleasing environment, to look after the needs of others, and to mediate disputes in ordinary social situations. If we regard this experience as inseparable from oppression, then we might agree with Nietzsche that what I am describing is merely "slave mentality." But if we analyze the experience, we find considerable autonomy, love, choice, and consummate skill in the traditional female role. We may evaluate the experience as essential in developing fully human beings.

Women have learned to regard every human encounter as a potential caring occasion. In nursing theory, for example, Jean Watson (1985) defined the moment in which nurse and patient meet as a "caring occasion." It is not just that the nurse will provide care in the form of physical skills to the patient. Rather, it is a moment in which each must decide how to meet the other and what to do with the moment. This is obviously very different from defining a medical encounter as a problem-solving event. Problem solving is involved, of course, but it is preceded by a moment of receptivity—one in which the full humanity of both parties is recognized—and it is followed by a return to the human other in all his or her fullness.

If we decide that the capacity to care is as much a mark of personhood as reason or rationality, then we will want to find ways to increase this capacity. Just as we now think it is important for girls as well as boys to have mathematical experience, so we should want both boys and girls to have experience in caring. It does not just happen; we have to plan for it. As we will see, such planning is complex and loaded with potential pitfalls.

Some schools, recognizing the needs just discussed, have instituted requirements for a form of community service. This is a move in the right direction, but reflection produces some issues to worry about. The practice provided must be with people who can demonstrate caring. We do not want our children to learn the menial (or even sophisticated) skills of caregiving without the characteristic attitude of caring. The experience of caregiving should initiate or contribute to the desired attitude, but the conditions have to be right, and people are central to the setting. This is a major point, to which I will return.

Next, practice in caring should transform schools and, eventually, the society in which we live. If the practice is assimilated to the present structures of schooling, it may lose its transformative powers. *It* may be transformed—that is, distorted. If we were to give grades for caregiving, for example, students might well begin to compete for honors in caring. Clearly, then, their attention could be diverted from cared-fors to themselves. If, on the other hand, we neither grade nor give credit for such work, it may inevitably have second-class status in our schools. So long as our schools are organized hierarchically with emphasis on rewards and penalties, it will be very difficult to provide the kind of experience envisioned.

The fourth component of moral education from the perspective of caring is confirmation. Martin Buber (1965) described confirmation as an act of affirming and encouraging the best in others. When we confirm someone, we spot a better self and encourage its development. We can do this only if we know the other well enough to see what he or she is trying to become. Formulas and slogans have no place here. We do not set up a single ideal or set of expectations for everyone to meet, but we identify something admirable, or at least acceptable, struggling to emerge in each person we encounter. The person working toward a better self must see the attribute or goal as worthy, and we too must see it as at least morally acceptable. We do not confirm people in ways we judge to be wrong.

Confirmation requires attribution of the best possible motive consonant with reality. When someone commits an act we find reprehensible, we ask ourselves what might have motivated such an act. Often it is not hard to identify an array of possible motives ranging from the gross and grubby to some that are acceptable or even admirable. This array is not constructed in abstraction. We build it from a knowledge of this particular other and by listening carefully to what she or he tells us. The motive we attribute has to be a real, a genuine possibility. Then we can open our dialogue with something like, "I know you were trying to help your friend . . ." or "I know what you're trying to accomplish. . . ." It will be clear that we disapprove of this particular act, but it will also be clear to the other that we see a self that is better than this act. Often the other will respond with enormous relief. *Here is this significant and percipient other who sees through the smallness or meanness of my present behavior a self that is better and a real possibility.* Confirmation lifts us toward our vision of a better self.

It is worth repeating that confirmation cannot be done by formula. A relation of trust must ground it. Continuity is required, because the carer in acting to confirm must know the cared-for well enough to be able to identify motives consonant with reality. Confirmation cannot be described in terms of strategies; it is a loving act founded on a relation of some depth. When we turn to specific changes that should occur in schooling in order to meet the challenge to care, I will put great emphasis on continuity. Not all caring relations require continuity (some, as we have seen, are brief encounters), but teaching does require it.

Confirmation contrasts sharply with the standard mode of religious moral education. There we usually find a sequence of accusation, confession, penance, and forgiveness. The initial step, accusation, causes or sustains separation. We stand in moral judgment and separate the other from ourselves and the moral community. In contrast, confirmation calls us to remain in connection.

Further, accusation tends to produce denial or rationalization, which we then feel compelled to overthrow. But the rationalization may in fact be an attempt on the part of the accused to find that possible motive and convey it to us, the accuser. Because we have to reject it in order to proceed with confession, penance, and forgiveness, offenders may never understand their own true motives. This sequence also depends heavily on authority, obedience, fear, and subordination. We can be harsh or magnanimous in our judgment and forgiveness. Our authority is emphasized, and the potential power of the offender's own moral struggle is overlooked.

I do not mean to suggest that there is never a place for accusation and confession in moral education. It is not always possible for us to find a motive that is morally acceptable; sometimes we have to begin by asking straight out, "Why did you do that?" or "How could you do such a thing?" But it is gratifying how often we really can see a better self if we look for one, and its identification is a first step in its realization.

This whole way of looking at ethics and moral education challenges not only parts of the religious tradition but also the ideas of Freud and like-minded theorists. Freud believed that our sense of morality develops out of fear. The superego, Freud said, is an internalization of authority—of the father's voice—and its establishment results from resolution of the Oedipal conflict. Sons fear castration by the father if they disobey or compete with him. Resolution of this desire to rebel and compete involves acceptance of the father's power and authority, and the superego (Freud's guide to acceptable behavior) takes up residence within the son. This account of moral development led Freud to conclude that women must be morally inferior to men. Because girls need not fear castration (having been born in that dread condition), their moral voice never attains the strength and dependability of men's.

Recent criticisms of Freud suggest that more attention should be given to the preoedipal period. Nancy Chodorow (1978) has theorized that girls and boys develop different psychological deep structures because females are almost exclusively the primary caregivers for both. Girls can find their gender identity without separating from their mother and, hence, develop a relational personality structure and perhaps even a relational epistemology or way of knowing (Keller, 1985). Boys, however, must construct their gender identity in opposition to all that is female. Here we have the possible roots of the different moral voices described by Gilligan. We will consider other alternatives as well.

Eli Sagan (1988) has also suggested that moral development begins and is strongly affected by preoedipal life. Without rejecting the Freudian framework entirely, Sagan recommends a shift in emphasis. If we give due weight to early childhood, we see that conscience (a sense of right and wrong, not mere internalization of authority) develops as much out of love and attachment as out of fear. Further, the primary fear is not of harm and punishment but, rather, of disappointing a loved parent and, at worst, losing that parent's love. This is a major challenge to masculinist psychology and a suggestion compatible with an ethic of caring and the model of moral education outlined here. Love, caring, and relation play central roles in both ethics and moral education.

I want to suggest that caring is the very bedrock of all successful education and that contemporary schooling can be revitalized in its light. Before describing a broad plan to make caring central in education, I need to explain why the current ideal is inadequate. Liberal education has been the Western ideal for centuries. Even when it is poorly funded in comparison with technical and professional education, it is still the ideal that puts pressure on precollegiate education. It is the form of education—done well or poorly—that most of us experienced. What is wrong with it, and why should it be rejected as a model of universal education?

Questions

1. Is caring a relation or a virtue?
2. What are the characteristics of a caring relationship?
3. Are intellectual caring and interpersonal caring related?
4. How is caring for ideas and objects different from caring for people and other living things?
5. Why does an ethic of caring reject universalizability?
6. How does traditional moral reasoning (Socrates, Plato, Kohlberg, etc.) differ from the ethic of caring?
7. What is the role of a carer in a caring relationship? Of the cared-for in a caring relationship?
8. Why is dialogue so important in a moral education that is based on the ethic of caring?
9. Is it possible to teach someone to care? Is it possible to develop the capacity to care for others?
10. What are the connections between the ethic of caring and the experiences of women?
11. Why is confirmation an essential component of the ethic of caring? How does this differ from more traditional, religious approaches to moral education?

15

Philosophy for Children: Matthew Lipman, Gareth Matthews, and Kieran Egan

Time Line for Lipman

1923	Is born August 24 in Vineland, New Jersey.
1948	Receives B.S. from Columbia University.
1950–1951	Is Fulbright Scholar to Sorbonne University, Paris.
1953	Receives Ph.D. from Columbia University.
1954–1957	Is assistant professor of philosophy at Columbia.
1957–1961	Is associate professor at Columbia.
1961–1967	Is professor of philosophy at Columbia.
1967	Publishes *What Happens in Art*.
1972	Is named professor of philosophy at Montclair State College.
1973	Publishes *Contemporary Aesthetics*.
1974	Establishes the Institute for the Advancement of Philosophy for Children at Montclair State.
	Publishes *Harry Stottlemeier's Discovery* and the accompanying manual, *Philosophical Inquiry*.
1976	Publishes *Lisa*.
1977	Publishes *Philosophy in the Classroom*.
1978	Publishes *Growing Up with Philosophy* and *Suki*.
	Initiates publication of *Thinking*: *The Journal of Philosophy for Children*.
1980	Publishes *Mark*.
1981	Publishes *Pixie*.
1982	Publishes *Kio and Gus*.

1987	Publishes *Elfie*.
1988	Publishes *Philosophy Goes to School*.
1993	Publishes *Thinking in Education*.
1994	Publishes *Thinking Children and Education*.
1996	Publishes *Natasha*.
	Ed.D in Pedagogy—specialization in Philosophy for Children—offered at Montclair State University.
2002	Retires from Montclair State University as Professor Emeritus.
2003	Publishes *Thinking in Education* (2nd Edition).

Time Line for Matthews

1980	Publishes *Philosophy and the Young Child*
1984	Publishes *Dialogues with Children*
1994	Publishes *Philosophy of Childhood*
1999	Publishes *Socratic Perplexity and the Nature of Philosophy*
2002	Publishes *Augustine: On the Trinity*

Time Line for Egan

1981	Publishes *The Erosion of Education: Socialization and the Schools*
1986	Publishes *Teaching as Story Telling*
1997	Publishes *The Educated Mind: How Cognitive Tools Shape Our Understanding*
2002	Publishes *Getting It Wrong From the Beginning*
2008	Publishes *The Future of Education: Re-Imagining the School From the Ground Up*
2010	Publishes *Learning in Depth: A Simple Innovation that Can Transform Schooling*

INTRODUCTION

Philosophy for Children began in the late 1960s while Matthew Lipman was a professor of philosophy at Columbia University, but it was not until Lipman became affiliated with Montclair State University in New Jersey that the program began to take shape. It was here that Lipman—in collaboration with Ann Margaret Sharp and the late Fred Oscanyan—established the Institute for the Advancement of Philosophy for Children (IAPC) and embarked upon his life's work of turning philosophy inside out by restoring its natural connection with education.

While others have contributed to making Philosophy for Children an internationally acclaimed thinking skills program, it is Lipman's genius that created the traditional corpus (novels and manuals) that—albeit in modified and expanded from—are being used throughout the world to engage children and youth in the philosophic enterprise.

In addition to the seven Philosophy for Children novels and accompanying instructional manuals, Lipman is single or lead author of *Philosophy in the Classroom; Growing Up with Philosophy; Philosophy Goes to School; Thinking in Education;* and *Natasha.*

Lipman is often asked how he came to write the pedagogical novel, *Harry Stottlemeier's Discovery.* Usually the real question is "How did he come to develop this innovative approach to dramatizing philosophy?" and "When did he first realize that the erudite and highly professionalized field of philosophy could be made accessible to a larger audience?" Though Lipman's skill in dramatizing philosophy has improved significantly since he created an inquisitive fifth grader in 1969, one can still find in *Harry* the essential components that characterize all Philosophy for Children materials.

Harry's persistent struggle to figure things out is a thread that permeates all of the Philosophy for Children materials. Caught in the act of daydreaming, Harry unsuccessfully attempts to reason his way out of a predicament. Experiencing embarrassment as a result of his failure, he turns his reasoning inward and tries to figure out his own mistake. Through such reflection, along with a little help from his friends, Harry begins to unravel the mysteries of thought and subsequently to apply his discoveries to his everyday world. In the first of a series of pedagogical novels, Lipman offers children and youth a practical and largely Deweyan model of how humans think. To the degree that students in the classroom identify with Harry and other characters in these novels, they are likely to emulate them in discovering and applying the rules of reason. As a literary work, *Harry is* contrived and overly simplistic. But as a vehicle for enabling children and youth to participate in the philosophic enterprise, it has few equals.

In suggesting that Philosophy for Children "is the only valid representative of Dewey's education theory put into practice,"[1] Lipman acknowledges his indebtedness to John Dewey. Lipman's first exposure to Dewey's thought occurred while in the army during World War II, participating in a special program at Stanford University. Here Carl Thomas introduced him to philosophy in general and—indirectly—to the thought of John Dewey. From Professor Thomas, young Mat Lipman learned the importance of grounding "one's theories in *concreta.*"[2]

As Lipman was leaving Stanford to rejoin in his infantry unit, Professor Thomas gave him a paperback copy of Irwin Edman's *Philosopher's Holiday.* A member of Columbia University's philosophy department, Edman's book was largely about "his recollections of Dewey."[3] Purchasing a copy of Dewey's *Intelligence in the Modern World,* Lipman understood little of it but carried it in his duffel bag as his division traversed Europe.

Before receiving his Ph.D. from Columbia in 1953 and accepting an academic appointment there as a professor of philosophy, Lipman returned to Paris on a Fulbright scholarship to study at the Sorbonne. Here—as a complement to Dewey's influence—Lipman discovered that it was "possible to discuss profound philosophical ideas with ease and clarity."[4] Resonating to Diderot's and other encyclopediasts' attempts to "establish a *rapprochement* between the expert and the man on the street, between theory and practice, and between art and craft,"[5] Lipman

---

[1] Matthew Lipman, "Dramatizing Philosophy," unpublished manuscript. 1993, p. 279.
[2] Ibid., p. 59
[3] Ibid., p. 60
[4] Ibid., p. 65
[5] Ibid.

acknowledges that "Diderot did much to shape my convictions about the role of philosophy in the public sphere."[6]

In Paris, Lipman also read an article by the German exile, Berhard Groethuysen, titled "The Child and the Metaphysician" published in the French periodical *Deucalion*. Using Kierkegaard as illustrative, the article demonstrated "how intimately the thinking of children and the thinking of philosophers resemble each other."[7] These European seeds were planted in the mind of a young Matthew Lipman, awaiting the right circumstances to germinate and bear fruit.

Upon returning to the states, Lipman settled into a promising, if somewhat ordinary academic career. Concerned that neither students nor faculty –including philosophers— exhibited good judgment during the riots of 1968, Lipman began to question the efficacy of teaching philosophy to undergraduates. Gradually, he concluded that both his students and his peers had been miseducated and no amount of philosophy could remedy the situation at this late hour. It was too late to help the current generation of undergraduates, but philosophy—as conceptualized by Socrates, Diderot, and Dewey— might still save future generations.

In a sense, the disturbances of the late sixties proved to be fortuitous for Lipman, for they enabled him to identify his mission in life. In his mid-forties and after achieving the rank of a full professor at a prestigious university, Lipman consciously set out to turn philosophy inside out and to restore its natural connection to education. Lipman's strategy for accomplishing this ambitious task "was to change the supply of students coming into the university,"[8] thus eventually forcing a change in the faculty. Harking back to the similarities between a child's thinking and that of a philosopher, the key was to keep alive the natural inquisitiveness and sense of wonder that children bring with them to kindergarten.

The Importance of Dialogue

The goal of the Philosophy for Children program is to transform elementary, middle, and high school classrooms into self-corrective communities of inquiry. Key to such transformations is the appropriate use of dialogue as a teaching strategy. Socrates, as portrayed in the Platonic dialogues, offers an excellent model of how discovery and understanding are enhanced through dialogue. Often conversing with the youth of Athens, Socrates models a process of intellectual inquiry that is rigorous but never condescending. Rather than imposing his own ideas and beliefs upon impressionable young minds, Socrates demonstrates that thinking is hard work that no one can or should do for someone else. Socrates demands that his charges think, but more importantly, he shows them how to think. He demonstrates that dialogue compels us to be on our toes, intellectually. In serious conversation, there is no place for mindless banter and slovenly reasoning. When engaged in serious dialogues, listening is thinking because one needs to understand before one can evaluate other points of view. Speaking is thinking for one must weigh carefully each word to ensure that it

[6]Ibid.
[7]Ibid.
[8]Ibid.

conveys the intended meaning. To engage in dialogue is to rehearse in our minds what others have said, to assess the relevance and significance of these remarks, to recognize perspectives other than our own, and to explore possibilities that heretofore were unknown to us. As Socrates demonstrates, genuine dialogue avoids indoctrination by holding all points of view, including one's own, to the same rigorous standards. To do this is not easy, but as Socrates demonstrates, the establishment of a community of inquiry enhances the cooperative search for greater understanding.

In order to transform classrooms into self-corrective communities of inquiry, children need a Socratic model to emulate. They need to read and talk about children who—like themselves—are struggling to figure things out. The Philosophy for Children materials help meet that need. Just as Socrates modeled a process of inquiry for the youth of Athens, the characters in the novels provide elementary, middle, and high school students with appropriate models of good thinking. Lipman, as the primary author of these works, has improved as a literary craftsman, but none of the novels qualify as great literature. They are intended as pedagogical novels, designed to offer children and youth a substantive intellectual diet around which to build a sturdy and lasting community of inquiry.

Matthew's Contribution

Gareth Matthews is one of the four leading contributors to the development of Philosophy for Children. Matthews did not participate with Lipman, Ann Margaret Sharp, and Frederick Oscanyan in piecing together a kindergarten-through-high school curriculum, but he supported this initiative by writing a regular column on children's literature for the journal, *Thinking*, published three very well received books about children and philosophy, and gave numerous lectures on philosophy and children at national and international conferences.

Matthews has been content focusing on understanding what children are like and to what extent they can be called philosophical. In pursuit of that understanding, he has accomplished three things of importance to the larger Philosophy for Children movement. First, he has scrutinized children's literature and found many of them to be philosophically rich, complex, and interesting. They (*Frog and Toad; Lulu;* and *The Flying Babies,* for example) present activities that are interesting and perplexing for mature philosophers as well as children.

Second, Matthews—by recording and analyzing scores of children's conversations—demonstrates how subtle and intelligent children can be when confronted with philosophical problems. In his three books derived from these conversations, Matthews illustrates that at least some children are capable of the same level of philosophical sophistication as adults.

Finally, Matthews engages children in dialogue in a gentle and caring way that is reminiscent of Socrates' conversation with a slave boy as portrayed in *Meno.* When so engaged, Matthews demonstrates that children exhibit the sort of intellectual curiosity and sense of wonder that characterizes the best of philosophers and philosophy. When exposed to this kind of caring dialogue, Matthews demonstrates that children make philosophical moves parallel to and at times surpassing those found in Plato's dialogues. Through these demonstrations and by remaining independent of Lipman's efforts to integrate philosophy into the school curriculum, Matthews provides a credible and respected academic voice in support of philosophy's contribution to the education of children and youth.

Enter Egan

Though not formally associated with the work of Lipman and Matthews, Kieran Egan's emphasis on imagination, story telling, and other tools of understanding add credence to Bruner's assertion that "any subject can be taught effectively in some intellectually honest form to any child at any stage of development." Egan's work illustrates the crucial connection between the philosophical question of what it means to be educated and the educational question of how we teach for understanding.

Egan suggests that not enough attention is given to the role imagination plays in education or in our vision of what it means to be educated. Instead, he explains, the modern world has embraced a set of ad hoc principles which continue to "have a pervasive and profound influence on teaching practice and curriculum design." According to these principles, education proceeds "from the concrete to the abstract, from the simple to the complex, from the known to the unknown, from active manipulation to symbolic conceptualization."[9] Egan contends that our over-reliance on these ad hoc principles has produced a model of curriculum and lesson planning that thinks of knowledge as a static entity and that denies or minimizes the role of imagination in the education process.

Egan offers numerous counterexamples, not to debunk these ad hoc principles, but to suggest that they are not always the most effective way to educate and that they are not the totality of education. To balance the widely accepted dictum that "children learn best from concrete, hands-on experiences," Egan counters that much of the literature for young children depends upon the child's prior understanding of various underlying abstract concepts. To illustrate his point, Egan explains that five-year-old children understand and appreciate the *Cinderella* story even though such understanding is dependent upon grasping such abstract and conflicting concepts as fear/hope, kindness/cruelty, and good/evil.

Egan's argument is important for it adds credence to Lipman's and Matthew's claim that children possess sophisticated conceptual tools at a much younger age than the ad hoc principles allow. The ability of children to make sense of rather complex fantasy stories reinforces Lipman and Matthews' arguments that philosophy and children are well suited for each other.

FROM *PHILOSOPHY GOES TO SCHOOL* (1988)

Did Plato Condemn Philosophy for the Young?

We all know that philosophy emerged in Greece about a hundred generations ago, and for this achievement we honor such figures as Thales, Anaximander, Anaxagoras, and Anaximines. Apparently philosophy was first embodied in aphorisms, poetry, dialogue, and drama. But this variety of philosophical vehicles was short-lived, and philosophy became that which, by and large, it has remained—an academic discipline, access to which was limited to college and university students.

[9]Kieran Egan, *Teaching as Story Telling: An alternative approach to Teaching and Curriculum in the Elementary School* (Chicago: University of Chicago Press, 1986) p. 28.

For the most part, these students in the upper echelons of education have been expected to *learn* philosophy rather than to *do* it. Often they study the history of systems of philosophy (perhaps from the pre-Socratics to Hegel, or from Aristotle to St. Thomas, or from Russell to Quine) in preparation for final examinations, or they prepare extended philosophical arguments on obscure but respected topics to qualify for academic degrees.

Yet philosophy is a survivor. In an era in which most of the humanities have been driven to the wall, philosophy has somehow managed to stay afloat—if only barely—largely by converting itself into a knowledge industry: *pace* Socrates! But the price of survival has been high: philosophy has had to abdicate virtually all claims to exercising a socially significant role. Even the most celebrated professors of philosophy nowadays would be likely to admit that, on the vast stage of world affairs, they appear only as bit players or members of the crowd.

Oddly enough, despite the continued social impotence of philosophy, it has remained internally a discipline of incredible richness and diversity. Only in the past few centuries has a new note sounded, suggesting that philosophy has practical applications undreamt of by academicians, and here and there are those who marvel (like Descartes amazed that mathematics offered such powerful foundations but was unused) at the great, sweeping panorama of its applicability.

Nevertheless, *applying* philosophy and *doing* it are not identical. The paradigm of doing philosophy is the towering, solitary figure of Socrates, for whom philosophy was neither an acquisition nor a profession but a way of life. What Socrates models for us is not philosophy known or philosophy applied but philosophy *practiced*. He challenges us to acknowledge that philosophy as deed, as form of life, is something that any of us can emulate.

Any of us? Or just the males? Or just the adults? To many philosophers, reasonableness is found only in grown-ups. Children (like women) may be charming, beautiful, delightful, but they are seldom considered capable of being reasoned with, logical, or rational. Descartes, for example, and the young Piaget seem to have thought of childhood as a period of epistemological error that is fortunately sloughed off as one matures. The adult/child dichotomy has an obvious parallel in the dichotomy between ideal industrial management ("rational") and ideal workers ("cheerful"). Nevertheless, it is likely that the dichotomy between adults and children, insofar as the capacity to pursue the philosophical form of life was concerned, would have seemed absurd to Socrates.

Generally, when a discipline is available only on the college level or above, it is because it is considered a discipline inappropriate for children or inessential to their education. However, this has not consistently been the case with philosophy, and Jacques Derrida has shrewdly noted that, until the Reformation, philosophy had been part and parcel of the education of adolescent princes and princesses.[10] But the Reformation put an end to all that: philosophy appeared utterly superfluous when it came to the preparation of future businessmen and scientists. With the ascendency of the business

[10]Jacques Derrida, *Qui a peur de la philosophie?*

ideology, philosophy was banished from the scene as far as the education of children was concerned. Not even Dewey, easily the most insightful of all philosophers of education, could bring himself to advocate philosophy as an elementary school subject, but that was because he had already committed himself to rebuilding education along the lines of scientific inquiry. For others, philosophy appeared too difficult for children or too frivolous or too arid; some even thought it too dangerous. What was it about philosophy that gave rise to these misgivings?

Let us turn back to Plato and re-examine his attitude toward teaching philosophy to the young. In the earlier dialogues, it will be recalled, Socrates talks to young and old alike, although just how young they are is not clear. (Robert Brumbaugh, for example, places the ages of the two children in the *Lysis* at eleven.) There is no indication that Socrates has any misgivings about these conversations with children (although on other occasions he is certainly capable of expressing the unease he feels about what he is doing: we have only to recall here his bizarre conduct in the *Phaedrus*). But then comes a seemingly dramatic reversal: in Book 7 of the *Republic,* after genially admonishing us to keep children to their studies by play and not by compulsion and after having perhaps overgenerously praised dialectic ("he who can view things in their connection is a dialectician; he who cannot, is not"), he urges that children not be exposed to dialectic, for "its practitioners are infected with lawlessness" [537]. Young people, he says,

> when they get their first taste of it, treat argument as a form of sport solely for purposes of contradiction. When someone has proved them wrong, they copy his methods to confute others, delighting like puppies in tugging and tearing at anyone who comes near them. And so, after a long course of proving others wrong and being proved wrong themselves, they rush to the conclusion that all they once believed is false; and the result is that in the eyes of the world they discredit, not themselves only, but the whole business of philosophy. [539][11]

Certainly this latter remark is not to be taken too lightly. The situation of philosophy in those turbulent times was precarious enough, without incurring additional risks by encouraging logic-chopping and speculation by Athenian urchins. Nor can we forget that even Aristotle had to make a hurried exit from Athens so as not to afford Athenians an opportunity to do to him what they had done to Socrates and thus "sin twice against philosophy."

This, then, is one reason for sequestering children and philosophy from one another: doing so is for the protection of philosophy, for if children are allowed to do it, philosophy will appear unworthy of adults. The other reason is for the protection of children: dialectic will subvert them, corrupt them, infect them with lawlessness. These reasons, it must be presumed, have been taken

---

[11]Plato, *Republic*, Book 7, trans. Francis Cornford. New York: Oxford University Press, 1945, p. 261.

as conclusive ever since Plato wrote, and his authority has been invoked to deter educational initiatives that might have given children access to philosophy earlier on. What are we to say about this? Was Plato wrong to have opposed dialectical training for children so vigorously in Book 7? Here it may be helpful to consider the picture of intellectual Athens painted by Gilbert Ryle. Ryle offers us a highly speculative portrayal of the manner in which the procedures and techniques of eristic or dialectic were taught to students. Intellectual contest was paramount: debaters were assigned theses to defend or attack, regardless of their personal beliefs, and it was through these "moot court" procedures, Ryle contends, that cogency in argumentation was fostered and achieved. These moot conditions "proved to be the beginning of methodical philosophical reasoning." Nothing in Ryle's account indicates that he found these forensic or sophistic techniques of instruction objectionable in any way.

Elsewhere, indeed, Ryle seems to feel that Socrates likewise was not inclined to distinguish between philosophical reasoning and philosophy. Thus he argues that in the *Apology* Socrates provides "only a perfunctory answer to the charge of impiety but a protracted defense of the practice of elenctic questioning." Ryle identifies such questioning as "the Socratic method" and tells us that it was the right to engage in such questioning that Socrates was most concerned to justify.[12]

Here we must tread with great care. It is one thing to say that debate and argument can be useful disciplinary devices in the preparation of those who are to engage in philosophical reasoning; it is quite something else to assume that philosophy is reducible to argument. The eristic method of teaching, probably introduced into Athens by the sophist Protagoras, may have been suitable for preparing future lawyers and politicians, but was it really serviceable for the preparation of everyone else (including would-be philosophers) who sought a more reasonable view of life? It would be strange indeed if Socrates, for whom the shared examination of the concepts essential to the conduct of life was of the greatest urgency, would have been content to equate that all-important pursuit with the dry, technical procedures of dialectical argumentation. What Socrates stresses is the continued prosecution of philosophical inquiry by following the reasoning wherever it leads (confident that, wherever it leads, wisdom lies in that direction), not the heavy breathing and clanging of armor in dialectical battles, where the premium is not on insight but on victory.

What made classical rhetoric and dialectic dangerous, for young people at any rate, was their separation of technique from conviction. Children should be given practice in discussing the concepts they take seriously. To give them practice in discussing matters they are indifferent to deprive them of the intrinsic pleasures of becoming educated and provides society with future citizens who neither discuss what they care about nor care about what they discuss.

Forensic education, the preparation of lawyers who can argue for any side regardless of their own convictions (if they have any), should be

---

[12]Gilbert Ryle, "Plato," in *The Encyclopedia of Philosophy*, ed. Paul Edwards. New York: Macmillan, 1967.

considered a very special case, in no way a model for the rest of education. The breeding ground of amoralism is the training of technicians who assume that ends are given (or do not matter), so that their concern is merely with means, with tactics, with technique. If children are not given the opportunity to weigh and discuss both ends and means, and their inter-relationship, they are likely to become cynical about everything except their own well-being, and adults will not be slow to condemn them as "mindless little relativists."

One may readily conjecture, therefore, that what Plato was condemning in the seventh book of the *Republic* was not the practice of philosophy by children as such but the reduction of philosophy to sophistical exercises in dialectic or rhetoric, the effects of which on children would be particularly devastating and demoralizing. How better to guarantee the amoralism of the adult than by teaching the child that any belief is as defensible as any other and that what right there is must be the product of argumentative might? If this is how philosophy is to be made available to children, Plato may be supposed to have been saying, then it is far better that they have none at all.

Plato's condemnation of eristic argumentation by children is consistent with his general suspicions regarding whatever it was that the sophists were up to in Greece. Evidently he saw them as his rivals in subversiveness: they seemed to him to be undermining the foundations of Greek morality, while he was trying to undermine the foundations of Greek *immorality*. When they glibly equated dialectic with philosophy—equated, in short, the part with the whole—he and Socrates were not taken in. Nowhere does Socrates ever draw the line when it comes to doing philosophy with people of different ages, for doing philosophy is not a matter of age but of ability to reflect scrupulously and courageously on what one finds important. Indeed, when Callicles suggests to Socrates that philosophy is unworthy of grown men, we may imagine Plato's amusement at being able to implant so seditious an idea into the conversation.[13]

It can hardly be doubted that the traditional prohibition of philosophy for children is much indebted to citations from Plato's *Republic*. Nevertheless, it must be concluded that, insofar as that prohibition has rested on an appeal to Plato, it has rested on a mistake.

Philosophical Inquiry as the Model of Education

The contemporary educational system is frequently depicted as monolithic, inflexible, and impenetrable. However, it is considerably more pluralistic than these accounts suggest—more loose woven, open-textured, and diversified. Within its many crevices and interstices are school administrators to whom philosophy for children, for whatever reason, seems irresistible. Some prize it for its promise of improving reasoning skills; others admire it because students seem to enjoy it for its own sake rather than for the sake of grades or because it is relevant to their vocational aspirations. Some see it as the central stem of the elementary

---

[13]Plato, *Gorgias* (p. 485), in *The Collected Dialogues of Plato,* ed. Edith Hamilton and Huntington Cairns. Princeton, N.J.: Princeton University Press, 1961.

and secondary school, out of which the specialized disciplines can emerge; others see it as a wholesome preventive to drug and alcohol abuse. These educators may be familiar with the traditional rejection of philosophy for children, but they are pragmatic enough to reject it in turn. They like what philosophy does when children do it. They may be quite unaware that philosophy for children happens to fulfill Plato's pedagogical admonition that education be conducted "not by compulsion but by play." Although it may not be easy to put philosophy in place, it is enough for them that it works when it is put in place correctly.

Under these circumstances, philosophy for children will continue to find its way into the elementary schools. After all, word of a good thing gets around; already, children who take philosophy are boasting of it to those who do not, and far from being viewed with odium and contempt, philosophy has become a status symbol of elementary school. But all of these changes may be merely symptoms of a shift in fashion. How can philosophy as a required elementary school discipline—perhaps even as the core or armature of the curriculum—be justified?

This will not be easy, because it relentlessly demands of us the kind of self-knowledge that we, as educators, know to be highly elusive but that Socrates was wont to insist is indispensable to the worthwhile life. We must put aside any illusions we may have about the benign influence we exercise as educators and speak frankly to one another as Santayana speaks of the "magnificent example" Spinoza offers us

> of philosophic liberty, the courage, firmness, and sincerity with which he reconciled his heart to the truth . . . . Many a man before Spinoza and since has found the secret of peace: but the singularity of Spinoza, at least in the modern world, was that he facilitated this moral victory by no dubious postulates. He did not ask God to meet him half way: he did not whitewash the facts, as the facts appear to clear reason, or as they appeared to the science of his day. He solved the problem of the spiritual life after stating it in the hardest, sharpest, most cruel terms. Let us nerve ourselves today to imitate his example, not by simply accepting his solution, which for some of us would be easy, but by exercising his courage in the face of a somewhat different world.[14]

If we examine the present educational system with such candor, it is fairly predictable that we will be bound to conclude not simply that our educational system is imperfect but that its imperfections are more responsible than we have cared to admit for the grave circumstances in which the world currently finds itself. If we deplore our leaders and electorates as being self-centered and unenlightened, we must remember that they are the products of our educational system. If we protest, as an extenuating factor, that they are also the products of homes and families, we must remember that the unreasonable

---

[14]George Santayana, "Ultimate Religion," in *Obiter Scripta,* ed. Justus Buchler and Benjamin Schwartz. New York: Scribner's, 1936.

parents and grandparents in these families are likewise products of the selfsame process of education. As educators, we have a heavy responsibility for the unreasonableness of the world's population.

Socrates must have known that the tincture of self-knowledge provided by philosophy would in itself hardly suffice to deter an Athenian state hell-bent on its own destruction. Nevertheless he persisted, even to the point of demonstrating that what he was doing was worth more to him than life itself. (Always the teacher, even his final act was intentionally instructive!) Surely Socrates realized that the discussion of philosophical concepts was, by itself, just a fragile reed. What he must have been attempting to show was that the doing of philosophy was emblematic of shared inquiry as a way of life. One does not have to be a philosopher to foster the self-corrective spirit of the community of inquiry; rather, it can and should be fostered in each and every one of our institutions.

There is, then, a narrower and a broader case for philosophy for children. The narrower case is simply that it makes a wholesome contribution to the present curriculum and the classroom. But the broader justification would have to rest on the way in which it paradigmatically represents the education of the future as a form of life that has not yet been realized and as a kind of praxis. The reform of education must take shared philosophical inquiry in the classroom as a heuristic model. Without the guidance of some such paradigm, we will continue to drift and the curriculum will continue to be a hodgepodge.

What Is It To Be Fully Educated?

Some educators today see philosophy for children as prefiguring a thorough going reappraisal of education, and they are eager to recite the characteristics of elementary school philosophy that they think the educational process as a whole should exhibit. This is without a doubt an appealing approach, but it should be accompanied by a comprehensive rationale. One does not usually attempt to redesign something unless one first knows what to expect of it or what to try to accomplish by means of it. The Greeks were probably the first people to insist that institutions (and not only people) needed to be perfected and that only by means of ideals such as justice and freedom could the reform of existing institutions be measured and judged. The notion of perfection is unlikely to stir us in quite the way it did the Greeks. Nevertheless, we may still agree with Dewey that nothing in human society commands our admiration as much as the way human institutions such as science and art, medicine and law seek in their practice to approximate their respective ideals of truth and beauty, health and justice.

What, then, is the ideal that educational practice seeks to approximate? This would seem to be the primary question that the redesign of education must confront. Thus put, the question may be too formidable to answer. Perhaps we should try putting a different question first: in what respect has education most greatly disappointed us? Here our response need not be in the least equivocal, and in answering the second question, we automatically answer the first: the greatest disappointment of traditional education has been its failure to produce people approximating the ideal of reasonableness. (This is not to say that all who are reasonable must have been educated, but rather that whoever is educated ought to be reasonable.) It may well be that in previous centuries unreasonableness was a luxury that human beings could afford, even though the costs were high. It should be evident, however, that the costs of our tolerant attitude toward unreasonableness are now far beyond our reach. We may still smile indulgently as we read of the legendary figures of history who were splendidly capricious and magnificently illogical: they savaged their victims, but they did not endanger everything. This is no longer the case; we will have to reason together or die together.

Traditionally, education has been conceived of as initiation into the culture, and the educated person has been thought to be the "cultivated" person or even the "cultured" person. But a closer look at traditional education might reveal students studying the disciplines, and in fact learning them, while yet failing to think in terms of them or to appropriate them fully. Seldom has traditional education been able to meet Vico's challenge—that the only way really to understand something is to re-enact it in some fashion. (One can understand what it is to be a story-teller only by becoming a story-teller, a painter only by becoming a painter, a dancer or a worker or a slave only by becoming a dancer or a worker or a slave.)

To be fully educated, one must be able to treat every discipline as a language and to think fluently in that language; be cultivated in one's reasoning as well as in everything else, remembering that reasoning is most effectively cultivated in the context of philosophy; and demonstrate educational accomplishments not merely as acquisitions of intellectual properties or as the amassing of spiritual capital but as a genuine appropriation that results in the enlargement of the self. Because philosophy is the discipline that best prepares us to think in terms of the other disciplines, it must be assigned a central role in the early (as well as in the late) stages of the educational process.

Converting Classrooms into Communities of Inquiry

It would be unrealistic to expect a child brought up among unjust institutions to behave justly. Abusers of the rights of others often turn out themselves to have been abused. Likewise, it is unrealistic to expect a child brought up among irrational institutions to behave rationally. The irrationality of institutions must be considered preventable. There is no excusing them, for to do so permits them in turn to become the excuse offered by children who have been reared in such institutions and who adopt the irrationality of the institutions that fostered them.

The institution with which we as educators have primary concern is education. The irrationalities or "socially patterned defects" that permeate education have to be rooted out because they do not die out on their own: they have a marvelous capacity for self-perpetuation. This involves our bringing a greater degree of rational order than currently exists into the curriculum, into the methodology of teaching, into the process of teacher education, and into the procedures of testing. The adjustments made within each of these must in turn be determined by the interrelationships they have among themselves, as components of education, just as the structure of education depends on what kind of world we want to live in, since it will have much to do with the character of that world.

All too often the components of education have that kind of bizarre interrelationship of which the best analogy is the tail wagging the dog.

Testing, which should have only ancillary status at best, tends to be the driving force of the system. The content of the tests structures the curriculum, which in turn controls the nature of teacher education. (This is not to deny that current practice in schools of education is consistent with the ethos of higher education generally, just as that ethos is in general consistent with that of the larger society of which it is a part. Schools of education tend to reflect the values of their societies, rather than the other way around.)

As long as the major goal of education is thought to be learning, as is the case in all tribal societies, the recall model will dominate testing, and teachers will find it difficult not to teach for the tests. Equally sad is that the information-acquisition model that dominates education, rather than encouraging children to think for themselves, is a failure even on its own terms, for we are constantly appalled at how little our children seem to know about the history of the world or about its political and economic organization. The effect of the tribal model is to stifle rather than to initiate thinking in the student. This does not mean we need to begin by producing better tests; we need to ask ourselves what kind of world we want to live in, what kind of education is most likely to contribute to the emergence of such a world, and what kind of curriculum is most likely to produce such an education. We must then set about producing that better curriculum.

There is good reason to think that the model of each and every classroom— that which it seeks to approximate and at times becomes—is the community of inquiry. By inquiry, of course, I mean perseverance in self-corrective exploration of issues that are felt to be both important and problematic. In no way do I mean to imply that inquiry sets a greater premium on discovery than on invention or a greater premium on rule-governed as opposed to improvisational activities. Those who produce works of art are practitioners of inquiry no less than those who produce new epistemological treatises or new discoveries in biology.

If we begin with the practice in the classroom, the practice of converting it into a reflective community that thinks in the disciplines about the world and about its thinking about the world, we soon come to recognize that communities can be nested within larger communities and these within larger communities still, if all hold the same allegiance to the same procedures of inquiry. There is the familiar ripple effect outward, like the stone thrown in the pond: wider and wider, more and more encompassing communities are formed, each community consisting of individuals committed to self-corrective exploration and creativity. It is a picture that owes as much to Charles Peirce as to John Dewey, but I doubt they would quibble over the credits if they thought there was a hope of its realization.

As so often happens when people describe the cloud castles of their dreams, the nitty-gritty realities are all too easily overlooked—realities such as the ladders by means of which the cloud castles are to be reached and the fearsome dragons and lurking trolls that are to be avoided along the way. . . .

Appropriating the Culture

The tribal model of education, in which the child is initiated into the culture, in effect provides for the assimilation of the child by the culture. In contrast, the reflective model of education provides for the appropriation of the culture by the child. A good case in point would be the textbook. As it currently stands, the textbook is a didactic device that stands over against the child as an alien and rigid *other*. It has this obdurate nature because it represents the final end-product of the received or adult view of the discipline. As Dewey would put it, the textbook (a century after *The Child and the Curriculum*) is still organized logically, like a table of contents or a sequence of lectures, rather than psychologically, in terms of the developing interests and motivation of the child. It is not something the child wants to enjoy and possess in the way one enjoys and assimilates a story or a picture; it is instead a formal, dreary, oppressive, and in many ways unintelligible summary of the contents that the child is expected to learn.

All of this is unnecessary, since we know from the work of Bruner and others that the child views material that is contextualized (i.e., presented in the form of a story) as something to be appropriated rather than rejected. If children are to learn to think in the disciplines so as to appropriate their humanistic heritage, they must begin with the raw subject matter of the disciplines and refine it for themselves. Masticating it for them in advance, the way mother birds masticate worms for their fledglings, is hardly the way to provide an education. Children presented with logic as a finished discipline find it repugnant, but they can find it delightful to discover it bit by bit and to see how it all interlocks and applies to language if not the world. This is how logic was probably discovered, and we can surmise that the early Greeks felt the same excitement and sense of power and mastery in discovering the same logic. Indeed, to learn something well is to learn it afresh in the same spirit of discovery as that which prevailed when it was discovered or in the same spirit of invention as that which prevailed when it was invented. When this spirit, which is truly the spirit of inquiry, prevails in the classroom, children will eagerly work through the materials of the arts and sciences and humanities for themselves and will appropriate them to themselves.

FROM *PHILOSOPHY IN THE CLASSROOM* (1977)

Guiding a Classroom Discussion

A thoughtful discussion is no easy achievement. It takes practice. It requires the development of habits of listening and reflecting. It means that those who express themselves during a discussion must try to organize their thoughts so as not to ramble on pointlessly. Very young children may either wish to talk all at once or not talk at all. It takes time for them to learn sequential procedures that a good discussion requires.

One of the reasons that the process of discussion is so difficult for children to learn is that they are so frequently lacking in models of good discussion with which they can identify. If neither the home nor the school offers them examples of thoughtful discussion—whether of adults with children, or even of adults with adults—then each generation of children must in effect invent the whole process of discussion by itself, because no one ever shows it how. In short, it is useful to have an established tradition of discussion that each child can automatically assimilate and identify with and engage in if dialogue is to enter meaningfully into the educational process.

One of the merits of the novels of the philosophy for children program is that they offer models of dialogue, both of children with one another and of children with adults. They are models that are non-authoritarian and anti-indoctrinational, that respect the values of inquiry and reasoning, encourage the development of alternative modes of thought and imagination, and sketch out what it might be like to live and participate in a small community where children have their own interests yet respect each other as people and are capable at times of engaging in cooperative inquiry for no other reason than that it is satisfying to do so.

Perhaps one of the most distinctive features of the philosophy for children program is that it suggests how children are able to learn from one another. This is a problem that is encountered today at every level of education: there are students in colleges, secondary schools, and elementary schools who try to "make it on their own" without really seeking to learn from one another or to assimilate the life experience of their peers even when, through discussion, it might be readily available to them.

While some children speak up readily enough but fail to listen to one another, others listen intently, follow the line of the discussion, and may then respond to it by making a contribution that goes beyond, rather than merely repeats, what has been said. The teacher should, of course, be aware of the possibility that the child who does not always listen may be developing a very unusual set of ideas, and needs to disregard the conversation for a while in order to do so. (The harm some children do to themselves by not listening is therefore likely to be considerably less than the harm other children do to themselves when, having failed to listen, they are constantly forced to cover the same ground that others have already gone over.) On the other hand, there are children who seldom speak up, but who listen intently and constructively to the class discussion. They are alert and involved, even though they fail to join in the discussion.

A discussion should build by way of its own dynamics. Like children in a playground building a pyramid by standing on one another, a discussion builds upon the contributions of each of its members. In asking questions, the teacher is not merely trying to elicit answers already known. Encouraging philosophical thinking is a matter of getting children to reflect in fresh ways, to consider alternative methods of thinking and acting, to deliberate creatively and imaginatively. The teacher cannot possibly know in advance the answers that children are going to come up with. In fact, it is just this element of surprise that has always been so refreshing about teaching philosophical thinking: one never is quite sure what thought will surface next.

It is, of course, important to keep the discussion going. As the children hear about each other's experiences and begin to learn from each other, they begin to appreciate one another's points of view and to respect one another's values. But when it appears that the discussion of one of the leading ideas of the episodes has ceased to be productive, the teacher must be prepared to direct the discussion tactfully to another topic.

The Role of Ideas in a Philosophical Dialogue

You may well be wondering what is distinctive about a philosophical discussion. In what ways may a philosophical discussion be contrasted with other kinds of discussions? Here we may distinguish philosophical discussion from discussions of two other types: scientific and religious.

Scientific Discussions

A scientific discussion is generally concerned with matters of fact, and with theories about matters of fact. The questions raised in a scientific discussion are in principle answerable questions. They can be answered by discovering relevant evidence, or by consulting acknowledged scientific authorities, or by making appropriate observations, or by citing pertinent laws of nature, or by conducting relevant experiments. Discussions in a science class can be very intense and very lively, especially if there is some disagreement as to how certain evidence is to be interpreted, or as to whether a given theory explains all the relevant factual data.

By and large, the scientist is dealing with how some portion of the world is to be described and explained. Therefore, a science class may involve discussion of such questions as what are the causes of sun spots, what is the temperature of dry ice, how does the heart work, how does the blood circulate, what was the Stone Age, what causes earthquakes, and so on. In general, the issues raised by these questions can be clarified and grasped by adequate discussion and analysis of elementary scientific theories and available scientific evidence. So a scientific discussion is subject to the authority of empirical evidence, as such evidence is interpreted within the accepted framework of scientific understanding. In principle, therefore, the resolution of scientific disputes is always possible.

Discussion about Religious Beliefs

Many children in your class are already in possession of a set of religious beliefs acquired from their parents, from their religious schools, from discussion with their peers, and sometimes from their own observations. These beliefs may relate to the purpose of destiny of the world, the question of personal immortality, the existence of a God, the expectation of divine reward or punishment, and so on. These are not generally the sorts of questions that can be decided by factual evidence one way or another. In no way is it part of the role of a philosophy teacher to criticize a child's religious beliefs, or to seek to undermine them even in an indirect fashion. The teacher simply cannot infringe upon the realm of children's religious beliefs without becoming guilty of indoctrination. On the other hand, there can be no serious objection to affording the child a view of the range of alternatives from which human beings throughout the world select their beliefs. After all, if it is not indoctrination to suggest to children who profess to believe in many gods, or in none at all, that there are conceivable alternatives to their views, why should it not also be possible to suggest to those who believe in a solitary supernatural being that there are many numerical alternatives?

It is always unfortunate when a teacher, out of self-righteousness or ignorance, attempts to modify the religious beliefs of children in the classroom. Such invasion of the child's intellectual integrity represents not only a lack of respect for the child but also a misconception on the teacher's part of the nature of science, the nature of philosophy, and the nature of education. Some individuals think that children's religious beliefs are unsound in light of what we know of science and philosophy, and can be corrected with a healthy dash of scientific or philosophical information. But there are no such facts that can dispel religious beliefs one way or another. To the extent that religious beliefs are matters of faith, it is a question whether they are matters that can be resolved by either science or philosophy.

It is, of course, quite possible for children to have religious discussions, just as they may discuss their families, their friends, their fears, their joys, and other private matters among themselves. An informal religious discussion among children typically involves a comparing and contrasting of their respective feelings and thoughts about religious matters. It does not usually involve the search for *underlying assumptions,* or the analysis of the meaning of concepts, or the search for clear definitions that often characterize philosophical discussions. In other words, religious discussions usually do not explore the assumptions on which religious beliefs rest, while a philosophical discussion cannot rest content unless it does explore its own assumptions.

To repeat, teachers must be very careful that this course in philosophical thinking does not serve as a tool in their hands or in the hands of the students to disparage the religious beliefs of some of the children in the class. The course optimally should serve as a tool by means of which children can clarify and find firmer foundations *for their own beliefs*. The teacher's role is twofold. It is not to change children's beliefs but to help them find better and more sufficient reasons for believing those things *they* choose, upon reflection, to believe in. And further, it is to strengthen their understanding of the issues involved in their holding to the beliefs they do hold.

Philosophical Discussions

We have tried to show that science and religion represent very separate areas of human interest in terms of their relevance to the classroom. In other words, from an educational point of view, scientific discussions and religious discussions are separate things and should not be confused with philosophical discussions.

Philosophical discussions need not just take up where science and religion leave off. Philosophical discussions can frequently become involved in questions of science and questions of religion, as philosophical discussions may lead into any other subject. Philosophy may or may not be a party to the dispute over factual descriptions of the world of religious interpretation of reality. As an objective onlooker, a philosopher is no more party to these disputes than an umpire is one of the contestants in a game that he referees. If anything, the umpire represents the spirit of impartiality that tries to see that the game proceeds in the fairest possible fashion. In a somewhat similar fashion, philosophy is concerned to clarify meanings, uncover assumptions and presuppositions, analyze concepts, consider the validity of reasoning processes, and investigate the implications of ideas and the consequences in human life of holding certain ideas rather than others.

This is not to imply that philosophy is concerned only with the clarification of concepts: it is also a fertile source of new ideas. For wherever there is a threshold of human knowledge, those who think about that particular subject area can only grope and cast about speculatively in an effort to understand what is there. Gradually, as methods of investigation of the new subject area are developed, as methods of observation and measurement and prediction and control are perfected, the period of philosophical speculation is replaced by one of scientific understanding. In this sense, philosophy is the mother of all sciences, for as philosophical speculation becomes more rigorous and substantiated, as measurement and experimentation and verification begin to occur, philosophy turns into science. In this sense, philosophy is a source of ideas that precedes the development of every new scientific enterprise.

Now what does all this mean for the role of the teacher in guiding *philosophical* discussions? First, the teacher has to keep in mind the distinctions just made between scientific, religious, and philosophical discussions and must retain these subtle distinctions as guideposts in encouraging children to think philosophically. The teacher must be aware that what began as a philosophical discussion can easily turn into a dispute over factual information that can be settled only by looking up the empirical evidence that is available. It is the teacher's role, once the discussion has taken this turn, to suggest where the empirical evidence may be found, rather than continue along speculative lines. For example, it is not a philosophical dispute if an argument develops in a classroom over the sum of 252 and 323. It *is,* however, a philosophical question to ask, "What is addition?" or "What is a set?" It is easy enough to look up in a book the exact year when Columbus landed in the Western Hemisphere. However, this in no way settles the question of "who was the first person to discover the Western Hemisphere?" a notion that is rich in ambiguity and in need of clarification. We assume that it takes *time* for light to reach the earth from the sun. But we do not have a science of time itself, and therefore, when children ask, "What is time?" they are asking a philosophical question, and there is no reason why, through dialogue with their peers and teachers, they should not be exposed to some of the alternative views that have been offered by philosophers if these views can be phrased in terms that they can understand.

Philosophical discussions can evolve out of a great many of the demands children make for the *meaning* of an idea. It is up to the teacher to seize upon these opportunities and use them as entries into philosophical exploration. If the child wants to know what the word "authority" means, or what the word "culture" means, or what the word "world" means, or what the word "respect" means, or what the word "rights" means, the teacher can take any of these as a starting point for getting as many views out on the table as there are children in the classroom, exposing the children to additional views that have been thought up by philosophers, examining the consequences of holding one view over another, and clarifying the meaning and the underlying assumptions of each view.

REVIEW OF ARNOLD LOBEL'S *FROG AND TOAD*

Together (1985)

Frog and Toad Together, I often tell my students, half-jokingly, is a philosophical classic. They smile indulgently, as is appropriate for a half-joke. Then I elaborate.

Each of the five stories in the collection, I explain, introduces a philosophical problem, or set of problems. Thus "A List," the first story, illustrates an interesting worry about completeness. Toad decides to write down a list of *all* the things he will do that day. When the wind blows his list away he complains that he cannot run after it because running after it was not on his list of things to do that day. Would reading the list, or even following the list, be inappropriate because "Read this list" and "Follow this list" were not on the list either?

Another story in the collection, "Cookies," takes up weakness of will. (See the very first of these columns, *Thinking,* Vol. 1, No. 1.) It invites us to puzzle over the question, "How could one ever try hard not to do what one really wants to do? If one tries hard enough to succeed at, say, *not* having another cookie, won't it be because one actually wants to stop having cookies?"

The story, "Dragons and Giants," explores the idea of bravery. Can I see in a mirror whether I am brave? Is there anything to look for? Must I do something dangerous to tell whether I am brave, something like slaying a dragon or facing down a giant? And suppose I am scared the whole time? Or don't realize how dangerous it really is? Or think it is dangerous when it isn't, really?

The last story in the book, "The Dream," suggests familiar problems about deception and the dream world. "Frog," Toad asks after a dream episode, "is that really you?" Frog assures him that it is. If the reassurance is real, it is entirely appropriate that Toad should be reassured. But it might also be appropriate that Toad should be reassured. But it might also be appropriate *in a dream* that Toad be reassured.

The story I have left out, the second one, called "The Garden," is about inductive reasoning. Toad plants some seeds and, becoming impatient about their growth, shouts at them to grow. Alarmed at the noise Toad is making, Frog tells him that he is frightening the seeds. Toad is not amused. He burns candles to keep his seeds from being frightened. He sings songs, reads poetry and plays music to them. When these efforts produce no visible result, Toad laments, "These must be the most frightened seeds in the whole world." Exhausted, he falls asleep. Frog wakes him with the joyful news that the seeds have sprouted. Toad mops his brow and sighs, "You were right, Frog, it *was* very hard work."

The textbook name for Toad's error in inductive reasoning is given in the Latin phrase, *"post hoc, ergo propter hoc."* (After this, therefore because of this.) Even very small children laugh at Toad's comment and thus show some awareness that *post hoc, ergo propter hoc* is a fallacy. But it is difficult even for a sophisticated adult to be clear about what makes the reasoning fallacious. David Hume sometimes says that causation is conjunction plus a certain human expectation. ("We may . . . form another definition of cause, and call it, *an object followed by another, and whose appearance always conveys the thought to that other."—Enquiry 7.2.*) So why won't singing to seeds in the fervent expectation of bean sprouts be their cause so long as bean sprouts result?

Hume also speaks of "constant conjunction" (singing always followed by bean sprouts sprouting) and even suggests a stronger condition, a counterfactual requirement: singing won't be the cause of the sprouting of bean sprouts unless, *if* one were now to do such "hard work," seed growth *would* result.

Understanding causality is a difficult job, at least as hard work as making seeds grow. Though it is hard work, it can also be, as Arnold Lobel's story should remind us, lots of fun.

Review of Arnold Lobel's *Frog and Toad Together* by Gareth Matthews in *Thinking,* Vol. 6, No. 2, p. 1. Used by permission of Matthew Lipman.

From *Teaching as Story Telling* (1986)

Story Rhythm

Stories are narrative units. That they are units is important. They are distinguishable from other kinds of narratives in that they have particular, clear beginnings and ends. The most basic story begins "Once upon a time" and concludes "they lived happily ever after." "Once upon a time" *begins* something and "ever after" does not refer to anything in particular except that what began is now ended. "Once upon a time" creates an expectation of a particular kind. We are told that at some particular time and place something happened. This something will involve a conflict or problem of some kind, which the rest of the story will be taken up resolving.

The story does not deal with anything except the problem set up in the beginning once it is underway. Everything in the story is focused on that central task. The weather is not incidental or arbitrary—it will affect either the action or the mood. If it does not, in a good story it will simply be ignored. Stories, then, have clear means of determining what should be included and excluded. We recognize as bad stories those that include things that do not take the story forward. Each such item lets interest sag, and if there are too many of them we stop reading, or watching, or listening.

"What happened next?" has to be answered by an incident or action that takes us towards some complication or resolution of the conflict set up in the beginning. There is, then, at the simplest level a rhythm in stories. They set up an expectation at the beginning, this is elaborated or complicated in the middle, and is satisfied in the end. Stories are tied beginning to end by their satisfying the expectation set up in the beginning. Anything that does not contribute to or fit in with this rhythm is irrelevant to the story and should be excluded. If in *Cinderella* we were to follow one of the ugly sisters through her daily round the story would sag: such events are irrelevant to resolving the particular conflict set up in the beginning of the story.

So we can observe a powerful principle of coherence and a criterion for selecting what is relevant at work in any good story. Such stories hold their power over us as long as all the events stick to and carry forward the basic rhythm. If we consider teaching in light of this cohesive principle of stories we may conclude that the general observation is hardly novel, but it encourages us to look at it in a new way. The principle of organizing a lesson coherently is obvious, but the comparison with the story form suggests new ways in which we might better achieve such coherence. How do we decide what and how much to include in a lesson? More material towards answering this will come in the next section, but here we might draw a first implication from the form of a well-wrought story.

In those stories which children find most engaging there are only those events and details which further the underlying rhythm. Other facts and events that might be connected to those in the story, even if interesting in their own right, are left out. Each irrelevant item, each item that fails to carry forward the story, lets our engagement sag a little. Most stories can obviously bear some of this, but too much and the story is lost. Think of the classic folk-tales. One thing that has happened to them in their centuries of transmission is that they have been honed down to the point where only essential details are included.

Classic folk-tales are, in this regard, a little like jokes. They both set up an expectation in the beginning that is ruthlessly followed to the end. The rhythms of jokes and classic folk-tales are clearly memorable. We might forget stories and jokes, of course, but once started on one the rhythm will usually carry us forward and fit the pieces into place.

A model for teaching that draws on the power of the story, then, will ensure that we set up a conflict or sense of dramatic tension at the beginning of our lessons and units. Thus, we create some expectation that we will satisfy at the end. It is this rhythm of expectation and satisfaction that will give us a principle for precisely selecting content. Consider how much content is forgotten after a lesson or unit is finished. What purpose did that forgotten content serve? Well, no doubt, some purpose is served occasionally. We do not want to neglect the fact that some forgotten content nevertheless may remain in the structure of children's understanding of a topic ("I don't remember who opposed the settlement, but I know there was some opposition"). Nevertheless, it is surely reasonable to conclude that much forgotten content—and no doubt much that is remembered too—plays no significant educational role. It remains in Whitehead's sense "inert" (Whitehead, 1929). The implication from this reflection on the power of the story form is that we should concentrate more on simplifying and clarifying our selection of content according to the rhythm set up at the beginning of our lesson or unit. We need, then, to be more conscious of the importance of beginning with a conflict or problem whose resolution at the end can set such a rhythm in motion. Our choice of that opening conflict, then, becomes crucial. Our first consideration must be on what is most important about our topic, and we will identify importance in terms of those profound abstract concepts which children clearly already understand—good/bad, survival/destruction, security/fear, brave/cowardly, and so on.

The rhythms that stories follow are a reflection of further conceptual abilities of children. That is, whatever conceptual abilities are involved in recognizing conflicts and problems and following their elaboration and knowing when they have been satisfactorily resolved, children clearly have. Nor are these trivial intellectual abilities. They are complex and profound. As the study of linguistics has enlarged our understanding of the great complexity of the intellectual task of mastering language, so the study of poetics gives us some hints of the even greater complexity involved in mastery of the story-form. Our educational task is not to analyse these skills in detail, but rather to observe them and recognize more clearly something of the range and profundity of the learning power that children have.

Binary Opposites

One of the most obvious structural devices we can see in children's stories is the use of binary opposites. Embedded in the story or embodied by the story, are conflicts between good and bad, courage and cowardice, fear and security, and so on. The characters and events embody these underlying abstract conflicts.

These abstract binary opposites serve as criteria for the selection and organization of the content of the story and they serve as the main structuring lines along which the story moves forward. Let us consider these connected functions one at a time.

If we set up a story with a wicked step-mother and a good girl, like *Cinderella,* we begin with a conflict between these embodiments of good and bad. The selection of incidents and further characters, then, will be determined by the need to show the goodness of the one and the badness of the other. The incidents in which the step-mother is cruel to Cinderella and favors her own unkind and vain daughters all elaborate the one binary pole. The unfailing kindness and self-sacrificing modesty of Cinderella place her as embodiment of the opposite pole. The story is the embodied conflict of the good and bad. In this way, then, the binary opposites that underlie our story serve as criteria for the selection of the "content"—the characters and incidents—which form the story.

These binary opposites, connectedly, provide the main structural lines along which the story moves forward. Having gathered the conflict at the beginning, we monitor the development of the story through the incidents showing the badness of the step-mother. She tries to frustrate all of Cinderella's wishes and to destroy her one modest hope of attending the Prince's ball. Our expectation is to see contrasting developments of Cinderella's goodness. Once these are vividly clear the conflict can then go forward through the actions of the good helpers, the attempts to frustrate these actions by the bad opposition, and so on to the final satisfying resolution in favor of the good. We even get some mediation in some versions of the story as the step-mother and ugly sisters recognize the error of their ways and, through Cinder's goodness, they too live happily ever after.

Wherever we look in children's stories, and in their own, no doubt derivative, narratives, we find such binary conflicts. We are not here concerned with psychological explanations, so much as simply observing their functions and power in making clear and engaging structures of meaning. Also, we should not use such observations to suggest that these features of children's thinking are somehow unique to children. If we pause and consider how we make sense of events we hear about on the news, say, we can see these kinds of binary opposite organizers busily at work. They seem to be the first stage in our organizing and making meaningful new information. If we hear, for example, that there has just been a revolution in an African or South American state, we first search with our binary organizers to orient ourselves to the event. We want to know whether the rebels were supplied with arms by the C.I.A. or whether they had Cuban advisors, for example. That is, we first search for events or facts that allow us to fit the information into our already formed binary ideological structures. If we cannot fit the news account clearly into such structures it remains in danger of being meaningless.

Unfortunately perhaps, the news media that are eager to engage us tend to present information already embedded in such contexts. This tends to restrict our understanding of the world's complexity to the basic unmediated binary opposites of childhood. So our media present political information very much in terms of good and bad competing superpowers, and news-stories that can be fitted to that most easily engaging structure get prominent display, and those that cannot tend to get short shrift. In children's stories, however, the mediation that is appropriate for adults has not yet taken place, and so clarity of meaning requires that we structure information on binary opposites. (This does not mean that we have to present things crudely as good or bad, as I will show in the following chapter.)

So these binary opposites are not only of use in organizing stories, but we see them prominently in all kinds of areas in which we organize and make sense of things. If our concern in planning teaching is to communicate clearly an array of material we might wisely consider how binary opposites might be used to help. For my model then I will build in a way of using binary opposites as a means of organizing and selecting content. Because our aim is educational, unlike that of most news media, we will also want to build in a reminder that we should be seeking mediation of the binary opposites we start with.

Affective Meaning

Clearly stories are concerned with affective responses. A good story-teller plays our emotions, as a good violinist plays a violin. We resonate with the rhythm of the binary conflict, the events that carry it forward, and its resolution. Education, seen through the dominant planning and research models, is a largely logical and narrowly rational business. In this view, education is an area where there is little room for our emotional lives. For this reason, the "affective" is usually considered a matter only for the arts—the educational margin or "frills."

As I tried to show in the previous chapter, this view is a product of a misplaced empiricism and of a restricted conception of learning and, not least, of the child. We make sense of the world and experience "affectively" no less than "cognitively." Indeed the separation of the two is a product of the same research programs. Do we make sense of a story affectively or cognitively? Well, of course, both work together. We are not divided into two distinct parts. As we hear melody and harmony as one—though we can separate them in analysis—so we make sense of the world and experience in a unitary way—regardless of what distinctions we might make for research purposes.

The dominant model and its associated research programs have tended to suppress the affective aspects of learning. Consequently they have drawn on only a divided part of children's capacities. A further contribution to teaching that can come from drawing on the story form is a more balanced appeal to children's learning capacities. By using the story form in planning teaching we can reinstate this important and neglected aspect of children's thinking. How stories engage our affective responses, then, is important for us to notice. We will want to build such powers into our model as far as possible, allowing for the differences between typical fictional material and typical classroom instructional material. We can observe at least two ways in which stories engage us affectively.

First, we can observe that stories are largely *about* affective matters—they are about how people feel. These feelings can either provide the motives for actions or they can provide the point and result of actions. If Cinderella's motives were not kind, springing from generous feelings, much of the point of the story would be lost. Also we can readily understand such emotions as causal elements that provide the dynamic of stories. "Jack was angry and decided to get his own back. He stood up, crossed the room, and opened the door." Clearly Jack is going out to get his own back. Such causes of actions present no comprehension problems to young children.

From this observation we can see the importance of human emotions and intentions in making things meaningful. To present knowledge cut off from human emotions and intentions is to reduce its affective meaning. This affective meaning, also, seems especially important in providing *access* to knowledge and engaging us in knowledge. This lesson from our observation of stories will become particularly significant in the discussion of teaching mathematics and sciences in Chapter Four. These are the areas that suffer most from being stripped of their affective associations. We tend to teach mathematics and science as inhuman structures of knowledge, almost taking pride in their logical and inhuman precision. There are two problems with this approach. The first is that it is not true in any sense, the second is that it is educationally disastrous. Later I will discuss ways in which we can rehumanize mathematics and science, seeing the knowledge in its proper, living context of human emotions and intentions.

The second way in which stories engage us affectively follows from the fact that they end. I dwelt earlier on some implications of the obvious point that stories end; they do not just stop but rather they satisfy some conflict set up by their beginning. It is this wrapping up of the story that gives it also a part of its affective power. In life or in history there are no endings; just one damn thing after another. The patterns we impose in order to determine meaning are unlike those of the story. The patterns of our lives or of history are always provisional—something may happen to make us reinterpret, repattern, them. The uniqueness of the story form is that it creates its own world, in which the meaning of events, and thus what we should feel about them, is fixed. Even real-life ugly sisters are on Cinderella's side. We know we have reached the end of the story when we know how to *feel* about all the events and characters that make it up. What is completed by the ending of a good story is the pattern that fixes the meaning and our feelings about the contents.

From this observation we can see that our model needs to provide some way of ending a lesson or unit that has something more in common with the way stories end than with ending because we have "covered" all the content identified as relevant. Our beginning, then, needs to set up some binary conflict or problem and our end needs to resolve it in some way, if we are to take advantage of stories' power to be affectively engaging.

Metaphors, Analogs, and Objectives

In the ancient world and through the medieval period people felt their hearts pumping away in their chests just as we do. But they did not know what was going on in there. There are endless accounts in ancient medical speculation and in the myths and stories of the world of what that bumpety-bump in the chest might be. It seems so obvious to us. The heart is a pump. Blood comes out in spurts when we cut an artery because the pump is working at the rate the blood spurts.

The function of the heart became clear only after the invention of the pump. Indeed, as Jonathan Miller (1978, Ch. 5) argues, the function of the heart became *knowable* only after the invention of the pump. Once people understood how a pump worked, they could use that knowledge to make sense of the heart's function. With the advance of technology an analogy was provided which enabled understanding of things which were otherwise mysterious.

We have within us, of course, another functioning organ whose workings are not at all clear to us. We have no adequate mechanical analogs of the brain. We have seen constant attempts to make sense of it in terms of increasingly sophisticated technology. The earliest analogs were natural. Late medieval textbooks represent the brain as a kind of tree with knowledge categorized in various ways as leaves or branches from a trunk representing, often, theology. Later it is represented in terms of clockwork. Then, with a better understanding of the mechanics of the body, we find the brain represented as made up of parts that functioned like muscles—leading to faculty psychology. In this view, the parts, or faculties, of the brain grew and remained limber through exercise, much as a muscle does.

Once the telephone and then telephone exchanges were built we find those providing an analogy for thinking about the brain. This was considered especially appropriate as it was discovered that there was also some kind of electrical activity going on in the brain itself. It seems fair to say that behaviorism, as an overall theory about human behavior, owes more to the telephone exchange than it does to observations of behavior.

To say this about behaviorism is not intended as a contemptuously dismissive criticism. Our thinking is suffused with metaphors and analogies. There is an important sense in which we use the world to think with. We can use the telephone exchange as a tool with which to think about the brain. The analogy is hidden in the theory, but it has provided the means whereby we can get some conceptual grasp on it. We need, however, to be constantly concerned that our analogies are adequate. The pump is an adequate analogy for making sense of the heart. The telephone exchange is, it seems to be becoming increasingly recognized, an inadequate analogy for the brain.

In any scientific field, however, a bad theory is better than no theory at all. It is the inadequate analogy that yields a bad theory, but it is in perceiving the inadequacy of the theory that we can construct a better one. The demise of behaviorism, one might reasonably argue, owes less to the assaults of competing theories, and more to the development of the computer. The computer allows us, analogically, to think about brain functioning in a more sophisticated way than does the telephone exchange. The computer tends thereby to destroy the basis of behaviorism. But it is itself, of course, merely a relatively simple machine, and so provides us still with mechanistic analogies for thinking about the brain.

While it might be fun to continue with such notions, I should return to the point! These comments on metaphorical thinking and the use of analogies are intended as an introduction to reflecting on the adequacy of the dominant model used in planning teaching. In what way? Well, another great technical innovation in this century was the assembly line. Instead of building, for example, an automobile in one place, bringing the components to it and having the same gang of workers do all the different constructive jobs, the assembly line maximized efficiency by the methods now familiar to us all. The various bits and pieces of the automobile were gathered together at different places along the line ready to be slotted into place at the appropriate time. The workers each had specialized functions which they performed in time to the movement of the line. The initial design determined every detail of the process. It is perhaps trite to ask: What does that remind you of?

One thing it might remind us of is the curriculum. We have our overall aim and the problem becomes how best to organize its components into a sequence in order to attain that aim at the end of the process. Education is not so much like an assembly line as that the assembly line provides an analogy which people can use to think about education. Such analogical thinking need not be conscious. No doubt people could understand the heart without conscious reference to the pump, and behaviorists might even resist consciously connecting their conception of behavior with the telephone exchange. But once we understand the pump or the telephone exchange we can make sense of processes which we see in analogous terms. Even though the analogous connection may not be conscious, there is a strong tendency for the language associated with the comprehended process to invade discussion of that which it is used to comprehend. Thus Cubberly early in the century could write that schools are "factories in which the raw products (children) are to be shaped and fashioned into products to meet the various demands of life" (in Callahan, 1962, p. 152).

And so the process of planning teaching can be represented in a model that is an analog of the assembly line. We first design our final product or state our objectives, then we assemble the parts or decide what materials and content we will need in order to achieve those objectives, then we organize workers with appropriate skills along the line or choose the methods appropriate to organize most effectively the teaching of that content, and finally we arrange some means of determining whether each product is satisfactory or we evaluate whether our objectives have been attained.

Now this does not mean that there must be something wrong with planning teaching by means of a model that is an analogous extension of the assembly line. The pump made sense of the heart. The question here, however, is whether the assembly line leads to a model that is adequate for its educational task. The adequacy of such a model is not usually *raised*, however, because we forget that it is an analogous extension from a stage of technological development.

Let us, then, raise the question of whether the dominant model *is* adequate for its educational task. A number of points might be made that can leave us feeling at least uncomfortable about the adequacy of the model. Most generally, derived from the assembly line analogy, is the requirement that the first step in planning teaching requires that one prespecify precisely one's objectives. As the plan of the automobile determines every aspect of the assembly line so our "educational objectives become the criteria by which materials are selected, content is outlined, instructional procedures are developed and tests and examinations are prepared" (Tyler, 1949, p. 3).

Now if we use the dominant model, and its hidden, persuasive analogy, as the means to think about planning teaching, this first requirement will seem obvious. Of course you have to start with precise objectives or you will not know what to do—as you cannot organize an assembly line without a precisely designed automobile to provide the criterion for the construction and organization of the parts and the arrangements of the requisite tools and construction skills. What we have to do here, however, is try to use our understanding of the reality of education to reflect back on the adequacy of this model. This is difficult. Normally we use the model to think *with;* here we are to try to think *about* what we usually think with.

The first simple observation to make is that in education we do not expect, nor should we aim, to have each student become identical "products" in general and in particular we do not expect each student even to learn a particular lesson the same way as any other student. There are endless ways of being and becoming educated. We may try to specify certain necessary conditions, which may form a "core curriculum," but the sheer diversity of individual students and of social and cultural contexts makes even this a most problematic task. Our observation in the classroom shows us the endless and unpredictable ways in which students *use* knowledge. What we properly value in education are these unpredictable and spontaneously creative uses of knowledge. Clearly we can say that the imaginative creativity of children does not prevent us specifying certain objectives precisely. Children can then use in individually unpredictable ways what was the objective of the lesson. But the point here is that it is the unpredictable use, the spontaneity, the creative imagination that is at the educational heart of the matter. What the model does is leave this out in the cold, and suggest that the heart of the matter is the controllable, predictable, prespecifiable part. It is by such means that a model can deform an enterprise it is supposed to serve. This is not an argument against the model, in the sense of a logically convincing refutation. Rather it is one reason why we should feel uncomfortable with the model: what is most valuable is left out, and teachers are not encouraged to focus their attention on it.

Relatedly, if we reflect not just on the diversity of things a teacher might hope to have happen in an average class, but the ways in which all kinds of associations of ideas, particular hobbies or interests, wonder and humour, that might purely incidentally be stimulated, we may consider whether the reality of educational engagements is inappropriately represented as planned means working carefully along a prespecified path to precisely delineated objectives. Of course we can organize our curricula and lessons this way. But such a process seems not to *fit* some obvious features of education.

In the assembly line, and the analogous model, the product is made up of the pieces put together in the right way in the right sequence. The educated person is not merely the accumulated product of all that has been learned. The more basic problem at the heart of this objection is subtle and, again, not a compelling argument so much as a point of view from which the inadequacy of the model is pointed to. The assembly line model sees the educational product as a carefully planned accumulation of parts. Human understanding, however, does not seem to accumulate this way.

Perhaps I can better point to the inadequacy of the old-technology derived model by contrasting it by analogy with a newer technology. In the old model, human understanding is represented as analogous to a two-dimensional picture. In order to compose the picture, we need only get all the pieces together and fit them in their places. But if we think of human understanding as more like a hologram than a two-dimensional picture, we see the poverty of the older view. If a hologram is broken in pieces, each piece contains an image of the whole. The laser will not show simply a part of the picture, but will show a fuzzy image of the whole. As pieces are added the whole picture becomes clearer. The curriculum is not adequately conceptualized if it is viewed as like a two-dimensional picture that can be completed by putting the pieces together one by one. Rather it is a matter of coalescence and increasing clarity, in whose composition linear processes are inadequate.

My point, again, is not that the dominant model is in any sense *wrong*. Rather, it embodies a way of thinking about education, and encourages ways of thinking about teaching, that are in profound and subtle ways *inadequate*. The alternative I will describe in the following chapter is also, of course, inadequate, but its virtue I think is that it is less inadequate than what I am proposing it should replace. (Without the dominant model, of course, there could not have been this recommended alternative.)

The assembly line has become a fairly general metaphor for dehumanizing working conditions. Some automakers have tried a number of alternatives to the assembly line in order to reduce the deadening and deskilled routines it encourages. The assembly line is saved, however, by its perfectly attuned robot servants. The dehumanizing carries over, it seems to me, into the planning model for teaching derived by analogy from the assembly line. It has tended to reduce and deform education into a process of accumulating sequences of measurable knowledge and skills. It has tended to suppress, in the name of greater efficiency, the organic complexity of education, and to disguise the fact that we can adequately measure or evaluate only relatively trivial aspects of education.

In conclusion to this rather imprecise discussion—imprecise, because we are dealing with things we have no adequate analogies to enable us to make precise sense of—we might briefly reflect on how well the assembly line works as an analogy for telling a story. Part of my point is the sense of strain we feel thinking of a story in terms of an assembly line. And yet we can do so: we need to have our product or objective clear at the beginning, we need to organize the content, decide on our narrative procedures, and prepare some way of discovering whether we have successfully got the story across. The point is that this just is not a very useful way to think about how to plan telling a story. The analogy at the basis of the comparison simply does not fit very well. It misses the point of the story form in the way that a clockwork orange misses the point of fruit. What I will turn to now is trying to show that telling a story is a better analogy than the assembly line for teaching and that the story form provides a more adequate model for planning teaching.

Conclusion

Telling a story is a way of establishing meaning. Fictional stories tend to be concerned largely with affective meaning, whereas in education our concern is more comprehensive. We want "cognitive" and "affective" meaning together. Because the dominant model has tended to emphasize the cognitive at the expense of the affective, drawing on some aspects of the story form for planning teaching can enable us to achieve a better balance. The result in practice of such abstract matters is clearer access to material for children and greater engagement with it.

The sense of story I am dealing with here is not so much the typical fictional kind, but something nearer to what a newspaper editor means when he asks his reporter "What's the story on this?" The editor is asking for an account of the particular events embedded in some more abstract context which readers already understand. The editor basically wants to know how the particulars fit into some binary conflict: How do these particulars give body to the ongoing story of good vs. bad, or security vs. danger, or political right vs. left, etc. The editor's question is one about how this particular knowledge is to be made meaningful and engaging to readers. So when I advocate use of some features of the story format it is in order to make new knowledge meaningful and engaging to children.

I will want to build into my model then some means of establishing at least some degree of story-like rhythm. This requires a particular kind of beginning that sets up an expectation, and a conclusion that satisfies this expectation. Such an overall form wraps the beginning and the end of a lesson or unit more tightly together than is usual. The new model also will be alert to the importance of underlying binary opposites for engaging interest and carrying it along. They also will provide a key criterion for the selection and organization of content.

I have spent some time discussing the inappropriateness of thinking about teaching by means of a model analogous to the assembly line because the major "heresy" of my model is that it does not begin with a statement of objectives. Indeed, objectives are not mentioned anywhere. In telling a story one does not begin by stating objectives, and yet stories are wonderful tools for efficiently organizing and communicating meaning. A major point of this book is that teaching is centrally concerned with efficiently organizing and communicating meaning, and so we will sensibly use a planning model derived from one of the world's most powerful and pervasive ways of doing this. Objectives based models are products of a particular phase of industrialization. They are the result of attempts to technologize teaching in inappropriate ways. They result in clockwork oranges. It is time to move to something more fruitful.

From *Teaching as Story Telling* by Kieran Egan (Chicago: University of Chicago Press, 1986), pp. 25–38. Used with Permission.

Questions

1. List some reasons why attempts to introduce thinking into education may have failed.
2. What are the unique characteristics of Philosophy for Children?
3. For Lipman, what does it mean to be fully educated?
4. Distinguish a "community of inquiry" model from other models of teaching.
5. When Lipman says that a "discussion should build by ways of its own dynamics," what does he mean?
6. Distinguish among scientific, religious, and philosophical discussions.
7. Discuss some of the philosophical problems in *Frog and Toad*.
8. What is meant by the rhythm of a story?
9. What is the relationship between the rhythms of stories and the conceptual abilities of children?
10. How do binary opposites assist in organizing and making sense of our world?
11. How do metaphors and/or analogies assist us in understanding otherwise mysterious things?
12. Why is story telling a more effective tool for understanding than an assembly line?

16

Parker J. Palmer

Time Line for Palmer

1939	Is born into an upper-middle-class family in Chicago, Illinois.
1962	Starts his Master in Sociology at the University of California at Berkeley.
1970	Receives his Ph.D. from UC at Berkeley.
1974–1985	Takes a sabbatical at Pendle Hill, the Quaker retreat center near Philadelphia, where he becomes the Dean of Students before leaving in 1985.
1979	Publishes *The Promise of Paradox*.
1983	Publishes *The Company of Strangers: Christians and the Renewal of American Public Life* and *To Know as We Are Known*.
1990	Publishes *The Active Life*.
1993	Wins the national award of the Council of Independent Colleges for Outstanding Contributions to Higher Education.
1993–1994	Is appointed the Eli Lilly Visiting Professor at Berea College in Berea, Kentucky.
1994–1996	Undertakes the "Courage to Teach" program while at the Fetzer Institute.
1998	Publishes *The Courage to Teach: Exploring the Inner Landscape of a Teacher's Life.* Is named as one of the thirty "most influential senior leaders" in higher education and one of the ten key "agenda setters" of the past decade by The Leadership Project, a National survey of 11,000 administrators and faculty.
2000	Publishes *Let Your Life Speak*.
2001	Is granted the Distinguished Alumni Achievement Award by Carleton College.
2004	Publishes *A Hidden Wholeness: The Journey Toward an Undivided Life*.
2008	Publishes *The Promise of Paradox: A Celebration of Contradictions in the Christian Life*.
2010	Publishes *The Heart of Higher Education: A Call to Renewal*.

INTRODUCTION

Parker J. Palmer characterizes himself as "a Quaker, a would-be pacifist, a writer, and an activist." Noting that what he has become is compatible with his unique human nature, Palmer suggests that he had not always known what he wanted to be. As is typical of much of his writing and teaching, Palmer draws upon his own experiences to illustrate that every human being has a unique nature with potentials and limitations. Palmer warns us against "wearing other people's faces" and suggests that asking the questions "Who am I?" and "What is my nature?" is the first step toward achieving "the joy that every human seeks" and toward the "path of authentic service in the world."[1]

A reoccurring theme in Palmer's life and work is a fondness for and the ability to simultaneously embrace seemingly contradictory or paradoxical positions or beliefs. As Palmer himself explains, "my vocation is the spiritual life, the quest for God, which relies on the eye of the heart. My avocation is education, the quest for knowledge, which relies on the eye of the mind. I have seen life through both eyes as long as I can remember—but the two images have not always coincided. . . . I have been forced to find ways for my eyes to work together, to find a common focus for my spirit-seeking heart and my knowledge-seeking mind that embraces reality in all its amazing dimensions."[2]

Parker J. Palmer grew up in the 1940s and 1950s in a white, upper-middle-class family in suburban Chicago. With his father associated with the same Chinaware company for more than fifty years—first as an employee and eventually as Chairman of the Board and owner—Palmer experienced a stable and relatively affluent home environment. As Palmer himself explains, his father taught him to rely on a "larger and deeper grace" and modeled for him compassion and generosity.

While love and respect characterized the boy's relationship with his father, Palmer was not interested in a career in business. As a young boy, Palmer expressed an interest in flight which contributed to his goal—announced in high school—of becoming a naval aviator. This interest in aviation manifested itself in a young Parker Palmer spending long hours developing ten- and twelve-page books on aviation. The logical consequence of this fascination with aviation seemed to lead to a career as an aviator or aeronautical engineer, but—as Palmer later discovered and explains—this adolescent compulsion of making of books about aviation, when coupled with his fascination with language, enabled Palmer to find his true calling as a writer.

Graduating Phi Beta Kappa from Carleton College in Minnesota with a major in philosophy and sociology, Palmer moved on to the Union Theological Seminary in New York. Quickly learning—thanks to mediocre grades and a pervasive boredom—that the ministry was not for him, Palmer soon pursued his master and doctorate in sociology at The University of California at Berkeley. Beginning there in 1962 and finishing his doctorate in 1970, Palmer experienced Berkeley during the tumultuous 1960s. Characterizing his Berkeley experience as an "astounding mix of shadow and light,"

---

[1] Parker J. Palmer, "Now I Become Myself," *Yes!* (Spring 2001), p. 2.
[2] Parker J. Palmer, *To Know as We Are Known: Education as a Spiritual Journey* (San Francisco: Harper Publishers, 1993), p. xxiv.

Palmer was drawn to the "light" and left Berkeley with a "lifelong sense of hope, a feeling for community, a passion for social change."[3]

While pursuing his master and doctoral studies, Palmer taught for two years (1965–1967) and loved it. Though he considered a university career, the "light" of his Berkeley experience fueled his belief in the possibility of real and lasting change. Instead of pursuing an academic career, Palmer accepted a position as a community organizer in Washington, D. C.

Describing his work in Washington as teaching in a classroom without walls, Palmer remained there for five years, interlacing his work as a community organizer with his duties in the sociology department at Georgetown University. After five years of this work, Palmer took a year's sabbatical at Pendle Hill, the Quaker retreat near Philadelphia.

One year stretched into ten, with Palmer eventually assuming the role of Dean of Students at Pendle Hill. Here at the retreat, Palmer found God in the silence of the Quaker meetings. As suggested in the selection included here, Palmer's understanding of and advocacy for dialogue as a pedagogical process has its origins in his Pendle Hill experience of the Quaker way of living and thinking. Until coming here, religion and faith in God had been largely an intellectual exercise.

While he was at Pendle Hill, Palmer's writings began to attract attention. In pamphlets on community and the power of paradox, and in books on spirituality, education, and on Christianity and the renewal of public life, Palmer began to attract a national following.

Following his decade at Pendle Hill (1975–1985), Palmer remained active as a writer, speaker, workshop facilitator, and consultant for educational, community, and religious organizations. Employed by a variety of institutions, including colleges and universities, Palmer continued to teach and write, sharing with an ever-expanding audience his faith that an education that integrates the head and the heart can produce effective social change. Becoming an associate of the American Association of Higher Education and a senior advisor to the Fetzer Institute provided Palmer with a forum to inspire changes in education and in the broader community of our modern world. Through presentations, speeches, and his writings, Palmer has established himself as one of the most influential leaders active today. Nearing his seventies, Palmer is considering leaving the public arena—as he puts it—"to make space for whatever else is out there."

Permeating much of Palmer's writings and teaching is the theme that contemporary human beings live disconnected or inauthentic lives. Palmer attributes this lack of integrity or this disconnectedness in the way we live to the way that the modern world answers the questions "How do we know what we know?" and "By what warrant can we call our knowledge true?"[4] Fearing the intellectual chaos resulting from a society where truths are no more than the personal whims of individuals, Palmer suggests that modern society has embraced a scientific *objectivism* as the only or ultimate reality. To acquire pure or untainted knowledge of this ultimate reality, humans

---

[3]Parker J. Palmer, *Let Your Life Speak: Listening for the Voice of Vocation* (San Francisco: Josey-Bass Publishers, 2000), p 20.

[4]Parker J. Palmer, *The Courage to Teach: Exploring the Inner Landscape of a Teacher's Life* (San Francisco: Josey-Bass Publishers; 1998), pp. 50–51.

must disconnect themselves from it both physically and emotionally. The modern human being has been socialized to believe that genuine or real knowledge is derived through scientific reasoning and must not be contaminated by subjective or spiritual elements. To the extent that the subjective or spiritual side of the human being survives, it is isolated or segregated from the rational or scientific self.

Palmer does not deny the importance or validity of "objectivist" knowledge but refuses to accept the either/or reasoning that offers a kind of mindless egalitarianism as the only other option. Searching for a way of avoiding the horns of this dilemma, Palmer suggests that the truths discovered and/or created in a complex, resourceful, and interdependent community of inquiry are at least as powerful as those derived from the more dominant *objectivist* model.

The modern world views the world through analytical lenses. In doing so, Palmer argues that we have fragmented reality into an endless series of binary opposites. While Palmer acknowledges that binary logic has resulted in significant scientific achievements, he suggests that our overreliance on it has destroyed or is destroying our ability to understand and appreciate the wholeness and wonder of life.

To Palmer, there is a reality that transcends either/or or binary thinking. Referring to Niels Bohr's assertion that "the opposite of a true statement is a false statement, but the opposite of a profound truth can be another profound truth," Palmer encourages us to entertain the possible truths of seemingly opposite yet profound both/*and* statements. In certain situations, in which "truth is a paradoxical joining of apparent opposites," it is more sensible to "stop thinking the world into pieces and start thinking it together again."[5]

We ignore life's paradoxes at our own peril. One need only to look at education today to observe the consequences of broken paradoxes. As Palmer explains, the separation of facts from feelings produces "bloodless facts that make the world distant and remote and ignorant emotions that reduce truths to how one feels."[6] In what for him is a kind of spiritual journey, Palmer encourages us to open our minds to a kind of paradoxical thinking that leads to a creative synthesis of the spiritual reality derived from the heart and the objectivist reality derived from the mind.

To prepare us for such paradoxical thinking, Palmer suggests that we need good teachers. While it is necessary for good teachers to know their subject matter, how to teach it, and for what purpose, these skills and/or attributes are not sufficient. According to Palmer, the key question to ask is "Who is the self that teaches?" In order to empower others to embrace the paradoxical nature of reality, teachers must know their own hearts. They must become authentic beings who are comfortable in their own skins. In Palmer's words, "good teachers join self and subject and students in the fabric of life. . . . They are able to weave a complex web of connections among themselves, their subjects, and their students so that students can learn to weave a world for themselves."[7]

For Palmer, the goal of education is for each individual to develop his or her authentic self. This can best be accomplished in what Palmer calls a community of truth created by teachers who know their own hearts, individuals struggling with the question "Who is the self that teaches?" Palmer's community of truth is grounded in

[5]Ibid., pp. 62–63.
[6]Ibid., p. 66.
[7]Ibid., p. 11.

the claim that "reality is a web of communal relationships, and we can know reality by being in community with it."[8] As one who knows her own heart, the teacher facilitates active participation of members of the group. As the group focuses on a common subject worthy of their respect, they engage in increasingly complex patterns of communication. Members share observations and interpretations, correct and complement one another, engage in conflict with others, and experience consensus almost simultaneously. As the community develops, members take ownership of a "circular, interactive, and dynamic" process that has meaning. In the community of truth, as in real life, "truth is an eternal conversation about things that matter, conducted with passion and discipline."[9]

Since Palmer's graduate work focused on philosophy and sociology, it is no great surprise that his educational ideas are closely aligned with those of Matthew Lipman's Philosophy for Children program (see Chapter 15). Both emphasize the importance of dialogue as a pedagogical tool, and both suggest that the role of the educator is to create learning communities that are eventually owned and maintained by the participants themselves. For Lipman, this is a self-correcting community of inquiry where a group of children begin with a well chosen text—a selection from a novel, short story, poem, piece of music, or scientific discovery—that is philosophically interesting. Using carefully crafted questions much like those Palmer advocates to create space that is both bounded and open, the teacher stimulates discussion among members of the group on issues and ideas of importance to them. Palmer labels his process as a community of truth and offers a more thorough analysis of the kinds of questions teachers or facilitators need to ask to foster the development of such a community.

A careful reading of Palmer's work suggests that his thought has been significantly influenced by Aristotelian and Socratic ideas. In addition, his rejection of either/or thinking is reminiscent of John Dewey's critique of modern thought. Still, he is unwilling to be limited by Dewey's naturalism but embraces instead seemingly paradoxical opposites as an essential component of his spiritual journey.

FROM *THE COURAGE TO TEACH*

The Hidden Wholeness: Paradox in Teaching and Learning

There is in all visible things

> an invisible fecundity,
> a dimmed light,
> a meek namelessness,
> a hidden wholeness.
> This mysterious Unity and Integrity
> is Wisdom, the Mother of all,

Natura naturans.

—THOMAS MERTON, "HAGIA SOPHIA"

[8]Ibid., p. 95.
[9]Ibid., p. 104.

Thinking the World Together

The culture of disconnection that undermines teaching and learning is driven partly by fear. But it is also driven by our Western commitment to thinking in polarities, a thought form that elevates disconnection into an intellectual virtue. This way of thinking is so embedded in our culture that we rarely escape it, even when we try—and my own words will prove the point.

In earlier chapters, I tried to correct several imbalances in the way we approach teaching. To correct our overemphasis on technique, I stressed the teacher's identity and integrity. To correct our obsession with objective knowledge, I stressed subjective engagement. To correct our excessive regard for the powers of intellect, I stressed the power of emotions to freeze, or free, the mind.

My intent was to rebalance the scales. But in a polarizing culture, it is hard to do that without slamming the scales in the opposite direction. In arguing for the neglected pole, I may be mistaken for someone who excuses poor technique, urging teachers just to "be themselves"; who believes there are no standards for truth, just "whatever you think it is"; who doesn't care about the content of your thoughts, just as long as you "share what you feel."

It is obvious (I hope!) that these are distortions of what I have said. But we distort things this way all the time because we are trained neither to voice both sides of an issue nor to listen with both ears. The problem goes deeper than the bad habit of competitive conversation some of us have: tell me your thesis and I will find any way, fair or foul, to argue the other side! It is rooted in the fact that we look at the world through analytical lenses. We see everything as this or that, plus or minus, on or off, black or white; and we fragment reality into an endless series of *either-ors*. In a phrase, we think the world apart.

Thinking the world apart, like thinking at a distance, has given us great power. Just as I respect the power of objectivity, rightly understood, I respect the power of analysis—in its rightful place. I have used analytical tools to develop my thesis in this book, and the remarkable machine on which I am writing it is driven by millions upon millions of either-or decisions. Without binary logic, we would have neither computers nor many of the gifts of modern science.

But for all the power it has given us in science and technology, either-or thinking has also given us a fragmented sense of reality that destroys the wholeness and wonder of life. Our problem is compounded by the fact that this mode of knowing has become normative in nearly every area, even though it misleads and betrays us when applied to the perennial problems of being human that lie beyond the reach of logic.

How can we escape the grip of either-or thinking? What would it look like to "think the world together," not to abandon discriminatory logic where it serves us well but to develop a more capacious habit of mind that supports the capacity for connectedness on which good teaching depends?

Niels Bohr, the Nobel Prize–winning physicist, offers the keystone I want to build on: "The opposite of a true statement is a false statement, but the opposite of a profound truth can be another profound truth."

With a few well-chosen words, Bohr defines a concept that is essential to thinking the world together—the concept of paradox. In certain circumstances, truth is found not by splitting the world into either-ors but by embracing it as *both-and*. In certain circumstances, truth is a paradoxical joining of apparent opposites, and if we want to know that truth, we must learn to embrace those opposites as one.

In the empirical world, as Bohr makes clear, there are choices to be made between true and false, choices that must be informed by fact and reason. If the question before us is whether a particular tree is an oak or a maple, we can examine its pedigree in full confidence that it cannot be both and that certain empirical markers will reveal what kind it is.

But Bohr also affirms another realm of knowing where binary logic misleads us. This is the realm of "profound truth," where, if we want to know what is essential, we must stop thinking the world into pieces and start thinking it together again.

Profound truth, rather than empirical fact, is the stuff of which paradoxes are made. But profound need not mean exotic or esoteric. We encounter paradoxical profundities every day simply because we are human, for we ourselves are paradoxes that breathe! Indeed, breathing itself is a form of paradox, requiring inhaling and exhaling to be whole.

The first two chapters of this book are full of ordinary truths about teaching that can be expressed only as paradoxes:

- The knowledge I have gained from thirty years of teaching goes hand in hand with my sense of being a rank amateur at the start of each new class.
- My inward and invisible sense of identity becomes known, even to me, only as it manifests itself in encounters with external and visible "otherness."
- Good teaching comes from identity, not technique, but if I allow my identity to guide me toward an integral technique, that technique can help me express my identity more fully.
- Teaching always takes place at the crossroads of the personal and the public, and if I want to teach well, I must learn to stand where these opposites intersect.
- Intellect works in concert with feeling, so if I hope to open my students' minds, I must open their emotions as well.

None of these truths about teaching can be approached as a simple either-or, though in academic culture we constantly try to do so. When I speak with faculty about the fear students bring into the classroom and how it paralyzes their ability to learn, often some critic will say, "So, you want us to stop being professors and become therapists."

No, that is not what I want. What I want is a richer, more paradoxical model of teaching and learning than binary thought allows, a model that reveals how the paradox of thinking and feeling are joined—whether we are comfortable with paradox or not.

Behind the critic's comment is a trained incapacity to see that heart and mind work as one in our students and in ourselves. They cannot be treated separately, one by the professor, the other by the therapist. When a person is healthy and whole, the head and the heart are both-and, not either-or, and teaching that honors that paradox can help make us all more whole.

When Things Fall Apart

It takes training to think the world apart because we arrive in this world with an instinctive capacity to hold paradoxes together. Watch a young child go through the day, and you will see how action and rest, thought and feeling, tears and laughter are intimate and inseparable companions.

In a child, the opposites commingle and co-create each other with the animal fluidity of breathing in and out. But that easy embrace of paradox is soon drummed out of us. Early in our journey toward adulthood, we are taught that survival depends on our ability to dissect life and discriminate among its parts.

The ability to discriminate is important—but only where the failure to do so will get us into trouble. A child must learn the difference between hot and cold to keep from getting hurt and the difference between right and wrong to keep from hurting others. But it is equally important that we retain, or recover, the ability to embrace paradox where discrimination will get us into trouble—the kind of trouble we get into when we enter adulthood with partitions between thinking and feeling, personal and professional, shadow and light.

We split paradoxes so reflexively that we do not understand the price we pay for our habit. The poles of a paradox are like the poles of a battery: hold them together, and they generate the energy of life; pull them apart, and the current stops flowing. When we separate any of the profound paired truths of our lives, both poles become lifeless specters of themselves—and we become lifeless as well. Dissecting a living paradox has the same impact on our intellectual, emotional, and spiritual well-being as the decision to breathe in without ever breathing out would have on our physical health.

Consider our paradoxical need for both community and solitude. Human beings were made for relationships: without a rich and nourishing network of connections, we wither and die. I am not speaking metaphorically. It is a clinical fact that people who lack relationships get sick more often and recover more slowly than people surrounded by family and friends.

At the same time, we were made for solitude. Our lives may be rich in relationships, but the human self remains a mystery of enfolded inwardness that no other person can possibly enter or know. If we fail to embrace our ultimate aloneness and seek meaning only in communion with others, we wither and die. Other-directedness may serve us well in certain roles or at certain stages of life, but the farther we travel toward the great mystery, the more at home we must be with our essential aloneness in order to stay healthy and whole.

Our equal and opposite needs for solitude and community constitute a great paradox. When it is torn apart, both of these life-giving states of being degenerate into deathly specters of themselves. Solitude split off from community is no longer a rich and fulfilling experience of inwardness; now it becomes loneliness, a terrible isolation. Community split off from solitude is no longer a nurturing network of relationships; now it becomes a crowd, an alienating buzz of too many people and too much noise.

As Dietrich Bonhoeffer said, "Let [the person] who cannot be alone beware of community. Let [the person] who is not in community beware of being alone." In a culture that rips paradoxes apart, many people know nothing of the rich dialectic of solitude and community; they know only a daily whiplash between loneliness and the crowd.

We even have personality technologies to make the whiplash stronger. I am thinking of the psychological tests we use, or misuse, to categorize ourselves as personality "types." Am I introverted or extroverted, inner-directed or other-directed, intuitive or sensate, feminine (and made for community) or masculine (and made for competition)? We put ourselves in either-or boxes, or are put there by others, and fail to embrace the paradoxical nature of the human self.

The world of education as we know it is filled with broken paradoxes—and with the lifeless results:

- We separate head from heart. Result: minds that do not know how to feel and hearts that do not know how to think.
- We separate facts from feelings. Result: bloodless facts that make the world distant and remote and ignorant emotions that reduce truth to how one feels today.
- We separate theory from practice. Result: theories that have little to do with life and practice that is uninformed by understanding.
- We separate teaching from learning. Result: teachers who talk but do not listen and students who listen but do not talk.

Paradoxical thinking requires that we embrace a view of the world in which opposites are joined, so that we can see the world clearly and see it whole. Such a view is characterized by neither flinty-eyed realism nor dewy-eyed romanticism but rather by a creative synthesis of the two.

The result is a world more complex and confusing than the one made simple by either-or thought—but that simplicity is merely the dullness of death. When we think things together, we reclaim the life force in the world, in our students, in ourselves.

The Limits and Potentials of Self

Paradox is not only an abstract mode of knowing, it is a lens through which we can learn more about the selfhood from which good teaching comes.

In workshops on teaching and learning, I invite faculty to look at their own classroom practice through the lens of paradox. I ask each teacher to write brief descriptions of two recent moments in teaching: a moment when things were going so well that you knew you were born to teach and a moment when things were going so poorly that you wished you had never been born.

Remembering such moments is the first step in exploring one of the true paradoxes of teaching: the same person who teaches brilliantly one day can be an utter flop the next! Though we normally take that paradox in a fatalistic or self-mocking manner, in this exercise we are asked to take it seriously as a source of self-knowledge.

Next, I ask people to gather in groups of three to focus on the positive case and help each group member in turn identify his or her gifts—that is, to name the strengths and capacities of the teacher that helped make the case in question an authentic learning experience.

Conducting this exercise on paper, as I am about to attempt, is not nearly as engaging as doing it face to face. I hope you will try it with a few colleagues, if for no other reason than the opportunity it offers to affirm one another as teachers, something we rarely do. Not only does the exercise help us understand ourselves in the light of paradox, but it can deepen our sense of collegiality as well.

Here is a moment from my own teaching experience at a small college in Appalachia, whose students come primarily from that economically depressed region:

> In my 1 P.M. senior seminar, we had been reading *Habits of the Heart* by Robert Bellah and his colleagues, whose main themes I had outlined in a lecture the preceding session. Now I wanted us to take the book's thesis that expressive individualism has replaced community and tradition—a thesis built largely on data from the urban North—and test it against the experience of these students from Appalachia.
>
> I asked them—first in small groups, guided by focus questions, and then in our large group, guided by me—to explore what they had been taught and what they believed about "freedom" (one of the key elements of individualism explored in *Habits*), especially "freedom from . . ." and "freedom to . . ." The small groups seemed very animated, and in the large group, more than three-fourths of the students contributed to an open and engaging discussion.
>
> Most of them said the same thing: they wanted "freedom from" things like unhealthy family ties, narrow religious beliefs, and prejudiced communities, and they wanted "freedom to" be themselves, choose for themselves, express themselves, and even "be selfish." Their comments seemed to fit the *Habits* thesis perfectly—and yet I had the sense that there was more to their lives than they were able, or willing, to articulate.
>
> Then one of the students—a popular young man, well known on campus for his religious faith and humane spirit—found some excuse (I cannot remember what it was) to tell the story of his false arrest earlier that term for drug-dealing in what turned out to be a case of mistaken identity. Given his character and the irony of his arrest, it was a very funny story, and he had everyone laughing uproariously until I intervened with a question: "Why didn't you sue the police for false arrest? You might have gotten rich overnight."
>
> The room quieted while the student explained that he would never have sued, that he was just happy that his mistaken identity

had eventually been cleared up. Then, defending and excusing the police, he said, "Everyone makes mistakes." Almost all the other students quickly made it clear that they agreed with his moral position.

I pursued the inquiry: "Let me hold a mirror up to you. You talk in terms of individualism and self-seeking, but underneath all of that you have such a strong sense of communal membership that you are willing to forgive the police their mistake rather than try to make money off of it. The kind of individualism the authors of *Habits* are talking about is not softened by that sense of community. The stereotypical individualist would have hired a lawyer that evening and filed suit the next morning."

In discussion, the class members seemed to find this interesting and insightful, and they agreed that this mix of individualism and community described them well. I ended up feeling that together we had accomplished two things: a deeper understanding of the book and a deeper understanding of the students' lives. I also had a sense of what the next item on our agenda should be: Why the gap between their individualistic rhetoric and their instinctively communal behavior?

What gifts do I possess that helped make this moment possible? Answering that question here may seem a bit self-congratulatory. I ask only that you reserve judgment until you read my second case. Then it will become clear that there is less to me than my gifts!

Here are some of the strengths other teachers have ascribed to me when I have offered this case in workshops:

- A capacity to combine structure or intentionality with flexibility in both planning and leading the class: clarity about my objectives but openness to various ways of achieving them
- Thorough knowledge of the material I assigned to my students and a commitment to helping them master that material too
- A desire to help my students build a bridge between the academic text and their own lives and a strategic approach for doing so
- A respect for my students' stories that is no more or less than my respect for the scholarly texts I assigned to them
- An ability to see my students' lives more clearly than they themselves see them, a capacity to look beyond their initial self-presentation, and a desire to help them see themselves more deeply
- An aptitude for asking good questions and listening carefully to my student's responses—not only to what they say but also to what they leave unsaid
- A willingness to take risks, especially the risk of inviting open dialogue though I can never know where it is going to take us

Receiving such affirmation is like getting a massage, which is reason enough to welcome it. But there are two additional and important reasons for doing so. First, becoming aware of our gifts can help us teach more consistently from our identity and integrity. Acknowledging our gifts is difficult for many of us, either because we are modest or because it is risky to stick one's head up. But when we are not reminded of and honored for the gifts we bring to teaching, it is easy for us to revert to the dominant pedagogy, even if it has little relation to who we are.

Second, we need reassurance about our gifts in order to take the next step—examining, with others, a moment when our teaching became all pain and no joy. Looking at our "failings" is always hard, but it is easier when done against the backdrop of our strengths. It can even be fruitful, as I hope to show in a moment, when we use paradox to transform a litany of failings into a deeper understanding of the identity from which good teaching comes.

Here is my second case. It comes from the same college, the same semester, and the same course, though a different section—thus proving that you never step into the same stream twice!

In my 3 P.M. senior seminar class, I was troubled from day one by a sense that a fair number of my students were cynical about what we were doing and were determined to stay disengaged. No matter what I tried, their entire emotional range seemed to go from silly to sullen to silent.

Three young women in particular behaved in junior high school mode, passing notes back and forth, ignoring printed items I circulated for discussion, talking to each other during both lectures and discussions, rolling their eyes in response to comments made by me and by other students, and so on. The whole class annoyed me, but these three were a particular needle in my eye.

After several sessions, I spoke to the class, said I was not happy with how it was going, named the behaviors I found distracting, and asked people to tell me what I needed to change—or else to get engaged with what we were doing. No one made any suggestions for changes, and as time went on, some students became marginally more involved with the class. But the Gang of Three continued to misbehave.

So I confronted them outside of class one afternoon when I happened to run into them on campus. "Confronted" is not an excessive characterization—I spoke with anger. They responded by telling me three things: (1) I should not "take it all so personally"; (2) I had made a mistake by disagreeing too vigorously with something one of them had said in class, which had made her mad at me; and (3) they were seniors who were tired of the college's required courses, of which mine was one, and had decided before the term even began to "blow it off."

All of that added to my anger, so I kept pressing for an apology until I got one. At that point, I apologized for my anger (which I realized was excessive, because I had become obsessed with these three) and suggested that perhaps we could start over. The young women agreed to try—probably to keep me from blowing up again.

Following that encounter, one of the three made a few real contributions to the class, but the other two—though they stopped misbehaving—remained disengaged. The class as a whole was dull and distracted, and I simply wanted to get the whole thing over with. I had found my sea legs with the group and was no longer thrown off by anyone, simply because I had lowered my expectations for any given session: *I made peace with the class by giving up on it.* I hate to teach, or live, that way, but with this group, that seemed to be the only way out.

I have reread and relived this miserable episode many times. It causes me so much pain and embarrassment that I always try to leap quickly from the debacle to the natural question, "What could I have done differently that might have made for a better outcome?" But when I lead this exercise in workshops, I insist that participants avoid that question like the plague.

The question is natural only because we are naturally evasive: by asking the question too soon, we try to jump out of our pain into the "fixes" of technique. To take a hard experience like this and leap immediately to "practical solutions" is to evade the insight into one's identity that is always available in moments of vulnerability—insight that comes only as we are willing to dwell more deeply in the dynamics that made us vulnerable.

Eventually, the how-to question is worth asking. But understanding my identity is the first and crucial step in finding new ways to teach: nothing I do differently as a teacher will make any difference to anyone if it is not rooted in my nature.

So I ask the small groups to look at this second case in the light of a particular paradox: every gift a person possesses goes hand in hand with a liability. Every strength is also a weakness, a limitation, a dimension of identity that serves me and others well under some circumstances but not all the time. If my gift is a powerful analytical mind, I have an obvious asset with problems that yield to rationality. But if the problem at hand is an emotional tangle with another person and I use my gift to try to analyze the problem away, the liabilities that accompany my gift will quickly become clear.

What are we to do with the limits we find on the flip side of our gifts? The point is not to "get fixed" but to gain deeper understanding of the paradox of gifts and limits, the paradox of our mixed selves, so that we can teach, and live, more gracefully within the whole of our nature.

When I explore my second case with fellow teachers, I always learn important things about my teaching, as long as my colleagues are able to avoid the fix-it mode. Most important, I learn that my gift as a teacher is the ability to dance with my students, to co-create with them a context in which all of us can teach and learn, and that this gift works as long as I stay open and trusting and hopeful about who my students are.

But when my students refuse to dance with me, my strength turns to weakness. I get angry, although my relational nature often keeps me from expressing my anger in clean and open ways. I become silently resentful and start stepping on the toes of my unwilling dance partners, occasionally kicking their shins. I become closed and untrusting and hopeless far more quickly than need be, simply because they have rejected my gift.

I have no wish to learn distanced methods of teaching simply to satisfy students who do not want to relate to me: teaching from afar would violate my own identity and integrity and only worsen the situation. Instead, I want to learn how to hold the paradoxical poles of my identity together, to embrace the profoundly opposite truths that my sense of self is deeply dependent on others dancing with me *and* that I still have a self when no one wants to dance.

Using *and* rather than *but* in that sentence is important because it expresses a true paradox. My sense of self is so deeply dependent on others that I will always suffer a bit when others refuse to relate to me; there is no way around that simple fact. At the same time, I still have a self when relationships fail—and the suffering I experience is evidence of it.

I need to learn that the pain I sometimes experience in teaching is as much a sign that my selfhood is alive and well as the joy I feel when the dance is in full swing. If I learn that simple but profound truth, I might stay closer to my gift and farther from repressed anger and be more likely to teach in ways that will work for both me and my students.

The root cause of this low point in my teaching was not a failure of technique, though there are techniques that could help me in such moments. The root cause was a sense of self-negation, or even self-annihilation, that came when my students were unwilling to help me fulfill my nature.

It is embarrassing to put it that baldly. I know, intellectually, how naive it is to assume that other people, especially students, are here to help me fulfill myself—naive at best and arrogant at worst. But that assumption is what did me in as that class unraveled, and my own growth as a teacher requires that I face such awkward facts.

To become a better teacher, I must nurture a sense of self that both does and does not depend on the responses of others—and that is a true paradox. To learn that lesson well, I must take a solitary journey into my own nature *and* seek the help of others in seeing myself as I am—another of the many paradoxes that abound on the inner terrain.

Paradox and Pedagogical Design

The principle of paradox is not a guide only to the complexities and potentials of selfhood. It can also guide us in thinking about classroom dynamics and in designing the kind of teaching and learning space that can hold a classroom session.

By *space* I mean a complex of factors: the physical arrangement and feeling of the room, the conceptual framework that I build around the topic my students and I are exploring, the emotional ethos I hope to facilitate, and the ground rules that will guide our inquiry. The space that works best for me is one shaped by a series of paradoxes, and I think I understand why.

Teaching and learning require a higher degree of awareness than we ordinarily possess—and awareness is always heightened when we are caught in a creative tension. Paradox is another name for that tension, a way of holding opposites together that creates an electric charge that keeps us awake. Not all good teachers use the same technique, but whatever technique they use, good teachers always find ways to induce this creative tension.

When I design a classroom session, I am aware of six paradoxical tensions that I want to build into the teaching and learning space. These six are neither prescriptive nor exhaustive. They are simply mine, offered to illustrate how the principle of paradox might contribute to pedagogical design:

1. The space should be bounded and open.
2. The space should be hospitable and "charged."
3. The space should invite the voice of the individual and the voice of the group.
4. The space should honor the "little" stories of the students and the "big" stories of the disciplines and tradition.
5. The space should support solitude and surround it with the resources of community.
6. The space should welcome both silence and speech.

I want to say a few words about what each of these paradoxes means. Then, to rescue the paradoxes and the reader from death by abstraction, I want to explore some practical ways for classroom teachers to bring these ideas to life.

1. *The space should be bounded and open.* The boundaries around a teaching and learning space are created by using a question, a text, or a body of data that keeps us focused on the subject at hand. Within those boundaries, students are free to speak, but their speaking is always guided toward the topic, not only by the teacher but also by the materials at hand. Those materials must be so clear and compelling that students will find it hard to wander from the subject—even when it confuses or frightens them and they would prefer to evade its demands. Space without boundaries is not space, it is a chaotic void, and in such a place no learning is likely to occur.

   But for a space to be a space, it must be open as well as bounded—open to the many paths down which discovery may take us, to the surprises that always come with real learning. If boundaries remind us that our journey has a destination, openness reminds us that there are many ways to reach that end. Deeper still, the openness of a learning space reminds us that the destination we plotted at the outset of the journey may not be the one we will reach, that we must stay alert for clues to our true destination as we travel together.

2. *The space should be hospitable and "charged."* Open space is liberating, but it also raises the fear of getting lost in the uncharted and the unknown. So a learning space must be hospitable—inviting as well as open, safe and trustworthy as well as free. The boundaries around the space offer some of that reassurance, but when those boundaries hold us to difficult topics, additional reassurance is required. So a learning space must have features that help students deal with the dangers of an educational expedition: places to rest, places to find nourishment, even places to seek shelter when one feels overexposed.

But if that expedition is to take us somewhere, the space must also be charged. If students are to learn at the deepest levels, they must not feel so safe that they fall asleep: they need to feel the risks inherent in pursuing the deep things of the world or of the soul. No special effects are required to create this charge—it comes with the territory. We only need fence the space, fill it with topics of significance, and refuse to let anyone evade or trivialize them.

3. *The space should invite the voice of the individual and the voice of the group.* If a space is to support learning, it must invite students to find their authentic voices, whether or not they speak in ways approved by others. Learning does not happen when students are unable to express their ideas, emotions, confusions, ignorance, and prejudices. In fact, only when people can speak their minds does education have a chance to happen.

But a teaching and learning space must be more than a forum for individual expression. It must also be a place in which the group's voice is gathered and amplified, so that the group can affirm, question, challenge, and correct the voice of the individual. The teacher's task is to listen for what the group voice is saying and to play that voice back from time to time so the group can hear and even change its own collective mind.

The paradox of individual and collective voices is most clearly illustrated by an example from outside the classroom: making decisions by consensus. Here, no decision can be made as long as even one voice dissents, so the group must learn to listen to individuals with care. But as a corporate voice emerges through honest dialogue, the group makes a claim on each person, compelling us neither to roll over nor to be defiant but to seek, and speak, our truth more thoughtfully. In a learning space shaped by this paradox, not only do students learn about a subject, but they also learn to speak their own thoughts about that subject and to listen for an emergent collective wisdom that may influence their ideas and beliefs.

4. *The space should honor the "little" stories of the individual and the "big" stories of the disciplines and tradition.* A learning space should not be filled with abstractions so bloated that no room remains for the small but soulful realities that grow in our students' lives. In this space there must be ample room for the little stories of individuals, stories of personal experience in which the student's inner teacher is at work.

But when my little story, or yours, is our only point of reference, we easily become lost in narcissism. So the big stories of the disciplines must also be told in the learning space—stories that are universal in scope and archetypal in depth, that frame our personal tales and help us understand what they mean. We must help students learn to listen to the big stories with the same respect we accord individuals when they tell us the tales of their lives.

5. *The space should support solitude and surround it with the resources of community.* Learning demands solitude—not only in the sense that students need time alone to reflect and absorb but also in the deeper

sense that the integrity of the student's inner self must be respected, not violated, if we expect the student to learn. Learning also demands community—a dialogical exchange in which our ignorance can be aired, our ideas tested, our biases challenged, and our knowledge expanded, an exchange in which we are not simply left alone to think our own thoughts.

But there are forms, or perversions, of community that are inimical to deep solitude, that do not respect interiority and are invasive of the soul. When the group norm asserts, however subtly, that everyone must speak, or must speak in a common voice, then both speech and dissent are stifled, the solitude of the individual is violated, and no learning can occur.

An authentic learning community is not just compatible with solitude; it is essential to a full realization of what the inner teacher is trying to tell us. In a community that respects the mystery of the soul, we help each other remove impediments to discernment. Given certain sensibilities and safeguards, nourished and protected by a teacher, a learning community can help us see both barriers and openings to the truth that lives within us.

6. *The space should welcome both silence and speech.* Words are not the sole medium of exchange in teaching and learning—we educate with silence as well. Silence gives us a chance to reflect on what we have said and heard, and silence itself can be a sort of speech, emerging from the deepest parts of ourselves, of others, of the world.

Psychologists say that a typical group can abide about fifteen seconds of silence before someone feels the need to break the tension by speaking. It is our old friend fear at work, interpreting the silence as something gone wrong, certain that worthwhile things will not happen if we are not making noise. But in authentic education, silence is treated as a trustworthy matrix for the inner work students must do, a medium for learning of the deepest sort.

These six paradoxes add up to sound pedagogy—in theory. But what do they look like in practice? I will try to answer that question, with one proviso: what follows is not a "formula" for teaching but rather a personal account of how I have tried to hold these paradoxes together in my own work.

The principle of paradox can help illumine the selfhood of any teacher and the construction of any teaching and learning space, but the particular pedagogy I am about to describe emerges from a self-hood that may bear scant resemblance to your own. By saying yes—or no, or maybe—to what follows, you may discover something about the sources of teaching that have authenticity for you.

Practicing Paradox in the Classroom

To show how these six paradoxes might be implemented in the classroom, I want to look in detail at the moment described in my first case study—in full awareness of the humility required by my second case! When I sat down to plan the session described in case one, I began with the first paradox: the learning space should be open and bounded. To implement that principle, I turned to the text we were reading at that point in the course, *Habits of the Heart*.

A good text embodies both openness and boundaries—the boundaries created by a clear and compelling set of issues and the openness that comes from exploring those issues in a reflective manner. By choosing such a text and immersing myself in it, I can often get a sense of the learning space I want to create in class. So I reviewed the issues central to *Habits,* finally settling on what Americans believe about freedom as the one I wanted to pursue.

But taking pedagogical clues from a text does not imply slavish adherence to it; the most boring classes I ever took (or taught) stayed so close to the text that we might as well have stayed home. By a good text I mean one that is fundamentally sound and—another paradox—one with enough unexplained gaps that it cannot be followed like a cookbook.

Students do not learn to learn from a text that is without sin, one that raises all the right questions and gives all the right answers. But a text with discontinuities and ambiguities demands our engagement, giving students space to move into its field of discourse and think their own thoughts. Taking pedagogical clues from a text means looking not only for what the text can teach us but also for what we can teach the text.

Habits of the Heart, it seems to me, is blessed by certain gaps in its data, which are based on interviews with a narrow range of Americans from which the authors draw some wide-ranging conclusions. From my vantage point at a small Appalachian college, I was aware that *Habits* had little to say about the large number of Americans who live in poverty and nothing at all to say about the unique experience of poverty in Appalachia.

To honor the first paradox—a learning space should be open and bounded—I decided to create boundaries by asking my students to focus on the picture of freedom that *Habits* paints and then to open that space by asking them, "What's wrong with this picture" based on their own experience. (Of course, the questioning approach itself honors the first paradox by creating clear boundaries around the subject while leaving students free to make their own responses.)

By inviting data from my students' lives into the conversation, I was honoring that part of the second paradox that says the learning space should be hospitable. Hospitality in the classroom requires not only that we treat our students with civility and compassion but also that we invite our students and their insights into the conversation. The good host is not merely polite to the guest—the good host assumes that the guest has stories to tell.

This second paradox requires that a learning space be charged as well as hospitable, a space where students are challenged as well as welcomed. I hoped to create this charge by lifting up freedom as the concept I wanted my students to reflect on. I knew that freedom was a major issue in their lives: some were still rebelling against their families, and others felt that the college unduly constrained their lives.

So my focus questions—"What have you been taught in the past about freedom, especially 'freedom from' and 'freedom to'? And what beliefs about freedom do you now hold?"—were chosen because I thought they might be hot buttons, and so they were. They got my students' attention, emotionally and intellectually, drawing them so deeply into the learning space that they could hardly avoid the challenge to think real thoughts.

To honor the third paradox—that the learning space invite the voices of both individual and group—I began by asking students to take a few minutes to reflect on the question in silence, the silence that most students require to think their best thoughts. Since simple silence is awkward for most people, I asked them to make notes as they reflected, giving them something to do. Then, in a subtle but shameless attempt to concentrate their minds on the task at hand, I said, "I will tell you in a minute what the notes are for."

Because my students did not know whether I would gather and grade their notes (which I would never do) or ask them to use their notes for personal reference in small groups (which I eventually did), all of them made notes, "just in case." Here is a small but significant flashback to the educative value of a charged ethos!

Then I made a gradual movement from the voice of the individual to the voice of the group. Following the personal reflection time, I asked students to gather for ten minutes in self-selected groups of three to share their reflections before the large group dialogue began. Small groups give everyone a chance to speak in a relatively safe setting, and the winnowing that they allow makes it more likely that students will have something of value to say when the large group discussion begins.

When the large group gathers, holding the tension of the third paradox—the voice of the individual and the voice of the group—depends heavily on the teacher's ability to facilitate rather than dictate the discussion. On one hand, the teacher must invite and affirm each individual's voice. That does not mean agreeing with everything that is said, no matter how ludicrous, as cynics sometimes suggest. It means helping each person find the best meaning in what he or she is saying by paying close attention, asking clarifying questions, and offering illustrations if the student gets lost in abstraction.

On the other hand, this paradox requires the teacher to give voice to whatever thought pattern may be emerging from the group: the group does not have a voice until the teacher gives it one. This means listening carefully and holding all the threads of the conversation in mind so that one can eventually lift up a fabric of thought and ask, "Does this look like what you have been saying?" I did this when I showed my students how the self-centeredness they claimed when questioned about their theory of freedom contrasted with the communal ethic they revealed when confronted with an actual dilemma.

The fourth paradox—that we must honor both the little stories of our lives and the big stories of the disciplines—is woven into all the pedagogical moves I have described. It is a hard tension to hold—not only because academia discredits the little story but also because the little stories are the ones students feel most comfortable with. Given free rein, they will hide out in their little stories and evade the big ones.

Though our little stories contain truths that can check and correct the big story (as my students' Appalachian experience corrected the big story in

Habits of the Heart), the teacher must keep using the big story to reframe the little ones. I did this when I used concepts from *Habits* to point out that my students' resistance to suing the police for false arrest revealed a stronger communal ethic than their talk about freedom had suggested.

The key to holding this paradox is the knowledge that though students can tell their own stories, they, like the rest of us, rarely understand the meanings of the stories they tell. How could they, when education so seldom treats their lives as sources of knowledge? The teacher who wants to teach at the intersection of all the stories, big and little, must continually make interpretations that students do not know how to make—until they have been "heard to speech" often enough to do it for themselves.

The fifth paradox—that the space should support solitude and surround it with the resources of community—is usually implemented only in a metaphorical sense. In most educational settings, we cannot send students off for solitary reflection in the middle of class. But what we can do, even as we are developing a collective voice around a given issue, is to honor the soul's need for solitude within the group.

For example, I tell my students that much as I value dialogue, I affirm their right not to participate overtly in the conversation—as long as I have the sense, and occasional verbal reassurance, that they are participating inwardly. This permission *not* to speak seems to evoke speech from people who are normally silent: we are more likely to choose participation when we are granted the freedom to do so.

Honoring the solitude of my students' souls also means that as I listen to them speak, I must discern how deeply to draw them into a topic with my questions. There are some places where the human soul does not want to go—not, at least, in full view of other people.

I came to such a moment in case one when that young man told the story of his false arrest. I knew immediately the question I wanted to ask him, a question that would raise the issue of freedom versus accountability that had yet to surface in our discussion: "Why didn't you sue the police for false arrest? You might have gotten rich overnight."

But that question has sharp edges, especially in a context of poverty. It could easily be heard as "What are you—stupid? You blew a chance to get rich." So before I could ask the question, I needed to ask myself: Can this student handle the question? Do he and I have the kind of relationship that would keep him from being wounded? This is the metaphorical meaning of protecting a student's solitude: inviting the whole truth while refusing to violate the vulnerability of his or her soul.

The sixth paradox involves creating a space that welcomes both silence and speech. In the session I am examining, there was much talk but only one clear period of silence—when I asked students to collect their thoughts and make notes on the questions I had posed. That was a valuable interlude. But the silences that interest me most are the ones that occur midstream in a discussion, when a point is made or a question is posed that evokes no immediate response.

As the seconds tick by and the silence deepens, my belief in the value of silence goes on trial. Like most people, I am conditioned to interpret silence as a symptom of something gone wrong. I am the salaried leader of this class-room enterprise, and I live by an ethic of professional responsibility, so in the silence my sense of competence and worth is at stake: I am the one who must set right what has gone wrong—by speaking. Panic catapults me to the conclusion that the point just made or the question just raised has left students either dumbfounded or bored, and I am duty-bound to apply conversational CPR.

But suppose that my panic has misled me and my quick conclusion is mistaken. Suppose that my students are neither dumbfounded nor dismissive but digging deep; suppose that they are not ignorant or cynical but wise enough to know that this moment calls for thought; suppose that they are not wasting time but doing a more reflective form of learning. I miss all such possibilities when I assume that their silence signifies a problem, reacting to it from my own need for control rather than their need to learn.

Even if my hopeful interpretations are mistaken, it is indisputable that the moment I break the silence, I foreclose on all chances for authentic learning. Why would my students think their own thoughts in the silence when they know I will invariably fill it with thoughts of my own?

The particular way of practicing paradox I have just described may have more to do with my identity than with yours. But practicing paradox in the classroom is not unique to the kinds of subjects or students I teach.

I have been in high school science labs where the paradox of the individual and group voice is honored as students look into microscopes, one by one, then gather to seek consensus on what they have seen and what it means. I know teachers of grade school mathematics who understand that the charge of math's mysteries must be held in paradox with an ethos of hospitality, especially if girls and minority youngsters are to overcome a culture that says they are less capable of quantitative thinking. I have visited college literature courses where the big story and the little stories are held in paradoxical tension as the teacher helps students understand the drama of the family in *King Lear* by relating it to family dramas that the students know firsthand.

The principle of paradox offers no cookbook fix for teaching. But if it fits who you are, it offers guidance on any level of education and with any field of study.

Holding the Tension of Opposites

Holding the tension of paradox so that our students can learn at deeper levels is among the most difficult demands of good teaching. How are we supposed to do it?

Imagine yourself in a classroom. You ask a well-framed question, and then you wait and wait as the great silence descends. You know you should wait some more, not jump, but your heart pounds then sinks, and finally feels helpless and out of control. So you answer your own question with an emotional mix of anxiety, anger, and authoritarianism that only makes things worse. Then you watch as the opening to learning offered by the silence vanishes—and teaching becomes more and more like running headlong into walls.

That scenario—which could apply to holding any of the paradoxes, not just silence and speech—suggests a simple truth: the place where paradoxes are held together is in the teacher's heart, and our inability to hold them is less a failure of technique than a gap in our inner lives. If we want to teach and learn in the power of paradox, we must reeducate our hearts.

In particular, we must teach our hearts a new way to understand the tension we feel when we are torn between the poles. Some clues to such an understanding are found in E. F. Schumacher's classic text, *Small Is Beautiful*:

> Through all our lives we are faced with the task of reconciling opposites which, in logical thought, cannot be reconciled. . . . How can one reconcile the demands of freedom and discipline in education? Countless mothers and teachers, in fact, do it, but no one can write down a solution. They do it by bringing into the situation a force that belongs to a higher level where opposites are transcended—the power of love. . . . Divergent problems, as it were, force us to strain ourselves to a level above ourselves; they demand, and thus provoke the supply of, forces from a higher level, thus bringing love, beauty, goodness and truth into our lives. It is only with the help of these higher forces that the opposites can be reconciled in the living situation.

Schumacher's words help me understand that the tension that comes when I try to hold a paradox together is not hell-bent on tearing me apart. Instead, it is a power that wants to pull my heart open to something larger than myself. The tension always feels difficult, sometimes destructive. But if I can collaborate with the work it is trying to do rather than resist it, the tension will not break my heart—it will make my heart larger.

Schumacher's illustration of this point is brilliant because it is true to ordinary experience: every good teacher and every good parent has somehow learned to negotiate the paradox of freedom and discipline. We want our children and our students to become people who think and live freely, yet at the same time we know that helping them become free requires us to restrict their freedom in certain situations.

Of course, neither our children nor our students share this knowledge! When my thirteen-year-old announces that he will no longer attend religious services or a student submits a paper on a topic other than the one I assigned, I am immediately drawn into the tension—and there is no formula to tell me whether this is a moment for freedom or discipline or some alchemy of both.

But good teachers and good parents find their way through such minefields every day by allowing the tension itself to pull them open to a larger and larger love—a love that resolves these Solomonic dilemmas by looking past the tension within ourselves toward the best interests of the student or the child.

As always with profound truths, there is a paradox about this love. Schumacher says that a good parent or teacher resolves the tension of divergent problems by embodying the transcendent power of love. Yet he also says that resolving the tension requires a supply of love that comes from beyond ourselves, provoked by the tension itself. If we are to hold paradoxes together, our own love is absolutely necessary—and yet our own love is never enough. In a time of tension, we must endure with whatever love we can muster until that very tension draws a larger love into the scene.

There is a name for the endurance we must practice until a larger love arrives: it is called suffering. We will not be able to teach in the power of paradox until we are willing to suffer the tension of opposites, until we understand that such suffering is neither to be avoided nor merely to be survived but must be actively embraced for the way it expands our own hearts.

Without this acceptance, the pain of suffering will always lead us to resolve the tension prematurely, because we have no reason to stand the gaff. We will ask and answer our own questions in the silence of the classroom (thus creating more silence); we will ride roughshod over the dissenting voice that confounds our learning plan (even though we said we welcomed questions); we will punish the student who writes outside the assignment (no matter how creatively) to bring him or her back in line.

We cannot teach our students at the deepest levels when we are unable to bear the suffering that opens into those levels. By holding the tension of opposites, we hold the gateway to inquiry open, inviting students into a territory in which we all can learn.

How to do this is not a question that can be answered, for it is done in the teacher's heart: holding the tension of opposites is about being, not doing. But some words from Rilke may help. They offer no technique for embracing suffering, because one does not exist. But they offer hope for what might happen if we tried.

The words are from *Letters to a Young Poet,* in which Rilke writes as a teacher. He had received a series of respectful but demanding letters from a neophyte who admired Rilke's work and sought advice on how to follow in his path. Rilke not only took the time to respond but did so with astonishing generosity.

In one exchange, the young poet presses the older one with question after urgent question, and Rilke replies with this counsel: "Be patient toward all that is unsolved in your heart and try to love the *questions themselves.* . . . Do not now seek the answers, which cannot be given you because you would not be able to live them. And the point is, to live everything. *Live* the questions now. Perhaps you will then gradually, without noticing it, live along some distant day into the answer."

His words could easily be paraphrased to speak to the condition of the teacher whose heart is unable to hold the tension of opposites in the classroom: Be patient toward all that is unresolved in your heart. . . . Try to love the contradictions themselves. . . . Do not now seek the resolutions, which cannot be given because you would not be able to live them—and the point is to live everything. Live the contradictions now. Perhaps you will then gradually, without noticing it, live along some distant day into the paradox.

The hope Rilke gives me lies partly in his notion that on "some distant day" I might find that I have lived my way into a more confident understanding of how to hold the tension of paradox than I have at this moment. Surely he is right about that: having lived into the tensions of teaching for some time now, I am better able to hold paradoxes together than I was years ago.

But my deeper hope comes with Rilke's words "and the point is to live everything." Of course that is the point! If I do not fully live the tensions that come my way, those tensions do not disappear: they go underground and multiply. I may not know how to solve them, but by wrapping my life around them and trying to live out their resolution, I open myself to new possibilities and keep the tensions from tearing me apart.

There is only one alternative: an unlived life, a life lived in denial of the tensions the teaching brings. Here, I play a masked professional role, pretending outwardly that I have no tensions at all while inwardly all those tensions I pretend not to have are ripping the fabric of my life.

Pretending is another name for dividedness, a state that keeps us from cultivating the capacity for connectedness on which good teaching depends. When we pretend, we fall out of community with ourselves, our students, and the world around us, out of communion with the common center that is both the root and the fruit of teaching at its best. But when we understand that "the point is to live everything," we will recover all that is lost.

I give the last word on this subject to Florida Scott-Maxwell, who, writing toward the end of a long and well-lived life, speaks with authority: "Some uncomprehended law holds us at a point of contradiction where we have no choice, where we do not like that which we love, where good and bad are inseparable partners impossible to tell apart, and where we—heart-broken and ecstatic—can only resolve the conflict by blindly taking it into our hearts. This used to be called being in the hands of God. Has anyone any better words to describe it?"

From *The Courage to Teach* by Parker J. Palmer. Copyright © 1998 by John Wiley & Sons. Reprinted with permission of John Wiley & Sons, Inc.

Questions

1. Explain why "who is the self who teaches?" is the key question for Palmer.
2. Compare Lipman's community of inquiry with Palmer's community of truth.
3. Explain Palmer's assertion that "we fragment reality into an endless series of either-ors."
4. Explain in your own words each of the six paradoxes of teaching and learning. Think of a personal example that illustrates each of the six paradoxes.
5. Do you agree with Palmer that "the place where paradoxes are held together is in the teacher's heart"? Explain your answer.
6. What does Palmer mean by either-or thinking, and explain how such thinking diminishes the "wholeness and wonder of life."
7. Compare Palmer's views of either-or thinking with John Dewey's discussion of such thinking.
8. In your own words, describe the ideally educated individual from Palmer's point of view.
9. Which of the other thinkers included in this volume do you think is most like Parker J. Palmer?
10. Explain what Palmer means by his vocation and avocation and how each are joined in his vision of the ideally educated individual.

NAME INDEX

SUBJECT INDEX